New-World Education Series

The Teacher

Yonkers-on-Hudson, New York

in School and Society

An Introduction to Education

HAROLD RUGG
Teachers College, Columbia University

B. MARIAN BROOKS
City College of New York

23103

WORLD BOOK COMPANY

Editorial Foreword

THE TASK of keeping teacher education abreast of social change and of the results of research in the various areas of learning constitutes an important challenge to educators. With complex discoveries growing out of the integration of widely separated fields of knowledge, it is becoming increasingly difficult for the lone teacher to understand and to interpret for students the forces of our civilization and their impact upon the educational program. Clearly, the writing of a series of books that will fuse the scattered bits of our potential teacher-education curriculum requires the coöperative effort of scholars of diverse capabilities.

Out of these considerations has evolved the plan for producing *New-World Education Series* through the collaboration of a working board of editorial consultants. Each member of the board has his own chosen professional area of specialization, yet all believe in the principle of integration and the unity of knowledge. Guided by this belief, the editorial consultants are coöperating with the authors of individual books in designing together, during a period of several years, a comprehensive body of textbook material for the professional education of teachers.

While each book of the series is distinctly the product of its own authorship, it has also had the benefit of early group planning and criticism by the other authors and editors. Each volume draws its materials from current scholarship in the foundational areas of sociology, psychology, philosophy, æsthetics, and history, and these materials are applied directly to the professional tasks of a special field, be that curriculum development, the practice of teaching, the guidance of learning and growth, the evaluation of results, or the organization and administration of schools.

The editors of *New-World Education Series* are convinced that today enough is known of our culture, of man and his behavior, and of the first principles of conduct to provide the makings of a great education.

But these makings lie scattered in many places. The purpose of this series is to gather and organize them for use in teaching.

For invaluable coöperation in developing the individual titles of New-World Education Series, the various authors and the publishers are deeply indebted to the following board of editorial consultants: Theodore Brameld, New York University; Lawrence E. Cole, Oberlin College; Harold Rugg, Teachers College, Columbia University; B. Othanel Smith, University of Illinois.

Author Preface

OF THE MANY problems in teacher education none is more important than that of presenting to the student a true and challenging introduction to the profession. Indeed, no task is more baffling than that of determining the proper content of the first course for college students who are planning to become teachers. In fifty years at least one hundred textbooks have been written in the endeavor to solve this problem. Some introductory books are miniature encyclopedias, others are essentially reference books or handbooks; many have stressed the American educational system, its structure and administration, others the profession of education and how to achieve a career in it; still others deal with abstract principles of the educative process.

The present book, because it was developed as a part of *New-World Education Series*, has benefited by the professional wisdom and searching criticism of the Board of Editorial Consultants and the authors of other volumes. It is our belief that such coöperative group design can go far toward producing a definitive first course in education. It is our hope that the present book will meet the demanding requirements of such a course.

The book is organized around the most pressing concern of the student: "What is to be my role, and my work, *as a teacher?*" The crux of that work, as planned in successive chapters, is *guidance*. The chief factor that shapes it is American culture. In harmony with the social and psychological sciences, the changing culture is interpreted as the chief molder of American childhood and youth, and of the schools in which they develop. To the extent that personal leadership can direct the culture-molding process, the teacher can play an effective role. In the first half of our book, therefore, the teacher's work in the common and higher schools, in the national school system, in adult education, and in the profession of education is studied in the matrix of the changing culture.

In the second half of the book the attention of the student is centered more directly on his future work *in the school.* Guidance continues to be the crux of that work, but in Part Two it is applied more specifically to the learning, growth, and development of pupils. The fruits of modern scholarship and the experience of artist-teachers, oriented toward the high goal of maturity of personality, are interpreted in successive chapters. These speak concretely to the student — "You and the Children" . . . "You and the Parents" . . . "You and the Curriculum." The same insistent concern of the student — "What is to be my role?" — guides his introduction to the problems of organizing and administering schools, of evaluating personal development and measuring abilities, and of the wise use of materials and equipment.

The principle of guidance, which is emphasized throughout the textual matter, is also put to work in each chapter, in three special instruments. The first is the chapter Forepage centering the student's attention on key ideas, problems, and relationships. The second, based on the psychological principle that we learn only what we have done, is the section immediately following the text, suggesting "things to do." The third, a "what to read" section, closes each chapter. The student is guided through the bewildering maze of educational literature by suggested readings and some analysis of what can be learned from each source.

H. R.
B. M. B.

Contents

ix

The Teacher in School and Society

An Introduction to Education

PART ONE
The School in the American Culture

CHAPTER 1

"TEACHING has been a good life to me!"

So said Mary Ellen Chase in her autobiography of a teacher's life, A Goodly Fellowship. So say the fine teachers of the world to all those who are going to be teachers. If you have any doubts about it, the great teachers will reassure you. There is no dissent in their autobiographies. In unison they welcome you to a life of stimulating and creative experiences, rich in personal companionships, and rewarding in its profound sense of contribution to the world. For all who love it and work at it, and all who are truly endowed for it, education can provide a good life and a great career.

This praise of teaching will sound strange to you if you have grown up hearing it belittled. Perhaps your enthusiasm has been dampened by such scornful remarks as: "If you can't find anything better to do, you can teach"; or, "Those who can't do, teach." It is true that in your fathers' day, education was all too often regarded as a way-station job — something to do while waiting for something better to turn up. But that was a generation ago. A new civilization has grown up since that time, and with it a new view of the role of education and the teacher.

Teaching: a Great Adventure

TODAY, CONFRONTED by the baffling problems of an industrial society, one distinguished leader after another has turned to the education of mankind as one of the fundamental solutions. H. G. Wells's statement of a quarter-century ago: "It is now a race between education and catastrophe," is being echoed today even by the politicians. Distinguished professional men, believing this, give their time without financial recompense to serve on boards of education. Successful young businessmen and women not infrequently give up their larger incomes for the more deeply satisfying work with growing human beings. Gone are the old days when teaching was turned over to those who had nothing else to do. Education is one of the supreme professions of man.

Cultivating the Human Garden

Why have the great teachers always so loved to teach? Francis Wayland Parker, one of America's renowned teachers, gave us his answer:

> "I can say that all my life I have had a perfect passion for teaching school. . . . I remember when I was teaching in the Grammar School in Piscataquog, I had . . . a bit of rocky, gravelly garden, that I used to tend and hoe, morning and night; — beans and corn and so on. Always it seems to me when I was hoeing I was dreaming when I said to myself, 'Why do I love to teach school?' And then I looked around on the growing plants and said, 'It is because I love to see things grow.' If I should tell the secret of my life, it is the intense desire I have to see growth and improvement in all

5

living things, and most of all in human beings. I think that is the whole secret of my enthusiasm and study . . . my intense desire to see mind and soul grow, to provide them with proper conditions for growth — for that is the best thing one person can do for another." [1]

It is true that a person cannot be a good gardener unless he loves growing things. That was the secret of the greatness of Francis Parker: his love of children. Ida Heffron, one of his teachers, pictures him in the famous Practice School of the Chicago Normal School:

"Often, as he strolled through the halls . . . he would be heard humming . . . like the loud hum of a bee. . . . Some older boys affectionately dubbed him 'our bumblebee.' In the yard the children swarmed about him, girls and boys — the younger ones followed him or walked with him hand in hand, beaming with pride. . . . All the children in the neighborhood played in his garden and, often out of breath, the little ones would come tumbling after him with flowers, stones, or insects for his admiration, calling, 'Colonel Parker! Colonel Parker!' . . . It is impossible, in mere words, to convey the confidence which he invariably inspired in children." [2]

Julia Weber, a teacher in a one-room school in a mountain neighborhood, felt much the same way:

"Friday, June 5, 1936. I visited today the little school in which I shall begin to teach next fall. It gave me a strange excited feeling as I drove up to the front door of the clean, white boxlike structure, shining in the sun. I have a deep faith in one-teacher schools and in the opportunities they afford to prepare children for a continually developing creative and democratic life. Here I shall have an opportunity to live closely with a group of children and to learn to know them intimately. I shall have them long enough to watch them grow and develop their capacities under guidance in as rich an environment as it is possible to make for them. I paused for a moment at the door and looked around at the woods surrounding the little schoolhouse. The recent rain made the leaves shine and the woods smelled so nice. 'All this will be our laboratory,' I thought. . . ."

[1] William M. Giffin: School Days in the Fifties, page 133. A. Flanagan Company. Used by permission. (Extract quoted here from Heffron's Francis Wayland Parker, pages 26–27.)
[2] Ida C. Heffron: Francis Wayland Parker, page 60. Ivan Deach, Jr.; 1934. Used by permission.

To Francis W. Parker, teaching was cultivating a garden. He loved to see things grow — most of all the minds and spirits of children. (Photo by courtesy of Flora Cooke.)

Three years later, as Miss Weber reflected upon the little school and her teaching experiences, she added these words to her diary:

"All those things that I want for the boys and girls I teach, are coming to me too. I, too, am becoming increasingly aware of my capacities and of my place in the world. . . . I am also aware that many of the things I now think I know, will take on new and fuller meaning as I continue to experience consciously. . . . I, too, can meet life creatively. . . ." [1]

The biography of great teaching furnishes abundant testimony of the feeling of exaltation. William Lyon Phelps, Yale's popular and beloved teacher of English, found acute joy in his work:

"I had rather earn my living by teaching than in any other way. In my mind, teaching is not merely a lifework, a profession, an occupation, a struggle: it is a passion. I love to teach. I love to teach as a painter loves to paint, as a musician loves to play, as a singer loves to sing, as a strong man rejoices to run a race. Teaching is an art — an art so great and so difficult to master that a man or woman can spend a long life at it, without realizing much more

[1] Julia Weber: *My Country School Diary*, pages 1 and 197. Copyright 1946 by Harper & Brothers. Used by permission.

than his limitations and his mistakes, and his distance from the ideal. But the main aim of my happy days has been to become a good teacher, just as every architect wishes to be a good architect, and every professional poet strives toward perfection." [1]

It was said of President Mark Hopkins of Williams that "To carry forward a class of ingenuous youth, watching them as they conquer new positions and gain broader views, filled him with the same ecstasy as Wordsworth felt when he beheld a 'rainbow in the sky.'" In his fifty years of teaching Hopkins became so famous throughout the country that President Garfield's well-known picture of him as a great teacher has been quoted perhaps a million times: "Give me a log hut, with only a simple bench, Mark Hopkins at one end and I at the other, and you may have all the buildings, apparatus, and library without him." And Vincent D'Indy said that César Franck, the great French music teacher, "never taught by means of hard and fast rules . . . his whole teaching was inspired by . . . love itself. Such an atmosphere of love radiated from this pure-minded man that his pupils not only cared for him as for a father, they were attached to each other in and through him."

It is not merely facts they teach — but life itself. The great teacher loves his work because its satisfactions come to him from the responses of other human beings; his satisfactions are as real and endearing and warm as life itself. The degree to which a person gives himself to teaching is a measure of the delight and success he will find in his work. He is the best and happiest teacher who shares enthusiastically with his students what he himself has learned, who gives unstintingly of himself, his strength, his passion. Every craftsman loves his material — the sculptor his stone, the musician his tone and rhythm, the writer his words. The teacher, too, must care deeply for the most precious of all materials, the growing and developing human life. Listen to Francis Parker again:

"I felt that there was only one study in the world, and that is the study of life . . . the function of the human being; to take the truth that comes in from all the universe and give it back being created and ever creative. . . . the supreme joy of being is to take in this life and give it out to others. . . . The steps of progress that I can see are the concentration of this truth in an ideal school, in an ideal education."

[1] William Lyon Phelps: *Teaching in School and College.* Copyright 1912 by The Macmillan Company.

Imparting Enthusiasm for Life

Life, not the subject, is what the true teacher teaches. That was what Yale of sixty years ago said of William Rainey Harper when the registrations of students in the Hebrew department were rising surprisingly. One Yale administrative investigator reported to the faculty: "It is that young cub Harper! He can teach Hebrew as though it were a series of hairbreadth escapes." Two hundred years after his death, Pestalozzi, the Swiss educator, admittedly an impractical administrator and not particularly important as a philosopher, still held his place in the educational Hall of Fame. Why? Because he was an enthusiast for life with "an unconquerable passion to minister to the lower classes of his country, to shelter and elevate the vagrant, homeless, uncared-for children who swarmed in his neighborhood." Energy and enthusiasm for life! "Be passionate in your interests and searches," the eighty-seven-year-old physiologist Pavlov admonished the young men engaged in research under his direction.

What the profession of teaching can do is well illustrated by the account given by the great architect Louis Henry Sullivan of his first class with Moses Woolson. Woolson came in, looked around, and said: "Boys . . . you have come here to learn and I'll see that you do. I will not only do my share, but I will make you do yours. . . . I accept the responsibility involved as a high, exacting duty I owe to myself and equally to you. I will give you all that I have; you shall give to me all that you have." Sullivan exclaims:

> "At last a Man! I was amazed, thunderstruck, dumfounded, overjoyed! I had caught and weighed every word as it fell from the lips of the master; to each thrilling word I had vibrated in open-eyed, amazed response. I knew now that through the years my thoughts, my emotions, my visions, had been formless and chaotic; now in this man's utterances, in a flash, they became defined, living, and real. In that first explosive contact a veil was parted, as it were by magic, and behold! there stood forth, not alone, a man, but a TEACHER of the young." [1]

These teachers with energy, passion, and enthusiasm for life serve as burning torches to keep the human fires ablaze. If you are a builder

[1] Louis H. Sullivan: *The Autobiography of an Idea*, pages 156–160. Copyright 1934 by W. W. Norton & Company, Inc. Used by permission.

of wood fires, you know that a single burning log will soon die down even though it has been blazing on all sides. But if, while it burns, another log is brought up beside it at just the right distance, the second one will burn, and "the contagious enthusiasm" of the two will keep each ablaze. So it is with the lone individual; even though he has rare power of self-propulsion, the fire slowly subsides. But bring close another responsible human being, and the interradiating heat keeps the two of them ablaze. Thus the enthusiastic teacher kindles and re-kindles the human spirit.

Providing Mooring Masts for Searching and Insecure Youth

The great teacher is more than a wise human being with an urgent enthusiasm for imparting his wisdom to his students. He or she is a person of character, strength, and spiritual force. Biographies are replete with revelations of students' dependence on their teachers. Helen Keller — deaf, dumb, blind — lost in a world of utter black silence, speaks of the day when her teacher came to guide her upward into a world of light and joy and security: "The most important day I remember in all my life is the one on which my teacher, Anne Mans-field Sullivan, came to me. I am filled with wonder when I consider the immeasurable contrast between the two lives which it connects." [1] Here was indeed a great teacher of another great soul. Louis Lasagna, who knew Miss Sullivan well, summed up her life: "It is no mean epitaph for any teacher to have it said of him that 'He rendered all whom he taught less deaf, less dumb, less blind.'" [2]

The freshman Becker asked the upper classmen at Wisconsin about Frederick Turner: "What does he teach?" And this was the reply he received: "American history, but it's not what he teaches. . . . Its what he is, the personality and all that sort of thing. It's something he gives you: inspiration, ideas, a fresh light on things in general. It's something he makes you want to do or be."

Thus, these teachers give forth deep faith as well as contagious enthusiasm, a faith and confidence needed by youth. They give a sense of standing foursquare, of being strong mooring masts in the midst of the stormy emotional turmoil of life. They contain the strength that

[1] Houston Peterson: *Great Teachers*, page 5.
[2] Quoted from a letter to Houston Peterson in his *Great Teachers*, page xxi.

comes from knowledge; they see with the perspective born of years of successful living. These strong souls are sorely needed today; for most people, grownups as well as children, feel insecure. No doubt you know this all too well; for your own parents, born probably around the early 1900's, have known little real security. During most of their lives the world has been torn by terrible wars or hurt by long depressions; few Americans have escaped the anxiety of foreign war, or the fears of unemployment and consequent loss of income. All the more honor to the teacher who is at one and the same time a guide to youth searching for answers to life's problems and a strong human anchor to cling to in a time of insecurity.

Being a Friend and a Guide to Living

How can these mature teachers reach out and affect the lives of younger people? How do they establish the respect and understanding that are the basis for real living and thinking together? There is no royal road, but certain conditions and human qualities are indispensable. The first is the feeling of friendliness and good will. "He loved the children," they said of Francis Parker. "He *liked* his students" is a frequent commentary on the successful teacher. Turner's students said that the great historian gave them the impression that they were "expected and welcome." He always seemed "out for adventure, up to something, in the most casual friendly way, inviting you to join in." Simon Patten of Pennsylvania frequently would say to students who came to him for advice: "Let me see; suppose we take breakfast together tomorrow morning." The next day, breakfast at the University Club would start at eight and go on, in some cases, until noon.

Professor Gummere of Haverford was to Christopher Morley "never the teacher, always the comrade. His was the strong friendly face behind the desk, . . . searching us and sizing us up." The charm of a friendly personality "shone from his sparkling eyes; it spoke . . . in his characteristic gesture of leaning forward and tilting his head a little to one side as he listened, patiently, to whatever juvenile surmises we stammered to express." It was Gummere's way "to pretend that we knew far more than we did; a measure of his constant respect for his students." He always "suited his strength to our weakness. He would tell us things almost with an air of apology for seeming to know more than we; pretending that we doubtless had known it all along, but it had just slipped our memory."

Thus the true teacher keeps the channels of communication open by going out to his students, feeling and showing a genuine interest in their concerns. He may create an opportunity of doing nonacademic things with them outside of class. Here the more formal order of the classroom or the laboratory gives way to the spontaneous, offguard revelation of the deep interests, understandings, and excitements of personal life.

Not only through the pathway of good will do teachers get their ideas and feelings over to their students, but also by building mutual respect. "He respected his students," "he treated them as equals," "he never talked down to them," the students say of a teacher whom they, in turn, respect. The artist-teacher assumes that the student is a person to be respected and treated as an equal in importance with himself, even though he may be younger and less mature. It is all in the mood of the clarion note sounded by Walt Whitman. "Had you thought that there was but one Supreme? I tell you that there are unnumbered Supremes." In the class of the true teacher every student is treated as a Supreme.

But even with a genuine will to treat his students with friendliness and respect, the teacher must solve the baffling problem of bridging the gap that is bound to exist in interests, vocabulary, experience, and maturity of understanding. This gap must be recognized and solved at the various levels of education. Great sensitivity and skill are required if the teacher is to note the capacities and needs of the student at any given moment and bring to him just those experiences and materials that will help him over the next learning hurdle.

Sometimes when we see the extent to which these artist-teachers are masters of understanding and communication, we recognize that there is a great deal of truth in the old saying: "Teachers are born and not made." It is probably true that not everyone can teach, for great sensitivity is demanded to understand and respond to the emotional and psychological needs of a much less mature human being. Well may we marvel at the true teacher's artistry of gesture of face and hands, at the perfect choice of vocabulary, the wise choice of dramatic episode and illustrative analogy, the subtle use of synonym, metaphor, and simile, the skillful alternation of suspense and definition, and the sensitive timing of the whole complex learning and teaching process. To do this and tune it all to the young student requires deep feeling as well as high intelligence, and these are the qualities of the artist-teacher.

Developing the Ability to Think

The biographers of great teachers are unanimous on still another characteristic: The best educators, they say, succeed in making their students think. To do this they endure the ordeal of teaching the hard way, not the easy way. The easy way is to tell both the facts and the conclusions; the hard but effective way is to set the stage so that the student can and will find out for himself. Dickinson S. Miller said that his friend William James's lectures were conversational, hesitant, "at times struggling for expression." James could never "speak ex cathedra from heights of scientific erudition." In his remarks there was always an atmosphere of if's and maybe's, and he gave the students the feeling of "his own exploration . . . his mind at work."

The philosopher Irwin Edman, speaking of a slow, halting lecture by John Dewey, says that he later discovered that he "had been listening to a man actually thinking in the presence of a class. . . . To attend a lecture of John Dewey's was to participate in the actual process of thought. . . . These hours came to seem the most arresting educational experiences, almost, I have ever had."

In his lectures Sigmund Freud, the eminent psychoanalyst, also exemplified the spirit of the "if's and maybe's," the qualifying "perhaps." He presented the facts, dissected basic principles, surveyed possible objections, and introduced conclusions with such caution, "that when he moved on in an unexpected direction it seemed the most natural thing to do. When he had to leave an argument unfinished, or incomplete, he pointed it out and went back to it at the right moment. In this way he led his hearers insensibly on, never giving them the impression that they were participating in a difficult and quite original investigation."

Garman of Amherst said that his aim "was to develop not disciples but apostles." His student, Dyer, said of him that, like many great teachers, he did not leave his students "with an airtight conclusion but with a certain conviction that they had acquired a method by which conclusions could always be found." Becker says that Turner never made him feel that he was "before the judgment seat . . . he criticized, and in the most honest friendly way, without leaving any aftertaste of personal depravity in the mouth." He seemed to believe "with Mr. Justice Holmes that one important article of his creed as a scholar was that he was not God." He always asked, but seldom answered; and when he did answer, it was preceded by "perhaps."

Teaching: a Life of Intriguing Problems

From those who do not like teaching, who do not give themselves completely to it, one might get the impression that it is largely drudgery: keeping unruly children quiet, marking their papers, keeping records, always correcting mistakes. It is true of teaching, as of every occupation, that there is a certain amount of routine work to be done; but it is doubtful if any other profession can offer a life of greater variety and of more intriguing problems. Naturally so, for the teacher's life is lived with stimulating men and women who are working at the most exciting and compelling problem of mankind — namely, guiding the growth and development of human beings. To work with curious, searching, growing youth is a constant challenge, for in the company of young Americans every day presents new problems. Every student is unique, and every changing situation is unique. No two days, no two group meetings, are alike. The very business of learning and growing is marked by constant change. Life in a truly active school provides not monotony and repetition but variety, excitement, and challenge.

And there are equally intriguing social challenges, especially in a period of tremendous social change such as that in which we live. Simon Patten, distinguished student of industrial society, was fond of saying: "The place of the teacher is on the firing line of civilization." Scott Nearing, one of Patten's students, and another social frontiersman, said of him, "the characteristic that distinguished Professor Patten from most of the other teachers at the University of Pennsylvania was that while he always had one eye on the classroom, the other eye was forever on the community." That is what the true teacher does — keeps one eye on the student, the other on society.

It is from this interrelationship of the student and the community in which he lives that the teacher finds the materials with which to teach and the method of teaching those materials. The dynamic teacher is alert to the necessity of observing the changing conditions and problems

ELIZABETH IRWIN was a great teacher and a pioneer experimentalist in public education and in teacher training. Her own brilliant teaching evolved from her rich background as settlement worker, free-lance writer, and psychologist. Her deep belief in public schools was intensified during her eleven years as Principal of P.S. 41, the school which became the private New York City school so loved and well-known as "The Little Red School House."

As a charter member of the Bureau of Educational Experiments — the parent of the Bank Street Schools — she helped to organize the Coöperative School for Teachers. For 26 years she was an active worker in this private teacher-education program centered in the concept of fitting the school to the child. Lucy Sprague Mitchell says of her:

> "She loved life. She loved common earthy things. Her way of living — was robust. . . . She had amazing courage. She was never afraid to think or say anything. . . . She was in deadly earnest. . . . Yet she never failed to extract the full humor from any situation."

of the people. No matter what subject or level of education he is especially trained to teach, he regards himself as a student of civilization as well as a student of the psychology of learning. Every day he keeps in touch with the kaleidoscopic current of events and teaches within the framework of the world's happenings.

The good teacher aims to interpret current happenings against a background provided by his sound knowledge of the people's history. He is less impulsive in his judgments of human problems. He is more apt to be right about the future, for his is the long-time view. Patten used to say: "I am a great deal more interested in what will happen five hundred years from now than I am in what will happen tomorrow."

"But five hundred years is so long ahead," they would protest. "Why not be interested in tomorrow?"

And Patten would answer: "Because the things that will happen tomorrow have already been settled. They were decided by the people and by the forces of yesterday. They are fixed — inevitable. But we can take a hand in deciding the events of the coming centuries." Perhaps we would shorten his time span. In an age of swift change, we must be interested in what will happen ten, fifteen, twenty years from now. Those coming events too are being settled today.

In a complex and changing world young teachers may perhaps feel overwhelmed by the staggering size of our social problems. Whenever you feel that nothing you can do will count, remember that the history of great social change is merely the accumulated experience of single individuals. It is the efforts of single, strong individuals that have changed the lives of communities, even of nations. For example, since 1890 the Americans have developed a new national style of architecture. It stemmed straight from the many original buildings designed by a single architect, Louis Henry Sullivan, and the many more built by his young assistant, Frank Lloyd Wright. So, too, modern education was brought about by the pioneering of a few leaders: Pestalozzi and Froebel and Herbart teaching their students and these students, in turn, teaching students of their own. All together, cumulatively even if slowly, these early teachers transformed the education of hundreds of millions of people. James William Crabtree led in the transformation of the National Education Association from a provincial little group of some 7000 to a great national organization of 216,000. In his autobiography, *What Counted Most*, Crabtree ascribes much of his accomplishment to the inspiration of Lizzie Moore, his country schoolteacher.

Finally, on the social side, there is another reward in teaching. It comes from standing close to the pulsing heart of the community. Teachers who have worked intimately with community groups understand the people more deeply and sincerely: their ways of living and their contributions to one another and to communal life. The teacher, in turn, wins the respect and coöperation of the community. His life as a teacher becomes enriched as he assumes the role of community citizen.

Teachers and Teaching: a Class Round Table

From the life histories of those who knew it best, we have been making a case for the intriguing life of teaching. But it needs to be studied much further. Do it in two ways: Study teaching as it affected your own life, and read the interesting books about it that have been written for us.

First, look back into your own life. Recall your good teachers. That teacher in the fourth grade — or was it the seventh — that made learning come alive for you; that woman who made mathematics an adventure, that science teacher who taught physics as though it were a "series of hairbreadth escapes." Why were they good teachers?

Look back over your childhood and youth. Scan again the personalities in home and neighborhood and town, in the school, the church, and the social groups. Which ones had the greatest influence on your life? Were they your father or mother, or were they other persons outside the home and the school? Would you describe them as teachers? Why? What was there about the way they lived and worked that made them that?

Write a description: *The Best Teacher I Have Ever Known.*

Introducing the Library on the Art of Teaching

Fortunately for you who are entering teaching, many of our country's great teachers, or their biographers, have put down their lives in vivid books.

For an overview of the dynamic spirit of the great teachers, don't miss Houston Peterson's *Great Teachers*; it is unique in the teacher's reading shelf, a series of long excerpts from a score of biographies portraying the personalities of a score of America's much-loved and long-remembered teachers. From this, go to some of the autobiographies and biographies of individual teachers. See H. G. Wells's *Story of a Great Schoolmaster*, the poetic life of Sanderson, the headmaster of the British school, Oundle. You will find a multitude of *Creative Power.* Mary Ellen Chase's *A Goodly Fellowship*, an account of the American — Louis Henry Sullivan, his *Autobiography of an Idea.*

From the rich experience of a great teacher of young children and youth have come several interesting books. More than any other teacher in our time, Hughes Mearns opened the eyes of teachers to the creative capacities of children in school. In the first hundred pages of his *Creative Youth* he describes how he introduced the writing of poetry, essays, and short stories to the children at Lincoln School. Read, also, Chapters I and II of his *Creative Power.* Mary Ellen Chase's *A Goodly Fellowship*, an account of her teaching days from rural schools in Maine to college work at Smith, will hold you from beginning to end.

If you are going to teach in a rural school, Julia Weber's *My Country School Diary* will give you many glimpses of her day-by-day experiences. Ida Heffron's *Francis Wayland Parker* is the story of America's first progressive schoolmaster.

CHAPTER 2

The Key Question of Education

WE BEGIN our study with the key question that will always dog your steps as a teacher: What does it mean to educate?

You will find that "to educate" means different things to different people and different things in different times. For example, if you focus your work on the great concept of *growth*, you will make your central task that of *guiding the living* of your students in the richest possible way. But if, on the contrary, you are chiefly concerned with "disciplining the mind," you will be more concerned with the cultural heritage of the past than you are with the living experience of the present learners.

The key question — What does it mean to educate? — will also compel you to ask: Where does education take place? Only, or primarily, in the school? Or, also in the home, the community, and the larger social world? Your study will lead you to see your task with a deeper and broader outlook; *the educativeness of out-of-school living* will become as important to you as that which goes on in a more limited way within the school.

Thus, in searching for the meaning of "to educate," you will get your first glimpse of the importance of two great foundations of education — *the psychology and the sociology of growth and development*. Through it all you will perceive the crucial importance of the teacher as a guide to the best possible living. But the end point of the study, as well as its initiation, will be in the conception: What Are the Conditions of Educativeness?

What Does It Mean "to Educate"?

IN YOUR LIFE as an educator in a school system you will have many different kinds of work. You may teach. You may become a principal or supervisor, a counselor, a librarian, a playground director, or a specialist in a clinic or a laboratory. You may be engaged in curriculum planning, critic teaching, or any one of the many activities involved in the work of the schools. But, irrespective of your special work you will be an educator; your primary job will be to educate. Constantly you will be confronted with the question: *What does it mean to educate?*

The Newer Conception of "to Educate"

Education as Guidance in Living

From the examples of Chapter 1 you could probably give a pretty good over-all answer to the question: To educate is to guide the growth of another person. As Francis Parker used to say, the school is a human garden, and the teacher is the cultivator of living beings. John Dewey merely uses other words: "Education is all one with growing." The life of any social group can be said to be an enterprise in living. It is, however, the unique function of the school to insure that *the living is consciously guided.* You and your fellow teachers are the guides.

There is no function of life higher than that of guiding the education of another person. It is, perhaps, the most subtle as well as the most crucial of all the professions. It requires the sensitive anticipation of the finest living that resides potentially in another human being. Hence, this obligation is placed upon the teacher — to perceive the rich potenti-

19

alities for living in other people. He must bring within their reach the best possible facilities for this growth. Thus the life of the school cannot be left to the casual circumstances of whim or chance. On the contrary and in a profound sense you, the teacher, must make it a "design for living."

Altogether in the past — perhaps too much so in the present — the formal school regarded its task as giving out information and examining the students to find out how much material had been mastered. Teaching was regarded as telling, examining, and policing; as assigning tasks and checking on their execution. But during the past fifty years a new view of this problem has developed. As educators came to see that it is the element of *guidance* that distinguishes a truly educational experience from any other episode of living, the newer schools have come to regard the teacher primarily as a guide; only incidentally is he a monitor and a judge. An incident will illustrate this point.

Recently we sat for an hour with six teachers, the school psychologist, and the director of a school in Menlo Park, California. They were discussing one of the boys in the school. The records brought out facts of physique, intelligence, temperament, school achievement, creative accomplishment, powers of leadership, and ability to get along with others. Detailed individual episodes of behavior were discussed back and forth. Strengths and weaknesses stood out. Finally, it was agreed that this case with its recommendations should be discussed by the director and the psychologist with the boy and his parents.

"Do you analyze and discuss every boy and girl with this care and detail?" we finally asked.

"Yes, we try to. It pays dividends in the smooth working of the school as well as in guiding each individual into a happy and growing life."

Fortunately, throughout our country today there are many schools where each young human being is treated as a person — not as a standardized cog in a great mass-production factory. A deep awareness of the *personal problems of youth* has been growing among educators, and in community after community something is being done about it. It is fortunate indeed that this is so, because there has never been a time in modern history when young people have been in greater need of wise guidance. On every hand young people see their parents baffled and

bewildered by the problems of employment and world conflict, and by the whirling change in ways of living and in social institutions. Children see their parents losing their jobs and losing confidence in themselves. They feel frictions and emotional disturbances in their homes. Many of them grow up surrounded by a sense of failure.

In a later chapter you will study this problem of guidance more thoroughly. For the moment, however, enough has been said to point out that the primary job of the educator is to guide the growth of young people. Education means, among other things, watchful, sympathetic, intelligent guidance.

This modern conception of education was not widely held during the youth of your fathers and mothers. The meaning of "to educate" has changed profoundly since their day. To make this clear in the early stage of your introduction to education, we shall compare and contrast some characteristic examples of the education of a generation ago with today's newer ideas and practices.

The Meaning of "to Educate" in Bygone Years

In your parents' school, education was regarded as something that went on in a schoolhouse between 9 A.M. and 4 P.M., Monday to Friday, September to June, from the age of six to the age of fourteen. "Being educated" merely meant going to school. Education was something you did in preparation for your life's work but was not looked upon as a part of life itself.

The pattern of school life was drab and standardized. The child's abode, for eight years or more, was a grim, rectangular, brick building housing four or five hundred children. If it was an eight-grade school, for example, it had eight classes, eight classrooms, and eight cloakrooms arranged along bleak, dark corridors. Rooms the same size, blackb the same size, wall paint in rooms and corridors all the same, te desk in front center — everything standardized. Children, pige in long rows, sat quietly, studied their lessons silently, obeyed t promptly, spoke or moved about only when permission was g "lesson" meant children sitting with hands folded, forty of eyes fixed on the same paragraph; memorizing and re

This was the listening school, where the children rea dull textbooks, and where daily the teachers gave cha

blackboards and raised tired voices in strident pursuit of elusive young attention. The tradition had grown that education consisted primarily in making people literate: preparing them to read, write, and reckon. Hence, the curriculum was thought of as the Three R's — as something one did with words, numbers, and other symbols. Bodies of facts called subjects were learned in short periods or recitations by reading out of books or writing down what was said by the teacher. Critical problems of our national life or the dynamic social changes taking place throughout the Western world were ignored in the classroom. Not "What do you think?", but "What does the book say?" — rote and routine.

Even today you may encounter these views and practices in some of the schools to which you go; but, as we said, great changes have come about in the last fifty years. Before we give some examples of the newer concepts of "to educate," sum up for yourself just what this earlier view meant. In doing so, think through the answers to these questions:

–Did education emphasize growth and the all-round living of the young people?

–How did it see the role of the teacher?

–How directly was the curriculum connected with the lives of the young people; their interests, their needs, their problems?

–Did the terms "education" and "school" have the same meaning?

Young Democracy at Work

Come now into some schools and take a look at a very different conception of education. The examples are all from schools in which we have been recently or from actual reports on activities in other schools.

First, a glimpse of a whole school working together:

As we walk down the shady path from the main building to the assembly hall, John French, the Director, says: "The school is gathering for an important town meeting."

"Oh, have you student self-government?"

"Well, you come now and have a look. Judge for yourself."

In a moment we are in the simple but attractive little theater where hree hundred boys and girls, twelve to eighteen, have come together. fine boy of perhaps seventeen serves as moderator through an hour

and a half of orderly but spirited discussion of recent student elections. The whole proceeding is in excellent temper and decorum; no artificial forensics, none of the competitive eagerness to beat an opponent but, on the contrary, the give-and-take of the open forum of fact and argument. As we watch, we feel a community mood of trying to get at the facts, see the problem, and find the best solution. A score of teachers, scattered about the room, rise now and then as members of the school community, and speak briefly. The Director sits quietly at one side, speaking only when called upon by the students for information or advice. A faculty adviser, intimately acquainted with the problem, speaks from time to time but without dominating the discussion.

We leave at 10:30 with the exclamation: "That seems to us to be self-government! But whether or not, it's good education."

"Yes," the Director agreed. "After twenty years we think it *is* education. We have this assembly several days a week, the first thing in the morning. Sometimes it is a fifteen-minute gathering for announcements and a brief exchange of views. Occasionally a group presents a project; or, as today, we may have a school forum. After twenty years we have come to know its educational possibilities, especially in building a sense of what democracy means. Young people can learn what government is only by practicing government. The root question in the problem of government is *competence*: "In planning and operating the school we must ask in connection with each activity, 'Who is competent?' The young people are competent to discuss, even to help make, decisions about many things in the school. Our job is to find the areas of competence and govern the school accordingly."

All over America children in elementary schools as well as young people in the high schools and colleges are studying problems and issues — either their own personal ones or those of town or country — in this same give-and-take of democratic discussion.

In a junior high school we might join the Social Problems Club. They are discussing the merits of the Marshall Plan for the economic relief of Europe. Maps and charts are displayed around the room; reference books, pamphlets, and magazine articles are being organized by the young leaders of the discussion. Here, as in the other groups, the teacher, though not presiding, is a potent leader behind the scenes, subtly guiding by asking questions and suggesting resources.

Social understandings come to children from meaningful experiences. These children are in a car constructed from boxes and other odds and ends. (Play Schools Association photo.)

Such responsible, independent activities of young people in the new schools are not confined to the high schools. Here is a fourth-grade group with a nine-year-old boy leading in the discussion of a joint pupil-teacher plan for the day. A trip is to be taken to an experimental farm, and the committee in charge is reporting the plans they have made. They distribute mimeographed directions to guide the tour. Another committee, working with the teacher, has prepared a statement of the problems and questions that have come out of earlier discussion meetings. All arrangements for the trip have been carefully planned, and every possible significant and contributing experience considered.

In another school we enter the science room just in time to see a motion picture being shown to some fifty biology students. They are studying Mendel's Law. Utter informality exists in the crowded room, but the students' intense interest makes for perfect quiet. Absorbed for twenty minutes in scientific study, they follow the film. Then follows a half hour of vigorous discussion, with much questioning and argument by the young people. A graphic fifteen-minute lecture is interjected by the teacher, who seizes upon the central thread of these questions and certain phases of inheritance which the film illustrated.

Now imagine yourself in a large Midwest city, observing a ninth-grade class as it takes up its month-long study of the water supply of that community. Day after day we go with their committee groups. One group visits the city engineer's office and other municipal offices — to collect, study, and report on maps and bulletins. Another assembles library materials that deal with the problems. Still another prepares maps, graphs, and other pictorial representations of the various phases of the system. Other groups visit the purification plants; they report on methods of purifying water, make a working model of the purification plant, study principles of hydraulics and other scientific problems involved in the pumping and distributing systems, and write historical accounts of the development of the system.

Thousands of examples like these could be given. What light do they throw on the meaning of education?

–In what sense are the teachers guiding the growth of these young people?

–How narrow or how wide is the knowledge they are getting?

–What role do facts and skills play in the school program?

–How does the practice in the give-and-take of discussion function educationally?

–What are the potentialities for growth in the experience of expressing oneself, of criticizing others' positions and statements, of appraising the validity of evidence of judging the value of sources?

Teachers Working with Individual Pupils

For two generations educators have struggled with problems involved in breaking the lock step of the public school. They have tried one device after another to motivate academic work and make it both interesting and challenging. Of all the devices the most publicized was the Dalton Plan [1] — a plan to individualize the education of its youth.

[1] See H. Parkhurst, *Education on the Dalton Plan*, for the founder's description of what she thought she did. But the best book on individualizing the work of the public schools is Carleton Washburne's *A Living Philosophy of Education*.

Let us visit a splendid modification of it in the Cambridge school in Massachusetts.

As we walk back across the lawn to the main building of classrooms the Director tells us: "Now you are on your own until lunch time. Go in and out of any of the rooms in this building, and you will find the Laboratory Plan in action. Yes, we have a kind of modified Dalton Plan for an hour and a half every morning. We do it with all the academic parts of the program. In each room you will find a teacher of one general department working with individual boys and girls. In that room, for example," pointing across the corridor, "you will find a teacher in charge of the social studies; over there mathematics. Across the hall in the library is what we still call English; up on the hill, in that long, low, white building, are the sciences."

For the rest of the morning we go from room to room. All the young people are at work, various activities are afoot, and there is opportunity for each student to probe into his own interests. Books are everywhere, not just in the library, which has several thousand volumes, but in all these laboratory rooms. We see many children working at problems in science and mathematics. In the mechanical-drafting laboratory they are drawing maps and charts. Here and there groups are in close discussion; individuals are quizzing one another. Now and then a teacher stops his work with a boy or girl to gather around him students who need assistance on the same idea or type of problem.

The program of the Laboratory Plan seems really to be built for individual needs. The teacher studies with the pupil, gives advice, points out errors, suggests new sources, appraises, approves, or corrects. Certainly the spirit of responsibility for one's work is being built up, and the children accept school as their work. The Bill of Duties as well as the Bill of Rights thrives here.

–How does this Individual Laboratory Plan give you new meanings for "to educate"?

–Can you state a principle of education that it illustrates?

Socially Useful Work in School

One of the hardest educational problems to solve these days is to arrange the program so that young people really can work, that is, engage in work interesting to them and also of real social use. At one of the

Work is fun for these five-year-olds who are hauling materials to cover a bare, muddy playground. (Photo from Louise M. Gross, State College, Cape Girardeau, Missouri.)

schools we visited, both a day school and a boarding school for twelve-to eighteen-year-olds, the Director said to us as we sat with him in the lunchroom at noon: "One of the features of this school — and we have been concerned with it for years — is that we provide real work. This thing you see going on now is an example: this dining-room work is all done by the young people themselves." Boys and girls were serving at the tables and from the kitchen to the table. "The work is allocated among all the grade groups on a year plan," the Director went on. "Cleaning is done after school hours in the afternoon, and the bigger jobs on Saturdays and in vacations."

Later, as we walked up toward the Shop, he went into the problem of work again: "I don't feel that we have really solved the problem of building a program of real work, yet we have made a beginning. This Shop, the Science Building over there, the Studio down under the big elms where the graphic and plastic arts are housed — all were built by the boys and girls themselves under the direction of our leading shop man, who is a skilled builder."

In the late afternoon we saw a number of young people in blue jeans starting out from the school. "To the school farm?" we asked.

27

"No, we have no school farm. Those youngsters work on the near-by farms and in the shops in town."

Then, a very wise remark: "Of course we must not overlook the fact that *going to school should itself be the chief work of young people.* Learning to be skillful in using the typewriter, solving an equation, mastering a language, making working drawings, creating a work of art — all of these, from the educational standpoint, are *work.*"

Let us mention another school where the entire life is imbued with the work spirit. Everybody works hard, enthusiastically, happily. Every boy and girl is required to give an hour and a half a day — from 3:30 to 5, three days a week — to nonscholastic work. The school of 160 boys and girls is divided into sixteen work crews, each one under a supervising teacher. The woods crew cleans the woods and chops wood for heating, cooking, and the fireplaces. The outdoor crop crews work in the fields. The barn crews clean the stables, cow barn, and chicken houses, care for the animals, milk the cows, and gather the eggs. The kitchen and dining-room crews set the tables, serve, wash dishes, and clean up. Clerical crews carry on office and paper work. Other crews repair the buildings and furniture. These 160 boys and girls work at every kind of socially necessary and desirable job that the actual carrying on of a community of young people and adults requires, and they go to college, too!

In another community, through the coöperation of the National Youth Administration and the board of education, almost the entire high school student body was involved in the work program. After school hours, on Saturdays, and in the long vacations, boys and girls worked as grocery clerks, dishwashers, janitors in drug stores and post offices, stenographers, waiters, and "baby sitters." The older boys rebuilt and renovated the entire high school plant, redesigned the school grounds and athletic facilities, and built a modern field house, bleachers for 800 spectators, a vocational shop, and hog-scalding vats. Through their Future Farmers of America they operated a low-cost service in butchering hogs. And the academic work went on apace.

To Know Oneself as a Person

In many schools education has come to mean helping the child find his rightful place in his social environment through the acquisition of facts, knowledges, skills, and abilities. But there are other essentials to a well-adjusted, happy personality, in other words, to a rich personal life. The child must be helped to know himself as a person. When he is confronted by puzzling, confusing attitudes, beliefs, and ideas about himself and about his reactions to his friends and his home life, he must be helped to handle them satisfactorily for himself and others.

From nursery school through high school the teacher will often hear such personal queries or affirmations as:

"Where did I come from?"

"Would it be nicer to be a boy than a girl?"

"I know how to dissect a caterpillar or a frog, but I know nothing about myself."

"No, I don't want to play with the others today. I don't like them; I want to play by myself."

When confronted by such questions and affirmations, will the teacher hush them up, evade them, or consider them as rude and resort to disciplinary measures? Or will she accept such queries and affirmations as being as natural as: "Why isn't oil found in the eastern coastal states?" Is education meeting these personal needs and interests?

Let us look into the schools and see. In the nursery school we find a family of rabbits. An excited little boy tells us how "last week the mother rabbit had five babies." Or, in the first-grade room we find a gray mother cat sleeping peacefully on a sunny window sill. We are told, "Don't wake her, for she needs lots of sleep because in three more days she will have some babies." As we go on through the elementary school, we find a continued and growing interest in biological and animal life, from which the children receive information and learn to adjust themselves to life experiences. We know from conversations with the child that on each age level these experiences in life increase and become deeper and broader. In the high school we find a problem area centered around personal living — the problems of growing up: understanding my body, looking my best, being happy in my home and with my friends, my beliefs, my national and spiritual values, my individual abilities and interests. The student, then, comes to know himself and his social group. As his emotions and attitudes change and he meets new experiences, he makes new interpretations of his personal reactions and beliefs.

In schools all over the country there is a change with respect to the health of young people and the community. In the Wells High School in Chicago, for example, there is under way a reconstruction of the work of the school pointed directly at improving the health of the students. A Health Center is operated by the science department under the leadership of the head of the department, himself a practicing physician. This serves as a practical clinic.

Elsie Clapp's Community School at Arthurdale, West Virginia — in a region that had no health services — provided clinics, district nurses, and school dentists to a people who had accepted sickness as inevitable. The nutrition needs of the school were served by the parents. They came every day, prepared the lunches, and assumed the responsibility of the lunchroom. Miss Clapp insisted that one beginning point in the development of a community school is the improvement of the health of the community itself.

Thus we see the process of growth and living as the interrelation of the personal problems of the individual with his social problems in home, school, and community.

–What points would you now add to your definition of "to educate"?

–What new materials do you see that are educative?

–How are new facts brought to the student?

To Express Oneself

To know oneself is also to express oneself — to express oneself with color, with sound, with movement, with words, and with many other materials. In the conventional school we called these activities English, art, music, and dramatics. Today these hold a broader meaning. Let us see what this meaning is.

First, we go to the art studio. In one room a group of high school students is modeling with clay; three are working at a kiln, firing some of their recently completed clay models. In an adjoining room others are painting. The teachers are working artists. One is a sculptor, the other a painter. Paintings on easels around the room show several human figures. "You have a life class in the high school," we remarked.

"Oh yes, we have done it for years. These paintings are some of our more successful results."

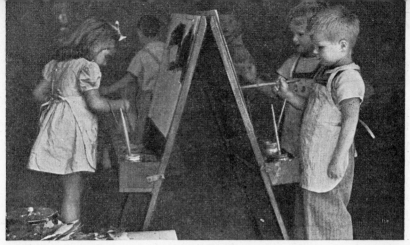

Crude as such painting may seem to an adult, it is nevertheless rich in creative experience for the child. (Louise M. Gross photo.)

"What a far cry this is," we said, "from the copybook drawing of our childhood days. How about architecture?"

"We study architecture and industrial design in several ways. Whenever a new building is going up, the members of the older groups are brought into the discussion of its design. They make sketches, criticize ideas and plans, and do a great deal of reading from the story of architecture. We also have built up a fairly good file of pictures and plans of modern schoolhouses."

One of the students goes to a cabinet and brings out pictures of the beautiful Crow Island School in Winnetka, Illinois. "We were crazy about this," he said, "and wanted to build our school something like it. But, of course, since we build of wood, there are lots of things in that building we couldn't use. Still, we are learning to use new materials even in our own homemade plant."

In Hughes Mearns's John Masefield Club, which took the place of the old English I in the Lincoln School,

"a single hour . . . would show that here is freedom to think and abundant exercise in that freedom; that child expression is based upon child experience; that to answer 'right' is to speak out of the fullness of living, not solely out of a book but out of life itself. One feels the freedom even from language self-consciousness; the thought follows a natural child form, clumsy and even comic from an adult standpoint, but adequate always for the end in view. Two fears are notoriously absent, the fear of not saying the right thing, and the fear of not speaking the correct set of words." [1]

[1] Hughes Mearns: *Creative Youth*, page 61. Copyright 1925 by Doubleday & Company, Inc. Used by permission.

In Mearns's classes the young people *created* remarkable essays, poems, and short stories. Mearns *was himself* a creative writer and had the approach of the poet to the young people. "I can't tell you what you should write about," was his frequent approach to a new pupil, "because I don't know what you know; but I could tell you what I want to write about myself." Then followed a vivid picturing of recent and remote experiences, so personal that no one else would dream of using the material. "That's the sort of experience I am having, but, of course, you wouldn't know enough about that. Now you — what sort of experience have you been having? Where have you been? What have you done recently? What do you think about most of the time?" [1]

In the child's creative play in these newer schools the story is the same:

> "A five-year-old group at the Rosemary Junior School visited a railroad station. They met the engineer and the fireman, who talked to them and let them climb into the engine. They saw the fire; they blew the whistle and rang the bell. About a week later they built a train in the court with out-of-door materials. They used a pail turned upside down for a bell, with a rope attached to it leading into the cab of the engine.
>
> "DAVID (*climbing onto the coal car*): All aboard! All aboard!
> "JULIA: "You be the fireman and I'll be the engineer. Your name's Mr. Smith, but I must call you Jim.
> "DAVID: All aboard! We're going to New York!
> "JULIA (*ringing the bell*): Ding dong! Ding dong! Toot! Hoo-oo-oo-oo-oo-oo! You must shovel the coal, Jim.
> "DAVID (*chanting*): Port Chester, New York. Now we're at New York! Now we're at New York!
> "In this case the dialogue of the engineer and the fireman was more truly a characterization of the real workers they had met, and because of the vividness of experience, the engine itself was a more complete construction, showing a new understanding of parts and how they worked." [2]

Here, then, are examples of newer ways of educating in the arts of expression. How much new light do they throw on the meaning of education?

[1] Gertrude Hartman and Ann Shumaker (Editors): *Creative Expression*, page 25. Copyright by E. M. Hale & Company. Used by permission.
[2] *Ibid.*, page 277.

HUGHES MEARNS (1875–) has won national recognition as a true artist-teacher. In his inspired teaching in the Lincoln School, Teachers College, Columbia University (1920–25), he was the chief initiator of the "creative youth" movement. In New York University (1925–46) he extended his work into the adult field. The subject-minded teacher of facts, says Mearns, neglects the creative impulse, failing to quicken feeling and to arouse "the sense of awe, wonder, insight, and delight" in which the facts should be set. Creative education, he explains, is not a subject-in-itself but an approach to all subjects of study. . . . It is a way of using the mind, the feeling, and the imagination.

Mearns sees the task of educators as that of developing people through "cultural living," by the cultivation of taste and judgment and the creative use of one's own mind.

–Can you tell now what is meant by "expression"? by "creative"?

–How is expression an important part of education?

–How does the creative process differ from memorizing? from solving problems in everyday life, in science, in mathematics?

–What are the most favorable conditions for the arts of expression?

Pupil-Teacher Planning

Before we leave the schools, let us ask one final question: What part do the young people play in planning their own work?

In the lower grades, a little; in the upper grades, a great deal. It depends on the children's age and how mature they are. We let them decide things in every case so far as they are competent to do so. They are certainly not competent to plan the general program of their total education from infancy to maturity. Only a group of teachers with years of experience and with the help of the parents are competent to do that. But the students are competent to take part in the planning of the work of any given day or for an even longer period of time. The staff decides the scope and organization of the work for the year; the young people study this plan in light of their immediate needs and interests. Through this participation we build their acceptance of responsibility. Does the class meet together to plan the work of the day? Yes, if there is a need, and in groups whenever it is necessary.

This must conclude our in-school examples of the newer interpretation of education. Enough have been cited to enable you to define clearly what it means "to educate." Before we turn to a systematic review of that problem, we need to explore another matter.

The Educativeness of Out-of-School Living

Many educators today insist that the out-of-school life of children is educationally more effective than that in school. The home life, the newspapers, the magazines, and the books that the young people read; the interplay of conversation, criticism, and discussion in community and youth organizations and groups; the radio, the newsreels, and the motion pictures — all these, they say, play a more important part in the educational development of a young person than does the school itself. Is this statement true? Consider a startling fact:

Make some quick computations of the actual number of waking hours in the period from birth to the end of the eighteenth year. Figure school attendance liberally at 200 days a year with six school hours a day. Assume attendance in school from kindergarten at the age of four through the twelfth grade at the age of eighteen. What per cent of the waking hours are spent in school? out of school? Roughly, what per cent are spent under the active influences of the home?

What conclusions have you reached from this rough computation and comparison? Does in-school experience constitute the most important part of the educational life of the young people? Is it important, then, to study the educativeness of out-of-school experience?

The Educativeness of Home Life

Granted that a large percentage of a child's time is spent out of school, which institution gets the larger share? First and foremost, the home and the family. Here the child's life is centered with the father and mother, brothers and sisters. Here is the vital and socially-motivated nub of his life for a long period — eighteen, twenty, or more years — and here, potentially, is the greatest educational center. In the home, in the first four or five years, life habits are established and temperamental patterns of behavior are set. Everything in the life of the home — the work and play of the family, the relations with friends — all social activities are naturally motivated. Problems — every kind of problem the home encounters — can be used realistically, as the wise parents meet them *with* their children at the moment when they arise. The home, then, is the greatest possible educational force in the life of the young person.

Part-Time Work

For young people who live in the smaller towns and in cities, part-time work in the late afternoons and on Saturdays and vacations is another profoundly educative influence. By the independent shouldering of responsibility for paid jobs outside their homes, boys and girls learn the practical ways of the world, build up habits of industry and thrift that can be acquired in no other way, learn the real value of money, come to understand people through firsthand mature contacts with them, and see their neighborhood in new ways. Doing socially useful work brings them into the community as school education has never done.

Agencies of Fact and Understanding

After the home and work, probably the most important out-of-school agencies are the newspapers, the radio, and the newsreel. Perhaps these are not educational influences to you. But consider a moment: Where do people get most of their "facts" about public affairs, about community problems as well as community doings? Where do they get their news about the nation and the world outside? Primarily from the newspaper, the magazine, the radio, and the newsreel. Certainly *on the side of being informed* the people, youth included, depend greatly on these sources. The systematic forum discussions that come over the air several times each week bring facts organized and interpreted, national and world problems and issues presented systematically, and arguments logically stated. Here is *directed* study.

Other Educational Resources

In the so-called purely entertainment side of life there is also rich educational material. The theater, concerts, sports, and motion pictures all make their contribution. Through the radio and television many of these entertainment features now reach people in the most rural areas. How our new means of communication and transportation have changed the education of the youth of America!

Must not the unique American institution, the comics, be considered a source of education? Are the lives of the American young people influenced by such youth organizations as the Boy Scouts, the Girl Scouts, the 4-H Clubs, the CYO, community centers, and similar groups?

These few illustrations merely introduce you to the problems of the educational possibilities in the out-of-school life in America. They will be more fully discussed in Chapters 7 and 10. But even this brief glimpse is an impressive reminder that education today includes far more than that which goes on in even the best schools.

–Do you need now to revise your definition of "to educate"?

–What other out-of-school resources for education can you mention?

–Are these being used by the schools? If so, how?

We come, finally, to a summary step — namely, to find the key idea with which to answer our major question. It emerges from every one of the examples studied — namely, the conditions of educativeness.

What Are the Conditions of Educativeness?

First: One condition of educativeness has stood out above all others throughout modern educational history — *freedom to investigate and experiment.* Any experience, whether in or out of school, will have educational possibilities if it leaves the young people free to explore. It must stimulate them to inquire, to ask questions, and to try to find the answers themselves. Therefore, if we depend constantly on the teacher or the textbook to give the answer, the child is hampered in learning. To the extent that investigation on the part of the young people is stopped, the opportunity to educate has been lost.

Blocks, toys, little hands, and play experiences build docks, ramps, tunnels, and skyscrapers. (Photo from Play Schools Association, New York City.)

Second: Is the experience in question organized as a problem? A problem presents alternatives; it compels the learner to choose; it prevents the passive memorizing of answers. The first step in getting young people to think is to present a vital problem, the answer to which can be found only by study and the analysis of all its possibilities and their relationships to other experiences. Hence, one criterion by which we judge the educativeness of an experience to be used in the school is: Has it problem-solving possibilities?

Third: The extent to which an experience will be educative will depend upon whether or not it fits the maturity, mental capacities, and interest of the pupil. Does he understand its basic ideas? Is it adapted to his level of development? Is its complexity within his power of analysis? An experience will be of interest to the pupil if it supplies a real need in his life, a need which he consciously feels or can be brought to recognize. Interest and need go hand in hand. As one asks these questions, the great role of the teacher stands out: The teacher guides the whole learning process by selecting and interpreting experiences appropriate to the pupil's interest and capacities.

37

Fourth: But more than interest is demanded: The self-effort of the pupil must go hand in hand with it. Hence, we must ask of the experience: *Has the experience been so organized that the pupil's incentive to study and investigate will be stimulated?* It must neither be obvious, too easy of understanding and solution, nor so complex that it baffles and discourages the first efforts of curiosity and inquiry.

Fifth: Finally, *does the experience have within it the power to incite individual creativeness and bring about the coöperation of the pupil with others in the group?* While many educative experiences are markedly individualistic, some experiences of the school should make social demands upon the young people and bring them into coöperative group work. In your later study of curriculum planning, you will inquire more thoroughly into this criterion of educativeness. Ideally, there should be a fine fusion in the curriculum of experiences; many of those which develop the creative ability of the pupil as a person should also draw him into the social activities of the school.

At this point we should inquire a bit into the concept of growth as a criterion of educativeness. Of the several measures of growth we suggest three:

–*First:* Can the person manage himself better as a result of the experience? That is, has he "learned"?

–*Second:* Has he consciously generalized what he has learned? Has he thought out its significance and stated it to himself? This is something that the teacher (as active guide and friendly critic) must help the learner do.

–*Third:* Has the experience been so selected and organized that it is personal and important to him? This points to the critical role of the teacher in choosing and designing experiences with conscious anticipation of the pupil's fullest possible growth.

In presenting these three measures of growth as the supreme criterion of the educativeness of a situation, we have added another important psychological idea which will be of use to you in all your work as a teacher. This is the concept of *learning.* Throughout your work you will be constantly studying the learning process. You will ask: Under what conditions will the learner learn best? In one sense this is another way of asking: What are the conditions of educativeness? For one of the important outcomes of any educational experience is learning that results in changes in behavior patterns, in the learner's way of living.

These, then, are the important conditions of educativeness. Their statement carries us much further on the path toward a clear definition of educativeness. At this point you should make your own definitions, but we shall give you illustrative examples which you may criticize and evaluate. Suppose we try our hand in that direction and say —

> An experience is educative to the extent that the person who undergoes it is prepared, as a consequence of it, to live another experience more completely, more sensitively.

Or, using our criterion of growth:

> An experience is educative to the extent that the person who has undergone it has *grown* as a result of it.

Finally, another way to phrase all this is: Young people tend to learn if the experiences that have been developed by the teacher are genuinely related to them. We sometimes say the experiences must be "real," intimately related to the personal needs of the young people. Thus you will ask constantly: Upon what needs, interests, and problems of my young people shall I build my teaching?

This discussion of the vital process of human growth and learning gives you the needed material with which to discuss the question: "What does it mean to educate?"

Two Things to Do: Study Good Teaching in Action and Study Its Principles in Books

Seek out good teachers and observe their teaching — that is the way for you to begin. Better yet, get them to take you on as interne, to live and work with them and their students. Do as much of it yourself, as you can, even while you are a beginning student of education.

But — *read and study as you observe and teach.* Forward-looking teachers and parents have not only been building better schools across our America; in order to build, they found they had to have a philosophy of education and on it to create a design for education. They worked with the combined spirit of scientists and artists. The result, since World War I, is a magnificent library of new writings about education and teaching.

For example, while John Dewey was creating his famous Laboratory School at the University of Chicago (1896–1904), he was thinking out and writing down the principles of learning and teaching and the place of education in a society like that of America. The result was a series of great essays and books. Several were so right that they are read today as they were in 1900; we cite three: School and Society, Child and the Curriculum, and, for present purposes, Chapters II, III, and IV of Democracy and Education. In 1936, forty years after the school opened, two teachers in it, Katherine Camp Mayhew and Anna Camp Edwards (sisters), wrote its dramatic story in The Dewey School; don't miss it, or its two appendices, which give Dewey's own principles of education in a good school.

Chapters III and XVII of Harold Rugg's Foundations for American Education also describe and interpret The Dewey School; Chapter XXI does the same thing for the progressive schools that Dewey stimulated, and Chapter XVI describes the Englewood School at Chicago, carried on for eighteen years (1883–1901) by Francis W. Parker, whom Dewey described as "The Father of progressive education."

In dealing with the conception of the educativeness of out-of-school living, you will need to devote yourselves to the study of our changing civilization, for we and our young people are caught in a period of frightening social change and national and world conflict. (It might pay you well at this time to turn forward and scan Chapters 4 to 6 to get a preview of this task.)

A good introductory piece on guiding growth is Chapter XVIII, "Education for Change," of James S. Plant's Personality and the Culture Pattern. Since the close of World War II the Educational Policies Commission of the National Education Association has published several interesting volumes picturing imaginatively the fine schools that could be built today in America. See, for example, Education of all American Children for the elementary school, and Education for All American Youth for the high school. From them you catch a glimpse of what the meaning of education might become in a few years hence, through a new curriculum that reaches far beyond the academic school.

Ernest O. Melby has described the school and its newer programs as a "laboratory for democratic living," in "Newer Instructional Practices of Promise" in the Twelfth Yearbook, 1939, of the Department of Supervisors and Directors of Instruction of the National Education Association.

For the creative spirit that is in all of us — fashioning things out of wood, color, fabrics, clay, sounds, words — see Harold Rugg and Ann Shumaker's

The Child-Centered School. The first half is a graphic description and appraisal of the newer conception of education; the latter half deals with creative expression in the various arts. Hughes Mearns's Chapter XXI, "All God's Chillun," of his *Creative Power* should be read in connection with it, as also his introduction to his earlier book, *Creative Youth.*

Carleton Washburne has written the outcome of twenty years of putting the new conception into action in a small public-school system in *A Living Philosophy of Education;* Chapter XXXI, "Using Community Resources," describes the way the Winnetka schools used the life of the community as educational experiences. Chapter XXI, "The Curriculum: Shunned and Neglected Areas," of Rugg's *Foundations for American Education* shows how the new school can build its curriculum around work, home life, the intimate problems of personal living, religion, and the controversial issues of our society.

CHAPTER 3

Understanding the Development of Personality

IN CONTINUING the study of education, we now turn our attention to one question: *Who is the human being that is to be educated?* What traits, needs, motives, interests make him a distinct personality?

The first insight into personality is an understanding of the significance of the organism, and there are several practical terms to help center attention upon it: *The whole child . . . the total personality . . . the style of life.*

Needs is the second key to understanding the development of a personality. We shall search for their sources both in physiological drives and in the social-psychological environment. Thus our study of the individual's needs will include the entire scope of motives — from drives to purposes. Upon these we can found our educational program.

The third central idea — the Mature Person — is the end-point of our study. Studying growth and development of children and youth, we need a goal — a personality to hold before our eyes. We shall strive now to understand the mature person, who will serve in that respect.

The Child as a Developing Person

ONE QUESTION you will decide as you start your life as a teacher is: What shall be the focus of my teaching? Our discussion of what it means to educate shows that two very different answers have been given. The teacher in the formal school habitually said: "I am a teacher of mathematics," or "I am a Supervisor of Music," or "I am a Director of the Special Subjects." Thus the emphasis was upon the subject matter.

But since the days of Francis Parker and John Dewey a new note has been heard in the educational land. Parker's famous Practice School in Chicago was no subject-centered school. Parker taught his teachers for a quarter of a century that neither science, nor geography, nor history, nor language, but the child was at the center of the educative process. He made this graphic by drawing great concentric circles representing subject matter based on the life of the race, but their center was always a child — a child growing, developing. The drives and purposes radiated from the child; the subject matter of learning was pointed back to the child. It was a *child-centered school*. Dewey agreed, and a host of educational leaders later inspired by him, that the school must be a child-centered community.

Each Child a Unique Life Style

Since Dewey's time, the statement, "I teach the child, not subject matter," has become almost a shibboleth of education. Also, it carries the meaning of: "I teach each *individual* child, not the children en masse." But such teaching is neither simple nor easy. One teacher

43

confronted by the task said: "My first day at school I saw a group of thirty-five youngsters. I wondered when I would ever learn to know them." [1] She worked hard during the next few days, visiting in the children's homes, and then she said: "From the blurred whole every child emerged by the end of the first week, an individual, clear and distinct." [1]

Thirty-five personalities, each one different from every other one; that is what a class really is from the standpoint of a true teacher. In every class you teach there will be as many life styles as there are children. There will be the cheerful, active child; the anxious child; the willing, obedient child; the timid, withdrawing one. And there will always be at least one power-seeker who, hand waving in the air, simply has to be first. This idea of uniqueness of personality, of style of life, is so important that it should be studied carefully. Let us consider some examples.

The Case of Philip

Philip was only five years and eight months old when he entered the first grade. The teacher realized he was young for the class; but she felt he could do the work, for his Binet intelligence test had shown an IQ (Intelligence Quotient) of 132, the mark of a "superior" child. In the class he was bright and quick, reasoned clearly, and remembered what he learned. The other children liked him because he was full of ideas, resourceful in inventing new games, always ready with suggestions; his skill in running and climbing and his ability to throw and catch a ball gave him prestige on the playground. His friends were always inviting him to do things, and he was included in the groups that formed during recess or lunch. The children felt that when Philip was in the group things were exciting.

On the surface he seemed to have all the ingredients for a successful and happy school life; yet there were disturbing signs. More and more the teacher overheard his companions saying: "Phil, stop worrying." "Phil, why do you ask so many questions?" Yes, she thought, Phil *did* ask a lot of questions; these seemed to show a sense of worry, and he seemed tense and strained. The teacher listened more carefully to his

---

[1] Commission on Teacher Education; American Council on Education: *Helping Teachers Understand Children*, page 46. Quoted by permission of American Council on Education.

Children coloring eggs: the cheerful, the curious, the leader, the anxious one — each a unique personality. (Louise M. Gross photo.)

questionings: "Did I do the examples all right?" "Why did we go into assembly hall by another door today?" "Why does John wear a snow suit before the snow has come?" "What mark did I get on my paper?" "When will the music class be over?"

What did this constant, querulous questioning mean? "Phil doesn't really care which door the class used or whether or not John wears a snow suit," the teacher thought. She studied Phil's problem more carefully; and one day as she watched him during an arithmetic period, she felt sure she was on the right track. She realized that whenever he was under a strain or felt he was being *tested*, he became panicky. At this particular moment, though he knew the answers perfectly, he just sat staring at the addition examples written on the board, biting his pencil and then his nails. Finally he glanced furtively at the others writing busily; then got up, asking to be excused. In two or three minutes the teacher followed him out and found him standing in the hallway, crying.

That afternoon the teacher visited Phil's mother and learned the true cause of Philip's anxieties. His younger sister had been recovering from a long attack of polio, and the mother had devoted herself almost altogether to her. Sally had been receiving the mothering, the care and attention, and Philip felt left out. He worried a lot, thinking, "She loves me, too, doesn't she?", yet growing more and more frightened.

His worries about little things at school were merely symptoms of a deep feeling of insecurity. Whenever there was the slightest shift in the familiar patterns of things, he became uneasy. As teacher and mother talked together, the mother also came to see the problem more clearly, and the two made a plan: At home the mother would make a special point of welcoming Philip when he returned from school and talking with him about his day. Instead of the usual early bedtime, he would be allowed to stay up after Sally had gone to sleep — to be alone with his mother and father, to have supper with them, and a story, and be specially tucked in for the night. Thus, he would be definitely reassured of his importance to them. At school Philip's teacher would arrange to build his feeling of security, being careful to praise his work and to show him special marks of her warmth and affection.

The plan worked well. Within a week Phil's torrent of questions had stopped; his forehead no longer wrinkled with anxiety; he became a changed and happy boy.

The Wide Range of Life Styles

There are many anxious children, some in every school group, and each one is a special case for study and guidance. But there are also many other types of personality. A few quick sketches will give a glimpse of the range of styles of life in every school class. First, Lucille, the teacher's right-hand helper:

"What a leader! What an actress! Lucille enjoys to the fullest taking on responsibility — she is chairman of committees, reads to the group and does many other things to help the class. . . . Father is manager of a fertilizer company. He takes part — an active part — in all community life. Spoke at the community meeting. Far above the average in leadership among the parents. . . . Father and mother support the school at all times. The mother is young — very attractive. . . . When I visited her she talked about her housekeeping, her guests, going out to social events with her husband, her children. She seemed very happy." [1]

[1] *Ibid.*, page 37.

There are the aloof, indifferent ones with whom the teacher never seems able to connect:

"Jack is quite a problem to me. I would like to help him. He comes late very often. He is always dirty. When he does get to school he takes such a long time getting started on his work. He seems content to sit and dream. There is no expression of interest on his face. When he is told to get started, he moves slowly into action, but then he soon stops work again and dreams. He never accomplishes anything because he does not persist long enough. This pattern of behavior continues during reading, spelling, language, and arithmetic periods, in fact all day long. He has some ability, for the little that he does is well done.

"All through the grades he has had the same traits. Teachers in these earlier grades tell me that they considered Jack quite a problem, for he had to be forced to do all the work. Naturally he failed to accomplish much. These teachers tried many ways of handling the boy. Some worked temporarily, but no technique was found that would solve the problem.

"So far I have found no interest in any form of activity. He does not enjoy painting or modeling or construction of any kind. He is not concerned with any subject. He is careless in handling materials and is frequently having accidents with paint. He is extremely clumsy in the use of his hands.

"As a rule he does not disturb the group. Only once in a while does he have any difficulty in getting along with children." [1]

Then there are the average, run-of-the-mine ones, fairly easy to get along with:

"Ned is one of the most likable children in the class. He is pleasant and can be appealed to. He enjoys teasing and sometimes carries it too far but we can forgive him easily because of his disposition and attitude. He is slightly sullen once in a while but whatever he does he seems to be willing to do over again — to admit that he has done wrong and to show that he is sorry. For instance, once on the playground he was rude to another teacher. I tried to talk to him, but he would not listen. Later in the day he asked to go see the teacher and tell her he was sorry. He returned, saying, 'Now I feel better.' This is his usual attitude." [2]

[1] Ibid., pages 28–29.   [2] Ibid., page 28.

Uniqueness of Life Style Centers Attention
on the Whole Person

We have given descriptions of four children, four styles of life, four different personalities — yet there are twenty-five or thirty more in every school class. Each is an individual; each must be studied separately and guided separately. This concern with the life style of a child is an effective starting point in your study of education, especially because it fixes attention on *the whole person*. Not only will you be *teaching the child*, but, more precisely, *the whole child* — not just Philip failing to do the examples on an arithmetic paper, but Philip worrying about events at home, feeling insecure, not wanted.

When teachers say they teach the whole boy or the whole girl, they are implying that in observing human behavior you see in every instance the whole child or the whole man or woman revealed in the behavior. Witness a child conducting a school orchestra, or his forty-year-old father solving an engineering problem with his co-workers over a drafting board. Both are examples of the whole-human-being-in-action. In each case the physical being, the mind, and the mood and emotions all are in the act. This is true of the behavior of most of us practically all the time; we are whole persons in action. So it is true of each child in your class, whether reading, writing, doing arithmetic, making a good run on the athletic field, taking part in the social studies discussion, watching a motion picture in the assembly hall, carrying on an experiment in the science laboratory, or building a boat model in the shop. Not one is a disembodied mind, not one a bundle of exploding emotions. All are whole children or youths in action.

This tendency for the whole body, mind, and emotions to act simultaneously and in integrated form is the Principle of the Whole. No principle of physiology, psychology, or education is of greater importance to the teacher. Psychologists express it by saying that "the organism tends to react as a whole"; the parts do not act separately. Hence, as teacher and psychologist of personality, while you will be dealing with groups of twenty, thirty, or more, you will be chiefly concerned with the whole personalities of each one. Each will have a unique style of life, and your concern with it will make you constantly aware of the integrated *wholeness* of each person.

An Important Scientific Idea: the Integrated Organism

There is a single scientific term for this idea of the whole person. You will need to understand the term and use it in your psychological studies. The term is *Organism*. It is indeed one of the most fundamental ideas of all the human sciences. Every living creature is an organism composed of millions of parts, but no part can work by itself alone. As George Hartmann says, "Tickle a man's foot and laughter occurs in the facial area." A severe head pain may affect the digestive system. We hear a loud sound, and the whole body moves. Every human act is complicated and interdependent. Consider such an act as handwriting: You probably write with your right hand. Try writing with your left hand. Your first attempt is much less legible and graceful than the writing done with your right hand; but it *is* handwriting and it *is* legible, much more legible than were your first attempts with your right hand. Thus, more than your right hand, arm, and fingers have learned to write. Your whole body has been involved.

A host of scientific laboratory studies confirm this principle of integration of the manifold parts of the organism. Research study of such organs as the endocrine glands — the thyroid and parathyroid, the adrenals, the pituitary, and others — has been one of the most fruitful lines of investigation. Since the middle of the nineteenth century, the power exerted by these ductless glands over the emotions and in the total behavior of the individual has been revealed by a slowly accumulating body of evidence. Since the beginning of the twentieth century scientific physiologists have studied the action of the digestive organs under various conditions of emotional stimulation. Dr. Walter B. Cannon and his research associates of Harvard showed, for example, that emotional hysteria in animals invariably evoked in them not only fear and rage but an increased adrenal secretion in the blood; under conditions of pain and intense emotions there occurred a marked increase in the sugar content of the blood. These results they confirmed by experiments on human beings.

Thus the research of the physiologists has proved that the manifold parts of the human organism do not work as separate units; they are organized, integrated. The chief agent in the process of integrating is the central nervous system, consisting of the brain and the spinal cord.

Along with the central nervous system is the autonomic (involuntary) system, of which the sympathetic nervous system is a part. All of these act in a unified way upon each of the stimuli or influences received through the receptors and effectors of the body's nerve system.

While the organism is the total living creature, the part played by the body is primary; everything depends upon it. As Hartmann says:

"The body breathes, runs, and digests, but it also loves, dreams, and writes history — to name but a few of its varied activities. . . . What is called 'mental life' is just that aspect of life which appears distinctively in our more subtle adaptations as memorizing, painting, debating, etc. Essentially, however, it is the living body . . . and not anything separate and distinct from it which solves algebraic equations, composes sonnets, and predicts eclipses." [1]

We lay great stress upon the part played by the body because teachers habitually act as though they were dealing only with minds. You must remember that you will never encounter a mind acting alone; the kind of "mind" you will deal with is the total organism, acting-as-a-whole. Study your own behavior and you will see the important part played by the body even as it responds with the simplest meanings. Try some simple experiments upon yourself. Try to say and to think "broad" while bringing the arms and hands close together in a contracting manner; note the feeling of strain in the body. Note how the gesture of the body tends to correspond to the meanings of the words you are using. Note how your body tends to strike *physical* attitudes of recoil, repulsion, or attraction, *corresponding to the mental attitudes of rage, fear, disgust, and love.* Listen to John Martin, eminent authority on the dance:

"When we watch a pantomimist, without scenery or properties, we are in no wise perplexed by his actions provided he is a good pantomimist. We know perfectly well that he is now knocking on a door, though there is no door there for him to knock on; now writing a letter, though he has neither ink nor paper; now counting his money, though his hands are actually empty. They are all movements so closely attached to experiences of our own that it requires no effort for us to *reproduce the memory of the experiences at sight of the movements.*" [2]

[1] George W. Hartmann: *Educational Psychology*, pages 44–45. Copyright 1941 by American Book Company.

[2] John Martin: *America Dancing*, pages 119–120. Copyright 1936 by Dodge Publishing Company.

These illustrations will carry home to you the meaning of integration in human response and the all-important part played by the body in every human act. As you watch people, you will understand with increasing clarity that there is no separate mind, no separate spirit, no separate body. In the term "organism" we include all the human responses, and center our attention on the unity of the millions of interdependent parts. It is the human organism that walks and talks, breathes and eats, reproduces its own species, and has the capacity to read, write, reckon, and govern itself through the use of thought. The successful teacher is the one who teaches the whole boy or girl in light of the total situation.

What Shall Be the Starting Point of a Child's Education?

Granted that the whole human being is the focus of our attention as teachers, what is it about him that determines what we teach and how we teach? This question also has been debated for generations, the answers given today differing profoundly from those of older, more formal schools. In earlier times the tendency was to see the boy or the girl as a receptacle into which facts could be poured, an automaton whose skills were to be perfected. Both the needs and the purposes of the children were ignored, or at least misunderstood. The child was visualized as a "learner," as plastic, complacent material to be molded by an all-wise teacher. He was to accept what the teacher said and obey the directions of the school. The system of rewards and punishments saw to it that he learned. This system consisted of corporal punishment or the threat of being marked down, and the reward of a red star, a high mark, a prize, or being on the honors list. Thus the teacher acted as though he were utterly unaware of the separate children and of their needs, interests, and purposes.

It was Parker and Dewey and the other leaders of the newer schools who rediscovered the great principles of human purposes and needs. Some of the "progressive" schools after 1910, overenthusiastic about "freeing the child," went off the deep end, confusing what the child merely *wanted* to do, with his *needs*. The more extreme schools built their whole program on pupils' interests and desires; the curriculum of one — the Decroly school in Belgium — was built on what the director called "centers of interest." Most of the newer schools, however, had a much more balanced point of view. Instead of centering attention on the desires and spontaneous interests of the children, they studied carefully the problem of needs, and how these can be used in building worth-while purposes and interests. During the same years scientifically trained physiologists were clarifying the role of the basic body drives in child development and behavior, while the psychologists and psychiatrists were showing the tremendous part played by emotional and social needs. As a consequence, the child's total needs — physiological and social — have come to be accepted as the very starting point of building a plan for his education.

The Needs of the Human Being

We asked a college youth recently about this problem: "Which of your needs are so important that your education should have been developed around them?" He told us at great length. Above all things he needed to keep alive, he said, to know his body and how to keep it strong and healthy. He needed a wife, a home and children of his own, to understand sex, to know how to love and cherish his family, and to build a good home. To have all this, he added, he needed work, to know how to work, to respect work, and to enjoy it. To be a good citizen he needed to know his country and the world, their history and the true forces that make them what they are. He was deeply concerned with what makes unemployment and depressions and how to prevent them. He kept trying to say that he needed to express himself in many ways, to create his own statement and to appreciate to the fullest the fine statements about life made by our poets. He sensed that he needed ballast and balance in his life: a plan to help him keep the points of life's compass straight and to guide him in a direction. He ended his remarks with a fine comment: "I need to feel the purpose of my life, both here and in the universe, now and hereafter."

In this single paragraph are summed up practically all the needs around which the education of a child or youth should be developed: the physical needs of the body, the social-sexual need for family life, the great central need of work, the need of knowing about one's world, the need to express oneself, and the need for a philosophy of life. A whole school could be built upon such a statement of needs.

With this brief introduction to the problem of human needs, we turn to a more complete statement of those needs basic to what and how we teach.

Needs Are Twofold: Physiological and Social

The Heredity-Environment Problem In each child with whom you work visualize *the two important factors that make him what he is.* The first is the physical equipment with which he, as an organism, is born; the other is the social, human world in which he develops. Child . . . and society; organism . . . and environment. Of every child and grownup — for example, Philip, Lucille, Jack, and Ned — might we ask: What made him like that? Depending on whom you ask, you get two distinctly different answers. Some will say: "It's in him; the stock was good (or bad, or indifferent). Blood will tell!" Others will say: "That family is always in a turmoil," or "It's the bad company he keeps," or "It's the neighborhood he lives in." Thus the answers always reduce to two types: one stresses *heredity*, the organism and its physiology; the other the *environment*, the social factors.

Throughout your studies this heredity-environment controversy will always be with you. It is important here because it points inescapably to the two distinctive factors — physiology of the body and the effect upon it of the environment — these, working together, make it possible for the organism to grow up as a human person. There follow from these two factors two distinctive sets of *needs*: the deep-seated physiological needs of the organism and the profoundly important social-psychological needs that arise from its development in a social world of human beings.

The Physiological Needs of the Organism — The Principle of Self-Balance

There are many basic physical needs (sometimes called drives or tensions), but five are well known to you and will suffice as illustrations:

First: the periodic need for food and drink — recurring throughout life because of the deficits in chemical ingredients created by the exhaustive action of the body.

Second: the need for periodic elimination of waste from the body.

Rest time is an important part of the daily program. (Photo from Play Schools Association, New York City.)

Third: the need for rest due to the deficits in body tissues, depleted by activity of the body.

Fourth: the need of the body for protection against harm from the physical environment.

Fifth: the need for a mate of the opposite sex.

These are the basic physiological drives, or needs. A consideration of them leads us to one of the most important principles of human life: *The Principle of Homeostasis, or Self-Balance*.

Walt Whitman, the great American poet, perceived and immortalized in one line of his profound *Leaves of Grass* one of the most significant characteristics of the behavior of man:

"O, to be self-balanced for contingency."

He was recording the rhythmic ebb and flow of action and reaction, pressure and counterpressure, tension and release, that you can illustrate in many common experiences. Each human body tends to maintain a state of balance: a normal body temperature (ranging around 98.6° F), rate of breathing and of heartbeat, etc. Whenever this balanced state is disturbed — that is, whenever internal *deficits* occur or external forces threaten — the body organs counteract to *compensate* for the deficits or to offset the threats. To cite examples:

–The body adjusts with a thermostat-like exactness to a sudden drop in room or outdoor temperature.

54

–If a person, accustomed to living near sea level, exerts himself when at a high altitude, the body compensates for the depletion of oxygen supply by more rapid breathing.

–When a person runs fast, climbs a long flight of stairs, or engages in heavy manual labor, the heart "pounds" and breathing speeds up.

–When the stevedore or the structural worker puts a strain on his muscles by lifting heavy objects, the reduction in oxygen supply is compensated for by minute adjustments in the action of the heart.

In each case we have shown that when a normal state of balance is disturbed by bodily activity or by threats from the external environment which have created deficits, compensatory action is made by the body, supplying the deficiency and restoring the balance.

Two generations of physiological studies supply a vast amount of confirming evidence; the operation of the endocrine glands and the hunger cycle provide two examples. The endocrine glands supply the blood stream with delicately balanced amounts of secretions indispensable to the normal metabolism of the body. The thyroid, for example, supplies the critically needed calcium; the adrenals supply equally essential sodium. If the amounts supplied deviate ever so slightly from the individual's peculiar normal need, the deficit or excess will be revealed in his total physical condition, and the individual, either naïvely or consciously, will do something to restore the balance.

Dr. Curt Richter cites the case of the boy who literally "ate salt by the teaspoonful." His family doctor, ignorant of the role of the glands, ordered the mother to prevent the boy from eating salt; the boy died. A post-mortem examination revealed a tumor on the adrenal gland which had been reducing the normal amount of sodium needed by the body; hence the boy's compensatory action in eating salt (sodium chloride) which would restore the needed balance to the disturbed metabolism of the body. Other experiments on sodium deficiency, induced by removing the adrenal glands of rats, confirmed this knowledge; such rats, when offered both pure water and a three per cent solution of sodium chloride, always chose the salt solution, the action of the body thus being maintained normally in spite of the absence of the adrenal glands.

Other confirmations of the remarkable self-balancing ability of the physical organism are shown by the "hunger cycle." Dr. Walter B.

Cannon and his associates have shown the connection between the contractions of the empty human stomach and the feelings of hunger. Of the five steps in the cycle, the *first* two are physical: First, the chemical resources in the stomach are exhausted — a physical deficit; second, the stomach contracts, the muscles become tense. The remaining steps are partly psychological: Third, the person becomes aware that he's hungry, he craves food; fourth, he eats; fifth, as the stomach becomes full, the physical organs relax and the human being feels that he has enough. Thus the chemistry of the body initiates the action, and the muscles continue it; the psychological factors involved in knowing and feeling emerge later.

We can define physical needs as a tensional state of the organism produced by either an excess or a deficit of the body substances or the stimuli needed to keep it in perfect equilibrium. *These needs are physiological drives or tensions;* in fact the three words — *needs, drives,* and *tensions* — are used synonymously. Hence, physical life as the basis of psychological life is a recurring interplay of tension and release. Life might be said to consist of periodic swings: balance . . . imbalance . . . balance . . . imbalance.

We should ask ourselves what we can learn from our brief study of this important biological *principle of homeostasis,* as Dr. Cannon named it. To the teacher it should convey the realization that needs of the individual are so real, so powerful, so not-to-be denied that they must be recognized and accepted. The wise teacher will go farther; he will make use of these powerful drives by organizing the life of the school and the work of the class around these needs. Thus he will provide impetus for good living and learning. It is interesting here to conjecture with Dr. Cannon that the homeostatic process may well be operating in human beings to satisfy needs still unrecognized. These needs may be of physiological or psychological-social origin. The importance of this complicated process is bound to be increasingly appreciated, and the process itself may be more far-reaching than we now know.

The Social-Psychological Needs: Motives and Purposes

With these primary physiological needs in action, the social needs of the human being develop through the very process of living with other human beings. We sometimes call these social needs "secondary," but by this we merely mean that they appear after birth; they are developed from the interplay of the organism with its environment. In fact, they begin at the moment of birth because the baby's body, free from the mother's body, at once demands food, which is usually supplied from the mother's breast. This then becomes a "social" need, the first of myriads of human social needs in threescore years and ten. Because they are fused with the physiological needs, we call them bio-social.

Although they are secondary in point of emergence, they are just as important, just as primary, as the physiological needs. From the physical, social, and psychological needs spring the motives of men. These motives are the powerhouses of human behavior. Study the behavior of the children in your class, asking: What makes them do the things they do? Look about you at the grownups in your own community. What drives their behavior? Look back over our history. What motive power led America's distinguished men to perform heroic feats in building our country? In each case there existed a set of motives and purposes, and back of the motives, physiological and social needs. So it is with the children. Behind each act of a child there lie motives, purposes; behind these are physiological or social needs.

Needs Develop as Personality Develops

One of the clearest ways to understand the social needs of the human being is to see them emerging stage by stage in the life history of the individual. As we sketch briefly the developmental process, you will notice that several important concepts are building at the same moment. One of these concepts is that of the *self*.

The Rise of the Self in the First Two Years

Satisfaction for the newborn infant consists in experiencing pleasurable sensations, such as sucking, feeling warmth and support, and being cuddled. His first realization of himself comes as he responds to other people, especially the mother. His hunger is satisfied by her and as he is dressed by her, held in her arms, and loved, he experiences other satisfactions. It is in the social act that the self arises and that the

CAROLINE B. ZACHRY (1894–1945) was an outstanding leader in the study of child guidance and personality development in both private and public schools. After teaching English in the Lincoln School of Teachers College, Columbia, from 1922 to 1926, she served for some years as Head of the Department of Psychology and Mental Hygiene at the Montclair (N.J.) State Teachers College. She then became Director of the Bureau of Child Guidance of the New York City schools. Her wise influence was widely felt throughout the system.

She was interested in the more profound factors of personality development. Trained as a lay psychiatrist, she kept closely in touch with welfare, civic, and religious groups. In addition to maintaining a private practice she devoted time to meeting with teacher and parent groups, adding to the general understanding of child behavior and needs. She was a member of the board of *Parents Magazine*, and organized the Institute for Personality Development. After her death this Institute was named in her honor. She was on the Board of Directors, and was Director of Research on Personality Development, of the Progressive Education Association.

child's gestures take on significance. He identifies himself with the mother and the others in the immediate family. The act is twofold, building an attitude of dependence on the one hand and, on the other, of habit, discipline, and independence. These are the first social acts of the Self and Other. The first glimmer of self arises through the "consciousness of acts and thoughts as they are related to others," the Other being largely the mother.

"The baby's first love," says Zachry, "is himself. He is completely self-centered"; as he "discovers his own body . . . his feeling of self is strengthened." [1]   In his play life he learns to walk, talk, handle things, develop skills; he plays the roles of the father, the mother, or the workman in the house. As he assumes these roles, he identifies himself with others. It is in these activities that the child begins to see himself as others see him. Charles H. Cooley's records [2] of the language and behavior of infants dealt with such questions as, "How is 'I' learned and what does it mean?"   Cooley says: "The Self Idea is a social conception . . . 'I' is social in that the very essence of it is the assertion of self-will in a social medium of which the speaker is conscious."

[1] Caroline B. Zachry: "The Growth Process," *Democracy and the Curriculum, Third Yearbook of John Dewey Society*, page 319.
[2] Kimball Young: *Source Book for Social Psychology*, page 337.

Moreover, "I" does not mean the visible or tangible body; it "means primarily a self-assertive feeling linked with action or emphasis expressive of the same." In his conversation and in his play the child stresses *my* mummy, *my* dog, *my* bed. Let another child come into the nursery, and he grabs toys for himself or demands, "I want this."

The Nursery School Years

In every nursery school we must assume, then, a group of little egocentric Selves — asserting themselves, defending themselves, contradicting, commanding, and resisting interferences. For example, one of the authors of this book conducted studies of the personalities of kindergarten children.

> "In one investigation, a study of the language of four-year-olds and five-year-olds, we found that more than two fifths of all their conversation revealed a naïve interest in themselves and their own affairs. Only one twenty-fifth of the conversations was an overt expression of the child's interest in the group. Most of the remarks were indicative of the trait we call 'self-assertion'; that is, they showed a sense of personal power, self-display, injection of self into a situation, defense of one's feeling of ownership, resistance to interference, contradiction, commands, threats, and derision." [1]

At this age a child shows a complete absence of modesty. He is interested in his body, plays with it, and asks questions about it. Teachers and mothers must accept this behavior for what it is, namely, a normal stage in growing up. The child is learning about the world, and to him the most important and interesting fact in the world is himself and his body. At this stage the child has an intense need for security and depends on adults for it and for a source of authority. The child's questions must be answered; he must be both reassured and stimulated to further inquiry. The world begins pressing in upon him; "emotional cultural pressures" make demands on every side, and the school must handle him in an understanding, sympathetic way. "He wants cuddling, caressing, and comforting attention."

Home and school must make sure that the child is neither overprotected nor deprived of affection. Family and teachers therefore

[1] Harold Rugg: *American Life and the School Curriculum*, page 289. Ginn & Company; 1936.

must be careful not to hold him back in the building of responsibility, nor, on the other hand, demand independence in a young child too soon. Dangerous emotional tensions may be created by insistence on too rapid learning. In a nursery school the child learns, in playing with other children of his age, the fundamental principles of getting on with other human beings. By sharing toys and taking turns on play apparatus, he learns to be a coöperative part of a group; he finds that rules which benefit the group work also to his own advantage.   .

As he starts nursery school, he is experiencing for the first time a world outside the safe horizon of his own comfortable family circle. He is surrounded by strangers who may expect new and seemingly difficult things from him. The comfort and reassurance he receives at this point from his teacher will do more than insure the happiness of his first days at school; it may well establish in him a confidence in the friendliness of people outside his own family.

Childhood and the Elementary School

In its general over-all history, the growth of most children appears to be an uninterrupted, ever-continuous process. Actually, physical growth is sporadic. Periods of rapid growth are followed by plateaus of apparent standing still. Although every stage of development builds on the gains of former ones, it also inherits the patterns of behavior that cause difficult adjustments later. But large individual differences exist, and boys and girls move into the elementary school with widely varying behavior patterns.

From the time of birth to adulthood there are two periods in which young people are particularly dependent on grownups: first, during infancy and through the nursery school years; second, from eleven or twelve through the years of adolescence. During the years of the elementary school, children are freeing themselves from parents and other adults. So much so, in fact, that they need special understanding and wise handling. If they are coerced, or nagged, the resulting hostilities and antagonisms will stand as barriers to coöperation between the child and the grownup. During these years from approximately six to twelve, the intensity of infant dependency declines; the child relies less upon adults, even to the point of rejecting their interest. He tends to turn to his own mates, quite generally to gangs of his own sex. For a few years the

In nursery school, children learn to get along with others. (Louise M. Gross photo.)

gang seems to have more authority than the home. Manners and social habits deteriorate. As Zachry says, the boy may have washed his hands at six or seven, but at nine or ten he is "always dirty . . . prefers old and shabby clothes . . . glories in semiarticulate slang." The family is now alien. The gang is the in-group, and life must have its secrets. Strong loyalties and antagonisms appear. Intellectual interests develop and shift. Curiosity in the outside world grows. The boy "wants to know what things are made of and how they work . . . girls become interested in sewing and cooking . . . both like to work in the graphic and plastic arts. They are freer in creative expression."

During this period there is a real danger of miseducation and mismanagement; wishes of children and of adults seem to be sharply in conflict. Grownups are always "ordering them about"; the taboos of elders are frequent and emphatic. Parents worry over the slovenly habits of their children, and many adults are hurt by what seems to be a rejection of themselves. For the child this is a dangerous period of emotional tensions and insecurity; only sensitive understanding and mature judgment on the part of adults will assure the child all the freedom he is capable of using. Such opportunities for freedom will give him a sense of independence and invaluable experience in solving his own problems. Moreover, the realization that he is respected and trusted by adults will go far toward giving him the self-confidence he is seeking.

Here is a very real opportunity for the teacher of the young child — an opportunity to guide the child in making responsible choices within the range of socially acceptable behavior patterns. The teacher will

61

have to realize that much of his guidance is accomplished indirectly. To the child, pressure from the group is more convincing than any advice or control that may be given either by parent or teacher. A certain key to success in dealing with the child is a genuine interest in what the latter is thinking: his activities, games, jokes, hobbies, and organizations. Above all, the parent and the teacher must know that boys and girls of this age are now markedly widening their community and changing their loyalties. The sensitive teacher will make wise use of group activities by allowing the children to take leadership and, with her guidance, work out their own standards. Such childhood experiences will establish the basis for good adjustment in the coming adolescent years.

Adolescence and Youth: the Junior-Senior High School

From its Latin derivative the word adolescence means "growing up." It is a period of sharp transformation in the growth process — extending from ten, eleven, or twelve years of age to the ages of sixteen or eighteen, depending on the individual. It is a period when boys and girls seek the status of the adult — seek to free themselves from the domination of parents, teachers, and adults in general. This vital need of freedom and maturity is a natural expression, inherent in the physical developments of the body from that of a child to that of a mature man or woman. With this great physical transformation come changed emotional reactions and attitudes. It is also a period during which many boys and girls leave their school life and go into some kind of a vocation — a period in which they establish themselves as independent members of society, socially and economically.

During adolescence the individual emerges as a differentiated social being. His interests shift from club activities and gangs toward new individual and group loyalties. He displays intense interest in particular boys, girls, and older persons — another important phase of the weaning from home, of the extension of the self into the larger world. Significant physiological changes occur, which, to those children who earlier in their development have not been given some understanding of sex and the life processes, may seem at first mysterious, and even terrifying. The development of sex characteristics, menstruation, and glandular developments change the emotional and sexual needs. The curves of physical and emotional growth no longer keep pace with one another, for emotional maturity tends to lag behind physical development. The experience of "falling in love" bursts upon some adolescents with tremendous force. As this happens, companions who are developing more slowly look on with astonishment, amusement, or even teasing.

Among these maturing youths there is increasingly keen competition for social approval. New friendships are formed, especially with the opposite sex. The attitude of "I am grown up" appears, and there develops the desire to be independent of parents and teachers. For some it is the stage of "showing-off" and aggression. Plans are made for adult life — fantastic plans, egocentric plans — all subject to the pressures of social approval and disapproval. The self now extends even further into the Other with its three basic components — "self-assurance, self-reliance, and self-esteem." Character, the moral self, emerges as the guiding, organizing, impelling force. Interest grows in religion, in politics, in occupations. This is another expression of the adolescent in his effort to identify himself with something bigger than his past social groups of the home, the gang, and the school.

As competition and conflict increase, the youth experiences internal struggles; his attempts to establish the status of his self, to build up his integrity as a person, involve difficult decisions and painful adjustments. It is indeed a period of self-consciousness, of inferiority, of reticence about hopes and aspirations. The intellectual work of the school — the use that a youth makes of his intelligence — will depend critically on his social and emotional patterns of behavior and development. His family relationships are in a state of delicate balance and easily develop antagonisms. More than ever he needs comradeship, sympathy, and understanding, a sense of being accepted and of belonging. Even though the adolescent wants to be treated as an adult, he is insecure in this new role; he feels the need of tactful adult guidance.

It is apparent that most of the problems of youth can be eased if parents and teachers show insight into the difficulties and needs of this period of development. The adolescent must be understood as a normal, functioning personality. Social experiences in which he can resolve some of his emotional and physical conflicts are important; his need for interpersonal relationships is intense. The teacher must see that the school program is broadened to include many kinds of social activities — dances, parties, group discussions, creative group activities.

Through such easy, informal contacts, boys and girls gain a feeling for others. They develop respect for the opposite sex, for minority groups both racial and economic, and for the various contributions which can be made by different individuals in a group.

To summarize this discussion of the development of the individual, you as a teacher must understand

–the common characteristics of the several phases of a child's growth and development.

–that each child is born a unique individual, different from others in physical, mental, and emotional characteristics.

–that the child's characteristics are deeply influenced by the home and community experiences.

–that children are not "good" or "bad"; but that their behavior is the result of the child's own needs and strivings plus the forces that the home, school, and society bring to bear on him.

–and, lastly, that these facts of growth and the varied factors which formulate the individuals' behavior pattern are very closely associated with the learning and teaching activities of the school. The teacher's happy rapport with each child and her understanding and wise handling of his needs will do much to assure his good adjustment to school and his success in his work. Learning experiences and subject-matter materials must be so selected that they will be significant to the child. The latter point is more fully discussed in later chapters.

Social Needs Are Twofold

From the teacher's continuous study of development, one insistent question arises: Who . . . what . . . is this human being that is being educated? How can I know him better: learn his purposes, discover what problems confront him, what human conditions mold him? Ever in the center, the constant core of his personality, are his social-psychological needs. We can now sum them up systematically. The social

These boys are installing electric lights in a series of tunnels they have built. (Play Schools Association photo.)

needs of the human being are twofold: the need for security and the need for freedom. To what extent they are opposed we shall see in a moment, but first we must deal with the need for security.

The Need for Security

Time after time our sketch of human development pointed to the deep-seated nature of the craving for security. It was expressed in the first responses of the baby to the mother's cuddling, and in manifold ways as he identified himself with the elders of the family. Later, his constant barrage of questions revealed the need for reassurance and confidence. He wants cuddling, caressing, and comforting attention; but he must neither be overprotected nor deprived of affection. It is a nice problem of balance, of reassuring the dependent child of our love and loyalty, but also of helping him reach the point where he can stand alone. In the elementary school he needs the feeling of belonging to his childhood group as well as being warmly received by the teacher.

The Need for Affection As the craving for security exists in us all, so does the chief route to building it: the need to love and to be loved. That the individual needs the love of his mother, father, children, and

65

others close to him is a truism of common sense as well as of the technical study of personality. Certainly in our society the foundations for
personal security are laid in the family. The records of personal living
reveal love as a tremendous moral resource, in some instances producing
great acts of sacrifice. The impulse of love is a tremendous motive
power for constructive human behavior: Love your neighbor as yourself has been set before man as the supreme guide for conduct.

The Need for "Belonging" Interdependent with the need for love is
the deep emotional need for "belonging," for being wanted. Each
person wants above all to have *his place,* to be accepted and respected.
This urge can be seen very early in the baby's response to his mother.
It is continually evident as the child grows and matures in responding
to others in the family, in groups, and later in the community in which
he works and lives. Thus the need to have a special place in one's
group is important throughout life. Such security may be given in a
thousand subtle, and often indirect, ways. A word of praise from
the teacher or parent at just the right moment may change a child's
whole behavior; witness Philip's anxieties.

Perhaps the most common error in guiding children's growth is allowing them to have the feeling that while others in the group are normal,
they are misfits. Actually everyone has something special to give to
the total group, and teacher and parent must work together to help
each child find his special place in his group. For example, one teacher
in visiting a family heard a mother say: "Jan is a sloppy, untidy child!"
The teacher knew that at school this was not so; Jan had been very
helpful in keeping the class accounts for the milk. With her help and
encouragement he had accounted for the number of bottles received
each day, the number used, the number returned, and the cost per day.
His records were neat and accurate, and he felt keen and justified pride
in his accomplishment. Hearing about this from the teacher affected
the mother deeply and made it easier for the teacher to discuss with
her other problems of Jan's development.

The truth illustrated by this example holds for every class and family
group. With careful guidance each child can find his own special
place in every group — family, school class, or play group.

What, then, should a child be able to expect from the parent and
the teacher?

First: respect as a person — a sympathetic understanding of himself: his likes and dislikes, his temperament and other personality traits, his purposes

Second: his share, as a member of the family or class, in the responsibility for planning and carrying on the activities of the group

Third: many and varied opportunities to think independently and choose for himself: to choose his friends, the clothes he wears each day, his use of his time, etc.

Fourth: an environment with a minimum of strain: a happy atmosphere which emerges from an understanding appreciation of the personalities of all in the group

The Need to Achieve   The corollary to the need for affection and the need of belonging is the need for a sense of achievement.   The effects of achievement are twofold; the feeling of satisfaction at having done a job well, and the emotional warmth of being accepted, approved, and admired by one's peers.   Both build security.   This is particularly true in our highly competitive society, which places such a high value on achievement.   One of the first things asked about a newcomer is: "What does he do?"   Not "Who is he?   What kind of person is he? What are his interests?" — but, "What does he do?"   Each individual needs a teacher who understands his capacities, his need to be recognized as a person of potential ability, and his need for building a sense of having achieved.

There are needs for other kinds of security, which reveal themselves especially in adult life.   The one that haunts most people, most of the time, is the need for economic security — the need for uninterrupted employment and sufficient income to live securely.   As the adolescent becomes a youth, his thoughts turn more and more to leaving school, getting a job, having a wife and children, and building a home of his own.   Economic security — freedom from worry over lack of a job — becomes an ever-insistent need; witness, for example, the skilled worker's fear of being laid off in industries of seasonal unemployment, and, on the constructive side, the new social security agencies of government, the manifold annuity plans, the worldwide movement to develop national programs for social insurance.

Insecurity and the Sense of Inferiority

One effective way to recognize insecurity in children is through the signs of inferiority shown in their behavior. It is not an exaggeration to say that nearly all people suffer from a deep-seated sense of inferiority, which hampers their social relations as well as their work. In one investigation of 275 college students, 90 per cent reported that even in college they suffered from a sense of inferiority; one third reported feelings of moral inferiority; half expressed a marked sense of physical inferiority; most of them said that they felt socially inadequate.

This mood is even more prevalent among school children, and you must expect it in your classes. It will reveal itself in many ways: in the child who stands apart from others on the playground, in the one who is constantly begging off from taking part in games, in the class play, or in other activities requiring initiative and leadership.

Rationalization There are various ways by which children and adults try to offset a feeling of inferiority and insecurity. Rationalizing is one. A teacher gives these two examples; no doubt you can multiply them many times:

"A boy has hurt his foot slightly. When the time comes for the hike of his boys' club, his limping has become more pronounced and he decides that he cannot go. After his mother questions him a bit, however, he admits that the real reason for not wanting to go is that he dislikes cooking over an open fire.

"Two girls are overheard talking in a college hall. One of them is evidently much behind in her work. She has been invited to go to the theater and, upon debating with herself, decides to go. Her defense is, 'I am so tired that I know I'll do better work if I have some recreation.' "

These are both examples of rationalization, sometimes called giving the "good" reasons for our behavior rather than the real reasons. Someone has called rationalizing the "chief indoor sport" of mankind. It is only one of some half-dozen ways of defending ourselves from a sense of inferiority and insecurity, to which all of us resort to some degree.

Compensation Perhaps the most common self-defense is "compensation," so named by the distinguished psychologist, Dr. Alfred Adler. Kimball Young illustrates it:

It is a happy experience when each child has his own little task to do and feels that he is important in the group. (Louise M. Gross photo.)

"The concept of compensation has been used in at least two divergent senses. The most common one describes an individual who, lacking strength in some particular feature of his make-up, attempts to develop some other trait or characteristic to offset this. For instance, the boy who is too fat to run and jump with other boys on the playground, who is hailed as 'Tubby' or 'Fatty' or 'Butch,' gets his social approval, his prestige, his sense of security, by outdoing his tormentors and would-be playmates in arithmetic, geography, spelling, or declamation inside the schoolroom. Or at the level of physical activity, the boy with crippled legs may develop into a skillful person where his hands come into play; that is, he may make beautiful toys, do artistic wood carving, or learn to play the piano well. The man who is unsuccessful in love-making may boast of his conquest of women, or he may turn his attention to some other form of prestige-producing activity." [1]

One way to spot insecurity and inferiority is to get behind the tendency of some children constantly to rush into the limelight. Often you will find a child deficient in some respect trying to compensate for

[1] Kimball Young: *Social Psychology*, page 129. F. S. Crofts & Company; 1930.

69

it in some other way. Consider the case of Harry M., a Negro boy of decidedly inferior physical and mental ability, who established his status as a leader in the boy gang of the neighborhood.

"Harry M. is a colored lad, fourteen years old . . . perceptibly stunted in growth . . . 'knock-kneed' . . . and is sensitive of his difference from the physique of normal boys. Both his two brothers, ages twelve and seventeen, are well developed. Harry dresses mannishly, and assumes a studied air of self-composure. He does not talk freely even in play. His behavior suggests an attempt to conceal his physical weakness and deformity with the prestige which his unexpressed thoughts and *possible* strength might inspire . . .

". . . His parents have been separated for a number of years. One of his early recollections is of appearing in Court with his mother and father when divorce proceedings were in progress. He remembers distinctly that his parents were debating who should keep the children, each with emphasis on a preference to be relieved of the responsibility. . . .

"Harry has only reached the third grade in school. He thinks his teachers like to 'peck' on him. His teachers declare him dull and slow, and devoid of interest. . . .

"His grandmother works out during the day, and he and his brothers are left to their own devices. The family lives in the section of the Negro community that produces the largest number of delinquent colored children. The boy has never been in Juvenile Court, but a number of his chums have. His manual training instructor asserts that he is a gang leader, although the smallest in the bunch. . . .

". . . Incorrigibility, fighting, truancy, and lying are his principal delinquencies. His success in fighting is due largely to the fact that he can induce his pals to do his fighting for him. The boy has a remarkable influence with his 'bunch,' and can take an interest in useful as well as destructive activities. A test of this came recently when his instructor made him squad leader to shovel snow. . . .

". . . he seems to have compensated for his physical disability through his power over the gang." [1]

Rationalizing and compensating are the two principal ways people strive to offset a sense of inferiority and insecurity. The psychoanalysts,

[1] Quoted by Kimball Young in his *Source Book for Social Psychology*, pages 412–413, from E. W. Burgess, "The Delinquent as a Person," *Am. J. Soc.* 1922–23: XXVIII: pages 665–668, published by the University of Chicago. Used by permission of the publishers.

under the leadership of Dr. Sigmund Freud, have given us the clearest understanding of this human tendency and have brought to our attention several other "self-defensive mechanisms." To define them briefly:

–*Substitution:* to substitute another kind of behavior for some kind that must be repressed; witness the temper tantrum in child or grownup.

–*Projection:* to attribute our own deficiencies to others; witness the neighborhood gossip, the mudslinging of rival political candidates, and a list of others "as long as the moral law."

–*Escape:* the chronic tendency of most of us, much of the time, to dodge responsibilities; in extreme cases, unwilling or unable to face our problems we build an imaginary world in which to live.

Dominance and Submission in Child Groups

It is clear, therefore, that children as well as adults tend to arrange themselves in any school classroom or other group in a rank-order of superiority and inferiority. A psychological way of saying it is that some are "dominant" and others are "submissive." Two facts taken together account for this rank-order of *dominance and submission:*

1. a wide range of individual differences in all their traits, and

2. the competitive atmosphere in home, town, and school in which the children live and develop.

The Principle of Individual Differences   As we have frequently stated, no two of the thirty children in your class will be alike in any respect. No two are growing at the same rate. As babies they learned the skills of sitting up, standing alone, walking, and talking at widely differing rates. By the time they reach the third grade, one among them will weigh 49 pounds, another 75; one will be 47 inches tall and another 58; one will read 30 words per minute comprehendingly and another 300. In adult society, as well as in school classes, this principle of individual differences marks every group. Egocentric individuals will be in the center of every little scene, and each one will be unique — different from all the others. Every neighborhood group, every work gang, every social organization will reveal the tall and the short, the strong and the weak,

the domineering and the submissive, the adventurous and the timid —
and between the extremes, a vast body of less pronounced types. This
is *the principle of individual differences*; it is basic to the understanding
and guiding of young people.

The Ruthlessly Competitive Character of Society   The second fact that
explains the dominance-submission character of our human groups
in America is the competitive spirit bred in our children. They have
been born into a society in which a great premium is put upon individual competition. Since this characteristic of American culture will be
developed carefully in Chapter 4, we shall do no more here than summarize this condition of our culture. It is sufficient to point out that
most children grow up in family, neighborhood, and town surrounded
by egocentric personalities. Each person is striving to establish for himself the securities we have mentioned; as a consequence the child constantly has to defend himself against self-centered people and compete
with them for the rewards of life.

Putting these two facts together — a wide variation in individual
abilities in every social group and a competitive, individualistic, rank-
order society — will help you understand much more clearly the frequently appearing traits of inferiority and insecurity. The vigorous, aggressive ones, often striving to compensate for some felt weakness, will
be "dominant"; the more complacent, even-tempered ones, "submissive." Assailed by social-emotional pressures, the latter feel inadequate.
They are not chosen first; their suggestions are ignored; they are pushed
aside; others go ahead of them in the line. A sense of frustration and
insecurity grows.

The Need for Freedom

In guiding children and youth our problem is complicated by the
fact that while each one needs to feel secure, *he also needs to feel free*.
Each one wants to tell what *he* thinks, to make suggestions, to help plan
the way things shall be done. Every human being craves an opportunity
to make his own statement, and he strives to find practical ways to do it.
As the child grows up, he wants to arrange his room in *his* special way,
to help choose *his* own clothes, to do his chores *his* way. Later, he wants
to feel free to choose his occupation, to go out on his own, and to build

his family and his home. This need for expression is a deep-seated universal need, and the school can most surely satisfy this need by building in the children the feeling that they are free to make their contributions. "What do *you* think?" should be the constant query of the teacher. "What is *your* idea? *You* make a plan for it."

To any American it is a truism that the first concept of democracy is freedom, especially in these mid-century days when our people are doing all in their power to oppose the spread of totalitarian dictatorships. In fact, since the rise of Hitler and Mussolini after the first World War, as well as the emerging power of the Russian Politburo, our political leaders have talked constantly about "the freedoms"; witness Mr. Roosevelt's "Four Freedoms" and the National Resources Planning Board's new Bill of Rights — the "Nine Freedoms." The very enumeration of the latter reveals the American demanding freedom in every aspect of life — freedom to get his own job and bargain for his pay; freedom from want, sickness, unemployment, accident, or dependency in old age; freedom from compulsion by employers or arbitrary officials; freedom to move about without being spied upon; freedom to grow, to become educated, and to take advantage of all the opportunities of a democracy.

Living in a democratic society that later proclaimed such a charter of human rights, it was natural that Francis Parker, John Dewey, and the other leaders of the new schools should have put down freedom as the first article of their educational faith. They said: "Free the legs, the arms, the larynx of a child and you have taken the first step toward freeing his mind and spirit." They sought above all to assure children the freedom to develop naturally, to be spontaneous and unselfconscious. In his charter of educational principles for his Laboratory School, Dewey laid down that the teacher should build in every child, first and foremost, the feeling that he is free to investigate anything of interest or importance. It is true that in attempting to build democratic schools for a democratic society some of our leaders went too far: Some mistook license for freedom. Assuming that freedom is absence of restraint, they "took off the lid" and permitted children to do more or less as they pleased. This not only produced disorderly schools, but too often it produced, in the less balanced and confident children, a greater sense of insecurity. These excited and shortsighted schoolmen forgot that many children need to live in an orderly world in order to feel emotionally secure.

Other teachers, more balanced in their understanding, knew that each child's freedom stopped where that of the next one began. They knew that a delicate balance between freedom and order must be discovered and maintained, and that to do this, the teacher, in the last analysis, had to be in control. To maintain the balance, to enlist the motives of learners and make education truly developmental, the teacher had constantly to guide the work — to stimulate the slow and inert, to encourage and advise, to appraise and question. Although he was not obviously dominating the work of the group, he was always in it, and always in control. Thus, while he strove to give the maximum possible freedom to each individual, he accepted responsibility for the guidance of all. His was to be a wise control — but control, nevertheless.

The End Point of Development: the Mature Person

This brings to a close our study of the child as a developing person. Throughout we have regarded him as a whole person, characterized by a unique life style, striving to satisfy his personal and social needs and building these into motivating purposes. Only by discovering his controlling drives can we expect to succeed in guiding him. We know that we shall get nowhere working *against* his needs.

We must also set ourselves a goal toward which to aim our educative process. If the developing individual is to be stretched to his highest capacities, the sights at which we set our aim must be high.

That high goal, which will challenge our teaching to the utmost, we call *The Mature Person*. In pointing to the characteristics of such an ideal we have no illusion that it is what most Americans are; it is what thoughtful ones among us aspire to be. If it seems to set our sights too high, do not forget that the times call for maturity of personality as never before in our country's life.

Since the mature person is a man or woman of energy and purpose, you will want to seek every opportunity to capitalize on each child's potential drives. You will direct these into channels of spontaneous expression; you will encourage his feelings for his fellow men, helping him develop as a companion of warm, generous sympathies and of deep affection for those close to him.

While the child needs help in enriching and strengthening his capacities for personal relationships, the teacher should seize upon every opportunity to cultivate his interests in man's most vital problems. For the mature person is informed of the condition of man, and acts with effective intelligence. To him no problems of social controversy in the modern world can be shunned. Bring to him at all ages, therefore, the vital materials needed to build an understanding of the world in which he is growing up. Teach him to confront issues frankly, to let his mind conclude whatever the facts of life conclude. Guide his development so that his companions will respect and admire his competence and will know, at every stage, where he stands on questions that divide children, youth, or adults. Build in him a sound knowledge of men and their affairs, and make him familiar with the best ways of living in a social group. Encourage every sign of intellectual curiosity, cultivating widespreading interests. Teach him to put himself constantly in the path of mature persons who will stimulate and stretch him.

We must recognize maturity of personality as a developing human quality. You will find children of ten who are amazingly mature, and men of thirty who apparently lack the capacity to grow up. But the fundamental questions of ethical behavior — "What kind of life do I call good? On what does morality rest in our changing industrial society? What kind of man is it producing? What kind of man am I?" — have to be faced on every level of growth. Acquiring a philosophy of life cannot be postponed to adult life; it develops from earliest childhood. And it must be stimulated and guided by mature teachers.

Firsthand Studies of Child Development

As you continue your study of the child as developing person, make some firsthand studies of children to accompany your reading.

1. Visit the practice school, or a near-by town school. Observe a group of three-, four-, five-, or six-year-olds; another perhaps of twelve-year-olds. Notice the differences in interests at different age levels. Ask the teacher of each group what she is trying to do for children of that age.

When you are observing in a class, try to get back of the overt behavior of the children. What need is driving a particular child? — the need of recognition? of companionship? of achievement? Put your knowledge and imagination to work on these questions. Don't hesitate to conjecture about child behavior; guess and then try to check on your guesses.

2. Make a careful study of the cumulative record card of a particular child. Include in your study his medical record; note the chief facts of his physical development. Are there clues here that explain his intellectual successes or difficulties?

3. See some of the educational research films on child development. These throw light on child needs as well as on the course of growth itself. See, for example: "This Is Robert," a film that you can secure from Vassar College, Poughkeepsie, New York; write to the Child Study Department. Or films issued by Dr. Arnold Gesell, Child Development Clinic, Yale University.

4. Ask mothers you know about their children. You will probably find that the children in any one family differ markedly one from another. Explore these differences, trying to discover the extent to which the parents created different human environments for their different children. Study the styles of life of the individual children.

5. Pick various aspects of growth for special study; for example, the skills that children use in their everyday life. Think of ways to help children overcome inadequacies in social behavior through improvement of these skills.

6. Looking back on your own development, select any aspect of it, such as social skills. Review the obstacles to learning and development that you had to overcome. Can you profit from such an introspective study as you guide the development of children?

7. In light of our discussion of social and psychological needs, would you favor coeducation for young people in school, in camps, and in social organizations? Give the reasons for your opinion.

8. Make a list of the motor skills that you use daily. Which of these did you acquire at preschool age? in the elementary school? in the high school? Did you have difficulty in learning any of them? If so, as you look back upon that difficulty, what seems now to have been the chief factors?

9. Appraise our statement of the mature person. How would you modify it or extend it as a goal for the teacher's role in guiding child development?

What to Read

See the writings on the growth process by Caroline Zachry; for example, her Chapter XII in *Democracy and the Curriculum* (*Third Yearbook* of the John Dewey Society), and her *Emotion and Conduct in Adolescence*. Haggard and Fry's *Anatomy of Personality* presents many interesting styles of life through case histories; don't miss it.

For the study of the nursery and young child, see especially *Education and Training* of the Committee on Infant and Pre-school Child of the White House Conference. For research studies of behavior in nursery school children in relation to total personality, see Lois Murphy's *Social Behavior and Child Personality*.

Chapters 2 to 6, Cole and Bruce, *Educational Psychology*, will give you a fine interpretation of the style of life — of physical, intellectual, emotional, and motivational development; likewise, Chapters II to VI of *Educational Psychology* by Gates, Jersild, McConnell, and Challman. For one of the best appreciations of educational psychology as applied to progressive education, see Pressey and Robinson's *Psychology and the New Education*, Chapters 2, 3, 7, and 10. A developmental study of the patterning of behavior is given in Gesell and Ilg's *The Child from Five to Ten*; another helpful publication is *How Children Develop*, which can be secured from the College of Education, Ohio State University, Columbus. See also Gladys Jenkins and Others, *These Are Your Children*, a discussion enhanced by numerous photographs of children in home and school activities.

For advanced students: Barker, Kounin, and Wright's *Child Behavior and Development* is a fine book of important research studies. The most distinguished recent volume on the total problem of the psychology of personality is Gardner Murphy's *Personality*; see especially Chapters 20–22 on the Self. Also for advanced students, see Harold Rugg's *Foundations for American Education*, Chapter VI, "The Person and the Psychology of Personality."

For the study of the adolescent, see such case studies as are given in Peter Blos's *The Adolescent Personality*, including teacher's reports, creative writing as expression of self, family histories, etc. See also Zachry's *Emotion and Conduct in Adolescence*, and Dimock's *Rediscovering the Adolescent*.

On the problems of the exceptional child, see Heck's *The Education of Exceptional Children* and Scheidermann's *The Psychology of Exceptional Children*.

CHAPTER 4

The Environment as Molder of Personality

THE ORGANISM-ENVIRONMENT problem must still be kept before us, but our attention will be directed specifically to the part played by the social environment in which the child is developing.

A new concept, *The Culture,* focuses our study, and three distinct questions must be answered:

–*First: How* does the culture mold children and youth and teach them what to think, feel, believe, and value?

–*Second:* What beliefs, ideas, and objects of allegiance come out of this molding process?

–*Third:* What is the teacher's role in the culture-molding process?

To answer these questions two kinds of material are employed:

–*First:* case studies showing how family and neighborhood life give young Americans their social ideas, beliefs, and attitudes.

–*Second:* a sketch of the century-long conquest of the American continent which contributed so much to developing the characteristic traits, ideas, beliefs, and values of the unique American individualism.

From these materials we shall generalize the culture pattern of the people, the essence of the American way of life.

The Child in American Culture

IN SCHOOL and college classes all over America there are young Americans whose parents were born and brought up in other lands. The youths *look* Chinese or Mongolian, Burmese or East Indian, African Negro or Latin American; but they dress, talk, and act like Americans of many generations. Get under their skins and you will find that they think and feel like Americans and hold American beliefs and values; they insist that they *are* Americans. This was frequently said by the native white GI's of the American army in World War II about their Nisei or Negro comrades or those born of other foreign stocks. This is not to say that there were not vast individual differences among them; outwardly they were a mixed brigade, looking like a committee of the United Nations. But inwardly, in their everyday beliefs and opinions and in their fundamental life values, they were typical run-of-the-mine Americans.

This well-known fact directs our attention to the nature of the social world in which the children are growing up and its role in their development. For it is the ways of living in the family, the neighborhood, the town, and the country that make those men psychologically so much alike. It is the way of life that takes the child of Chinese parents, with Chinese eyes, hair, and facial characteristics, and turns him into a facile American businessman. It was the culture of modern New Zealand, Hawaii, and America that took Dr. Peter Buck, the child of Polynesian (Maori) parents, and transformed him into the world-distinguished director of the Bishop Museum in Honolulu, the scientific student of anthropology, the skilled linguist, and the professor in American universities. It was a sharp change in human environment that took a thirteen-year-old Negro boy, unable to read and write, out of a primitive Mississippi river hamlet and turned him into a University of Iowa Doctor of Philosophy at the age of 24.

Is a "Human" Environment Needed to Produce "Human" Beings?

Most people develop so naturally in their villages or cities that the indispensable role played by that human world in their own development never occurs to them. Suppose you were to ask most young people today: "What kind of creature would you have been if, at your birth (assuming that you had lived), you had grown up for some years without any human beings around you?" They would scoff and say: "How absurd! The kind we are, of course!" Yet there is grave doubt that such a person would really become a "human" being, walking, talking, eating, working, playing, as human beings do. Several startling examples have come to public attention in recent years which throw important new light on the role of the human environment. They are so arresting that we shall describe two of them briefly.

The Cases of Anna and Isabelle

A few years ago Dr. Kingsley Davis reported[1] the case of Anna, an illegitimate child born in 1932 in a nursing home and described at that time as normal. She was discovered, in 1937, in an upstairs storage room of the Pennsylvania farm home of her grandfather, who had refused to recognize her and compelled the mother to hide her. She had spent most of the five years in a crib or wedged tightly into an old chair. Throughout that time she had been given no solid food; she was fed milk and oatmeal gruel by a spoon. Described by the officer who discovered her as "just bones, with skin drawn over them," she was unable to stand, talk, chew, or drink. She had never been bathed, nor had she been given toilet training. Taken to a county home, she revealed all the symptoms of being deaf and blind. Utterly unresponsive

[1] Kingsley Davis: "Extreme Isolation of a Child," *American Jour. of Sociol.*, 45 (Jan., 1940), pages 554–565; and 52 (March, 1947), pages 432–435.

and expressionless, the muscles of her legs and ankles were so flaccid that her feet lay limp and straight, with the soles touching the bed.

Within three days — on receiving normal feeding, massage, and care — she sat up. Her arms, head, and mouth began to move, and she looked up when the door opened. She turned her head at sounds, frowned, scowled, smiled when coaxed, and revealed temper when restrained. After her sixth birthday, Anna was transferred to a private family, where, under a woman's devoted care, she learned in a month to drink from a glass, to get downstairs by sitting on each step, and to feed herself with a spoon. After four months in the new home, with good social-emotional conditions, she walked a few steps alone, responded to simple verbal commands of the foster mother, and began to show an interest in people. But at the age of six she was still classed as an idiot, equaling the score of a normal one-year-old on a standardized performance scale.

From seven and one-half until her death at ten and one-half, Anna was in a private institution for retarded children. At nine she could bounce and catch a ball, her toilet habits were firmly established, she could dress herself except for fastening her clothes, and had developed speech to about the two-year level. In her last report, at ten years, she was rated at the two-and-one-half-year level of intelligence — certainly not higher than imbecile.

In the case of Isabelle, illegitimate child of a deaf-mute mother, we have an instance of recovery from social isolation. She was discovered at six and one-half years in a dark room, where she had lived with her mother, shut off from the rest of the family. She was unable to use human speech, and an intelligence test gave her a mental age of two years with an estimated status of feeble-minded. However, under careful instruction in an institution, Isabelle learned rapidly to adopt human ways. In two years' time she learned to speak, covering the stage of learning that ordinarily requires six years of childhood. Although we lack detailed knowledge of Isabelle's infantile capacities, nevertheless the case again illustrates the profoundly important role of the social environment.

It is not too much to say that if the child of human parents is to become a thoroughly human being, he must grow up in a human environment. If he is to walk on two legs and talk, he must develop in a walking-on-two-legs and talking environment. Apparently there is no inherent capacity in the individual that makes it possible for him to achieve such skill unaided by a human environment.

Granted, then, that both organism and environment get into every human situation, because of the indispensable role of the latter, we shall now turn our full attention to the nature of the environment. In the most complete sense the environment is the total physical and human world in which the child lives and develops. In part, it is obviously the physical earth, its climate and other geographic conditions, and the universe in which it all turns. While this physical environment plays an important role in molding human ways of life, it is the ways of living themselves with which we, as teachers, are chiefly concerned.

The social anthropologists have made many studies of human ways of living in modern times. Some have gone to live for prolonged periods with primitive tribes in Africa, Asia, South America, and the South Seas, making careful records of the details of family and tribal life; others have made careful records of family, neighborhood, and community life in our own cities and towns of America. From these studies, to which we refer at the end of this chapter, teachers can get rich eyewitness material about the American way of life and how it is molding our children and youths.

The Culture: Its Three Levels

American life is the life of its 60,000 organized communities, with 51,000 villages of fewer than 1000 inhabitants each and 96 cities with a population of more than 100,000 each. In addition, there are the millions of neighborhoods. While each separate community is unique in some respects, all reflect the basic qualities of our way of life. Between the two World Wars our people became conscious of this "American way of life" as never before in their history. Its spirit was declaimed over the town meetings of the air, in the press, and in hundreds of books. It can best be summed up, perhaps, in the anthropologists' term "the culture," meaning the total life of the people. It will be helpful to distinguish the culture from "society." American *society* means the people — the nearly hundred and fifty million Americans working, playing, governing themselves, carrying on family life, and so forth. American *culture* means *what the people in that society do, think, feel, believe, desire, fear.*

The concept of the culture can become such an important educational instrument that we shall distinguish its three principal levels or aspects. Fortunately, these three levels also distinguish what can be done in the three divisions of the twelve-grade school — the elementary, the junior high, and the senior high school — in the building of an understanding of the local community. The first level, the physical civilization, can well be studied in the elementary school; the second, the social institutions, is appropriate material for the junior high school grades; the third, the psychology and philosophy of the people, is mature content for the senior high school. We turn to a brief discussion of each of these three levels.

1. The Physical Civilization: the Surface Aspect of the Culture

The most obvious of the three levels of the culture of a people is the physical or material means of carrying on life. If the school is in a great city, this external physical aspect shows itself in the producing and distributing of goods and services. The children can see it revealed in factories, power plants, massive business structures, railroad and automobile transportation, telephones, telegraphs, radios, department stores, schools, government buildings, and the workers of the town. The direct study of these in the elementary school will build an understanding of how our economic system produces food, shelter, clothing, and other physical requirements.

Through motion pictures, books, still pictures, and lectures of returned travelers the young children can build a similar grasp of the physical aspects of other cultures among the earth's people today. They will learn, for example, that in China and other agrarian countries food, shelter, and clothing are produced by the power of muscle, wind, or water — by handicrafts instead of machines; that animals and men are beasts of burden, and that goods are exchanged mostly by direct face-to-face bargaining. Thus both in industrial and agrarian societies the physical ways of living are the obvious external aspects of the civilization. These are meaningful themes for the study of community life in the elementary school.

RUTH F. BENEDICT (1887–1948), graduating from Vassar College in 1909, was first known as a poet, publishing in *Poetry*, *The Nation*, and other magazines. Beginning in 1922 she began the scientific study of primitive cultures and established an international reputation as a pioneer interpreter of culture patterns. This concept was given widespread circulation through her book, *Patterns of Culture*, and her pamphlet, *Races of Mankind*, written with her colleague, Gene Weltfish. Her contributions in this field were based on years of firsthand research among American Indian tribes (1922–39) under the sponsorship of the Medical Services Branch of the U. S. Office of Naval Research, and Columbia University. Her interest in liberal movements and in progressive education is shown by her work as an editor of *The Social Frontier* and of *Frontiers of Democracy*. Among her other books are *Race, Science and Politics*, *The Chrysanthemum and the Sword*, *Zuñi Mythology*, and *Patterns of Japanese Culture*.

2. The Social Institutions

By the time they have reached junior high school, young Americans should have learned to look beneath the obvious physical life that they see on the streets and highways, on the farms, and in industries to discover the social institutions of the people. One of the most important of these is the character of family life. The school can build an understanding of this by contrasting the one-generation family in America and other modern nations with, for example, the clan-family of China, in which children, parents, grandparents, great-grandparents, uncles, aunts, and cousins all live together, several generations in one group. Another social institution is government. At the junior high school level various kinds of democratic governments can be studied in close juxtaposition with the striking dictatorships in other regions. Still more subtle social institutions are hidden from a superficial observation; for example, the language of the people, the newspaper-magazine press, and the way things are measured. There are the rituals of the churches, lodges, and other fraternal organizations, and of courtesy and social life. There are the characteristic food habits of the people, their ways of dress, their speech, and their chief recreational interests and activities. Although some of these are too complex to be effectively studied in the junior high school, certainly they are proper subject matter for the senior high school.

3. The Basic Psychology and Philosophy of the People: Their Culture Patterns

Hidden from superficial study, but most powerful in determining a people's way of living, are their psychology and philosophy — the patterns into which their daily behavior tends to fall. This basic psychology determines what the people want and, hence, what they do. It marks their desires and their taboos. This also is the proper study of the adolescent and post-adolescent years. In the senior high school the social psychology of the people should become an important part of the social science curriculum. You as a teacher must become a student of this social psychology. It reveals itself, although only to close observation, in the general "climate of opinion" of the community; that is, the mental and emotional atmosphere that pervades the ongoing life of schools, churches, families, social organizations, labor unions, associations of manufacturers, and recreational groups. Each one has its characteristic attitudes and points of view, as well as typical ways of speaking and acting. As you study the groups of the community, you will note (in these groups) the role of dominating persons who appear to set the tone and standards of the climate of opinion — aggressive personalities in families, neighborhood clubs, unions, churches, and other social organizations.

These, then, are the three levels of culture: the physical ways of living, the social institutions, and the psychological culture patterns of the people. The concept is of enormous importance to the teacher. The children in our schools are growing up in American culture, in American families, in American neighborhoods, perhaps in a distinctive social class. It is impossible for us to understand them and plan their education except as we see them *in their culture*.

The Culture as Teacher of Beliefs and Values

The culture is no mysterious abstraction. We can illustrate that point very simply by considering the moment-by-moment episodes of everyday life and by studying their implications in the molding of young

personalities. Think of total human environment as a series of concentric circles, with the growing child at the center of all. Consider
especially two face-to-face groups of people that influence this development most of all:

-the family — father, mother, brothers and sisters — the smallest,
most intimate human circle

-the neighborhood — fifty, perhaps a hundred, families in the block
or down one street and around the corner. This, of course, is a
small part of the community: hamlet, village, town, or city.

Outside these face-to-face groups lies the region, embracing many
communities in river valleys, on mountain slopes, and on plains, and the
still larger continent, and the inhabited earth.

Each developing personality can be thought of, therefore, as a human
center on which multitudinous social pressures work their molding process. Under our modern conditions of communication the scope of these
social forces reaches actually around the world. But it is through the
first three — the 35,000,000 ramilies, the million and more neighborhoods, and the 60,000 communities — that the culture exercises its influence most profoundly. All of these are face-to-face groups, most of
them within the sight and hearing of the growing child. Since the
neighborhood is itself the integration of a score or two of family groups
and since family and neighborhood are so closely interrelated, we shall
consider them together.

We turn for a moment to a few examples of the culture-molding process. As we do so, remember that *you need to understand this process,
because you and your fellow-teachers will play an important part in
guiding it.*

Families Mold Attitudes and Beliefs

In a small New England country town the Abbott family of parents
and seven children was considered a happy group. Mr. Abbott, foreman
in a near-by mill, provided the family with a comfortable living; but their
friends thought of them as rich. The housework was not a burden; the
mother had help with the cooking, and each child accepted his special
chores cheerfully. A big downstairs room in the sprawling house was
given over to the children to be used as they liked. Here plays were

produced, and a neighborhood newspaper composed and printed on a hectograph. In one corner of the room was a workbench with tools hanging on the wall above. In a busy chemical laboratory in another corner two of the boys produced colors, smells, and minor explosions. A closet had been transformed into a darkroom by an earnest young photographer. In the Abbotts' house something was always happening — inside, and outside too. One small boy raised pigs, his sister kept hens, and two of the older children had a vegetable garden.

The family atmosphere was one of freedom to explore and experiment. The house was a place to be used, and it was used hard. Mealtimes, with all members of the family present, were like lively parties with fun and jokes, each one interested in what the others were doing. Every evening, for an hour after dinner, in the small room that was "Pa and Ma's living room," Mrs. Abbott read aloud to the assembled crowd. One book after another they heard together, the children developing familiarity with the great characters of literature and history and an appreciative feeling for fine language. These parents really enjoyed their children. They lived happily and closely with them, giving them freedom and encouragement to develop their own interests. They demanded of them only complete honesty and fair dealing.

Today each of the seven children is leading a fine creative life. Growing up in such a home they could hardly escape becoming useful citizens as well as happy human beings.

Often the current of events in the family molds feelings and attitudes more sharply than spoken words.[1] Here is a case of such molding of attitude in one youth:

"It wasn't so much what my father and mother said that made me grow up feeling such an inferior person. It was the unspoken things that happened in the family. By the time I was ten years old I became conscious that when Father came home tired out from his work, he almost always had to go down in the basement and work at repairing shoes and replacing worn-out things in the house. Sundays likewise rarely ever meant rest for him. He was slaving constantly to keep our little place looking well.

[1] These episodes are chosen principally from the senior author's file; some are adapted from his *An Introduction to Problems of American Culture*.

"Mother, too, worked long hours. She scrubbed floors, mended our clothes, and did the washing and ironing!

"And then the boarders! How I came to hate the boarders in our home. They seemed to me to be outsiders. Yet I knew that without the few dollars they brought into the family each week, we might not have enough to eat. Certainly we couldn't pay the interest on the mortgage, which came due every July and January.

"I don't think I grew resentful of the wealthy people on the hill, but I'm sure that I grew up with a sense of my own inferiority. In later years, even after going through college and being received everywhere, it was difficult for me not to adopt the attitude of humble respect with which I had grown up as a boy."

Every family is involved in the lifework of the community and the nation's economic system, and its daily life builds attitudes and opinions about problems of labor, property ownership, coöperatives, wages and dividends, prices, and the part to be played by the government. A young man once told us:

"As I grew older an attitude was developed against working people. Their fathers worked for someone else; my father had his own business and his own office. Their fathers carried tin lunch pails; my father came home to lunch. They lived in rented houses; we owned our own house. Their mothers worked; my mother didn't have to. We went away in the summer; they stayed home. And these things were because we were 'better off' than they. We had more money. All these influences made me believe that I was better than they."

In the family and the neighborhood the children form opinions and attitudes about other races and nationalities; in some cases these stick throughout life. One person told how an unjust attitude toward other Europeans was formed by his family:

"A family of Polish people moved in across the street. I never had an opportunity to see much of them — they were just a large litter of ragged children whose noses ran and whose mother never had her hair combed and always wore bedroom slippers in the street. I never knew them, because two weeks after they moved in, we moved away, and a 'For Sale' sign was put on our house. My mother explained that we were moving because you really couldn't live across the street from such people. Poles, it seemed, were even worse than working people! As a result of these family attitudes, I have always had little respect or liking for Poles or other Slavs."

One person who has little race prejudice says:

"I was taught that our religious teachings were based on Judaism, so I respected Jewish tradition. Until I reached normal school I knew only two Jews, a business friend of my father's (greatly respected by the family) and a rabbi friend of my uncle's. Predisposed to like Jews, when I came to New York I found I enjoyed talking with them. They interested me greatly. The irritation they cause some people merely amuses me. I understand it, but do not share it."

In millions of white homes children's attitudes are being molded about Negroes. Consider this case:

"Very early in my life I was given a strong sympathy toward the colored race. An escaped slave had been given shelter in the home of my grandmother, and this colored mammy lived the rest of her days as one of the family and gave her services to helping raise my father and his brothers and sisters. Colored people were rare in Canada, and sympathy for the slaves was strong. I was quite a grown boy before I realized that any people still held the Negro to be an inferior person."

Neighborhoods Build Attitudes and Beliefs

Since it is in the neighborhoods of a town or city that the impact of the culture is most directly felt, they are of great importance to the teacher as another aspect of cultural understanding. Here is a typical example of a lower middle-class neighborhood:

In the corner house on Garfield Street in Laneville lives the superintendent of the mill. Beside him lives a carpenter, who by a hard struggle has saved enough to buy his own little house, although there is still a large mortgage on it. Opposite lives the floorwalker in the local department store; next to him a master machinist; beyond him an elevator man, who is able to live in the neighborhood because of the combined earnings of three children who left school at an early age. Beyond the elevator man lives an automobile salesman; across the street the manager of the local hotel has his home. Then follow, in succession, a teamster, the driver of an ice wagon, and three clerks in stores on Main Street.

On the whole it is a middle-class neighborhood, on the border between lower middle and upper middle. In no single house is there much wealth. Yet the children of the carpenter, the machinist, the elevator man, and the clerks note the respectful ways in which their parents greet the superintendent of the factory and the manager of the hotel. They learn to notice, also, that these people have larger and better-kept lawns around their houses. They rarely, if ever, wear soiled or patched clothing. Now and then fine automobiles drive up to these houses. Thus the children of the working class learn a certain kind of respect for those of greater means. A feeling of "their place" grows in their minds. Sometimes a feeling of inferiority grows and works a bad influence on their lives.

In addition to these silent influences, attitudes and beliefs are being formed by neighborhood gossip and neighborhood opinions. When we are very small, we may listen to such neighborhood talk as the following: "Old Mrs. Adams complains that the foreign servants one gets nowadays don't know how to keep their place." On another porch, Mrs. Moller and Mrs. Sullivan exchange confidences about their children:

> "I don't know what I am going to do about George," says Mrs. Moller. "I had no idea we had so many Negroes in this part of the town until the other day I saw them all trooping out of the high school. And as for Mr. Hall's Academy, they say that he has more Jews than Christians!"

Mrs. Sullivan's problem is even more acute:

> "Here I have got myself a nice home in one of the best streets, and my boys run down to the Old Town playground almost every afternoon to play with their 'hunky' and Italian schoolmates. You should hear the language they bring home!" [1]

We overhear a conversation about Mrs. Smith and Mrs. Jones. We learn that Mrs. Smith has adopted a little orphan, and we conclude that she must be a fine person. We learn that Mrs. Jones hasn't paid her butcher bill for two months, and we decide that she is dishonest.

---

[1] These three episodes are adapted from *And Who Is My Neighbor?* published by *The Inquiry*, New York, page v.

Thus our opinions about Mrs. Smith, Mrs. Jones, and many other persons in the neighborhood, community, and nation are formed.

Other attitudes and opinions are formed in the neighborhood because the neighbors like or dislike, approve or disapprove, certain things. One person says:

> "In my neighborhood you had to be very careful of what the neighbors would think. Some girls in high school who didn't live in the neighborhood were getting jobs as waitresses in hotels for the summer. I wanted to get such a job. I was not allowed to. 'What would the neighbors think of your father if he let you do such a thing?' I had to be home very early from all high school parties, for late hours brought forth the question, 'What will the neighbors think?' "

Neighborhood influences in the Midwest are illustrated by the following account:

> "I was born in Iowa, where the leaders of all phases of community life were members of the 'old families.' My parents, too, belonged to this 'old family' group, both parents having been born and reared within the community. In my neighborhood, strangers and newcomers were looked upon with questioning and even dislike.
>
> "The leaders in this community were very religious, all Protestants, and very prejudiced against Catholics; in fact, as a youngster I had the idea that the Catholics were always plotting to get control of the United States government, and, if they did, all Protestants would be killed.
>
> "Negroes too were looked upon with great disfavor, the idea being held in our community that all black people were thieves. This anti-Negro feeling was so strong that the few colored families who came to town soon moved to Kansas City or Chicago, where they could escape this prejudice.
>
> "These three attitudes — (1) antipathy to strangers, (2) prejudice against Catholics, and (3) prejudice against Negroes — became my own, and it has taken time and effort on my part to overcome them."

Family and neighborhood also mold our politics for us. One man says: "The Martins have always voted straight Democratic. My wife and I do today. My boys will, too." Another tells how he became a Democrat:

"When I was six years old my father died, and my mother took me and went to live in a small house on her father's farm. Here it was that the hotbed of politics held sway.

"Every night in autumn and winter my mother went over to her father's house to read and discuss the daily news. Politics held the greatest place in the conversation, especially if election day were near. My grandfather was Irish, and he and all the members of his household were Democrats. Many a time I sat on a footstool at my mother's feet listening. Although the opposition was small, the speaker seemed to be facing hundreds of the opposing party; he would beat the air or strike the table as if trying to convert and convince them all.

"Much of the conversation I could not understand, but some of it I understood, such as 'The Democrats favor the working class.' . . . 'If the Democrats win, every honest man will be given a chance to rise.'

"I knew my mother and grandfather were splendid people and of course never doubted their political views. Their politics became my politics."

Another Way to Study American Culture

These brief illustrations must suffice to make clear the powerful role of the culture, especially family, peer groups, and neighborhood, in molding the ideas, feelings, and beliefs of our youth. Bear in mind that this observation of the American way of life in action, in village and town, is only one of the two ways in which you can study the culture of our people effectively. The other way is to steep yourself in American history, observing how the traits and culture patterns became established in the people as they cleared the North American continent and built upon it their modern civilization of 60,000 communities. This is such an important study for those entrusted with the development of our children that we shall introduce it to you now.

We can do no more than turn the spotlight on a few selected movements and events. Our purpose is to suggest the physical and cultural setting and point to the characteristic traits and objects of allegiance born from ten generations of civilization building. We now turn the history clock back to the first years of national independence and westward expansion.

The Development of the Continent as Fashioner
of American Traits, Beliefs, and Values

In 1790 the American frontier was beginning to blaze its way through the Appalachians. In 1890, one hundred years later, the last frontier had been obliterated. The entire continent from Atlantic to Pacific, the continent that Thomas Jefferson had said could not be settled in a thousand years, was conquered in a century. The physical pattern of the new nation had been sketched in, and the basic traits and ideology of the people had taken shape. The world's greatest attempt to build a civilization of abundance, part private and part socialized, under a democracy of free men, was under way.

And the greatest instrument with which to guarantee it — universal education at public expense — had been established for the first time in man's history. .

The Development of the Continent

Bred in such an orgy of clearance and settlement, it is little wonder that the American became a lusty, aggressive man of action, sure of himself in anything that had to do with physical construction. Nothing was too big to undertake.

Movement was the central mood . . . movement and expansion . . . bigger and better. For a hundred years the Americans trailed west on a moving frontier, thirty miles a year. Lap by lap the wilderness was claimed and cleared while behind it rose farms, crossroad hamlets, and expanding towns. The impulse was economic: the rich hinterland of resources and trade always lay "just over yonder." By the time Thomas Jefferson had argued the Congress into paying Napoleon $15,000,000 for the Great Plain between the Mississippi and the Rockies, thousands of prairie schooners were creeping through the passes of the Allegheny Mountains. In the first lap of the westward movement the prize was the Ohio Valley just behind the Appalachians, and to it the growing cities of the eastern plain built their lanes of trade in frenzied decades of road, canal, and railroad construction. Begun in 1817, the Erie Canal joined the Atlantic with the Great Lakes by 1825. .

The Ohio, so recently paddled by red men, became the scene of picturesque trade and travel. Whole communities moved in; then, sensing the better land farther on, moved out. The young Abe Lincoln, ferry boy at Anderson Creek, marveled at the downstream pageantry of the flatboat transportation, followed in no time at all by the new steamboats chugging upstream from New Orleans.

In the East and in Europe the first rumblings of the Industrial Revolution manifested themselves in an Atlantic scheme of manufacturing and merchandising. Acres of smokestacks reared themselves in the cities of the old world and in those newer ones of New England. At last, artificial power controlled and harnessed to wheels! The year 1828 saw the first horizontal boiler engine made in America, puffing along the little Baltimore and Ohio stub line. Bumpy, narrow-gauge railroads — all gauges different — spread from town to town. Terminals sprang up overnight. By 1855 Cornelius Vanderbilt had standardized the individualistic track gauges and joined New York and Chicago in the first true railroad system.

Not only was the trek westward; a new South also came to life. Across the Tennessee and Carolina mountains the youth of the old aristocracy hacked down superb timber, cleared the land, and established their Cotton Kingdom. The merchant marines of Massachusetts, Britain, and France swarmed into the harbors of Charleston, Savannah, and New Orleans. By 1825 the Creole Capital of the South was a world city of French, English, Dutch, Norwegians, Spanish, and Italians.

In the East — from New England to Ohio — Horace Mann, Henry Barnard, and Calvin Stowe were building the first graded public schools for the hordes of children that were crowding the new industrial towns.

In 1849 . . . gold in California! The torture of the western barriers endured, the pioneer had spanned the continent. Behind the moving frontier, hamlets appeared where a year before only gophers and jack rabbits lived. Hamlets became towns; towns, cities. The nation grew. As the smokestacks of the cities multiplied, a new agricultural civilization unfolded on the western prairie. While thieves and crooks governed brawling San Francisco, and the Vigilantes conducted a little revolution in the name of law and order, 459 wagons were counted in one ten-mile stretch in the Platte River Valley.

In the northeast zone embryo industrialism slowly formed, and the new immigrants concentrated in islands of foreign-born peoples. The inventive genius of Kelly, McCormick, Howe, and Goodyear broke the bonds of the old handicraft, which had held back mass production, automatic skill, and technical efficiency. The civilization of leather and wood gave way to one of iron and coal. In 1810 America produced 54,000 tons of iron . . . 347,000 tons in 1840. William Kelly had succeeded in blowing air through melted pig iron, and the Age of Steel

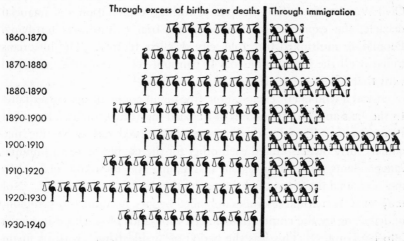

Each symbol represents an increase of one million people

Growth of population in the United States during the past 90 years. (Twentieth Century Fund, *U.S.A.: Measure of a Nation*, by Thomas R. Corskadon and Rudolph Modley; Macmillan.)

had arrived. The steel bridge and the 90-pound rail speeded urbanization. Cities of a million grew, and face-to-face neighborhood life slowly declined.

> The spirit of craftsmanship began to die in America, and the lazy giant — the public school — slept peacefully on, unaware of the shaping issues.

The War Between the States! Shirts, socks, belts, shoes by the 10,000 gross were needed. Generals wept for guns, production speeded up, and industrialism grew. Steel and the new railways helped prevent the division of the Union. Under the demands launched by the way, there began a tremendous expansion of machine-made goods. McCormick led it in agriculture, Carnegie in steel, Frick in coal and coke, Rockefeller in oil, Vanderbilt, Hill, Huntington, Stanford, and Harriman in railroads, Morse in the telegraph, Bell in the telephone, Armour in meat, Morgan in money and credit. In the short space of forty years handicraft was supplanted by large-scale, corporation-owned factory production of standardized goods. A single example: the U. S. Steel Corporation, capitalized in 1901 at $1,400,000,000, was the giant product of Andrew Kloman's little iron forge, valued in 1858 at $5800! From post-Civil-War reconstruction, in spite of ruthless exploitation and financial debacle, the expansion of the new industrial culture was terrifying. Population multiplied threefold, city dwellers tenfold. The historians called it all the Great Industrial Expansion; yet it was little compared with that which came after 1900.

It was a wild era of exploitation, free-for-all competition, laissez faire. In the '70's and '80's thousands of frenzied individuals drained the oil of Pennsylvania. Two hundred competitors turned out harvesting machinery, fifty owners knifed each other for the copper mines, a hundred independents took the silver out of Nevada, and thousands of lumbermen denuded the forests, fighting each other by fair means or foul. Not only were the natural resources despoiled by greedy competitors; ruinous underselling by the corporations forced thousands of small businessmen into bankruptcy. This was the period of "wildcatting," with its financial disaster for the many and the ever-pyramiding wealth for the few. Cornelius Vanderbilt was worth $10,000,000 in 1865; he died twelve years later leaving $104,000,000.

Here were unique problems for the new nation to solve. What was the content of instruction in its crude new national school system?

Speed and size! Make it big! Get it done! America can lick the world! These were the slogans. As the poet Carl Sandburg said of Chicago in 1900, it was "Bigness and Bedamnedness!" Nothing up to that time in modern life is more breath-taking than the speed with which the new industrial system was set up and the contrasts in living that emerged within the lifetime of a man. Out of hundreds of illiterate American families came children who made some of the world's revolutionary scientific discoveries, inventions, and creative statements. Americans who had been born in log cabins died in marble palaces. Youths who had grown up with their nearest neighbors fifty miles away, huddled in their old age in a city block housing 2000 human beings. The nation, illiterate at the beginning of the century, could read and write at its close. Thus the whole culture changed overnight as a modern industrial social order ousted a primitive handicraft society.

This is the picture, then, that comes to mind when we recall our fathers' world of 1890:

–Everything in "the little," but in the mood of "make it bigger."

–A new country, in cultural infancy, not yet having thrown off the grip of the mother culture of Europe, having barely begun to make its own indigenous, expressive statement.

–A face-to-face culture, insulated and isolationist, provincial, lacking a world view or world interest.

–A handicraft culture, just moving out of the first crude stage of industrialization . . . standing at the verge of the Second Technological Revolution but still a debtor country.

–The world's outstanding individualistic people . . . a private-enterprise country . . . apparently progressive, but actually one of the most conservative peoples on the earth.

Fifty Years of Technological Change, 1890's–1940's

Then, in a half century, came a still more startling transformation. The epoch-making discoveries in electromagnetism of Oersted and Faraday (1820's and 1830's), Maxwell's great theoretical achievement in writing equations of the electrical field of force (1870's), and Herz's contributions in the 1880's laid bare the laws of the electromagnetic field, and in the next fifty years produced undreamed-of technological and social change. It brought a new world into being.

The physical record is clear. In the period between 1860 and 1870 the United States Patent Office granted 80,000 patents; from 1930–1940 the total was approximately 485,000. Hundreds of machines and attachments were devised: power-driven lifting machines; crushing, rolling, shearing, stamping, loading, and unloading machines; machines to start and stop machines; machines to repair machines. Measuring instruments were improved. All these new inventions sharply changed ways of manufacturing. The central factory, driven by a central power station and owned by a single corporation, integrated all independent industries and processes under one efficient control. Economy and

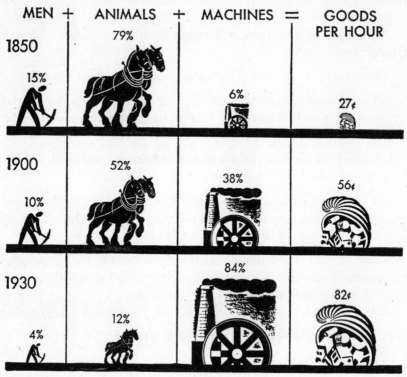

The development of machine power in the United States during its period of greatest industrialization. (Twentieth Century Fund, U.S.A.: Measure of a Nation; Macmillan.)

efficiency in production quickly advanced under the skill and vigor of the driving masters of capital, who built the great corporate industries. Concentration and integration of control became the chief characteristic of the social system.

Then came the First World War, 1914–1918. Under the enormous demand for goods, the new systems of heavy industry and mechanized agriculture *more than tripled their production and exporting of goods and materials.* Overnight the United States changed from a provincial, isolated debtor country to the leading manufacturer and creditor nation of the world. Invention itself became subjected to mass production.

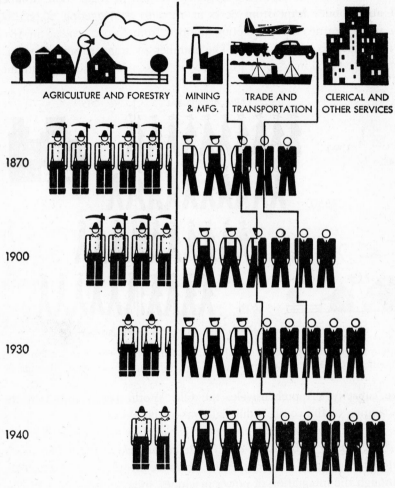

Each symbol represents 10 per cent of all gainful workers

Our jobs have changed during the past 70 years. (Twentieth Century Fund, *U.S.A.: Measure of a Nation;* Macmillan.)

A vast hierarchy of workers — executives and managers, superintendents, designers, foremen, skilled workers, technicians, office employees, and salesmen — all learned how to work as an efficient team.

By the 1920's the American economic system was becoming organized for efficient production. The volume of goods produced increased enormously; the curves of production rose, almost uninterrupted, from 1870 to the beginning of the Great Depression in 1929. The number of automobiles leapt from 8000 in 1900 to a staggering 26,000,000 in 1930. Farm crop production jumped from $2,000,000,000 in 1870 to $21,500,000,000 in 1920. The number of wage earners increased from 12,500,000 in 1870 to 48,000,000 in 1930. Here was huge produc-

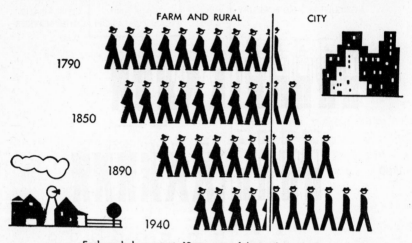

Each symbol represents 10 per cent of the total population

During the past 160 years, our population has shifted from farm and rural areas to the cities. (Twentieth Century Fund, U.S.A.: *Measure of a Nation;* Macmillan.)

tive capacity. Apprehensively, the Old World began to watch the awakening of the young industrial rival in the West.

But the increase in the productive capacity of the individual worker was even more astounding, and it altered his whole life. The nearly automatic factory had come into existence in the heavy industries. Through the integration of power machines, men, and processes in continuous straight-line design, the capacity of an individual to accomplish work increased almost incredibly. Increasing output per worker, as shown by decreasing man-hours per unit of production, doubled, then tripled, in fifty years.

In the summer of 1929 President Hoover said: "We shall soon with the help of God be in sight of the day when poverty will be banished from this nation." American workers were coming to believe that they would never be without jobs and high wages.

Between October 24 and 29, 1929, shocking things happened. Prices of stocks and bonds tumbled precipitously. Panic seized the speculators; fear and bewilderment spread over the country. The people began to save what money they had, buying only necessary goods. The business of stores and factories declined. One by one, factories closed, and such unemployment prevailed as America had never known before. The normal unemployment figure of 2,000,000 for the prosperity year of 1929 became 12,000,000 in 1932, and was variously estimated at 13,000,000 to 17,000,000 when President Roosevelt went into office.

By the winter of 1932–1933 the country was at the very depth of what the historians soon began to call "The Great Depression." The people were beginning to mutter "poverty in the midst of plenty!"

We need not recall at length the efforts of the Roosevelt administration to build up the morale of the people, to give millions of them a dole, to bolster up banks and utilities, and to create schemes of temporary made-work, including, finally, a huge federal program of public works. In fourteen great depressions this was the first time the federal government had made a bold and serious attempt to "prime the pump" of a potentially efficient and productive, but actually inefficient and stalling, economic system. The competitive conditions of private enterprise had failed to keep the system going; now let government try its hand. And try it did, creating a score of governmental agencies, many of which were shown to be unwise, but some, such as the Tennessee Valley Authority, the Soil Conservation Service, the Civilian Conservation Corps, and the building of the great land-reclamation projects, were magnificent permanent contributions to the reconstruction of our country.

But the consequences were baffling. The volume of production did revive; it was, indeed, practically as large in the spring of 1937 as in the summer of 1929. But the number of people employed did not rise in proportion; even in the autumn of 1939 there were still 10,000,000 employable workers out of work in America.

Then, in September, 1939, Hitler and the Nazi armies debauched Poland, and World War II, long predicted, was on.

In June France fell. The British, waiting for Hitler to cross the

Channel, murmured: "We'll evacuate to Canada!" Millions of star-
tled Americans, listening to their radios, imagined a Nazi conquest of all
Europe. The government sprang into action and moved the country
with it. Quickly the production of armaments speeded up. *Unemployment in the United States began to decrease, for the first time in
ten years,* as millions went back to work. A year passed; Britain, blitz-
bombed, waited for the blow. But Hitler stood still in France.

December 7, 1941 . . . Pearl Harbor. In a burst of national anger
most of America awoke and went to war. Businessmen and labor, bury-
ing the hatchet just below the surface, pulled together well enough to
design and build ships, planes, tanks, guns, and to transport seven million men overseas. Complete figures on our Gargantuan war production after January, 1943, are not yet available. We called it "total war,"
but what proportion of our economy and social system we organized in
1942–1946 we shall perhaps never know. Certainly we did not put all
our resources to work. But we did learn in those years of pressure and
planning that our economic system could produce five times as much as
it actually had produced in the middle years of the Great Depression.

Before we turn to an appraisal of the personal traits and beliefs that
came out of this physical and technological conquest of North America,
let us sum up the significant facts of American society in these mid-
century years:

–Land area relatively unchanged for a generation; no sign of popular
desire to increase it.

–About 150,000,000 people, second most populous industrial nation,
with an enormous mixture of peoples and a remarkable degree of
American assimilation, but increasing racial nobility and dangerous
friction; the concept of equality not yet implemented.

–United States, the No. 1 economic and military nation, creditor to
the world, possessor of the predominance of the earth's developed
natural resources and producing technology; a country capable of
producing an abundant life for all its people.

–15,000,000 of the 60,000,000 workers organized and participating in
the national struggle for power, already a successful political force.

–Popular interest in politics, which had seriously declined, partly revived after 1929 through increasing public study of issues by business, labor, and governmental organizations.

–A mood of bigness throughout the culture; concentration of population and of industrial wealth and power; the grave danger of increasing monopoly with the issue — shall it be private or public?

–For half the people, urban life becoming increasingly anonymous; hence, dangerous trends in lack of social discipline.

The Teacher's Part in the Culture-Molding Process

Let us pause a moment to recapitulate. The main theme of our study is twofold: *First* — How does the culture teach the children and youth what to think, believe, and value? *Second* — What ideas, beliefs, and objects of allegiance do they come to hold as a consequence of this molding process?

We have employed two kinds of material: *first* — case studies which have shown how family and neighborhood life give young Americans their social ideas, beliefs, and attitudes; *second* — a sketch of the century-long conquest and settlement of the American continent, during the course of which the characteristic traits, beliefs, and values of our people were developed. We turn next, therefore, to a discussion of what those beliefs and values were.

As we do so, bear in mind that the reason for all this discussion of the history and psychology of the culture is that the teacher plays a leading part in guiding the culture-molding process. The kind of man or woman that will emerge from that process will be determined by who guides it — who picks out the conspicuous things in the social world and directs the child's attention to them, and on what basis these are selected. It is the educator, in his twofold function of curriculum maker and teacher, who plays the chief role in selecting and interpreting the American way of life to the children. It is incumbent upon teachers, therefore, to become competent students of both the history and psychology of the culture and to be as objective as possible in critically appraising it and passing it on to the youth. The ideas and beliefs that teachers select, and the interpretation they give, will go far toward determining what the young people come to believe. This points, therefore, to the great responsibility of the teacher in guiding the culture-molding process.

It becomes of central importance, therefore, for *the teachers to see clearly what characteristic ideas, beliefs, and values come out of the ten generations of American history and are now reflected in the families and communities of our country.* It is these that we can draw from our brief studies of the social psychology of our people. We ask next, then: Who is the American? What are his beliefs? What does he value?

The Way of Life Taught Young Americans by the Culture

The ten generations in the new world turned the hardy pioneering European stock into a new brand of modern man. Above all, the American became an aggressive man of action, confident, in a casual sort of way, that he could "lick the world." Whether or not he could lead it out of its morass of confusion and political anarchy was a matter to be settled later, but that he would succeed at all tasks of physical construction, there was no doubt. Had he not shown that he could harness uncontrollable river systems, win two World Wars in thirty years (others helped, of course!), tunnel mountains, even move them? Could he refinance and arm and equip economic systems far and wide? Why not?

A Sturdy Individualism: Free Enterprise

Our fathers did not invent the idea of leaving every man free to work out his own salvation; it was in the air on both sides of the Atlantic, and the Europeans brought it with them to a favored spot where it could flower best. All the conditions favored the newcomers: a virgin continent of unmatched resources, the makings of a rich economy one to three months distant from the armed quarrels and political intrigues of class-conscious Europe, and a generally accepted mood of "everyman for himself" as the basis of practical life.

So it happened that in America the Individual, free and equal, was the center of every episode of civilization building. Driving and directing all behavior was a sturdy individualism. Its roots were nourished

by the deep belief in freedom in every kind of enterprise. And freedom
meant *absence of restraint*. Take off the lid! The sky is the limit!
"Don't tread on me," read the banners in the political torchlight pro-
cessions. It was generally believed that a people would achieve the
greatest possible wealth and well-being if each man were left free to develop his farm, business, mine, or bank as he saw fit. The less control
the better. The Founding Fathers agreed, and the twentieth-century
corporation leaders echoed them, that the best government is that government that governs least.

The Concern with Material Things

History had demonstrated that the American, in company with most
other peoples, should value the possession of property and money. The
masses of the European peoples had always been chronically poor; they
continued to be poor throughout their early generations in North America. Things were scarce — so scarce that most of the people lacked
the necessities of life, while only the few could have comforts and very
few the luxuries. Until recent decades physical things were still produced by handcrafts and wind and muscle power. So much human
effort went into their production, and so few things could be produced,
that things and the money to buy them were prized above all. Thus
things, as well as freedom, lured the people; and the possession of money
income seemed the sure route to success.

Of course the Americans did not invent the craving for property
and money. Their ancestors in Eurasia had long before laid the foundations for the acquisitive spirit. Even before the first landings in Virginia and Massachusetts the leadership of the new manufacturing
countries of Europe was safely in the hands of the traders, the manufacturers, and the money lenders. Three hundred years of life in the
new continent did not alter this. A man's status in the community, as
well as in the country, came to be measured by the size of his bank account, the size and style of his house, his horses or automobiles, his
wife's clothes, his summer vacations, and the exclusiveness and extent
of his children's education. Business became the norm of our institutions, and it was assumed that the practical man who has "met a pay
roll," and his lawyer, would make the best mayor, governor, congressman,
or president.

Naturally, therefore, in a world in which everyone knew that there was not enough to go around, the shrewdest, most aggressive, and most persistent would get the luxuries, and, as the slogan said, "the devil take the hindmost."And it was assumed, as the nationwide problems of relief in the Great Depression proved, that "the poor ye shall have with you always." It was not, indeed, until the World Wars that any considerable number of our people really knew that with our gigantic resources, machine technology, and skilled personnel a high standard of life could be given to every American family.

Each Man Responsible for Himself

In such a struggle for existence, traits of resourcefulness and independence are built in a people. Every American learned that he had to look out for himself. The central note of the creed of practical everyday life was expressed by a saying attributed to the British Puritan leader, Oliver Cromwell: "Put your trust in God; but mind to keep your powder dry!" The Americans paraphrased it: "God helps those who help themselves."

In a class-ridden society the little man is not only unfree; he is, on a minimum scale, cared for. But in a society of equals, each man is not only free; he must look out for himself. Hence, in every generation American fathers told their sons: "There stands the Ladder of Opportunity. Success, riches, glory, and power are at the top. You are free to climb it, but you must climb it under your own power. It will be hard, and you must school yourself for the effort. The higher you climb, the fewer will be the prizes, and the harder the competition. As you near the top, the rungs of the ladder will get smaller because the better things are always more scarce. Others will want them, too, and there will be more climbers than space on the rungs. You may have to push others off. Hence you must face up to your task; use every ounce of your energy, but use your common sense, and, above all, 'act right.' "

Cromwell's advice was paraphrased on twentieth-century playgrounds whenever mothers said to their complaining children: "No, I won't ask his mother to make him give it back. Get it yourself; he's no bigger than you are." "Don't be a sissy; hit him back if he hits you." But in all generations they have added, "Play fair." . . . "Don't hit below the belt." . . . "If you want to fight, pick on someone your own size."

The Belief in Success and Progress

Such an emphasis on things and competition puts a premium on individual success and social progress, and the nature of the emerging culture reflected its far-reaching influences. In each generation sons were pushed out to establish their own families. In frontier days the pioneering ones among them "moved west, to grow up with the country"; those left at home moved to other land to develop their own farms away from their fathers. The young were expected to find their own jobs, earn their own way, pick their own wives and husbands, build their own families. There were several routes to moving up the social scale: earning a larger income, marrying someone with money, or getting more education. But irrespective of how it was done, each generation was expected to go further than the preceding one.

The community climate of opinion increasingly reflected the belief in progress. Bigger and better! . . . Watch us grow! The American increasingly said: "I am a devotee of progress. I believe that by careful thought and planning my fellow citizens and I can build a better world in which to live. The justification is in the actual achievement of our fathers. By their efforts they actually doubled the length of life, raised the standard of living, and taught masses of people to read and write, thereby lengthening the radius of intellectual communication and human sympathy. The American way of progress is, therefore, a fact." Believing these things and passing on the beliefs to their children, the Americans cumulatively cultivated the spirit of innovation.

A Unique Individualism: "I" and "We" Doing It Together

Two brands of individualism have fought for supremacy over men's minds and actions: the exploitive tradition of rugged individualism and the great tradition of coöperative development of individuality. The exploitive tradition accepted laissez faire and acknowledged competition as the sole morality, and wealth the supreme goal. This was the standard of the empire builders, of the buccaneers of the coal and cotton kingdoms, of the giants of the Iron Age. It was the individualism of unrestricted rights — and no duties!

Yet this peculiar brand of individualism contained the potential germ out of which could grow a coöperative society of superior individuals. The great tradition held before men the goal of the person living the Good Life. In espousing freedom for the individual it sought to guarantee freedom for all. This was the spirit that has stood firm to the present day against oppression, confiscation, class violence, and dictatorships.

Thus, in the building of American civilization the problem of discovering the optimum relation between "I" and "We" has always confronted the people. Repeatedly we have been faced by such questions as: How can we reconcile the drives of the competitive individual with the needs of society? How combine individualism and coöperation? What is the proper role for each self in the large society? How can we allow each individual to express himself for his own soul's sake as well as for the good of his neighbors without encroaching upon those neighbors?

Such solutions as the Americans achieved of this problem of "I" and "We," they learned the hard way. Great crises taught them the value of tempering individualism with coöperative effort. Under a system of free enterprise in water supply, for example, Detroit, Chicago, and other cities burned down. Because of privately supplied impure water people of St. Louis died in a terrible epidemic of disease. Such tragedies awakened the Americans to the need of coöperative control. They "socialized" their water supplies, and these are now the pride of most of our cities. Similarly, the Americans "socialized" their roads, their harbors, their waterways, most of their schools and their colleges, many of their libraries and museums, and half of their hospitals. Yet, they do not regard this as socialism.

They tempered their individualism with varying amounts of public ownership and coöperative control. They advanced a new conception for the relation between freedom and control. Instead of laissez-faire free enterprise, their economic system became a mixed economy — much of it private, but some of it public; much of it decentralized, but some of its parts centralized. The most thrilling example came in the midst of the Great Depression with the founding of the Tennessee Valley Authority. The TVA revealed to the world what the American brand of democracy in action really meant: "I'll do this and you'll do that . . . each of us doing what he is specially competent to do . . . I and We doing it together." The federal government takes over those activities that can be managed successfully only by its sovereignty, wealth, and creative power. The more local governments, the coöperatives, individual farmers and businessmen, and private companies in the grass roots do, each in their own way, what they are most competent to do.

As a consequence of this example of the TVA, the peoples in the river valleys of the entire earth, as well as in the eleven great valleys of the United States, are now considering which brand of "I" and "We" doing it together will best fit their needs and cultural conditions. Here the American deservedly leads the world, foregoing all imperialistic ambitions to conquer it. It may be an inspiring portent of other fine kinds of world leadership to come.

Equal as Well as Free — no Caste!

One quality in our individualism that partially justified the Americans' insistence that their brand of democracy had more chance of surviving in a socializing world was their union of freedom with equality. Like other men, they knew that they differed widely among themselves, yet more than most other men they asserted equality. On every frontier the Americans left consciousness of class behind them. Pioneer life built respect for the competent man, irrespective of his birth, wealth, or social position. The laborer as well as his labor was admired and respected. The more successful ones of each generation did create physical symbols of their superiority over their less successful fellows through their acquisition of land, houses, clothes, jewels, and so on. But even they did not aspire to build a *caste system*, which would involve being born into a social class, taking on its attributes and passing them on to one's children.

This is not to say that they ignored the obvious principle of individual differences; the competitive struggle throughout the society taught that fact to every new generation. A rank-order of competence did emerge in every community and neighborhood. The strong and agile, the intelligent and understanding, the sensitive and persistent, the ambitious did tend to gather most goods and so gain the power and the glory. Yet, underneath the obvious differences in physical, mental, and creative abilities one basic quality was recognized in all: the dignity and worth of the personality of each man. Men were not only equal "before the law," and "in opportunity," but in the sovereignty of their personalities. The very essence of the American brand of democracy was the insistence on the supreme value of the individual. Hence, unlike many societies, both primitive and modern, which divided people into rigid groups or castes, American society tended to become a welter of constantly shifting social groups. Although wealth and achievement did produce apparent classes in every generation and in every community, the lines between them were blurred and ever changing.

Moreover, the people themselves do not feel rigidly divided into social classes. A recent Gallup poll asked American people the question: "To what social class do you belong?" Eighty-eight per cent answered middle class, 6 per cent placed themselves in the upper class, and only 6 per cent considered themselves in the lower class. This finding was confirmed by a recent Roper (*Fortune*) poll, and by such studies of community life as those of the Lynds in Middletown and of Alfred Winslow Jones in Akron.

Against this view, a vigorous presentation of the point of view that American society is definitely class ridden has been made by a group of social anthropologists under the direction of Dr. Lloyd Warner of the University of Chicago. These investigators maintain that our people divide themselves into six social classes, ranging from the "upper-uppers" of wealth, social influence, and political power to the "lower-lowers" of the poor, unskilled, immigrant dwellers down in the "clam flats" by the river or on "the other side of the tracks." One can, as they do, quote evidence of feelings of distinction from the running comments of citizens in many communities. An upper-class member, for example, looks down his nose at the lower-middles, saying, "They're not nice people; we don't have much to do with them." The upper-lowers reverse the comment: "They are the big shots; we're not in their class." Dr. Warner's several books on "Yankee City" give many personal histories to illustrate the process by which lower-lower immigrants from Eastern Europe become upper-middle Yankees — even "lower-uppers" — in three generations.

Rank-Order Society

In a competitive, success-and-progress society marked by individual differences in capacity the people inevitably arrange themselves in a rank-order of achievement and status. The tendency is for people in such a society to measure a man by comparing him with other men.

The accolade goes to "the richest man in America," the heavyweight champion, the Nobel Prize winner, but also to the high school boy who wins the state spelling contest. This rank-order idea gets into everything the people do — the appraisal of community life itself as well as the selection of officeholders, the award of prizes, the allocation of jobs and salaries.

Thus the community asks about its schools: "Are they as good as the schools of other towns of our size?" Not, "Are they as good as we, with our resources, can make them?" Within the schools, also, life is organized on the rank-order idea; witness the marking systems, the competitive contests for rewards and prizes, the effort to raise pupils' scores in the school subjects above the national norms. The promotion of the school child as well as of men in business, science, and government is rated on a rank-order basis. In home and school elders ask: "Have you done it better than the others?" Not "Have you done it as well as you possibly can?"

Man competes with man for the head of the line, brother rivals brother, town competes with town. The American child is taught to measure himself against his mates — to strive to get ahead of them all. That inner peace cannot be achieved by such an attitude has been difficult for Americans to realize.

Right and Wrong: Rewards and Punishments

The western peoples, including the Americans, developed the idea of every man for himself and every man responsible for himself into an elaborate code of behavior. Unlike most primitive societies, which rely on the spirits and the gods to punish wrongdoers, modern men take the responsibility on themselves. So children grow up under an elaborate system of rewards and punishments. The code of right and wrong is taught early and late: "This way of behaving is right; that way is wrong. Drink your milk. Eat your vegetables. Never tell a lie. Pay your bills. Don't touch others' property." Much of the time the teaching is authoritative: "Act right. . . . Be good — and everyone will love you. . . . God will be on your side if you are on the right side." Only in the wisest homes are the children taught that they must make their own decisions. Here they are told: "This is your problem. Is it a good thing to do, or not? You must decide." That some of the

homes and some of the schools have learned to put the responsibility on
the children promises much for the future of democracy.

Summing up the Culture-Molding Process: the Stereotype

We need not multiply examples. Those that we have given are
typical of the ideas and beliefs that are developed in the episodes of
daily living that constitute American culture in action. And our
examples are sufficient to drive home the point that family, neighborhood and town, school, church, movies, and radio — all taken together
tend to form the personalities of the young people. Surrounded by
older people, each one a self-oriented person somewhat predisposed to
make the child over according to his own pattern of opinions and beliefs, the child's learning and personality development go on by a
back-and-forth interactive process. The social environment — personi-
fied by the human beings of prestige — presses in upon him. He
presses back, sometimes accepting completely the meanings thrust upon
him, sometimes resisting, making over his responses to fit his own
predilections.

But the selective nature of the process is very clear. The social
world is indeed an overwhelming confusion of activities, words, meanings; too many meanings assail the child for him to react to them all.
He must select a few and respond to those. But how? He is young,
immature, inexperienced, easily swayed, and inclined to accept the
familiar or the obvious interpretation. So the adult world helps him.
It picks out the characteristics of objects: "This is sharp; it will cut you.
This is heavy; it will crush you." It catalogues people: He is a good
American; be like him. He is a crook, bad company; he'll lead you into
evil ways. He is a Red, subversive, not a real American; people will
suspect you if you associate with him." It forms in the child recognized attitudes toward disease, politics, religion, and morals. In every
situation the culture, through its interpreters and mouthpieces (father,
mother, teacher, pastor, scout leader, older playmate) picks out ideas,
beliefs, traits, and objects of allegiance and dramatizes and stylizes them
for the growing child. This is the personality-forming process called by
social psychologists — *the Stereotype*.

Studying How the Culture Molds Personality

1. As you turn to the college and town libraries for more reading, put our study of American culture to work. Make some firsthand personal observations of family and neighborhood life in the community where you are now living. Appoint committees to do it systematically. How do the current and local ideas, beliefs, and attitudes in your community compare with those discussed in this chapter? How does your estimate of the American way of life differ from the estimate given in this chapter? Do you now see that by culture patterns we mean the characteristic beliefs and attitudes which are the core of our way of life?

2. If you live in or near a cosmopolitan community, study the traits in the people of the foreign-speaking neighborhoods. Get data from the social agencies of the city. Talk to the teachers who have children or youth from these sections of the community.

3. Keep notes on outstanding characteristics in your own neighborhood behavior. Watch for signs of racial coöperation or intolerance and economic and political divisions in the community. Keep an informal record of conversations heard that indicate consciousness of class or of classlessness in your town.

4. Assume, for example, you were teaching a seventh grade. Make a list of things you could do with the children in order to build understanding of the group life of the community.

5. Look back into your own development as a young American and write a brief autobiographical sketch. Show the human beings and social forces that helped turn you into the person you are today. Cite conspicuous events that illustrate how your ideas and points of view were formed. Discuss personalities or groups that influenced you.

6. Reconstruct, as far as you can, the personality of one of your grandparents. Compare and contrast his social world — its economic and social conditions and problems, characteristic ideas and beliefs, likes and dislikes — with your own. How do you account for the striking changes?

7. Interview some old people in your community, discussing the culture of America of fifty years ago. Compare their ideas of it with those you have got from your historical reading.

8. See if your family has kept old letters, diaries, or other records that will give you a picture of the lives of your parents or grandparents. If each

student in the group will bring any such letters to class, a fine discussion may be had.

9. Look back into your own education. Did the history of American life given you by the school and the college leave a feeling for the traits and beliefs of Americans? What phases of American life would you now stress that were left out in your education? Which ones do you now feel were inadequately treated? What do you think might be the explanation?

More Reading about the American Culture and Way of Life

From the huge modern library available to guide your study of our America and how it grew, we cite only a few of the very finest readings, and the best adapted to your needs.

First, the newer histories: Don't miss Leo Huberman's *We, the People,* or the Beards' *Basic History of the United States.* Let your pupils (junior or senior high school) read them. You yourself, and perhaps the brighter high school students, will enjoy and get much from Charles and Mary Beard's *Rise of American Civilization.* Perhaps the various volumes of the Rugg series — for example, *Man and His Changing Society, Changing Governments and Changing Cultures, The Conquest of America,* or *Introduction to Problems of American Culture* — are in your library. See the hundred-page sketch of the characteristics and achievements of our industrial-democratic society in *Democracy and the Curriculum* (the Third Yearbook of the John Dewey Society). An excellent history of American education against the background of the great social changes is Edwards and Richey's *The School in the American Social Order;* see especially pages 439–867.

As for conditions and problems in America today, and culture patterns, John Gunther's book will take you, as its title says, *Inside U.S.A.* David Lilienthal's *T.V.A.: Democracy on the March* (Pocket Books) gives a magnificent picture of the American way of life in action — a moving story of three million people rebuilding their farms, businesses, and homes in the Tennessee Valley; it's a "must." Chester Bowles's *Tomorrow without Fear* will give you a glimpse of the tremendous potentialities for the abundant life in our giant economic system. Build up a library of the low-cost "Public Affairs Pamphlets"; see especially Nos. 25, 32, 45, 50, 80, 84, 85, 95, 99, 103, 119, 121, 129, 142, dealing with current American problems and issues.

Several firsthand studies of ways of life in American communities are given in the Lynds' *Middletown* and *Middletown in Transition*, and in W. Lloyd Warner's Volume I of the Yankee City series, *The Social Life of a Modern Community*; also in James West's *Plainville, U.S.A.* The molding power of Southern communities upon the Negro child and youth personalities is dramatized in Davis and Dollard's *Children of Bondage* and in Davis and Gardner's *Deep South*.

Five studies of the press, radio, movies, and other agencies in forming public opinion can be found in *A Free and Responsible Press* by the Committee on Freedom of the Press. See also Walter Lippmann's classic study, *Public Opinion*.

Five contrasts in cultures and culture molding may be got from Margaret Mead's *From the South Seas*, Ruth Benedict's *Patterns of Culture*, and Abram Kardiner's *The Individual and His Society*.

For two opposed views on the dangers in and the need for social planning see Von Hayek's *The Road to Serfdom* and Barbara Wooton's reply to it, *Freedom under Planning*.

One of the best recent publications stressing the group setting of the child and the cultural conditioning that inheres in group living is James H. S. Bossard's *The Sociology of Child Development*.

CHAPTER 5

Building the School for a Society of Free People

A COMPLEX industrial-democratic society requires a system of public schools for all the children, that will educate free and intelligent men. This, mankind has never had before our time.

To build such a school is a difficult thing. The Americans have been struggling to do it for over a century. To understand the school in American culture we must know the roots of that struggle.

In this present chapter we see the magnificent *physical* victory in the battle for free universal *elementary* education; in the next chapter, the gains in building *higher* schools.

We also see the ineffectiveness of the education which was set up — a static, formal, and authoritarian school that ignored the conditions and issues of our changing society.

But we take courage from the heartening examples of the pioneering educators who built many child-centered elementary schools after 1890.

THE GOAL AHEAD: *Schools and Colleges That Will Educate Mature Men and Women*

The Common School in American Culture

ON AN EVENING in 1941, the teachers of Little Tallapoosa School in rural Georgia brought 75 tenant-farmer parents and their children together to discuss what could be done through the school to improve their own living conditions in the neighborhood. Many suggestions were made: repairing the schoolhouse, building a kitchen and lunchroom, improving the general living of the community through the enrichment and revitalization of the soil, and the like. The teachers described how other rural communities had established canning plants, health centers, and other services through their schools.

Although the farmers were slow to be convinced, they were interested enough to attend other meetings. As these meetings continued, the parents gradually warmed to the possibilities, and formed study committees to look into the various proposals. Finally they organized a coöperative, with a state charter to enable them to engage in buying, processing, and marketing. The teachers and farmers together formed themselves into a board of directors, shares were sold at $2.50, and $500 was raised. They bought an old building, hauled it to the school grounds, on which a site had been leased, and there they established a canning plant. Under a local farmer who served as manager, and with the volunteer labor of their own members, they processed 15,000 cans of vegetables and fruits the first season. An electric pump was installed for the school and the cannery, tractors and other equipment were secured, and a community clubhouse was erected. Then came a school lunchroom, a community library, a community school health center, a gristmill, a feed mill, and a sweet-potato curing house.

The report of the third annual meeting of the coöperative, by

M. D. Folger, Director of Teacher Education at West Georgia College, gives a thrilling picture of accomplishments:

> "As night came the farmers from all parts of the community assembled at the little schoolhouse with their wives and children . . . to hear the reports of their president and treasurer and do some thinking about next year. The president . . . explained how a few members had advanced the money to buy the new tractor. There had been enough cash in the treasury to purchase the plows and harrows."

The treasurer in his report stated that

> "the money borrowed to install the gristmill had been repaid and the feed mill had been purchased from the earnings on the cannery and gristmill. The net profits from their enterprises were running around $125 a month. There was something over $500 in the bank. All bills were paid. The cannery had been in operation three years, and almost 100,000 pints of food had been preserved for use by the people in their homes and in the school lunchroom."

Then Mr. Folger added:

> "But how had this thing happened to a people who three years earlier had never had any experience in group action for the common welfare?"

How indeed! The Little Tallapoosa School was not much like the school of the three R's we described in Chapter 2. In Little Tallapoosa the community is the school, and vice versa. Children and parents and teachers plan and build together and discover both leadership and coöperation among themselves.

There are other places in America where such things are happening in education. Although the number is not large, there are enough to encourage us to feel that our people are awakening to the tremendous potentialities in their schools for leadership in community and national life. While the conception of an education-centered community is a product of recent years, its roots were planted by American leaders in the earliest days of national life. In Andrew Jackson's day they knew that if the new American experiment in democracy was to succeed, the people must be intelligently informed. Democratic government could be based permanently on the consent of the governed only if the people understood their conditions and problems, and were intelligent in their voting. This demanded that the people be educated to the extent at least of being able to read and write. A system of public education was imperative.

Horace Mann, the first secretary of the Massachusetts Board of Education, Henry Barnard, editor of the *Connecticut Common School Journal* and first United States Commissioner of Education (1867–1870), the Reverend Calvin E. Stowe of Cincinnati, and others prodded the people into building such a system. Between 1820 and 1840 the new state constitutions and school laws provided for the support of public elementary education by taxation. "The mind of every citizen in a republic is the common property of society," read one of the preambles. ". . . it is therefore considered the peculiar duty of a free government, like ours, to encourage and extend improvement and cultivation of the intellectual energies of the whole."

Decade after decade the battle for universal tax-supported education raged across the United States. Public-education societies published pamphlets, lobbied with legislators, and developed new educational experiments, while many property owners opposed their plans. In its creation of new states the federal government set aside sections of land for the support of common schools and a state university. Step by step the people defeated the old conception that education should be privately supported, that is, only for those children of the well-to-do who could afford to pay for it.

Thus, even before the War Between the States the concept of a public school system paid for by the taxes of the people and free to all the children was becoming an established American principle. Linked to this problem was the growing idea that the development of a truly democratic nation demanded compulsory school attendance. When voluntary measures did not seem to work, compulsory-attendance legislation began to appear. Massachusetts was the first to pass such a law (1852). It is important to understand that this principle was initiated by the grass-roots study, discussion, and campaigning of the people in the local communities. It was not imposed by a central government as in Prussia, France, England, and other European countries. It was the American attempt to build popular understanding of the problems of the culture through public education. The purpose was to help guarantee the success of democracy, of "government by the consent of the governed."

Building the System of Universal Public Education: 1840's — 1890's

Building the Structure of the System

In this background and from these unique factors, the educational system of the United States was swiftly created in the half century between 1840 and 1890. As you can see, our fathers did it all at the very moment they were setting up their economic system of factories and farms and binding them together by modern transport and communication. The entire physical structure of the civilization had to be set up at once — no single part could wait until others had been completely developed. To permit it to function democratically, the Bill of Rights was established and the suffrage developed. And the democratic idea was extended so that it would embrace a new idea in the history of the human race — namely, compulsory *tax-supported* and *universal education.*

Citizens who had never dreamed of financing public schools by taxation had to be persuaded to do so, and legislatures had to be brought to the point of passing compulsory education laws and codes that regulated school instruction. Buildings, teachers, curriculum — all had to be created for the first time in history. No normal schools, state colleges, or universities existed in which to train teachers; they had to be created. The first in Massachusetts, after 1839, were duplicated decade after decade, until by 1890 every state had a complete, even if crude, system of teacher training. It *was* crude; young men and women from the farms and from the mechanics' homes of the towns and cities were given a few months or a year or two of "normal" instruction and sent out to teach. Thus from extremely meager beginnings a teaching staff was trained to man the most extensive system of public education any nation had ever set up.

The same situation was true with respect to buildings, equipment, and courses of study. In a half century after the building of the Quincy Grammar School of Boston (1847), schoolhouses sprang up in thousands of communities. Bad as they were, they were the best in the world. It was all a tremendous physical achievement. Nothing like it had ever been possible before, and no people had been presented with so many gigantic tasks to be accomplished simultaneously.

Moreover, no people ever before had been given such a chance to capitalize on the democratic idea. The Americans inherited a long head start toward the idea of leaving the individual free to rise to his highest innate capacity, and this came to them *at the very moment that a virgin continent of untold riches was given to them to develop as they saw fit*. As we have seen, they saw fit to develop it, in theory at least, for *the good of the individual*. Certainly the authoritarian, dictatorial, or police state was furthest removed from their ideals. Although they made many mistakes, and did often exploit the people for selfish reasons, there came out of it the highest order of democracy to be enjoyed by any large country.

Perhaps the most significant development was the building of free public high schools. For more than a century from the founding of the Benjamin Franklin Academy in 1751, well-to-do Americans had been able to buy schooling for their children. The private conception of education grew so swiftly that by 1850 there were 6085 academies in the United States attended by 263,000 pupils and taught by 12,260 teachers. But these were *private* schools, financed by the rich parents of the pupils who attended them, not 5 per cent of all the population. But private education, even in the secondary school level, was not in tune with the growing democratic spirit of America. As early as 1821, therefore, Boston created the first American public secondary school — the English High School, and in the 30's and 40's public high schools were established by law in most of the states. From then on the private academies declined, and people turned more and more to the public high schools. By 1900 the number of private academies had dwindled to 1500, while the public high schools numbered 7000.

Thus America led the world in practicing the idea that everyone should have a secondary education. Think what that means — not less than thirteen or fourteen years of public education for all. Compare this with an average school attendance in most modern nations of less than eight years and in many others of only three to four. But the history of the last fifty years has established that it could be done. Today

Public Schools Enrollment, Teachers, and Expenditures [1]

SCHOOL YEAR ENDING	POP. 5 TO 17 YRS.	PUPILS	PER CENT OF POP. 5-17	TEACHERS	TOTAL EXPEND.
1880	15,065,767	9,867,395	65.5	286,593	$78,094,687
1890	18,543,201	12,722,631	68.6	363,922	140,506,715
1900	21,404,322	15,503,110	72.4	423,062	214,964,618
1910	24,239,948	17,813,852	73.5	523,210	426,250,434
1920	27,728,788	21,578,316	77.8	679,302	1,036,151,209
1930	31,571,322	25,678,015	81.3	854,263	2,316,790,384
1940	29,805,259	25,433,542	85.3	875,477	2,344,048,927
1947	29,317,000	23,659,158	80.8	833,512	3,124,550,348

[1] United States Office of Education figures.

there are over 7,000,000 young Americans in high school, 71 per cent of all those of secondary school age.

Looking back on it all: In 1840 public universal education simply did not exist; but by 1890, in a little more than a half century, the physical structure of a national system of schools had been built. Summed up quickly it was:

–Universal education an accepted American doctrine — elementary, secondary, and even higher education.

–A twelve-grade scheme of public education, free and tax-supported.

–A continuous ladder of educational development divided (with some exceptions) into two major types of schools: an eight-grade elementary and a four-year secondary school.

–School buildings for all children from the ages of six to eighteen.

–12,500,000 children in elementary and secondary schools.

–160,000 in undergraduate colleges and in professional schools and colleges.

–The groundwork for the American idea of providing opportunities for each individual to develop to his maximum stature — the very foundation of the American tradition.

A magnificent physical achievement — and accomplished in a very short time!

The School of 1890

But what kind of child development went on within that system of free public education? An example from a formal school of some years ago will recall its nature as described in an earlier chapter. A seventh-grade boy, interrupted in the exciting self-originated enterprise of stuffing a bird, gave E. R. Guthrie, the psychologist, the following juvenile description of what went on in a typical school day:

"We have a man teacher. He doesn't get mad much. We talk a lot. If somebody throws a pen or stuff like that, he puts you out in the hall. We have 20 words for spelling. We write them on Monday and Wednesday and Friday, but it only counts on Wednesday and Friday. Then we have social science. It's really history, but he likes fancy names for things. Then we study geography and then mathematics — really arithmetic, you know. He gives us some fancy doo-jigs to work with. About two boys get their seats changed if they've been poking somebody. Then the teacher gives us exams and stuff and we have recess — ten minutes — not much time for doing things. We mostly play marbles. Then the bell rings and we go in and the teacher talks a lot about notices. Then the music class. The music teacher talks a lot. We don't sing much. Sometimes we sing a review song, but mostly the teacher talks. Then we have reading. The teacher is nuts about ancient literature. Then we check our books at the book table. They have about 200 books. Some of them are good and some are corny. We have shop, too; make things. There's a jig saw and a lathe and a sander and a printing press. We use all those things. I made a record case and a broom holder and a box." [1]

Turn back to Chapter 2 and reread the description of the education that went on in those drab prison-like schools of 1890: grim two-story brick structures, eight-grade schools, rooms arranged in files four on a floor and two on each side of the darkly wainscoted corridor. That was the child's abode for eight years or more. The grammar of life that went on in it was as standardized as the drab rooms were standardized in size and equipment: forty-eight children in forty-eight ironbound seats and desks — standardized, in spite of the fact that no two of the four hundred children were alike.

[1] Forty-first Yearbook, National Society for the Study of Education, The Psychology of Learning, page 17. Quoted by permission of the Society.

Central to the elementary schools of the town was the high school. The young people were older, but the regimen was much the same. The bells rang the periods, in and out, and the pupils marched from room to room — from algebra to English, French to physics, Latin to manual training. In the deadly forty-minute periods the ancient curriculum of the seven liberal arts held sway: dissection of British classics, memorizing of verbs, seventeen ways of factoring, minutiae of battles and legislative enactments, and the rise and fall of dynasties.

The extracurricular activities, tacked on to the program in late afternoons and better adapted to individual interests and abilities, are just coming into American high schools: interscholastic teams, glee clubs, literary and debating societies, and class organizations — a beginning toward building the active life and program of the school.

Looked at in the framework of the whole country and the shortness of time in which it had been developed, much could be said in its favor. For example, bad as its content and methods were, it did succeed in teaching ninety per cent of the people to read and write and reckon. But tests showed that the people could not read very well and, more important, their semi-literacy did not imply that they really understood the conditions, trends, and problems of the Great Society that was taking shape all around them. And it was mass production in education, with its own assembly line of mechanized large classes, curriculum designed for the mass student body, and learning evaluated by the rank-order concept.

Four Conceptions of Education in 1890 [1]

1. *"Education" and "Going to School" were Synonymous* Education was conceived as a process that takes place in a schoolhouse, five hours a day, aloof from the community and national life which created it. Those children of 1890 seldom left their classroom, almost never left their school, between nine and twelve in the morning and one and three in the afternoon. Practically all of the educative process went on either in the seats or beside the seat in the aisle. In 1890 neither the legs of the child nor his larynx had been freed. The idea of using the whole schoolhouse was not understood; that of using the whole community and the region about it had not been dreamed of.

[1] Adapted from the senior author's appraisal of the schools of 1890 in his *Foundations for American Education*, pages 523–526.

This grim-looking schoolroom typifies the regimentation of our education up to the past two or three decades. (Photo from Association for Supervision and Curriculum Development.)

2. *Education Is Something You Do before You Enter Your Lifework* Pervading the work of the schools in 1890 was the conviction that education is preparation for life. For some children this preparation would last only six or eight years, for others twelve, for the select few, sixteen or more. But for all it was a getting-ready-to-do, not a doing-now. Almost nobody conceived education as an enterprise in living. It did not touch the practical doings in the family, the neighborhood, the occupational life of the people, or the government of the community. It was not concerned with the individual's growth, but was merely the learning of subjects during the periods of the school day. It was something abstracted from the real, active life of young people, something set aside from the ongoing stream of experience.

3. *Education Is Something You Do with Words and Other Symbols, Arranged in Subjects and Presented in Textbooks* These schools of 1890 were merely schools of literacy — teaching the people to read and write and reckon — but nothing else. The curriculum had become a mosaic of tools and "subjects." No consideration was given to the realistic use of these tools. The content of the subject was determined by the reading matter "set-out-to-be-learned" in compact books called

125

"textbooks." These books were well named, for they were literally
books of "texts," compendia of knowledge, made by the professors of
the liberal arts colleges.

As the nineteenth century wore on, the array of subjects became so
bewildering that administrators had grouped them in parallel courses,
combinations called "curricula": Classical, General-English, Latin-
Scientific, Engineering-Technological, Modern-Classical, Manual-Train-
ing, College-Preparatory, and others. Thus the curriculum was standardized. The state boards controlled the curricula of their "common
schools" by issuing state-wide courses of study. The College Entrance
Examination Board, desiring uniformity and continuity above all else,
developed the rigid standard of fifteen "academic units" for entrance
to college.

4. *The Subject Matter Was the "Liberal Arts," the "Great Books" of
the Past — Paraphrased* Our first common schools were created by
men and women who were themselves the product of a literate classical
education. For a century the trustees and boards of education as well
as the faculties of colleges and schools lived in the aura of Europe and
the rich literary heritage of the past. The "seven liberal arts" of the
classical education were the chief sources from which the professors
who made the books and courses of study got their subject matter. For
the past two thousand years the curriculum had consisted of these seven
liberal arts, divided according to the tradition of Latin Europe into
two parts: the *trivium*, consisting of grammar, rhetoric, and logic; and
the *quadrivium*, consisting of arithmetic, music, geometry, and as-
tronomy. Cultivated Europe had admired this curriculum and practiced it down to the present moment. Witness Thomas Huxley's
eulogy of it: "I doubt if the curriculum of any modern university shows
so clear and generous a comprehension of what is meant by culture as
this old trivium and quadrivium does." Naturally, therefore, when our
fathers' professors were confronted with the task of building a wholly or
completely new national system of schools, they followed the only
course they knew and built the curriculum primarily out of these classical studies.

We say "primarily," not entirely, for the substructure of the system had barely been hammered into place when both citizens and
professional educators began to tinker with its reconstruction. On all

sides there was denunciation of the medieval trivium and quadrivium. Just before 1890, the people of the middle classes demanded and effected the introduction into the curriculum of a vast array of new and practical subjects: home economics, drawing, the industrial arts and engineering, bookkeeping, typewriting, stenography, and other forms of business practice.

But the grip of the liberal arts was too strong to be broken. There was no discussion of the critical problems of our own national life or the dynamic social changes that were taking place throughout the western world. No reference was made to the technological revolution. There seemed, indeed, to be a contempt for the contemporary. The present, or even recent history, was no fit subject matter for education. The "local" was trivial! Since only the past and the remote could be documented, only those should be used as the subject matter of education for young minds. The educators believed in training for citizenship, but little democracy was actually practiced in the classroom.

This, then, was the point to which American civilization had developed a school system by 1890. While a few men of great insight saw how utterly inadequate it was, it is doubtful if even they had any pre-vision of the tremendous changes that would come during the next fifty years of American education.

The Great Transition in Education, 1890's–1940's

The technological changes which transformed our social-economic system had some parallels in education. Family and community patterns were altered profoundly, and an age of emancipation and creative expression emerged that found outlets in every phase of the life of the people. Of these outlets one of the most significant was our schools. Many progressive young fathers and mothers, surrounded by the popular revolt in politics and economic life and hating the repressive education of their own childhood, wanted the New Freedom in education for their children. In the next fifty years they built new kinds of schools all over our country. We have fallen into the habit of calling such schools "progressive."

New Elementary Schools, Centered in Child Development

The progressive movement in education is the product of the work of many people; in fact, we owe the better schools of the 1940's to the thousands of young progressive parents as much as we do to the similar thousands of teachers. However, there is always a spearhead in every movement, and in this case the creative force was two men — Francis Wayland Parker and John Dewey.

Francis W. Parker's Pioneering (1875–1901)   John Dewey, who is quite generally credited with the original pioneering, said himself, "Colonel Parker, more nearly than any other one person, was the father of the progressive educational movement. Did you ever hear of a man who, starting as superintendent of country schools, has reached a point in his career twenty-five years later, where the anniversary of that beginning was an event to be marked by the educators of a nation?" The celebration to which he referred was in recognition of Parker's quarter-century of work in building two types of new schools: first, as superintendent of the Quincy, Massachusetts, schools from 1875 to 1880; second, from 1883 to 1901, as the builder of the Chicago Normal School and especially of its great Practice School.

To understand the progressive movement we must understand Parker, "the evangelist of life," lover of children, and devotee of democracy, who grasped intuitively several of the great principles of growth and education and in Quincy built the first true School of Living in America. Although he stayed in Quincy only five years, the spirit and curriculum of the school were so imbued with new vitality that his work attracted attention throughout America and Europe. There was less emphasis upon the memorization of facts and textbooks and more upon firsthand, out-door observation. Reading became the acquiring of meanings, rather than an exercise in the learning of techniques of oral pronunciation. The schoolroom became a pleasant place of activity. Teachers were brought into the reorganization of the materials and methods of instruction. A central position in the curriculum was given to geography and nature study, "and the sand table in the schoolroom and the sand piles in the school yards were extensively used in the development of concepts of structure." The skills were taught in connection with content subjects, and language usage took the place of

FRANCIS WAYLAND PARKER (1837–1902) is generally regarded as the pioneer liberator of the American school child. After several years of teaching, he entered the Civil War as a private and, for many acts of gallant leadership, left it as colonel of his regiment. Following the study of education at the University of Berlin, he transformed the Quincy, Massachusetts, schools into a mecca for progressive educators. Visitors saw recitations alive with investigation and action.

Parker was Principal of the Cook County Normal School in Chicago from 1883 to 1901. Its Practice School became a world-famous center for the study and discussion of the newer principles of education. In 1901, with the collaboration of John Dewey, Parker organized the University of Chicago's School of Education.

grammatical analysis. Summer schools and institute classes developed for the education of teachers. Within a short time Colonel Parker and his Quincy schools became a national institution and educational leaders came from Europe to visit him.

The Dewey School, 1896–1904 Although Dewey had acclaimed Colonel Parker as the father of progressive education, the influence of John Dewey himself in the development of the progressive movement was far more profound and extensive than that of any other single person. It started in 1896 with his Laboratory School, now generally referred to as the Dewey School. It was created by himself, his wife, Alice Chipman Dewey, and several neighbors two years after the opening of the new University of Chicago. It was the first "laboratory school" in America. As Mr. Dewey said, its laboratory characteristic was "the key to the work of the school." During the eight years of the existence of the Dewey School its chief purpose was to conduct a designed experiment in education.

From the Dewey experiment and the many books of educational and psychological theory that came out of it, the principle of growth became the *core* in many educational programs. Everything in the life and work of the school — the curriculum, the activities of which the program consisted, and the teaching method — was geared to bringing about the maximum growth of children. The conditions for growth were carefully studied and the work planned in terms of them:

First: freedom for the child to investigate and experiment.

Second: choice of school experiences to fit the changing interests, attitudes, and capacities of the stages of growth through which the child passes from infancy to adolescence. The Dewey School recognized three stages: (1) from about four to eight; (2) from eight to ten; (3) from ten until the thirteenth year.

Third: education in the solving of problems, and this was considered important beyond all the rest.

Fourth: the use of scientific material and the scientific way of working.

Fifth: the fitting of education to the interests of young people. In the school they had learned that "classroom results were best when activities were in accord with a child's changing interests, his growing consciousness with the relation of means and ends, and his increasing willingness to perfect means and to postpone satisfactions in order to arrive at better ends."

Sixth: providing coöperative activity on the conception that the school is a miniature society, an actual community. Schoolhouse, rooms, furniture, equipment — everything was flexible and informal, on the assumption that a school was a miniature home, and pupils and teachers planned the program of work together.

The program of study was organized around the development of civilization, its most important center being "the social occupation"; that is, man's basic activities in providing food, shelter, and clothing for himself and his family. The teachers began with the present experiences of the children, their needs, interests, and aptitudes. They then selected a phase of the development of civilization which would supply the child with a greater material for understanding of and increased power over his own present life.

They carried on activities dealing with "primitive life, Hebrew life, early American settlements," not as mere tags, but used educatively, calling into play the imagination of the children. The historical material was always subordinated to the children's community life in the

JOHN DEWEY (1859————) is the world's leading interpreter of the modern educational doctrine of growth through the personal reconstruction of experience. On this and related principles he developed at the University of Chicago, 1896–1904, the first laboratory school in America. His two small books written at that time — *School and Society* and *Child and Curriculum* — provided the chief intellectual impetus stimulating the development of a new education. As Professor of Philosophy in Columbia University from 1904 to 1930, he clarified, in a dozen books, the scientific method of inquiry and the role in behavior of intelligence and problem-solving thinking.

Dewey has been a pioneer in bringing about two profound shifts in thought: he has turned men's minds from the doctrine of authority toward the doctrine of experience, and from mechanical to organic explanations of the universe, of human beings, and of their culture. Several of his writings are already becoming classics in education and philosophy — for example, *Democracy and Education, How We Think, Human Nature and Conduct, Philosophy and Civilization*, and *Intelligence and the Modern World*.

school. It was set in the framework of actual community life today, built by the children and the teachers, using tools, implements, construction, dramatization, storytelling, and physical material as resources. "Present family life was studied before primitive life; the settling of Chicago before the earlier colonial settlements of Virginia and Massachusetts." This was quite different from the old school curriculum which merely had the student learn the chronological facts of past history.

America Created a Score of New Schools Mr. Dewey left Chicago in the summer of 1904 to become professor of philosophy at Columbia University.[1] For nearly a decade little happened on the progressive educational scene. Miss Flora Cooke and some fifteen of Francis

---

[1] Although he never engaged in actual school experimentation again, he wrote several books in the next quarter of a century that have since been read by hundreds of thousands of educational workers. These books of Dewey's have perhaps been the largest single influence in the building of better schools since 1890. You should study carefully his *School and Society* (1899) . . . *Child and Curriculum* (1902) . . . *How We Think* (1909) . . . *Interest and Effort in Education* (1913) . . . *Experience and Education* (1938) . . . and the book which describes his experimental school — namely, K. C. Mayhew and A. C. Edwards's *The Dewey School* (1936).

Parker's former students were quietly developing the Francis W. Parker School of Chicago as a vigorous progressive school. Today it is still one of the best examples. In 1904 Junius Meriam established an experimental elementary school at the University of Missouri, and in 1907 Mrs. Marietta Johnson opened her school for Organic Education at Fairhope, Alabama. But throughout the country public schools remained conventional and rigid.

About 1912 there came the first signs of the impatience of thoughtful Americans with their medieval schools, and a few voices began to urge the claims of individual development. This was accelerated by the increasing power of the psychology of individual differences. In ten years a new wave of protest schools swept across the eastern section of the United States. Progressive parents and teachers joined hands to set up the various "Park" Schools in Baltimore, in Cleveland, in Buffalo, and in Dayton. In New York City, in 1913, Caroline Pratt opened her little Play School (now the City and Country School), and with the collaboration and support of Mrs. Lucy Sprague Mitchell organized the Bureau of Educational Experiments. Others followed in other cities and towns, and laboratory schools were started in a few universities.

By the close of the First World War these new schools were finding a great need for the exchange of ideas. In the winter of 1918–1919 their leaders organized themselves as The Progressive Education Association. Their purpose was to unite the scattered progressives, provide them with a national forum of discussion, enlist the interest of citizens, and build an informed educational opinion throughout the United States. The first two public meetings were held in Washington in 1919 and 1920. Every year from that time until 1941 an annual meeting of the Association was held in one of the Eastern cities. In 1924 a grant from Mrs. Avery Coonley, renewed each year for some years, made it possible to publish a magazine, *Progressive Education*, which soon achieved a national reputation.

All too briefly described, this is the manner in which new types of child-centered elementary schools developed in the generation after Francis Parker died and John Dewey closed his Laboratory School in Chicago. Before we turn to the striking developments in the high schools that came with the Great Depression of the 1930's, we should gather together these characteristics of a truly modern elementary school so that you will recognize them as you begin your teaching.

Lucy Sprague Mitchell (1878————), master teacher of children and of adults, has long pioneered in the search for better types of education. Following her work as a professor and as dean of women at the University of California, she taught at the City and Country School (New York), helped found the Bank Street Schools, and was chairman of the latter's Bureau of Educational Experiments. She has had wide experience as curriculum consultant and in conducting psychological surveys and tests in public and private schools.

She is best known as the author of such books for children as *Here and Now Story Book, Manhattan, Now and Long Ago, Young Geographers, North America,* and *Horses, Now and Long Ago.* Her work has been built on the conviction that the child is educated best through participation in the social world, and that, correspondingly, the teacher's education should involve active experiences with children and with adults in the community.

What a Good Elementary School
Looks Like Today

First: Its Active Life The first thing you will notice about a modern school is its lively, active atmosphere, which contrasts so sharply with the passive inertness of the traditional school. It is a well-known fact that to live and to grow is to be active. The pioneers who created our modern psychology — such men as Charles Pierce, William James, and John Dewey — discovered that *the first principle of growth is active response.* Things become meaningful in our early childhood only as we *use them* in some way. Living is acting, moving, growing.

Thus the psychology that you will study in your teachers college will frequently be called an "action psychology." A child, for example, learns the meaning of an object by making practical responses to it. Years ago Dewey said: "By rolling an object, the child makes its roundness appreciable; by bouncing it, he singles out its elasticity; by lifting it, he makes weight its conspicuous distinctive factor." Each of these illustrates that we "respond *with* meanings"; we do not get meaning in some mysterious way. The *meaning is something which we create for ourselves,* first and foremost by doing or feeling something with our bodies. This, then, is the first condition of growth — namely, that meaningful living is active response.

Second: Freedom — People Act Naturally if They Feel Free   No article of faith of the newer schools has been more preached in our times than that of freedom, and for more than a generation the advocates of freedom have been trying to practice what they preached.   They unscrewed the ironbound chairs and desks of the schools and put light, movable tables, chairs, and benches in their places.   Ironbound chairs are for listening, they said, but the new school is for working, for doing.   That means that the furniture must be suited to every need of the school's work; children should have light movable tables and chairs that can be moved aside or put together according to the work to be done.   "Free the legs and the larynx of the child" became the watchword.   The children must be free to go to the library, the laboratory, the shop, or the art studio to carry on their planned work, free to talk to one another when talking is natural and needed.   Thus as you begin your teaching, you may find that this spirit of freedom abounds in the school.   The old question-and-answer recitation will have given way to the lively, spontaneous committee conferences, group interchange of thought and discussion.

But freedom consists of more than feeling free to move about and talk.   We shall see, in just a moment, the important place taken by freedom of thought and expression.

Third: Interest — the Motive Power of Activity and Growth   As you observe the young people in these newer schools, you will no doubt ask yourself: "Why are they so industrious?   In the traditional schools the children seemed bored, listless, inattentive.   But here there is intense concentration on work.   Why?"

There is one good reason: *the children are interested in what they are doing.*   These teachers have built on their needs.   More than that, they have succeeded in building on what the children regard as their needs, on what is *real* to them.   Here is the route to true *educative activity.*   Here is the way to the greatest growth — Interest.   Parker and Dewey seized upon *child interest* rather than *adult purposes* as the motive power for a dynamic happy growing life.

Examine the curriculum, the facilities for the program of work in the daily schedule, even the vocabulary of the school program; these all point to the concern for needs and interests.   The emphasis on active working rather than passive listening is shown by the creative work periods, story hours, projects, creative music, industrial arts, and open forum discussions of the forward-looking schools; these have supplanted the "subjects" of the traditional schools. Hence schools have become places where the children can come early in the morning, where they linger late in the afternoon, and to which they come back on Saturdays. These busy, hard-working young people are interested, or they would not work as they do.

Fourth: Much Problem-Solving and Original Thinking   Come back to the problem of freedom in the schoolroom: True liberty is much more than freedom to move about and to talk. It is to *feel* free to think one's own thoughts and to exchange the results of one's thinking with others. Above all, the route to intellectual growth is *freedom to investigate,* to find out for oneself. Here is the major condition for real educative growth. The traditional school's requirement that the children memorize the words given them and give them back precisely on demand caused teachers to miss this great cue to learning and growth. While the traditional school asked the child: "What does the book say?," the new school asks: "What do *you* think?"   Which reminds us of a story from the boyhood of Angelo Patri, distinguished New York school principal. Patri tells of the frequent nightly discussions of his immigrant parents and their neighbors in the kitchen of his little Italian-American home. Here they talked of their new lives in America, of politics and local government in New York City. Angelo, then a boy of ten, had been permitted to sit near the grownups and listen. Suddenly one evening, without warning, his father turned to him and said directly: "Angelo, what do *you* think?"   Patri says that *at that moment he grew up; for the first time in his life he felt that he was expected to think.* Not only was he free to say what he thought; he was *expected to form his own ideas,* not just echo to his elders what they had thought. Here, then, is the sure-fire way to stimulate real intellectual growth: present young people with *real problems that they must solve.*

Fifth: Pupil-Teacher Planning   Another characteristic of the good school is that the children take part in planning the work. In the traditional school of the past the boys and girls had no part at all; in fact, even the classroom teacher took little part. The curriculum, the day's work, and the time schedule were all worked out by the officials

Children find greatest happiness in activities initiated by their own interests and purposes. (Louise M. Gross photo.)

in the superintendent's or principal's office. But go into one of the newer schools at the beginning of any morning, and you will see pupils and teacher planning the day's work together. Of course it will be done within the framework of the year's over-all outline of work made in advance by the teachers and administrators. But in the decision of how to use the day's time the children will play a vigorous part. No doubt you will hear committees of pupils reporting plans for various items of the day's work — a trip to be taken, a group discussion to be held, an assembly program before the whole school, individual reports of work accomplished or to be done, discussion of test results, news items to be placed on the bulletin board, plans laid for an inter-class project.

Such schools are rightly called "child-centered." More and more their life is organized around child initiative and child responsibility. Here is another revelation of the understanding of a psychological truth, namely — that one grows in ability to plan and govern one's life only through actual *experience* in planning and self-government. And this planning takes place under guidance — for there is recognition of the true role of the teacher. The teacher advises and encourages the children, checks and questions where necessary, and provides stimulation where that is needed. Thus, in the newer schools you will see boys and girls taking an active part in carrying on the life of the school.

Sixth: Creative Expression   These characteristics of a good school about which you have just read can be embraced by the one final idea — creative expression. Here again traditional education's *insistence on conformity* is opposed to modern education's constant *demand for expression.* For example, to consider your own experience. In the elementary school that you attended how much expressive activity was there on the part of the boys and girls? Did you write, and paint, and dance, and make music as you yourselves felt it? In the high school were you asked to make suggestions for the carrying on of the school? Did you produce original products in industrial arts or help design the buildings and equipment in the school? Were you expected and encouraged to think creatively about not only the problems that challenged your own personal life but also those of the larger social environment? If so, you were singularly fortunate, for, by and large, the school has centered its efforts on making the individual adjust to the existing order.

But the new school builds on the creative spirit within each individual. It assumes that every human being has some ability to invent, to create, to think, and to feel clearly and in unique fashion. Creative expression through the arts is one of the driving motive forces of the new education. The successful teacher creates in the class a climate of opinion in which every boy and girl tends to express what is within himself to say.

Summing Up: Conditions Favorable to Growth   Here, then, are six things you should look for in order to decide how far a school has moved from the traditional toward the newer point of view:

1. Is it active rather than passive and inert?

2. Do the young people feel free to investigate and experiment? Free to move about, to talk together, to work in groups as necessity demands?

3. Are the children interested in what they are doing? Do their activities fit their own needs and purposes?

4. Do young people take a vigorous part in the planning of the life and program of the school?

The mere availability of crayons and large paper are enough to encourage children to express their own feelings.   (Louise M. Gross photo.)

5. Are problem-solving and original thinking fostered, especially in the classroom but also in all school activities?

6. Is it a school of creative expression and a high order of appreciation?

To the extent that you find these conditions in a school, you will know that the teachers and the administrators are providing the conditions most favorable for achieving the central aim of education — namely, the full development of the whole person.

One other generalization: the two kinds of elementary schools are centered upon very different conceptions.   The traditional mass school has its eyes on subjects of study constructed primarily to pass on the social heritage of our civilization.   The better schools, on the other hand, emphasize the development of the child as a unique individual. The latter aim is fundamental, but alone it is insufficient.   There is another crucial focus of education.   An adequate educational philosophy would be centered on the society and the culture as well as on the young child.   The more forward-looking elementary schools are beginning to do this, and a group of educators have given themselves wholeheartedly to this aspect of education, with the result that they have brought im-

138

portant changes to the high schools and the colleges. To that development we turn in Chapter 6, for a discussion of the problems of youth in the American culture.

Investigating the Role of the School in the Social Order

There is much that you can do to add to your understanding of the struggle of thoughtful Americans to build effective schools for a society of free men. We suggest a few things; no doubt you can think of many more.

1. Visit two schools: the first an elementary school of the more formal type; the second, a progressive school. Evaluate, compare, and contrast the things you see in these schools on the yardstick of the six "Conditions Favorable to Growth" given in this chapter (pages 137–138).

2. Try to build for yourself a vivid picture of the old-fashioned, formal schools. See if you can find old prints or photographs, drawings, or lithographs of the schools of earlier days; look, for example, in such older histories of education as those of Cubberley or Graves. Ask your elderly friends or relatives for pictures of schools of their childhood days.

3. Write down anecdotes you have heard your parents or other older relatives and friends tell of their lives in the "little red schoolhouse." Describe the methods of instruction, the use of rewards and punishments, the reading matter used, the "recitation," etc.

4. Have Panel Discussions, or Forums, on such subjects as:

–How much freedom should be given to children in the elementary school?

–To what extent should the children be included in planning the curriculum of the school?

–To what extent should the life and program of the elementary school be built around the interests of the children?

–In building character, which was more effective: the old-fashioned school or the newer progressive school?

5. Write a paper describing the elements in the school that you attended which seem to you to have been rigid and formal; describe those which were in keeping with good modern educational practice.

What to Read

1. On the Rise of the American School

There is a growing library of readings on the school in the social order. Perhaps the best basic history of American education, particularly for the period since 1860, is Edwards and Richey's *The School in the American Social Order*. For an over-all story of the rise of the school in American industrial society, after 1840, see Harold Rugg's *American Life and the School Curriculum*, especially Chapters I to VI. A parallel and briefer account is in the *Third Yearbook* of the John Dewey Society, Chapters I–III. Chapters 21 and 22 of R. Freeman Butts' *A Cultural History of Education* shows the inter-dependence of the school and the social order. Chapters XII to XIX of Edgar A. Knight's *Twenty Centuries of Education* give a clear statement of the evolution of public school systems.

The NEA Educational Policies Commission's *The Unique Function of Education in a Democracy*, written by Dr. Charles A. Beard, is an excellent discussion of the nature and role of education in a society such as America; see also their *Education of Free Men in American Democracy*. George Counts' *Education and the Promise of America* reëxamines our fundamental traditions, their modifications, and the relation of the school to them.

2. On the Newer, More Progressive Developments

Harold Rugg's *American Life and the School Curriculum*, Chapters XII to XXV, gives an account of the progressive movement in American life and education; also Chapter IV of Rugg and Shumaker's *Child-Centered School* and, for the emergence of the creative artist in the schools, Chapters XI to XXI.

Several leaders of the progressive schools have written their own stories of the years from 1910 to 1930 or 1940. Caroline Pratt's *I Learn from Children* is the graphic story of the founder of the City and Country School in New York City; Agnes de Lima's *The Little Red School House* tells how Elizabeth Irwin, the parents, and the teachers developed the school of that name, first as part of the New York public school system, then as a private venture.

You can get a glimpse of what is actually being done in public schools from books like *Let's Go to School*, by Horrall and the teachers in a San

Jose, California, elementary school. School programs in four centers of America are described in *Organizing the Elementary School for Living and Learning*, issued by NEA's Association for Supervision and Curriculum Development. J. Wayne Wrightstone's *Appraisal of Newer Elementary School Practices* is just what its title states; see Chapter I for origins and development.

The principles of the new programs are stated in L. T. Hopkins' *Interaction: The Democratic Process* and in Hollis Caswell's *Education in the Elementary School*.

CHAPTER 6

Teachers and the Youth Problem

OUR STUDY centers now on the effective education of youth in high school and college. Nowhere in the culture have the effects of social change been felt more intensely than in the lives of youth. Our study focuses on the interests and needs of youth and the educational program of the higher schools. Note the important educational lag in the culture:

–The culture changes swiftly.

–The work and educational needs of youth change equally swiftly.

–The school and college administration changes slowly.

But again progressive pioneers give us courage; new and more effective colleges and high schools are emerging, loosening the strangle hold of ancient academic goals and practices.

In this scene the educational task again becomes clear:

*To build higher schools that will develop
a generation of mature men and women.*

Youth in American Culture: the Higher Schools

I$_T$ WAS in the economic depression of the early thirties, as unemployment in the United States reached frightening proportions, that the conditions and needs of youth gripped the attention of far-seeing citizens and educators. By "youth" we mean the middle of the three groups that comprise the American people. On one side is the adult population of perhaps 80 million people; at the other extreme are 35 to 40 million infants, children, and adolescents, the bulk of the school population. Between them is a large middle group of more than 20 million young people between the ages of 16 and 24. Any precise division of the population by ages is somewhat arbitrary. This particular scheme was employed by the American Youth Commission which, during the Depression, made an important study of the problems of youth, and we shall follow their definition.[1]

What Is "The Youth Problem"?

The youth group includes young people who are in the last two years of high school and those who are in the college, university, or technical and professional schools. It is, therefore, your own age group, and you no doubt will have a vivid personal appreciation of its problems. Problems there certainly are. So sharply do they stand out that we

[1] See their important summary volume, *Youth and the Future*, and the detailed study prepared for them by Howard Bell: *Youth Tell Their Story*.

143

have come to say: "There is a Youth Problem, and the American people must do something about it." The American Youth Commission, for example, certainly did not dodge it:

> "Recent social and economic changes in the United States have given rise to difficulties in the care and education of young people with which existing institutions are quite unprepared to deal adequately. The changes not only have greatly intensified the problems which confront the schools, but also have created an urgent need of protection and further education for millions of youth whom the schools are not now reaching. Without some provision for basic planning to meet this situation, there is serious danger that present conditions may constitute a fundamental threat to the national welfare." [1]

Howard Bell, in one of the Youth Commission's reports, put the problem bluntly. What, he asked, shall 21,000,000 young Americans "do with themselves during the ever-widening time when the school is through with them and jobs are ready for them?" The facts of what the youth are doing with themselves bear him out. Of the 21,000,000 young people in 1946:

–7,000,000 were in high schools.

–2,500,000 were in colleges, universities, and technical and professional schools.

–2,000,000 were at work.

–9,500,000 were neither employed nor in school or college.

Nearly half of the total group were drifting, idling; they were neither at work nor in school or college, not knowing what to do. Some of the young people themselves told the Commission: "Youth is in a muddle." . . . "Out of school too young, they don't know what to do or why." . . . "They're in the midst of a great social and economic change."

There is general agreement that this presents a difficult and dangerous problem for our people, one to which our young teachers should devote serious study. It is a problem of which there are two separate phases — work and education. All but the infirm, no matter how young or how

---

[1] The Report of the American Youth Commission, *Youth and the Future*, page x.

old, should have work — personally satisfying and socially useful work.
All, no matter how old, should spend part of their time in education.
The youth problem, then, is a twofold problem.

Youth's Need of Work

What *can* young people do with the working hours of their day?
Two acceptable possibilities lie before them — a job or school. Most
of them are old enough to go into permanent work, and in former times
they did. Fifty years ago most of them left school at 14 or 15 years of
age, taking unskilled work for a while, or learning a trade. By the time
they were 20 years of age they were journeyman workers. But in recent
years, as machines have come into industries, employment has become
harder to find for all grownups. Youth have been still further pushed
aside. For some of them the problem was temporarily solved by staying
in school longer. Even ten years ago 7,000,000 were in high school —
ten times as many as in 1900 — and 2,500,000 were in higher institutions.

Yet, out of 21,000,000 only one tenth — 2,000,000 — had found employment. They told Howard Bell: "Getting jobs is the main problem." . . . "Employers want experienced people, but I don't see how
you can get experience if they won't give you a job." Many wanted to
marry and make homes — but — "The problem is how to get married on
$15.00 a week."

Youth themselves insisted that the nub of the youth problem is economic security — getting a job at a decent wage. There was also the
need of getting more education and having healthful recreation and
leisure-time programs through which to build their spiritual lives. They
thought the wages of most employed people were much too low and that
government should do something about it, even to setting minimum
wages and maximum hours and standards of work.

During the years of the thirties the American Youth Commission and
several other national commissions studied the problem very carefully.
They all agreed that not only was the key to it economic — namely, work
for youth — but the factors that brought it about were economic, also.
Of the 21,000,000 youth, 10,000,000 grew up in working-class homes in
which the income was so low that the families could not have an "adequate diet standard of living." The American Youth Commission says
flatly that the crux of the youth problem is low income and large fami-

lies. Our society is dangerously divided into economic classes. Youth are not equal — equality is a myth, says the Commission. Economic factors drive millions of young people out of school into a job much too early and at much too low an economic level to enable them to marry and build up their own home life. Thus "a vicious circle of economic determinism" has developed in our society. Howard Bell warned in his book that the one thing a democracy must have if it is not to die "is a social order enriched with enough generosity and foresight to provide all its youth with opportunities to grow, and endowed with enough wisdom and courage to make these opportunities worth the taking."

The Government's Experiment in Socially Useful Work for Youth
During the depression of the thirties the federal government, for the first time in its history, took official responsibility for jobs for youth. It established the Civilian Conservation Corps in 1933, and in 1935 the National Youth Administration. In eight years the CCC gave employment to 2,500,000, of whom 84 per cent were under 19 years of age. Four out of five of them worked well; in eight years their work was valued at $1,500,000,000. The NYA provided part-time employment for men and women who lived at home and maintained their normal community lives. There were 1,750,000 out-of-school youth in the part-time project and 1,800,000 in-school youth in a student work program. This program gave to each one work totaling 60 hours a month at a compensation of approximately $16.00.

A broad range of work was provided, the largest number of youth being on construction projects. The men built thousands of public buildings, roads, parks, airports, and riverbanks. The women worked in clerical and service enterprises in schools, hospitals, libraries, and social agencies. The American Youth Commission, studying the results after eight years, said of it: "For the first time in their history the major conservation agencies of the federal government were provided with a labor force approximating the size of their task."

Work-Experience Programs in Schools Stimulated by World War II
The whole employment situation changed drastically when the United States entered the Second World War, and work for youth changed with it. Ten million men went into the armed services. Enormous demands were made upon farm workers, while the war industries multiplied their requirements several fold. By 1943 a serious shortage of labor was

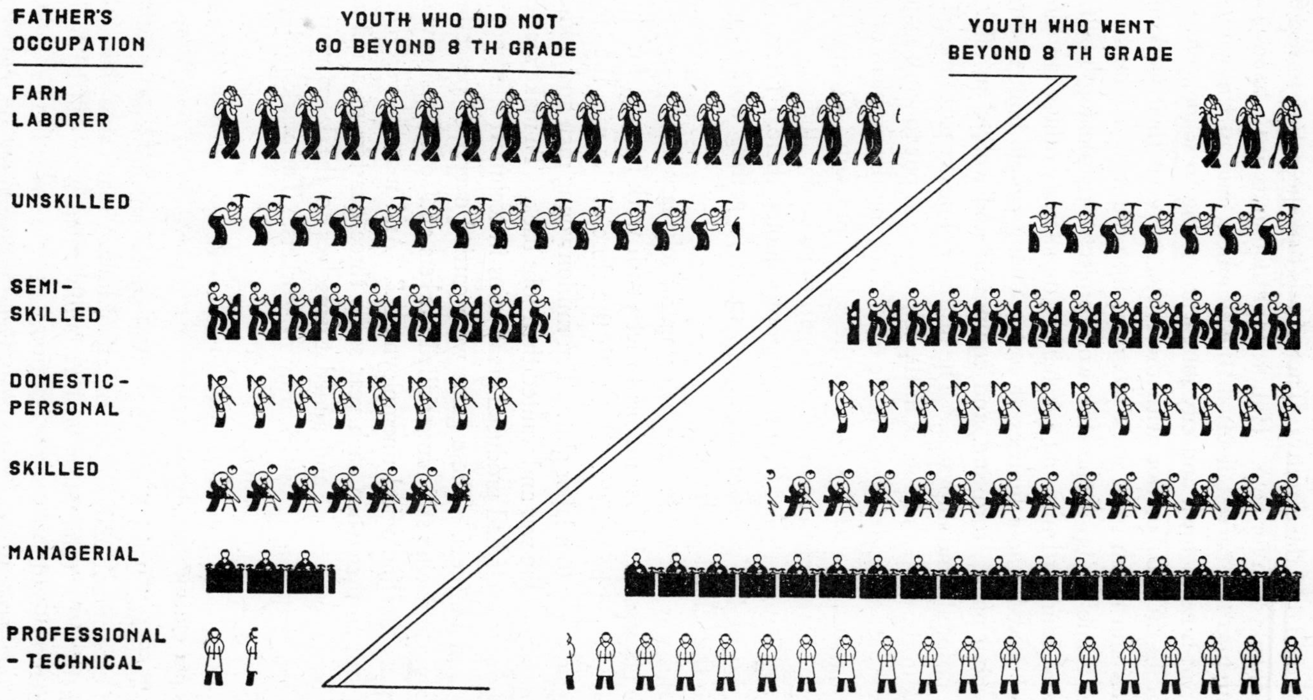

FATHER'S OCCUPATION

YOUTH WHO DID NOT GO BEYOND 8TH GRADE

YOUTH WHO WENT BEYOND 8TH GRADE

FARM LABORER

UNSKILLED

SEMI-SKILLED

DOMESTIC-PERSONAL

SKILLED

MANAGERIAL

PROFESSIONAL-TECHNICAL

The father's occupation as a determiner of the child's education. (From Howard Bell's *Youth Tell Their Story*. Courtesy American Council on Education.)

147

experienced all over the country.   Then it was that the nation turned to
its high school youth for help.   Hundreds of thousands of 16- to 18-year-
olds went into the harvest fields in the summers, and in the winters
worked part-time in town and city jobs while going to school.   Many
communities, in collaboration with the NYA, surveyed their work opportunities and began to fit work programs into the regular school curriculum.   Some set up coöperative work projects — gardening, poultry
raising, and canning fruits and vegetables "on shares"; others ran cafe-
terias and served school lunches at cost.   Young people built and repaired school plants, furniture, and equipment and worked in offices,
libraries, hospitals, and shipyards.   The historic Schneider part-time plan
— a week in the shop and a week in the school — was put to work again.

Thus at last a beginning was made toward solving the problem of in-
corporating socially useful work into the school program.   One of the
long-shunned areas of the curriculum began to be boldly studied.   Turn
forward to Chapter 13 and scan the examples quoted there.   These will
remind you of the effective beginnings made in getting work experience into the school program.

But this was war work.   It was comparatively easy in 1942–1945 to
persuade citizens and labor unions to let youth work for pay, for their
labor was needed by society.   But with the close of the war, the labor
shortage gave way to a labor glut.   Ten million young men and women
came home from the war and wanted their jobs back.   To make matters
worse, the war itself had produced great gains in technical efficiency in
industry and business.   These gains were carried over into peacetime
production, displacing still more skilled workers and so increasing what
is known as "technological unemployment."   And matters were complicated still further when each year some three quarters of a million
young people left school and added themselves to the labor market,
seeking places in the industrial army of workers.   The work problem
for youth bids fair to remain just as acute.

With this judgment the social prophets agree.[1]   Youth, one authority says, will be

> "shoved around pretty roughly.   Widespread unemployment, which
> will encourage youth to stay in school longer, may cause some fric-
> tion between veterans as well as family men, who will have job
> preference, and the rising generation."

[1] Goodwin Watson: *Youth after Conflict*, pages 209 and 217.

Another authority says:

> "Young people reaching the labor market on an average of two to three years after Armistice will be seriously disprivileged. The labor bloc will try to keep young people from entering the labor market either by extending the maximum educational age or by endorsing compulsory military training."

With the close of the war, youth experienced a letdown in their own earning power and in the amount of spending money they had. In the latter part of the war boys and girls in high school had much money to spend, money given them by their families or easily earned at highly paid jobs. Such well-paid work is now no longer available to boys and girls. However, there is a consensus that there will be many job opportunities for young people in such "service" fields as health, recreation, education, the arts and sciences, and public service; these occupations will require higher education. A college president predicts that in the years ahead:

> "we shall see more clearly than now the economic value of personal services of every description. (Within a few years) there will be a tremendous release of machine power and trained man power . . . this leaves as a major outlet for man hours, the development of the personal and the educational arts. No single gadget can take the place of a hundred teachers."

Goodwin Watson adds:

> "neither can automatic machines replace artists, scientists, designers, architects, doctors, dentists, nurses, psychologists, lawyers, housekeepers, athletic coaches, beauty parlor operators, actors, musicians, poets, dramatists, novelists, gardeners, or social workers."

Youth's Need of Appropriate Education

The Increased Holding Power of the Schools   It is with mixed feelings that one approaches the subject of the role of education for youth today. How many of the 10,000,000 should be in some kind of higher educational institution? It is almost impossible to tell, but that the number is large we can be sure. To understand the problem we must consider the social and educational conditions that have created the situation.

A generation ago the problem was much simpler. Most young people expected to go to work by the time they were seventeen or eighteen years of age; in fact, more than half of them were in gainful occupations at the age of sixteen.   Only a few — the well to do and the "intellectually minded" — counted on going to college.   Education was required for all children up to the age of fourteen; in a few states the legal age of leaving school was fifteen, in rare cases sixteen.   To the general pub-

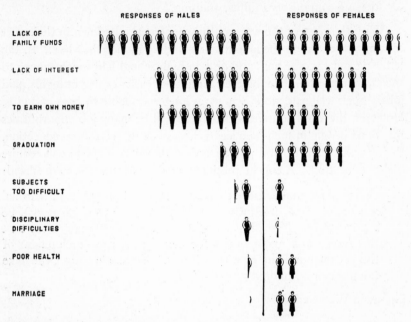

Why youth leave school.   (From Howard Bell's *Youth Tell Their Story*.   Courtesy American Council on Education.)

lic, education was something to be stopped at the point where the law so allowed.

But in recent years, partly because of the increasing difficulty of finding work for young people in an overcrowded economic system, partly because of changing views about life and education, a new situation has developed.   Not only has attendance in public high schools and in colleges and universities increased enormously, but more and more people have come to believe that both boys and girls should stay in school and even in college as long as possible.   As the holding power of the school increased, important changes occurred in the nature of the school population, and corresponding stresses and strains developed in the higher educational system itself.

The Changing Abilities and Interests of the Higher School Population
By the years of the depression of the thirties school administrators
and teachers were commenting on certain consequences of this increasing holding power of the high school and college. With the attendance
in high school and college of youth who would formerly not have pur-
sued their education thus far, there came a general lowering of the level
of the students' abstract intellectual ability. Shockingly large percentages of young people — 30, 40, even 50 per cent — failed to pass the
requirements of such academic subjects as mathematics, languages, ancient history, and the physical and natural sciences. The more old-
fashioned teachers tended to blame it on the young people — their lack
of ability, their unwillingness to work hard, and the slipshod habits they
had brought with them from the elementary school. Some said bluntly
that at least a third of the high school population did not have enough
"intelligence" to get a high school education, let alone go to college.
They meant, of course, an education made up of mathematical, scientific, and classical studies.

In the meantime, the use of objective measures of intelligence and
educational achievement had become widespread across the country.
As educators studied the results of these tests, taken by millions of young
people, they noted that the general level of mental ability of the high
school population seemed to be declining. It was pointed out that this
was to be expected; in the years prior to World War I, for example,
only the most intellectually able had stayed on to complete the high
school course and to enter college. Many studies showed, for example,
that whereas the average IQ for American children in elementary school
was about 100, the average IQ for students in the last years of the high
school was nearer 115, and that for the standard college was probably
nearer 120. But by the thirties the studies revealed a progressively lower
IQ for students in the junior and senior high school years — not more
than 106 to 110, while the average for the junior college was probably
not more than 112 to 115.

The Lag in the Academic Curriculum The schools of certain progressive communities tried to meet this problem of the changing nature,
abilities, and interests of the high school population by introducing new
courses of instruction. The curriculum was increasingly diversified;
scores of new courses covering a wide range of vocational interests were

introduced. Added creative opportunities were provided for the expression of individual aptitudes and interests. New plans were tried out for the organization of material. These steps were taken, however, only in a few of the more progressive communities. For the larger number of the young people who crowded into the senior high school, failure was still the order of the day. It became increasingly evident that one half, perhaps three fifths, of the high school population *could not profitably engage in the study of the current academic courses in mathematics, physical and natural sciences, and languages,* which constituted the great preponderance of the high school and college program of studies.

Loosening the Strangle Hold of the College

Causes of College Domination of Secondary Education   Even in the early years of the depression of the thirties progressive leaders saw that more drastic changes had to be made in the curriculum if the young people were to profit from its study. Certainly one of the problems was to loosen the stranglehold of the college on the high school curriculum. The chief obstacle was that the people as well as most of the teachers and administrators still believed in the academic education that had been adopted throughout America. Essentially it was the "liberal arts" of the 1890's, a secondary program composed of narrow academic subjects. More than half of the time was devoted to mastering the minutiae of algebra, geometry, grammatical and rhetorical styles and techniques in English, and the modern languages; the remainder of the time was given to memorizing specific facts in science, history, geography, and civics. This had prevented the high school from developing the reflective and organizing abilities of the students and cultivating their creative aptitudes. While industrial civilization had swiftly changed and while new and "practical" subjects had been added to the curriculum, the old academic setup still held sway.

The colleges had always been in control. This came about logically: first, through the fact that their professors had constituted the Committees of the National Education Association and other organizations whose recommendations for the curriculum were followed by the nation's schools; second, through the standardized machinery of their powerful College Entrance Examination Boards which tested high school graduates applying for college. For example, in 1948 the College Entrance

Youth work for a more attractive community — grading the school lawn. (Photo from Frank G. Dickey, University of Kentucky.)

Examination Board examined about 80,000 high school students. From the days of the first private academies and public high schools, instruction had been devoted to those subjects required for entrance to college, either through certification or examination.

But the biggest obstacle to changing the high school program was the educational philosophy of most of the administrators and teachers. These men had grown up in the academic high schools and colleges and had really come to believe in a curriculum of subjects dominated by mathematical and linguistic studies. These, they said, "discipline the mind." Although a totally new psychology of growth, development, and learning had evolved in the last fifty years, most of these educational workers had remained completely unaffected by it. They still knew nothing better than the academic course of study.

Against these suffocating conditions three forces struggled, during the twenty years between the two World Wars, to free the high school and permit its curriculum to be fitted more closely to the needs of the students.

Liberalizing the College Entrance Requirements Many college leaders had long been aware of the urgent need for improving this situation. As early as World War I the college examining boards took steps to loosen the hold of entrance requirements on the secondary schools by introducing broader types of Comprehensive Examinations. In 1920 the

153

College Entrance Examination Board established its Commission on New Types of Examinations and in 1926 set up the new Scholastic Aptitude Test, which has since been given annually. It is an objective type of examination with less emphasis on specific knowledge and skill, and more on general traits and on the ability to organize and use material and to solve problems. New tests in English composition were designed to measure the skills that young people normally use in written composition and to discover and measure their ability to organize material and to express themselves clearly and accurately. Thus, out of the twenty years of self-reform within the College Entrance Board came marked improvements in the examination and admission of high school graduates to college.

Growth of a More Progressive Spirit in the Colleges   Still more recently Harvard, Columbia, Chicago, Yale, Princeton, Minnesota, and other colleges and universities have gone far in accepting the long and steady trend toward general education. For more than twenty years Columbia's undergraduate college has given a general freshman course in Introduction to Contemporary Civilization. Many of the progressive colleges through the country — especially the newer ones such as Bennington, Sarah Lawrence, Antioch, and Black Mountain — have experimented with similar courses introducing young Americans to the history, conditions, and problems of western industrial civilization. Under the spur of this work, particularly since World War II, the colleges have swung into a general acceptance of this idea of general education for all. Thus the vanguard of the colleges and the secondary schools is beginning to take a stand for a treatment of general education in "broad fields" of study.

Important Study of the High School Curriculum   But the most important single event in the attempt to loosen the strangle hold of the college on the high school was the Progressive Education Association's "Eight-Year Study." This was made by its Commission on the Relation Between School and College (1930–1943). During the thirteen years which passed between the appointment of the Commission and the issuing of Volume V of its Report, three hundred colleges coöperated with thirty secondary schools, half public and half private, in an experiment in which the academic entrance requirements of the college were abolished and the secondary schools were permitted to build the curriculum as they saw fit. Each school was on its own so far as making its program of studies was concerned.

While some of the older private schools "loved their chains" and made few changes, many of them did build a new program of general education around the problems of youth and tied it in closely with the actual life of the community. The center was the study of civilization, present and past. In the public high schools particularly, socially useful work for youth was introduced into the curriculum. The young people dealt directly with such questions as: How do young men and women earn their living in this region? For what general field of work am I best fitted by ability, aptitude, and interest? How does one best go about getting a job? How can I hold one? What causes failure? They studied many problems relating to marriage and the home. Thus the boundaries between old subjects were broken down, realistic problems of youth and adult society were brought into the curriculum, and new "broad fields" of subject matter were substituted for narrow, old-time academic subjects.

The Eight-Year Study was perhaps the most distinctive large-scale educational experiment of the last half century. It was also a controlled experiment in which results were carefully measured. In all, 1475 pairs of students — each "experimental" student matched by a "control" student — were followed through the four years of their college course. Their grades, standings on tests, literary themes, prizes or other honors won, and other aspects of their personal records were tabulated and compared. They all filled out elaborate questionnaires giving data on their reading, health and personal problems, and extracurricular activities.

Did the progressives succeed in college? They did, indeed, and better than their mates in the conventional academic schools. One committee of presidents and deans of six of the colleges summed up the conclusions in the words of H. E. Hawkes, Dean of Columbia College, the chairman:

"The students from the schools whose pattern or program differed most from the conventional were very distinctly superior to those from the more conventional type of school. I should add that, in extracurricular interests non-athletic in character, the graduates of the thirty schools were markedly more alert than their group . . . It looks as if the stimulus and the initiative which the less conventional approach to secondary school education affords sends on to college better human material than we have obtained in the past."

This is the positive appraisal of distinguished college leaders who began the study with a deep skepticism as to its results. *Matched person for person, the graduates of the progressive schools were more competent, more creative, more alert and intelligent after four years of the new type of high school education than their mates in the conventional schools. They won more academic honors; they had more intellectual skill and information; they were more systematic and objective in their thinking, knew more about the meaning of life and education, and had a deeper and more active intellectual curiosity. They were markedly more concerned about the life of their own community and the crucial affairs of the world outside. They had more resourcefulness. They won more honors in student organizations, athletic teams, music, the theater, the dance, and the other creative arts. When left to their own resources, they initiated more important and stimulating nonacademic activities.*

These, then, are the chief gains of the last twenty years:

First: We have enormously clarified the *needs* of youth; a much clearer biopsychological picture of youth is beginning to emerge.

Second: We have shown that the traditional college requirements hamper the building of an education appropriate to the needs and wants of youth; that, when the grip of the college is loosened, schools and teachers who are truly progressive tend to produce young men and women better equipped to meet life.

Third: We have learned techniques of freeing the high school from the traditional demands of the academic college and have begun to experiment with new programs of studies.

These are undoubtedly important achievements, especially in the light of the times in which they have been carried out.

Society Changes — Schools Lag Behind

But while the schools and colleges have slowly tried to reform themselves, the world about them has changed more swiftly than ever before, creating even more difficult problems for educators. Especially is this true in the case of the youth, your own age group.

Forums help clarify the ideas for students of Adamson High School, Dallas, Texas. (New York Herald Tribune photo.)

You will be graduated from college in the 1950's. In what kind of world will you begin work? Certainly it will not be much like that in which your grandparents lived and worked. The social transformation of our civilization has replaced our fathers' quiet handicraft society with a restless, high-powered, machine-dominated nation of town and city dwellers. Although our resources and technology are capable of producing an abundant life for all our people, we are constantly menaced by the threat of mass unemployment. In spite of a spurt due to the war, population growth has slowed down, and while America is the second most populous industrial nation, recent generations have not been reproducing themselves. We are becoming a predominantly older people, and must look forward to providing security for old age as well as for youth. Our country has become the creditor of the world, but, stymied by two World Wars and confronted by the staggering task of reviving the earth's economic systems, the United States now faces economic exhaustion. Within our own borders the economic scene is marked by a struggle for power between owners and workers and by equally menacing racial and social frictions.

Surrounded by harassing social forces, the American family is baffled in its attempts to function as the cultural center for the nation. Whereas fifty years ago the mood of the Little was prevalent, the country is gripped today by the spirit of Bigness and by the danger of monopolistic control of industrial wealth and political power in a few hands. As life has moved from the Little to the Big, the intimate neighborhood life of our fathers' day has given way, for city dwellers at least, to an increasingly anonymous and unresponsible metropolitan existence with dangerous trends toward social license. Thus the entire society is being transformed, and thoughtful people are deeply concerned lest our democratic way of life become seriously endangered.

The Higher Educational Task: to Produce a Generation of Mature Personalities

There can be no dodging the task that is presented to the leaders of American education. It is nothing less than the building of a system of schools and colleges that will turn out a generation of men and women able to cope with the conditions and problems of the modern world. It must be a generation of young realists, as well as idealists, intelligently informed about the actual conditions and problems of the world-wide struggle for power and the trends and factors that produced them. For these youth have to create a *new and coöperative domestic and world order*, an order in which they and their contemporaries in Russia, Germany, China, Japan, and other countries may live together in peace. History has never before given such a problem to educators, for never before in man's life has such a combination of circumstances emerged. Hence, no society has ever come near achieving such a goal as we now set ourselves.

Since the task is urgent, and the time is all too short, its focus lies in the reconstruction of the higher schools. The long-term job is the creating of better nursery and elementary schools, but the immediate one centers in the senior high school and the college. It is youth now sixteen to twenty-four years of age, or thereabouts, who in a short time must be prepared to solve America's difficult and complex problems. It is on their education that the bulk of our post-war energies must be

centered. To meet the strenuous times ahead we must build a generation of young men and women of tougher spirits, of stronger moral
fiber, and of greater integrity than has emerged from the intellectually
anemic program of the "liberal arts" higher schools. The new generation must be willing to slave, even to die, for the democratic way of
life; for the present years witness a recurrence of the age-long struggle
between it and totalitarian dictatorship. Democracy's greatest chance
for success is here in America, and it is America that must lead in the
tremendous battle for its defense.

A New American College Emerging

Fortunately, in building a new educational institution for American
youth in these critical days, we do not start from scratch. It is nearly
a hundred years since pioneer students of education first tried to make
over the sixteen-grade scheme of school and college instruction and fit it
more closely to the needs of American youth. Even before the graded
structure had taken clear shape, some college presidents had put their
fingers on obvious weaknesses and tried to revamp the plan. It was
too long, they said, and wasteful of students' time and energy. The
most inefficient place of all, they continued, was in the last two years
of high school and the first two years of college.

From the days of the War Between the States to the present moment,
progressive college administrators have tried to shorten the school and
college course. Some wanted to shorten the period of general college
education to three years, some to two. *Some real radicals wanted to
join the freshman and sophomore years of college work to the junior
and senior years of the high school.* Eighty years ago President W. H.
Folwell of the University of Minnesota advocated this plan. Speaking
before the National Education Association in 1875, he said: "The work
of the first two years of the college is the work of the secondary school,
and there it can be done most efficiently and economically. Turn this
work over to the high school." The Board of Regents of Minnesota
actually adopted his plan but discontinued it in 1884 when Folwell
resigned.

Presidents Andrew D. White and C. K. Adams of Cornell also supported the plan. President Henry Suzzallo of the University of Washington and Dr. J. H. Baker, Chairman of the Committee on the

Economy of Time in Education of the National Education Association, agreed that the period of general education was too long. As early as 1876 President Daniel Coit Gilman advocated the elimination of one year at Johns Hopkins. President G. Stanley Hall at Clark agreed. Throughout his long administration of Harvard, President Charles W. Eliot advocated shortening the college course. In fact, his 1888 speech before the NEA on "Economy of Time in American Education" is credited with having launched the economy of time movement in public education. Actually, President Folwell's plan had been proposed twenty years before.

Almost without exception the distinguished executives of American universities were in agreement that that form of general education known as collegiate should close by the end of the sophomore year. Before Robert M. Hutchins of Chicago proposed it a few years ago, several presidents recommended the "granting of the bachelor's degree after two years upon what was at least the equivalent of the accomplishment demanded for that degree." From the twenty-first year of life most young Americans would devote themselves to occupational work. The small percentage who stayed on in an educational institution would be engaged in university or higher studies in the graduate professional and technical schools of medicine, law, dentistry, engineering, and education. Thus the graduate work of the university, while it was of advanced intellectual and professional caliber, would, nevertheless, be vocational. But every college president failed to bring about this change until the junior college movement was well established. Other presidents failed because the professors of the colleges would not have it. The academic faculties were conservative and were powerful enough in every institution to defeat the plan.

The Junior High School

Actually, in this reconstruction of the upper levels of education the middle grades of the twelve-year public school system — especially the seventh to the ninth or tenth, covering ages twelve to fifteen — were reorganized first, although no years were "saved" in the process. About 1910 school superintendents, principals, and professors of education, led by Charles H. Judd of Chicago, Charles Hughes Johnston of Illinois, and Thomas H. Briggs of Teachers College, Columbia, led a widespread discussion of the need for dividing the twelve-grade scheme into three divisions instead of two — each division to be an effective unit.

Combine your kindergarten, they said — and nursery schools wherever they exist, — with the six elementary grades to create an effective working unit covering the first eleven or twelve years of life. This will give a fine elementary school.

Create a separate school for ages twelve to fifteen, with a separate building, budget, administration, teaching staff, and a new curriculum. Break the old, rigid 8–4 system of the twelve grades into 6–3–3, or 6–4–2, or some such organization which will recognize the uniqueness of the period of adolescence and create a strong, effective, independent school. Thus you will get a fine new "junior" high school. This will leave the two or three top years, ages sixteen to eighteen, for the new senior high school.

The proposed reorganization was actually brought about. By the middle 1920's several thousand school systems had substituted either a 6–3–3 plan or a 6–4–2 plan, or some other plan in place of the earlier rigid 8–4 system. Certain obvious educational gains emerged from the setting up of the junior high school as a separate school. Being separately housed — often a new building, to which the community pointed with pride — boards of education increased its budget and gave it better teachers. Since it was separate and had a relatively new teaching staff, the school was able more easily to throw off the grip of the old seventh- and eighth-grade curriculum and build one better suited to the needs of the boys and girls. Thus many gains came from this movement toward grade reorganization.

Types of Public High Schools [1]

TYPE	4-YEAR PERIODS				
	1922	1926	1930	1934	1935
Junior high	387	1109	1842	1946	2372
Senior high	91	414	648	755	959
Junior-senior and undivided	1088	2003	3287	3936	6203
Regular	12,490	14,184	16,460	16,574	15,056
Total reporting	14,056	17,710	22,237	23,213	24,590

[1] Adapted from the United States Office of Education, *Biennial Survey of Education*, 1920–22, 1924–26, 1928–30, 1932–34, and 1936–38.

Enrollment in Public High Schools (Per Cent of the Total Number of High School Pupils)

TYPE	1937–38	1945–46
Junior high schools (6–9 grade)	19.0	18.4
Junior-senior (6–12 grade)	24.4	25.8
Senior high (9–12 grade)	13.1	16.8
Regular high schools (of 4 years or less)	43.5	39.0

The Two-Year Junior College

Throughout the past fifty years the few pioneering administrators from the colleges and senior high schools have never relaxed in their vigorous discussion of and experimenting with the problem of a better institution for our youth. During the very years in which the first nine or ten grades were being reorganized, just before and after World War I, new plans were being devised and tried out for the critical ages between sixteen and twenty. In planning for these years, four distinctive leads were followed:

–Progressive secondary school and college leaders greatly improved the methods of admitting students to college; this has already been sufficiently discussed.

–Many public school systems and private groups in local communities established two-year junior colleges covering the freshman and sophomore years.

–Several of the established private colleges were systematically reorganized and new "experimental" colleges were established.

–A few daring pioneers went the whole way and created a new four-year college by combining the last two years of high school with the first two years of college, giving the bachelor's degree at the close. Several universities created new "general colleges" within their structure.

As we have seen, forward-looking administrators were experimenting even before 1900 with junior colleges for the freshman and sophomore years. About that time, for example, President William Rainey Harper set off the first two years of the University of Chicago as an "academic" college, later called the junior college. President David Starr Jordan of Stanford University and leader in the University of California supported that plan, and several junior colleges were actually set up before 1900. The oldest one surviving today, Joliet (Illinois) Junior College, was started in 1902 under Harper's inspiration.

By 1915, seventy-four junior colleges had been created in one way or another, largely west of the Mississippi River. Then came World War I and, as always happened, such a great crisis brought about considerable educational change. By 1922 the number of junior colleges had jumped to 207. By the time we had reached the severe trough of the Great Depression, the number had doubled to 469. In 1945 there were 584 junior colleges in the United States — one third of all the higher educa-

Number of Junior Colleges and Enrollment, 1915–1945 [1]

YEAR	JUNIOR COLLEGES	ENROLLMENT
1915	74	2,363
1922	207	16,031
1927	325	35,630
1932	469	97,631
1937	528	129,106
1940	575	196,710
1945	584	249,788

[1] For 1915–1940: Walter C. Eells, *American Junior Colleges*, page 18; for 1945: Eells, "Junior College Directory, 1945," pages 17–39.

tional institutions — and in them were exactly a quarter of a million students. Nearly half, 45 per cent, were public institutions. Thus the American idea of *a free, publicly supported educational system reaching from infancy to adulthood is at last being put into practice.* And no stage of it is more important, in the light of the current need of an intelligently informed citizenry, than what is happening to these older girls and boys.

Steadily the nation's school system has grown from a few primary grades a hundred years ago to a public junior college covering the thirteenth and fourteenth grades. This is democracy in action, for education *is* the primary route by which the democratic way of life can be built in our nation.

Progressive Experimentation in Private Colleges

Meanwhile the progressive movement, as such, was making itself felt in the youth years. We have already discussed the profoundly important Eight-Year Study of the Progressive Education Association designed to free the senior high school curriculum from the grip of the conventional colleges. During the very years this study was being made, several colleges of a new type were started. Conspicuous among these was a new college for young women, Bennington, in Vermont, under the presidency of Robert D. Leigh and the sponsorship of William H. Kilpatrick and several prominent leaders of the Progressive Education Association. For the decade of the thirties it was outstanding among the private colleges in setting a new program of work in the social sciences, the humanities, and the arts.

A lasting contribution was made at Bennington in creating a great school of the expressive arts. The nub of this was the Bennington School of the Dance, where during the summer months the leaders of the modern dance in America created a truly national institution. There came Martha Graham, Doris Humphrey, Charles Weidman, and Hanya Holm; the composer Louis Horst; and John Martin, critic of the dance. This school was under the general direction of Mary Jo Shelly, the general coördinator of the arts in the College, and Martha Hill of Bennington and New York University. Here also were Arch Lauterer, building a new stage design in a college theater; Otto Luening in music, and Edward Park in the graphic and plastic arts. No other college in our times has so clearly exemplified the unique contribution of the private college as did Bennington under Robert Leigh.

Other outstanding new or rejuvenated colleges were Sarah Lawrence in Bronxville, New York; Antioch in Yellow Springs, Ohio, known now for twenty years for its conspicuously successful part-time occupational and educational program; Black Mountain in North Carolina; Mills near Oakland, California; Stephens in Columbia, Missouri. In all there was vigorous experimentation with new college curricula. Here was effective private experimentation with general education, based on the direct study of the needs and problems of young people and of adult society, and providing opportunity for creative production in each of the media of expression.

In the 1920's Teachers College, Columbia, launched one of the most promising experiments in teachers college education in our entire history. This was New College, designed primarily to give a new type of general college education for those who are going into teaching. Developed under the direction of Professor Thomas Alexander and staffed by a pioneering group of young educational experimenters, it was new in many respects: new in that students were selected for their all-round promise of future leadership; new in a curriculum developed around seminars, its courses constructed out of the interests and aptitudes of the students themselves; new in the requirement of four to eight months of foreign travel, which was regarded as an indispensable part of the college course; new in its examinations, which measured general culture, breadth of interests, and constructive creative work as well as general knowledge. In spite of the exciting nature of this first major experiment in building a new teachers college, New College was abolished in the 1930's by the dean and trustees of Teachers College, Columbia.

The New Four-Year General College (Grades 11 to 14)

But the type of reorganization that went directly at the problem of general education for youth between the ages of sixteen and twenty was the four-year general college. As we write, more than thirty of these are in existence, and more are being established every year. What Presidents Folwell, White, Adams, and others asked for seventy-five years ago has finally taken shape. It has come by various routes — from below in the vocational and liberal high schools, from above in the minds of creative college administrators, by reorganization of old institutions, and by the creation of totally new ones. But it has come at last, and already it is making an important contribution to the lives of young Americans.

Credit for being the father of this new four-year college really should go to Mr. George A. Merrill, for forty-five years (1894–1939) the head of vocational schools in San Francisco — including the California School of Mechanical Arts, the Wilmerding School of Industrial Arts, and the Lux Technical Institute. As early as 1908 he said, in a report to the president of California:

"The elementary school should end with the sixth grade. Grades seven to ten (the last two of the present grammar grades and the first two of the present high school) should be made to constitute a new intermediate or secondary school. . . .

"The last two grades of the present high school should be grouped with the two lowest grades (the freshman and sophomore years) of the present college course, to form a new high school or college. The actual teaching of trades, if that ever becomes a recognized function of the public schools, must fall within the province of this new high school, in which the pupils would range from sixteen or seventeen years of age to twenty or twenty-one." [1]

Here, forty years ago, are the beginnings of the 6–4–4 plan. During the ensuing years many leaders — William M. Proctor, Leonard U. Koos, John A. Sexson, Harl Douglass, Robert M. Hutchins in the vanguard — sponsored it.

The earliest and most continuously successful public school effort was that in Pasadena, California, under the progressive superintendency of Dr. John A. Sexson. There in 1928 the Pasadena Junior College was opened. Today under the principalship of Dr. John W. Harbeson it flourishes with 5000 students. In 1933 President Robert G. Sproul of the University of California, after carefully examining the plan in action, approved it, and praised it in these glowing terms:

"Apparent advantages of the four-year type of junior college are:

–a favorable grouping of students;

–an educational unit of satisfactory length;

–low instructional costs because of elimination of duplication in matters of building equipment and educational organization;

–educational efficiency, making it possible for bright students to shorten the period of formal education;

–continuity of curricula and elimination of educational duplication;

–especially favorable conditions for the development of four-year curricula in semi-professional fields; and

–a guidance system which is continuous throughout the four years, during which period for the average student there is perhaps the greatest necessity for sound advice."

---

[1] John A. Sexson and John W. Harbeson: The New American College, pages 27 and 28. Copyright 1946 by Harper & Brothers. Used by permission.

The Chicago Plan   The most publicly discussed of the many attempts to bring about the new four-year college was the so-called Chicago Plan, under the presidency of Robert M. Hutchins. At the University of Chicago, in the 1930's, the last two years of the University High School were joined to the first two years of the College to form a new four-year college. In 1942 President Hutchins made an announcement that stirred the college world:

> "On January 22 (1942) the University Senate, by a vote of 63 to 48, decided to authorize the College, which controls the four years from the beginning of the conventional Junior year in high school to the end of the conventional Sophomore year in college, to award the Bachelor's degree 'in recognition of general education as redefined by the College faculty' . . ." [1]

"General education as redefined by the College faculty" took actual form in a reconstructed curriculum of five groups of general courses — arts, literature, biological sciences, physical sciences, social studies, and the humanities. These preceded other subject-matter courses and were appraised at the end by seven comprehensive examinations. Units, grades, and compulsory attendance were abandoned. Professor-made syllabi built the courses for individual study, and each student was permitted to progress at his own rate of speed, taking the examinations when he was ready. Normal time of completion is two years. A few required three years; many have actually completed the seven units in one year, a very few in one semester.

The General College of the University of Minnesota   Another attempt to create a more effective college was the establishment of a General College at the University of Minnesota, under the direction of Dean Malcolm McLean. At first, as a two-year junior college, it was a reflection of the "progressive" activity movement in the college curriculum. It was designed as a new type of general education constructed out of the experiences, needs, and interests of the students rather than from adult society and the conventional college program. Like the Chicago Plan it was individualized; graduation and the granting of the degree depended on passing five comprehensive examinations, mostly of the objective type, and taken whenever the student felt he was ready. These

[1] John A. Sexson and John W. Harbeson: *The New American College*, page 67.

examinations were planned to measure broad powers, general understanding, attitudes, and grasp of principles, as well as mastery of factual knowledge and skill. The syllabi were made "on the spot" by both the instructors and the students, capitalizing to the fullest extent the interests and needs of the latter group.

Things to Do Now about the Youth Problem

America's twofold problem of work and education for youth is primarily the problem of your own age group. As you can see, forward-looking citizens and educators are profoundly concerned with it and are trying earnestly to do something about it. It is important that you and your classmates study it, and take your places as leaders in the emerging youth movement.

1. Make a study of "youth in the news" over a period of a week; for example, clip newspaper items dealing with things happening to youth. What generalizations can you make from these, regarding the problems and difficulties of youth? What should adult society do about it?

2. Make a diary record over a period of time giving actual conversations and episodes involving young people, indicating stress and strain among youth today.

3. Visit a juvenile court, or a juvenile session of a court, and study the difficulties youth are encountering today as shown by the problems with which the judge has to deal.

4. Prepare a list of the problems of young people today as revealed in plays, motion pictures, novels, or short stories that you have seen or read.

5. Study the catalogues of your own college, comparing its offerings with the courses and curricula given half a generation or a generation ago. What major changes seem to you to be coming about? Are these changes sufficient to provide the kind of education you think youth should have if they are to be educated for the social world of the years ahead?

6. Study the catalogue of the most modern or progressive college you can discover and compare its program of work with that of your college. A few of those that have been discussed in recent years are: Bennington College, Bennington, Vermont; Antioch College, Yellow Springs, Ohio; Sarah Lawrence College, Bronxville, New York; Black Mountain College, Black Moun-

tain, North Carolina; Stephens College, Columbia, Missouri; Roosevelt College, Chicago, Illinois; Goddard College, Plainfield, Vermont.

7. Compare these programs with the program in general education now developing in the older private colleges, such as Harvard (see *General Education in a Free Society*), Yale, Princeton, and Hopkins (see the December 1945 issue of the *Association of American Colleges Bulletin*), and Columbia (see a *College Program in Action*).

8. Make a study of the actual paid jobs which you and your classmates have held recently or are holding now. Get the facts on kinds of work done, pay, and potentialities for growth and development. Are these jobs "blind alleys," or are they fitting you for an effective lifework? Appraise the extent to which your school and college education has prepared you for these jobs. Did school and college help you in getting employment? Was the employment coördinated with your educational work?

9. Write an autobiography, beginning with your high school years, discussing your development in the light of the problems, social changes, and trends described in this chapter, showing typical effects and molding influences on your life. To what extent did your school guide you in meeting problems and in building understanding? What changes in school guidance would you make as a result of your experience?

10. Have a round table discussion on the study of controversial issues in the schools. In connection with this, discuss the problem of indoctrination in teaching.

What to Read

1. On the Youth Problem

The various reports of the American Youth Commission are indispensable; see especially Chairman Homer Rainey's brief over-all statement, *How Fare American Youth?* and the Commission's general summary, *Youth and the Future*. Howard Bell's dramatic case studies, in his *Youth Tell Their Story*, are a "must." Goodwin Watson's *Youth after Conflict* will give you an interesting account of the development of youth's problems since the 1920's, with predictions for the 1950's.

See Chapter XVII of Harold Rugg's *Foundations for American Education* for a comprehensive interpretation of the whole problem of society-centered foundations of education. See also Chapters V, VII, and VIII of the *Third Yearbook* of the John Dewey Society. Chapter IX of their *Eighth*

Yearbook deals with youth and its vast potentialities; Chapters I to IV plan for the future. For excellent statements of public attempts to develop work programs for youth see L. L. Lorwin's Youth-Work Programs.

2. On the Changing Social Order and Its Problems

We refer again to the reading suggestions given at the end of Chapter IV. See also Harold Rugg's Foundations for American Education, especially Chapters VIII to XIV and Chapter XVIII. See the selected reading lists given in Foundations for American Education.

3. On New Educational Programs in High School and College

From a vast and growing literature we pick a few of the best things. The Educational Frontier, W. H. Kilpatrick (Editor), lays a general foundation. These reports are interpretations of the work and findings of national commissions on the high school. The report of the Progressive Education Association's Commission on the Secondary School Curriculum is in Thayer, Zachry, and Kotinsky's Reorganizing Secondary Education; that of the NEA Policies Commission is in the fine programs designed for youth in Education for All American Youth; that of the North Central Association of Schools and Colleges is in B. Lamar Johnson's (Editor) General Education in the High School. Paul Hanna presented concrete descriptions of youth's participation in community activities in his Youth Serves the Community.

The chief points of view on the reorganization of the college are given in some eight or ten basic books. A general overview can be gained from R. Freeman Butts's The College Charts Its Course. The important conclusions of the Progressive Education Association's "Eight-Year Study" can be found in Chamberlain and Others, Did They Succeed in College? and in Aiken's Thirty Schools Tell Their Story. The North Central Association's report appears in the Yearbook of the National Society for the Study of Education, edited by Alvin Eurich: General Education in the American College.

The position of the modern scholastics (the Hutchins-Adler group) is well stated in Mark Van Doren's Liberal Education; the position of other private colleges in such works as the Harvard Report, General Education in a Free Society, and the Columbia report, A College Program in Action.

The development of the emerging four-year (11th to 14th grades) college is best stated in Sexson and Harbeson's The New American College. On the junior college see Walter C. Eells (Editor), Why Junior College Terminal Education? Alexander Meiklejohn reports on earlier and very interesting experiments in the reorganization of the first two years of college in his The Experimental College.

On the integration of high school and college see the five volumes of the Progressive Education Association's report of the Commission on Relations Between High School and College; also L. V. Koos's *Integrating High School and College*.

4. On Guidance

Among the new books on the guidance of adolescents and youth we recommend particularly the following: Peter Blos's *The Adolescent Personality*, giving case studies and interpretations of typical behavior; Caroline Zachry and M. Lighty's *Emotion and Conduct in Adolescence*, a "must"; and Dimock's *Rediscovering the Adolescent*, based on an elaborate two-year case study of 200 boys, ages 12 to 14.   Part II of Leslie Chisholm's *Guiding Youth in the Secondary School* is a practical guide to the solution of youth's personal problem.   And don't miss Katharine Whiteside Taylor's *Do Adolescents Need Parents?*, done for the Progressive Education Association's Commission on Human Relations.

CHAPTER 7

In a Democracy There Is No Terminal Point to Education

THE CHIEF GUARANTEE of the abundant life in a democratic society is *continuing adult education*. That the American people believe this is shown by the tremendous organizational machinery of adult education and by the 50,000,000 persons now devoting themselves to some form of education.

—A new phenomenon in world history: a third of a nation vigorously carrying on continuing studies of its needs, problems, and institutions, cultivating personal expressions and appreciations.

We see on the horizon:

—the School of Tomorrow, open and used seven days a week, fifteen hours a day.

—the resources of the community centered on education.

Government and Life in a Society of
Free Men Means Continuing Education.

The Teacher and Adult Education

SOME PEOPLE think of education as limited to the years spent in formal schooling. This is far from the truth! In the generation that has passed since World War I, the American continent has come alive with adult education. In hundreds of communities, and in most of the states of the Union, groups of grownups are doing things together which are truly educational.

In Kalamazoo, Michigan, on a little side street, you will find The Peoples Church. There the minister, as people in Kalamazoo will tell you, is "doing something real. He has a carpenter shop in the basement, he gets people together to study things: community needs, factory conditions, the schools. Not crowds of them — just a dozen or so in this group and that. He keeps one thing after another going. There's life in that church!"

And there is life in little adult education groups all over the country — from San Francisco to Boston. You can come upon them in little shops, in the offices of county farm agents, in a Grange Hall or labor union headquarters, a teachers college, a church, or a YMCA auditorium. In Detroit there is the Merrill-Palmer School for parenthood; in New York, the Child Study Association and The Peoples Institute; in many cities, the rooms of the American Association of University Women, which is "an educational association" . . . not a "federation of college clubs or women's clubs." Every week in the year and in the most unexpected places, you can find these educational activities going on outside the schools and colleges.

Consider what is happening in the offices of business corporations. Had you thought of these as centers of adult education? Probably not, but they are; witness the fine programs of health education reaching out all over the country from the main offices of the life insurance companies. Many of them now publish and distribute pamphlets to their policy-holders; this is not only conducive to better health and longer life, but also to the better use of leisure time. Good business it is, but good education, too.

A savings bank organizes classes in cooking and budgeting for its depositors so that they may get more from the use of their money, and thus save more. You say again: "Good business!" Yes, but good adult education, also!

Through a teaching program of pamphlets and correspondence, a national mail-order house conducts an educational campaign among low-income farmers in our southern states, encouraging the raising of diversified vegetable crops, both for the farmers' household use and for sale. The farmers have improved the health of their families, increased their income, and so have become better customers. So again, it is good business, but it is good adult education as well.

The personnel departments of large corporations are conducting schools for their own executives, in which they study human relations and develop understanding of their employees' problems and interests. Here is applied psychology, adult education in action.

New Leadership Creating a New Kind of Adult Education

A New Kind of Teacher

The best way to understand the real nature of adult education is to know its teachers. They are an unconventional lot, most of them having avoided training in our orthodox teacher-education institutions. Thanks to Harry and Bonaro Overstreet, who painted a graphic portrait of these teachers in their book, *Leaders for Adult Education*, we know much about them. Person after person told the Overstreets the same story: "It was mostly a matter of happy accident. I didn't wake up one day seeing a great light. I wasn't a crusader for a new world." These men and women simply began to teach adult groups, most of them never

HARRY OVERSTREET was Head of the Department of Philosophy of the College of the City of New York from 1911 to 1939, and has written many influential books for citizens and teachers; for example, *Influencing Human Behavior, About Ourselves, Town Meeting Comes to Town,* and the widely read *The Mature Mind.*

BONARO OVERSTREET was a teacher of creative writing in public schools but is known principally as a poet and essayist and as the author of such volumes as: *Search for a Self, Brave Enough for Life, American Reasons,* and *Freedom's People.*

The Overstreets, working as a potent team of two, have achieved a unique place as leaders in group discussions and consultants in adult education.

having taught before, and thereby "began to see educational problems and opportunities (they) had not thought about."

In the public evening school of one Midwest town, the Overstreets found a school for grownups "geared to adult wants and needs," studying problems of parenthood, citizenship, and counseling, and engaging in handicrafts and arts. But the remarkable thing was the teachers: "How do you get teachers like that?"

"We hand-pick 'em," was the answer. "Pick them through luncheon talks or long one-day get-togethers. . . . One out of twenty would turn out to be real possibilities." They got some from the local teachers college or high school. "But many of them we get by bringing in a lawyer or a doctor, a social worker in the community, a foreman in a factory. So we draw from the community and give to the community."

An Example: the WPA Educational Program The educational program of the Works Progress Administration was organized in the 1930's and,

handicapped though it was, "opened a new chapter in the education
of the American people." In the midst of nation-wide unemployment,
the WPA teachers were unable to find jobs in the schools, the welfare
agencies, or the libraries. So they were "forced to go out and find something to do." They "took neglected America as their portion," creating
their educational jobs by doing things that needed to be done but that
no one else was doing. They had to train themselves for the new tasks,
learn "how to walk country roads, hunt out the illiterates, and interest
these people in learning to read and write." They found many
unexpected examples of ignorance. Many of these illiterates were
"X-markers, who drove automobiles, but who could not read danger
signs on the road, and who had never opened any book or newspaper."

So the WPA teachers had to teach themselves by learning on the
job. They learned many things in addition to teaching. They learned
how to care about "changed lives, changed homes, and changed communities." They learned how to bring a sense of accomplishment to
people who knew little of life's resources. They learned a great deal of
what sound education is, and above all, they learned that education is
"experience-centered." What and how they learned was of the greatest
moment to adult education in our country.

Another Example: the CCC's Program Like the WPA program, the
education program of the CCC camps were American, "fashioned out of
adversity." These men and women also learned on the job. Their
educational programs succeeded only where they grasped the problem.
Their educational program also was experience-centered, "stemmed out
of specific felt needs." They went "directly at the job of training individuals to do the jobs that needed to be done." Each adviser "created
for himself the job of guide, counselor, friend, educational salesman,
and wise coöperator." Although for a long time there was much opposition to including education in the CCC camps — "messing in education with disciplined work!" — before the end of the Depression the
Corps came to accept "the mental, moral, and social growth of the
young men" as a primary obligation. The Overstreets concluded that
out of it "a profoundly significant form of adult education has developed."

A Third Example: Training for Workers' Education Then there was
workers' education, "the problem child of the adult-education move-

ment." Labor leaders saw that workers had to be enlightened about the social issues of the day — an enlightenment they had certainly not gained from their school education. The public forums had helped, but not much. So the workers had to plan their own methods, developing teaching techniques that would lead to effective social action. It was not easy to make a study of the current issues nor to link education to real social purposes. Yet the workers' education movement did it. The leaders in the movement organized workers' summer schools in which vigorous, alert union members studied social-economic issues, public speaking, labor union problems and techniques. These people became union leaders and union educators.

Episodes of Adult Teacher Education

Stories of teachers' experiences abound with illustrations of the nature of the new adult education. There was, for example, the city director of public libraries who had a unique method of training young librarians. She required each of her novices to spend several months going about the city, getting acquainted with it, talking to people of every walk of life to discover their interests and how the library could help them. More of the young librarians' training time was spent outside the library than within it — certainly a revolutionary method of library education.

There was the man who took the principalship of a little high school in the Midwest. He found that he learned most by studying the parents and ended by giving most of his energy to leading adult education in the town.

There was the successful owner of a business enterprise, shy, unable to speak in public, who, while continuing with his business, made himself the director of a conspicuously successful adult school.

One capable, but dull and academic, psychologist discovered the art of teaching through teaching a psychology class for labor union members. The workers' questions came from experiences of passionate interest, and only answers applicable to experience would do. The psychologist soon found himself in a new "world of the hopes and perplexities and fears generated by the working conditions of modern society." By trial and error he learned to find new kinds of illustrative material, new ways to present it, new ways to test it. When the course was over, he had become absorbed in teaching grownups. He had "stepped down from the status of well-trained college professor," but he had also "stepped up to the status of a searching human being." Today he is still at the job of learning from adult classes how to teach adult classes.

In one town the adult-education leaders invented an effective teaching technique. The Overstreets reported how the leaders of discussion groups attended a different discussion group, one night each week,

> "watching the ways of the leader . . . the audience's response, getting the feel of the whole thing. Then after the discussion they were to retire to some convenient meeting place, where, over a bite to eat, they could compare notes on the good and the bad they had heard."

This gave them concrete stuff with which to appraise the art of discussion; they had something real to talk about.

The School of Related Arts and Sciences at Utica, New York, requires every teacher to work as an assistant in one class and to be a student in at least one other. Thus they constantly practice the concept of "the experience of inexperience."

The best speaker in a recent adult-education conference in the Midwest was not a school or college teacher; himself a foreman, he was the leader in the education of other industrial foremen.

The director of the Boston Center for Adult Education put his finger on the qualities of leadership when he said about a certain teacher of adult groups: "He's getting better and better all the time, but if he ever stops getting better, he won't be any good." Continuous growth is the fundamental measure of the good teacher.

In one adult-education center in the Midwest there were two teachers — one a distinguished scholar, the other a journalist. Both started with large classes, but after the first meeting the attendance steadily declined. The two men discussed the problem with the director. The scholar said, "What is wrong with these people?" The journalist asked, "What is wrong with me?" The college professor soon quit, but the journalist stuck to his group and made a teacher of himself. This shows that a goodly amount of humility and self-criticism is a first requirement of developing a good teacher.

In the study of these practical programs the Overstreets discovered *why adult education really exists.* It is, they say:

"because there are men and women who are puzzled enough about life, or hungry enough for new experiences, to resume voluntarily the status of learners. They do not, however, resume the status of children. They remain adult. Indeed, by their puzzlement and hunger they prove themselves really adult. They may look clumsy, at times, . . . But let not the teacher who looks at them be deceived. These men and women who are willing to look clumsy in order to learn represent the most mature portion of our grownup population."

But enough of such examples of adult education. Certainly the old notion that education is something that goes on only in a schoolhouse from 8:30 to 3:30 is passing. Far from being closed after 3:30 in the afternoon, and on week ends and long summer vacations, the schoolhouse — even the formal kind — is open from dawn to midnight the year round. And the "schoolhouse" appears in the strangest and most varied places. The view that education is continuous from infancy to old age is indeed rapidly establishing itself.

Adults Can Learn

One reason for the prevalence of the idea that education is restricted to the early years of life was the generally accepted belief that "You can't teach an old dog new tricks." By the time they reached their maturity, human beings were supposed to have done their learning. From then on, what little they learned would come very slowly and with increasing difficulty. Some of the scientific facts you have encountered about growth may seem to you to confirm this idea; for example, the curves of physical and mental growth appear to indicate that most people reach maturity at about the sixteenth or seventeenth year.

But these established facts of physical and mental growth do not actually run counter to the potentialities of adult learning. In recent years psychologists have sought scientific answers to the question: "Can adults learn?" In 1927 Edward L. Thorndike reported the findings of experiments in adult learning that went far toward settling the matter. Thorndike showed that most persons forty years of age learned almost as well as adults of twenty and better than children of twelve. This was true in the learning of such skills as handwriting, typewriting and short-hand, and the new techniques in algebra, science, and foreign languages. On the whole, ease of learning rises steadily until about the age of twenty and continues at about the same level for some years, after which it very slowly declines but not more than one per cent a year. Thorndike's conclusion was that up to the age of fifty no person should be deterred from further education by the belief that he had lost his learning power.

These experiments of Thorndike's were widely discussed and acclaimed. Morse Cartwright, in his *Ten years of Adult Education,* calls Thorndike's findings the "most potent factor in the spread of the adult education idea in the last decade" (1924–1934). They greatly heartened those who were organizing the adult-education program.

The Long History of Adult Education in America

For more than two hundred years, if one were to include political enter-prises like the New England Town Meeting, various forms of adult education have been practiced in the United States. In agrarian days there was no lack of reality about the subject matter of these political meetings; they centered around the community's local issues. The citizens discussed their problems face to face and solved them by the ballot. It is often said that in the experience of the Town Meeting was born the leadership of the American revolutionary movement.

But recognizable examples of formal, adult education also have more than a hundred years of history. In the second quarter of the nineteenth century the farmers and mechanics of Massachusetts organized the first Lyceum "for the purpose of self-culture, community instruction, and mutual discussion of common public interests." So rapidly did the Lyceum idea spread across the country that by 1839 there were more than 3000 such forum and discussion groups. Their leadership included the most distinguished names in the nation: Henry Thoreau, Ralph Waldo Emerson, James Russell Lowell, Oliver Wendell Holmes — to name only a few. For several decades the movement continued unabated.

EDUARD C. LINDEMAN (1885————), Professor of Social Philosophy in the New York School of Social Work since 1922, has long been recognized as an outstanding national leader in adult education. His influence as a speaker on education and the community on such national and international forums as those of the Progressive Education Association and the New Education Fellowship, has been world-wide. Through his activities in the Workers Education Bureau, the American Civil Liberties Union, and the Institute of Propaganda Analysis, he has made distinguished contributions to adult education and community social work.

Such books as his The Meaning of Adult Education, Wealth and Culture, The Community, and Social Discovery interpret the educator's opportunity to build an understanding and practice of democracy in family, neighborhood, and community life. He conceives of the community and its organization as a comprehensive laboratory for the development of habits of democratic discipline.

In 1874 leading churchmen organized the Chautauqua Institution, which became famous in the history of adult lecture and study groups. Commercial lyceum circuits sprang up and prospered. These were followed by the university extension movement, the county farm agent movement, and the rise of the YMCA and the YWCA, each with its manifold educational activities. Then, near the turn of the twentieth century, the adult-education movement was dramatically accelerated by the sensational nation-wide building of public libraries.

Thus the Americans long ago built a tradition of adult education. On every frontier and in the hamlets and towns they came together to study their problems coöperatively. These meetings were not only for preserving the social spirit by the barn dance after the house-raising, the corn husking, and the "socials" of the churches, but also for studying the group's collective problems. Yet, for nearly a century no federal agency took charge of endowing, promoting, or appraising the manifold forms of adult education that were evolving.

The Role of Great Private Endowments

It fell to the lot, therefore, of the rich private foundations to promote adult education. One by one these were established in the early 1900's through the great fortunes made in steel, oil, railroads, meat, and urban land.   Conspicuous examples were the Carnegie and Rockefeller fortunes, which endowed several foundations for social, philanthropic, and educational purposes; witness the Carnegie Endowment for the Advancement of Peace, the Carnegie Foundation for the Advancement of Teaching, the Carnegie Corporation; the corresponding Rockefeller Foundation for the Advancement of Teaching, the General Education Board, and the Laura Spellman Rockefeller Foundation; also the Milbank Fund, the Rosenwald Fund, and others.   These endowments represented enormous financial resources, the Carnegie and Rockefeller running into hundreds of millions of dollars.   Even the smaller ones were wealthy, the Rosenwald Fund having $22,000,000.

Interpreted in the broadest sense, the preponderance of wealth in these foundations, which aggregated more than a billion dollars, was devoted to the development of education; much of it was education of the grownup population.   It would be difficult indeed to overestimate the powerful influence of these Funds.

The Radiating Power of a Single Study Group

At the other extreme from the rich foundation is the local study-discussion group.   Without funds, lacking the wide-reaching sounding board of press, radio, or movies, the true basis of adult education lies in the continuity and integrity of the grass-roots group of self-educating citizens.   An outstanding example of what one little group of pioneers did is found in the Teachers College Discussion Group, organized around William H. Kilpatrick in New York, in 1927.   In it a dozen professors of the social-philosophical and historical foundations of education joined together every other Monday night for dinner and a three-hour discussion.   Regularly from 1927 to 1934, intermittently from 1934 to 1938, and again for several years after war began in 1939, they held their bi-monthly study group, exploring informally the roots of every phase of our civilization.

In hundreds of hours of this friendly but incisive intellectual exploration they dug down to the social foundations of education.   Even by 1932, when the economic depression had slid into its deepest trough, they had become a cohesive group, agreeing fairly closely on the constituents of the democratic principle, and taking their stand together for the general conception of a welfare state.   All but two avoided leadership in political organizations, confining their efforts to studying and critically appraising platforms, creeds, programs, and strategies, and making manifesto statements on current issues.

For more than twelve years the group held together, practicing what they preached to other Americans. It was vigorous adult education; and it worked, for it resulted in far-reaching educational changes. These dozen professors believed in educational action as well as in study and discussion. They became the nucleus of the sixty "Fellows" in a dozen universities, who, in 1935, established the John Dewey Society for the Study of Education and the Culture, published eight *Yearbooks*, launched the magazine *The Social Frontier*, and influenced the social reconstruction of educational programs across the country.

Study-Discussion Groups of Civic Organizations

After World War I such organizations as the American Association of University Women, the League of Women Voters, the National Child Study Association, the General Federation of Women's Clubs, the National Association of Business and Professional Women, the YMCA and the YWCA, and the National Council of Jewish Women built up local branches across the country. Many of these have systematically organized their members for various kinds of adult education. For example, the League of Women Voters has established hundreds of branches in which the members study local conditions, problems and issues, needs for civic improvement, political reform, and the like. Through its state leagues the national organization provides systematic training in politics; it prints and distributes publications which are used in

"study groups, round tables, radio programs, public meetings, citizenship schools, and institutes of government and politics. Preelection work, consisting of voters' schools, election information booths, candidates' meetings, publication of candidates' records, discussions pro and con of election issues, are a regular part of these activities. Visits to legislative bodies, to courts and public institutions, and conferences with public officials and technical experts provide firsthand information. Some Leagues undertake surveys of units or functions of government, publish digests of laws, train speakers, issue publicity, and publish a regular bulletin giving current information. Members of the League of Women Voters do not merely learn *about* government; they take part *in* government."

Consider the nation-wide influence of the American Association of University Women. In the years 1937–1939 its 853 local branches had more than 2500 study groups carrying on regular study. From its national headquarters a staff of trained experts prints and distributes material for the use of these study groups in education, international relations, social studies, the economic and legal status of women, and the arts. It maintains a Research Information Service in Secondary and College Education, supports legislation and other public action, endows the education of gifted women scholars through graduate fellowships, and carries on research in the subject of the status of women.

The Consumers Coöperative Movement and the Coöperative League of America also maintain educational departments, including study-discussion groups, and distribute material for the use of these classes.

The National Child Study Association organizes many local councils in parent education, gives courses in the training of lay leaders, distributes printed material, and holds regional and national conferences and institutes on child study and parent education.

Perhaps the most impressive work is done by the labor unions. Each of the larger unions is building up a large-scale program of social and political education among its members.

The Work of Public Agencies

Side by side with the adult educational activities of these private organizations is the important work of countless branches of local, state, and national government. A generation ago (1914) the Smith-Lever Law brought under one plan of development the farm and home extension work of county governments, state agricultural colleges, and the federal Department of Agriculture. The aim was to instruct adults who were not in school in "subjects relating to agriculture and home economics." The public subsidy of $25,000,000 a year led to the building of a national staff of 6000 professional educational leaders, most of whom were involved in adult instruction.

While the original aim was the improvement of crops and the technical work of the farms, the philosophy of the leaders slowly changed to emphasize better farm life. The farm home as a more attractive place in which to live was made coördinate in importance with better use of farm machines, telephones, electricity, roads, automobiles, and radios. Group forum and study work became part of the program, lectures were given in the social sciences and the humanities, the women's movement was reinterpreted, and the farm people were encouraged to make more use of recreational facilities in consolidated rural schools and town schools. The work focused on the building of cultural and educational centers for adults. Thus the long-standing rugged individualism of the farm slowly gave way to greater community coöperation. It is the considered judgment of leaders in adult education that this movement has become of tremendous national importance; today they say: "Three farms out of every four have been affected by the program."

Paralleling these developments was the systematic building up of study and discussion groups by the federal Department of Agriculture. Today hundreds of thousands of farmers' study groups are in action across the country.

Local, state, and national departments of public health now conduct adult-education programs in hygiene, sanitation, diet, exercise, and the prevention of communicable diseases. These programs are systematically building understanding of the obligation of the community to create publicly aided housing enterprises. For a generation these departments have also contributed to the safety of public streets and highways and the development of more attractive parks and well-equipped playgrounds.

A similar change in point of view has come about in the education of public officials. Consider, for example, the new conception of prison work. The idea of personal rehabilitation of prisoners is taking the place of punishment. New York State now conducts a School for Prison Guards which includes a two months' training course in the psychology of understanding prisoners as human beings. State and county governments have been setting up police schools ever since August Vollmer, Chief of Police in Berkeley, California, started the first one years ago. This was a school in which prospective police officers studied the psychology of dealing with community groups and individuals as well as the defense of life and property. New York State police officers, for example, all pass through a course of preliminary training in matters of courtesy and tactics in dealing with the public.

The public library has in the past twenty-five years become one of the nation's most powerful agencies for adult education. Launched on a nation-wide scale nearly a half century ago by Andrew Carnegie's multi-million gift, the library was for a long time fairly isolated from the public education of the community. It was a depositary for books rather than a stimulus to the community-wide use of books. Just as in earlier times the insurance agent learned how to sell insurance, the social worker how to estimate relief needs, the prison guard how to force prisoners to obey rules — so the librarian had long confined his study to the specific technical library skills. Since World War I, however, a wholly new conception of library education has developed. The younger generation of librarians is today studying how to build community understanding through the library and how to study the community's needs for books. They ask: "Which books will help most to solve this man's or that woman's problem?" "What pamphlets, reports, and books will that sixth grade need in carrying on its next unit of work?" Thus the function of the library becomes educative rather than merely custodial.

Adult Education in the Colleges and Universities

Meanwhile one of the largest strands of adult education during the past twenty-five years has consisted of new graduate and special forms of education in the universities and colleges. Consider the summer schools run by these institutions — certainly more than a thousand each summer with several hundred thousand teachers in attendance. This is adult education on a mass scale. Witness also the late afternoon, evening, and Saturday classes of practically all the larger colleges and universities — annual attendance running into the hundreds of thousands.

Added to these are the countless staff meetings of city school systems, the meetings of state and regional teachers' associations, the scores of teachers' national meetings representing every department of learning, and adult-education workshops which in the past fifteen years have sprung up all over the United States.

ALVIN JOHNSON (1874———) has had a distinguished career as a liberal economist and as a leader in combating intolerance in human relations. The motives that have driven him as educator, he says, are the needs for: (1) the extension of higher education to the adult, which prompted him to build up the New School for Social Research; (2) the restoration of the unity of the social sciences, which led to his creating The Encyclopedia of the Social Sciences; (3) the international solidarity of scholarship, which led him to develop the University in Exile to help persecuted foreign scholars; (4) the abatement of discrimination on the basis of race, religion, color, or national origin, which inspired him to work successfully for laws against discrimination in education.

At a dinner in his honor Dr. Johnson said that we must "look forward and strive forward toward the era when perverse national ambitions, perverse ideologies, shall cease to torture and slaughter men, and the humblest may stand upright . . . , confident that the next man is his friend, destined not to curb and narrow his life, but to enrich it."

In recent years many colleges have created new and special kinds of adult-education programs. The New York State College of Agriculture at Cornell now offers summer courses for town and country ministers. Here for two weeks each summer they take courses in rural sociology, study the economic problems of agriculture, the family, farm and business coöperatives, the social problems of the community, rural education, and specialized forms of church work. The aim of the new adult education is not only to inform and inspire ministers concerning the opportunities of the church in community life, but also to build leaders for the nation's adult education.

The Continuation Center at the University of Minnesota periodically holds institutes for successful leaders who want to meet together for advanced study. One week you will find doctors meeting at the Continuation Center to try to work out answers to their own questions; another week superintendents of schools, or managers of coöperative stores, or public health nurses, social workers, or ministers.

In a California junior college a dozen faculty members — including a psychologist, a physicist, an economist, a historian, and two teachers of English — met once each week for the purpose of finding out the special contributions being made to man's knowledge by the various fields of work represented in the group.

For a generation now the universities have been taking over what
was first developed by private commercial schools, namely, education
through "correspondence." Most large institutions now offer home
extension courses; today such courses enroll tens of thousands of adult
students.

The American Association for Adult Education

It was not, however, until the 1920's that a single national center
was created for the formal organization and cultivation of adult education. This move can be traced to the imaginative initiative of the
leaders of the great educational foundations, particularly of Dr. Frederick
P. Keppel and the Carnegie Corporation of America, of which he became president after World War I. In the next twenty years the
promotion and endowment of adult education became one of the principal enterprises of the Corporation.

It was under Dr. Keppel's leadership that the American Association
for Adult Education was organized in 1926 with a Board of Sponsors
including James Earl Russell, Charles A. Beard, Everett Dean Martin,
Alfred E. Cohn, and Eduard C. Lindeman. Surveys were made of the
status of the nation's adult-education activities, and other researches
were launched. A series of some twenty volumes were published dealing with the entire scope of adult education. Regional and national
meetings were held, and the *Journal of Adult Education* was published. Distinguished national leaders occupied the presidency of the
Association — James Earl Russell, Newton D. Baker, Felix M. Warburg,
Dorothy Canfield Fisher, and Edward L. Thorndike, to name a few.

Into the development of the American Association for Adult
Education the Carnegie Corporation poured several million dollars.
When the work began in the middle 1920's, it was estimated that in
thirty specific types of adult education, 15,000,000 Americans were enrolled; by 1934 the number had risen to 22,000,000. Over 20,000,000
of the adults were enrolled as follows:

agricultural extension	6,000,000	public schools	1,500,000
private correspondence school	1,000,000	radio education	5,000,000
library adult education	1,000,000	indoor recreation	2,000,000
lyceums and Chautauquas	1,000,000	unemployed relief	2,250,000
men's and women's clubs	1,000,000		

Summing up the Potentialities of Adult Education

This impressive array of facts and figures is convincing evidence indeed that, although the federal government has done little to promote and endow adult education, the nation has a tremendous potential need for it. The recent *Handbook of Adult Education in the United States*, published by the American Association for Adult Education, discusses no less than thirty-two specific types of adult education now going on in the country. This includes:

–thousands of study-discussion groups of the federal Department of Agriculture and state and county agricultural extension groups.

–thousands of local branches of the National Congress of Parents and Teachers, YMCA, YWCA, YMHA, YWHA, American Association of University Women, National Federation of Professional Women's Clubs, General Federation of Women's Clubs, Child Study Association of America, National Association of Jewish Center Executives, local unions affiliated with the American Federation of Labor and the Congress of Industrial Organizations, the Workers Education Bureau of America — totaling at the latest estimate not less than 50,000 groups. The table on the preceding page sums up the statistical facts as estimated sixteen years ago. Today they are even more reassuring.

–several thousand public libraries now becoming active centers for the education of adults in the community, "the librarian with his non-partisan, non-sectarian library used as a rallying point and always reckoned upon as the chief auxiliary aid; town and village libraries as well as branch libraries in all the larger cities . . . hundreds of county libraries working with the study-discussion leaders in the Grange, the Farm Bureau, aiding the county agent and the home demonstrator, preparing special lists of books and other reading materials for self-education programs, building reading courses for individuals, planning lecture series, holding meetings, preparing study outlines for special groups, collaborating with the organizations engaged in the adult education of their members.

–a vast program of informal adult education going on through the motion picture, radio, television, the theater, music, and other arts.

–the museums of the country (estimated to total 1500) becoming vigorous leaders in adult education in the arts, sciences, and industries; . . . 170 museums reported 30,000,000 visitors in a year using art, scientific, and educational exhibits, lectures, conferences, study-groups, clubs, instructional courses; many have educational directors who are experimenting with library reading courses, radio broadcasting, nature study, art appreciation, etc.

–no less than a hundred associations, councils, conferences, committees, and boards affiliated with the American Association for Adult Education, maintaining paid secretaries, information services, and various kinds of experimental enterprises.

–perhaps a hundred commercial correspondence schools enrolling a million students or more, the more reputable ones organizing themselves as the National Home Study Council, with 37 institutional members.

–scores of formally organized adult-education centers in colleges and universities.

–schools for the elimination of illiteracy among the foreign-born in all the larger cities of the country, including evening classes in language and related subjects; sometimes incorporated as an integral part of the community public school system.

–many organizations of the foreign-born, memberships running into millions, fusing various types of adult education with their recreational and social functions.

–many community forums which periodically gather to listen to lectures on current topics, ask questions, and discuss — a continuation of the Lyceum and Chautauqua movements.

–and many others, totaling 32 distinctive types of adult-education enterprises in America.

Not only is the organizational machinery available for a powerful adult-education movement in America, but the physical means of communication is now perfected, ready for efficient mass use.   In less than two generations a huge mass communication industry has been invented and constructed: a radio and television industry reaching into more

Citizens of Front Royal, Virginia, hold a community-planning workshop. (Photo from Jesse F. Ogden, University of Virginia.)

than half the homes of America, a motion picture industry reaching a hundred million Americans a week, a massive newspaper-magazine-book press read by the vast preponderance of people. It is now possible to send words through the air, in print or on the screen, into every hamlet and most of the homes in the United States. Any officer of national or world prestige can at last actually be heard by the people. So with the physical means of communication so perfected, a part of the battle to get the facts interpreted clearly to the people has been won.

Resources Available for the Americans' Study of the World's Crucial Problems

The Development of Mass Communication

Let the teachers of America be of good heart. The task of getting the American people to understand and do something about the critical problems before the world is, indeed, a staggering one, but our resources are great. Not only is the physical machinery available, but powerful beginnings have been achieved in putting it to work. Certainly first steps have been taken: a fine body of clear-minded students has been setting the problems clearly before the people with an interpretation of the forces and factors that contribute to them. For example, we know vastly more about the problem of full production and full employment — basic to all our other problems — than we did a generation ago.

191

The radio and other mass communication agencies are steadily widening the horizon of our people's understanding.

The distinguished volumes of the Report of the Commission on the Freedom of the Press have stated clearly what our country needs from this mass communication industry in order to build a national program of adult education. Those needs are five:

-first, a truthful, comprehensive, and intelligent account of the day's events in a context which gives them meaning;

-second, a forum for the exchange of comment and criticism;

-third, a means of projecting the opinions and attitudes of social groups to one another;

-fourth, a method of presenting and clarifying the goals and values of the society;

-fifth, a way of reaching every member of the society by the currents of information, thought, and feeling which the press supplies.

The Capacity of the People for Social Understanding

The likelihood of success in building an intelligent public mind about the world in which we live depends upon the quantity and quality of the intelligence of the American people. And the past forty years has accumulated an encouraging body of facts about that also. We know that out of the hundred million grownup persons in America — if we include those who are in the youth and adult sectors of our population — we can count on a vast strategic minority of thirty million through which we can build widespread social understanding. Given the facts of our world and surrounded by an atmosphere of study and thought rather than one of propaganda and hysteria, this great American bloc represents enough mental capacity to comprehend the real working of our economic-social system, to judge roughly of the feasibility of political plans and policies, to estimate the abilities and characters of our legislative, executive, and judicial representatives and to appraise their success or failure in office.

These 30,000,000 Americans, if they are intelligently informed and imbued with good spirit and intentions, can build coöperatively a social understanding that will carry America successfully through her great crisis. But to do it educators must create a nation-wide program of adult education. Just as truly as in the years 1917–1918 and 1941–1946, we are at war! At war with forces that may indeed destroy mankind. This war situation must be met with a war-like psychological program. Every agency of communication must be coördinated in a great organism of education.

The Power of an Adult-Education Program in Creative Politics

With the head start that we now have in the use of adult study-discussion methods, imagine what a great central agency like the Office of Education of the United States could do now. Imagine in every community of the country a program of forums and discussion groups combined with the press, the motion picture, television, and the radio:

–a million study-discussion clubs — yes, a million — one in every one of the neighborhoods of America, organized around alert citizens, including teachers, as leaders;

–ten thousand weekly forums, panels, and round tables in the school-houses, theaters, and municipal auditoriums of the nation . . . conservatives of the center-to-right and progressives of the center-to-left on the same platform;

–national radio hookups of similar "town meetings," panels, and round tables, listened to and discussed by a million study clubs;

–"Four Minute" or "Ten Minute" men and newsreel shorts in the movie houses of the nation every week in the year;

–the curricula of a hundred thousand senior high school and college classes made over to incorporate this study of winning the peace.

And . . . as for materials! This campaign would require a pamphlet-bulletin-article-book-writing program that would dwarf anything ever dreamed of in this or any other country. The nation's finest novelists, poets, essayists, columnists, and other publicists, drafted to write. Drafted, we say. The nation's scholars in the social sciences — economics, politics, government, history, sociology, social psychology, and public opinion — drafted to organize topics, to outline material, to collaborate with the professional writers in preparing books, pamphlets, bulletins, and articles printed by government printing presses and syndicated at cost throughout the country.

We have merely lifted the curtain a bit on the kind of scene that we could stage in our educational drama in the next few years. This is our moment to make dreams come true. Long have we looked toward a millennial day when the American citizenry would become intelligent and alert, when understanding and tolerance would be abroad in the land. The dawn of that new day is now on the horizon.

Further Studies in Adult Education

1. Make a study of the available resources for adult education in your own community. Visit some of the groups that are now carrying on such work. (Analyze the conditions and factors in the community life that have brought them about.) Find out how well they are attended. How do the group leaders get people to join? Search for areas and needs that are not being satisfied by these programs of adult education.

2. Interview several people who are now taking part, or have taken part recently, in such programs. Find out what persuaded them to participate. What obstacles did they have to overcome? What are they getting out of it? Who are the teachers? Interview the teachers if possible.

3. Interview several people who are not engaging in such adult-educational ventures. As tactfully as possible try to find out why not. Discuss social problems of the day with them to see how much interest they have in such matters. Discover their recreational or creative interests. Do you think they might be persuaded to join in study and discussion groups?

4. Try to discover instances of older people in your community who in middle or old age have successfully taken up new kinds of study, creative work, or other means of personal cultivation; instances in painting, for example, like that of Grandma Moses. If there are such persons in your neighborhood, arrange to have talks with them about what they are doing.

5. Discuss how the teaching in an adult-education group would differ from that carried on in a high school or college class.

What to Read

One of the most interesting introductions to the recent development in adult education, especially for its many case histories of individuals and groups, is Harry and Bonaro Overstreet's *Leaders for Adult Education*. From that go to Elsie Clapp's *Community Schools in Action*, referred to earlier. For the exciting developments in adult education in the TVA see Maurice Seay's (Editor) *Adult Education*.

The problem of developing forums for public discussion is well discussed in former Commissioner of Education John W. Studebaker's *Plain Talk*. Mary I. Ely's *Adult Education in Action* discusses the same problem, indicating reasons for success and failure in specific instances.

The American Association for Adult Education has for many years published a periodic *Handbook of Adult Education in the United States*. The latest one (1948) is called *Community Education in Action*; it will bring you up to date on active programs based on community needs now going on in our country. Gaynell Hawkins' *Education for Social Understanding* reports types of programs of case work and group work agencies.

On the role of libraries see Alvin Johnson's *The Public Library — a People's University*; also *Libraries and Adult Education*, a report of the American Library Association. Other general surveys of the subject can be found in Ruth Kotinsky's *Adult Education and the Social Scene*, and in Lyman Bryson's *Adult Education*.

Part IV, "Social Chaos and the Public Mind," of Harold Rugg's *The Great Technology*, written at the depth of the depression of the 1930's, is a statement of the over-all problem of adult education in our changing society.

Advanced students should go to the four distinguished volumes of the Report of the Commission on Freedom of the Press: *A Free and Responsible Press*, the over-all interpretation of the Commission; Llewellyn White's *The American Radio*, its amazing growth and need for reorganization; Ruth Inglis's *Freedom of the Movies*, the social role of the film and attempts at self-regulation; and Llewellyn White and Robert Leigh's *Peoples Speaking to Peoples*, an analysis of international understanding through free access to the agencies of communication.

You should also have at hand one or more guides to the problem of group discussion. We suggest the following: Harrison S. Elliott's *The Process of Group Thinking*, M. P. Follett's *Creative Experience*, James H. McBurney and K. Hance's *Principles and Methods of Discussion*, Alfred D. Sheffield's *Creative Discussion*, and Frank Walser's *The Art of Conference*.

CHAPTER 8

Does Our Democracy Provide Education for All Children?

It is clear that the American people have the makings of a great and democratic school system. In spite of our tremendous physical achievement — 50,000,000 Americans doing something personally about education — we confront two startling sets of facts:

First: Of our gigantic financial resources we use only a tiny part for our schools.

Second: We believe in equality of opportunity for all our people . . . yet we practice a tragic inequality in the opportunity we provide huge numbers of Americans.

Why these contradictions?
We have two very important questions:

–Do the people understand how crucial is universal education of a high order for a democratic society?

–Do the people themselves actually decide how much educational opportunity the children of all the people shall have?

We introduce these questions here. Their full answers can be the result only of years of study.

The American School System

ONE HUNDRED YEARS ago there were almost no organized school systems in the United States. The Founding Fathers had not foreseen the need for public education; in fact, no definite plans for education can be found in the national Constitution. By 1820, however, state legislatures had drawn up partial programs. There were a few scattered state universities, boards of education, and school executives who did the work that superintendents do today. A little group of normal schools existed, but there were no colleges of education or teachers colleges as we know them today. As we write this book we are, in a sense, celebrating the hundredth anniversary of the first organized city "grammar school" — The Quincy Grammar School of Boston.

But today, what a transformation! Every aspect of education has changed. The entire continent has been covered by a huge network of schools, so that every one of the 18,000 chartered communities, every one of the 100,000 country districts, in fact, every one of the 1,000,000 neighborhoods of America can now send its children to school.

Continent-wide, our school system is one of the nation's biggest non-profit enterprises. It is perhaps the world's greatest social achievement, and it was all built in a century. For thousands of years human beings had lived in organized societies without popular systems of education as we know them today. The mass of the people were illiterate, in a sense ignorant. They were unaware of the enormous resources for the good life that lay undeveloped all around them. Then, in the second quarter of the nineteenth century there was launched in our United States one of the most thrilling adventures. We date the drama from about 1840, although the prologue was being enacted in the previous

197

decades. In the same century in which the entire continent was conquered for the social use of mankind, the Americans built the structure
of *the first free universal system of education* in the world.

Fifty Years of Growth — Testimony to the American's Faith in Education

Our Potentially Great Educational System Today

First, a few facts about our educational system in order to get the
whole picture before us. Some of these facts are so arresting that they
are scarcely believable, but remember that our statements are based on
official statistics gathered by our United States Office of Education.

First: Not less than 50 million Americans are devoting at least part
of their time and energy to education. This is more than one third of
all our people, for the total population now, at the mid-century, is estimated at nearly 147 million.

Second: Thirty million of these Americans are devoting their full
working lives to education. Over 25 million of them are children and
youth in elementary and secondary schools. Some three million are
in colleges, universities, and technical and professional schools. One
million three hundred thousand are teachers.

Third: Thus, the number of people being educated in America today
is more than the corresponding number in all of eastern Asia with its
500 million Chinese and 400 million Indians, and more than are being
educated in the twenty republics of Central and South America.

This fact of *a third of a nation personally concerned with education*
is the chief witness to our belief in the democratic way of life. For the
democratic way is based on intelligent understanding by the people, and
continuous education is the only route to understanding. Here is an
army enlisted in the carrying on of the good life — 30 million human
beings devoting themselves to trying to understand the world in which
they are living — 30 million people committing themselves to building
the good life and permanent world peace, for here is the one sure way,
even if it be gradual and slow, to build world peace. And here is the
way, the only way, to prevent Jim Crow laws, the poll tax, and frighten-

ing periods of unemployment. If we are to get a system in which all men really will be brothers and in which there will be no unemployment, the first step is in the building of understanding among the people.

Here, then, are the makings!

A half century of astonishing growth brought these makings into being. On the adjacent pages are some official statistics which you can keep at hand for reference. They show the swift speed with which the people invested their money in better schools and steadily kept their children longer and longer in school.

To make the comparison clearer, we also give the growth of population in the United States during the same years. As you study the tables, bear in mind that in the fifty years population in America practically doubled: 75 million in 1900, over 150 million for 1950.

Growth in Population of the United States

1900	75,602,515
1920	105,710,620
1930	122,775,046
1940	131,669,275
1950	150,500,000

Total Enrollment in Public Elementary and Secondary Schools

YEAR	ENROLLMENT	PER CENT OF 5–17 AGE GROUP
1900	15,503,110	72.43
1920	21,578,316	77.8
1930	25,678,015	81.3
1940	25,433,542	85.5
1950	26,635,000	88.0 (?)
1960 (estimate)	34,091,000	

The Slow Growth of the Elementary Schools

First, note that the total number of pupils in elementary and secondary schools did not grow so rapidly as certain special aspects of the school system. For example, there were 15 million in 1900 and 23 million in 1946; this was an increase of only about 60 per cent, three fifths as large as the increase in population. Why? For one thing, most of the children of elementary school age *were in school* in 1900; for another, the size of the family and the number of children have been declining steadily. This is driven home by the facts on the number of children in elementary schools; there were only 14 per cent more in 1946 than in 1900. Nevertheless, the increase in the percentage of children in school means that the drawing power and the holding power of the school was increasing.

Enrollment in Public Elementary Schools (Kdg. to 8th Grades)

	BOYS	GIRLS	TOTAL
1900.........	7,600,151	7,383,708	14,983,859
1920.........	9,781,793	9,596,134	19,377,927
1930.........	10,842,259	10,436,334	21,278,593
1940.........	9,681,465	9,150,633	18,832,098
1946.........	9,098,013	8,579,731	17,677,774

That the power of the schools to reach and teach the young people did increase markedly is shown by the number of days schools were in session each year. This number increased from 144 to 176 and the (average) attendance increased 50 per cent. Moreover, the teaching staff more than doubled in the fifty years.

Instructional Staff of Public School Supervisors, Principals, and Teachers

1900	423,062
1920	677,867
1930	880,365
1940	911,835
1946	867,248

If you add to these 900,000 *public school* staff members all those engaged in private schools, the instructional and directive staffs of colleges, universities, technical and professional schools, and adult educative institutions, *the total staff is 1,300,000.*

The Swift Expansion of the High Schools

But the next two tables tell the real story of the advancing faith of our people in education. *Thirteen times as many young people were in high schools in 1940 as there were forty years earlier:* 6,500,000 against 500,000. And *sixteen times as many were graduated from high school!* Only 71,000 were graduated in 1900; forty years later 1,100,000 were

Number of Pupils in Public Secondary Schools including Postgraduate

	BOYS	GIRLS	TOTAL
1899–1900.........	216,207	303,044	519,251
1920.........	992,664	1,207,725	2,200,389
1930.........	2,115,228	2,284,194	4,399,422
1940.........	3,250,952	3,350,492	6,601,444
1946.........	2,633,117	2,989,080	5,622,197

Number of Public High School Graduates

1900	71,410
1920	275,238
1930	605,457
1940	1,143,246
1946	974,407

graduated. And the figures on college enrollment and graduation drastically confirm the amazing expansion of education in our country during this period.

The People's Faith Shown by the Money Spent

Perhaps the best measure of the Americans' belief in anything is the amount of money they will spend for it. The next six tables give the chief changes in the facts about the financing of schools. In 1946 the American people had *ten times as much money invested per pupil* in school buildings, land, and equipment as in 1900: $35.00 in 1900, $351.00 in 1946. Moreover, they spent *fourteen times as much to run their schools* in 1946 as in 1900 ($2,707,000,000 against $180,000,000). And they spent eight times as much per pupil attending.

Average Value of School Property per Pupil in Average Daily Attendance

1900	$ 35.00
1920	112.00
1930	242.00
1940	300.00
1948	401.00

Current Expense per Pupil in Average Daily Attendance

1900	$ 16.88
1920	54.65
1930	86.70
1940	88.09
1948	178.71

Grand Total of Public School Expenditures

1900	$ 214,964,618
1920	1,036,151,209
1930	2,316,790,384
1940	2,344,048,927
1947	3,124,550,348

Another indication of the belief of the people in education is the money spent for summer schools and adult schools — nothing in 1900 . . . $3,000,000 in 1920 . . . almost four times as much twenty years later. The people's growing faith in the teachers is shown by the fact that they paid the typical public school educator nearly eight times as much in 1948 as in 1900 — $2440.00 per year against $325.00 per year!

Expenditures for Public Summer and Adult Schools		Average Salary of Teachers, Supervisors, and Principals	
1900	————	1900	$ 325.00
1920	$ 3,276,593	1920	871.00
1930	9,824,827	1930	1420.00
1940	13,367,139	1940	1441.00
1946	11,447,415	1948	2440.00

Finally, another test of the people's belief in education is the extent to which they are willing to put their children in private schools, and pay the fees of such schools in addition to supporting public schools by taxation. The figures show nearly 3,000,000 children in private and parochial schools in 1946, twice as many as in 1900. The increase in the

Pupils in Private and Parochial Schools

YEAR	ELEMENTARY	SECONDARY	TOTAL
1900..........	1,240,925	110,797	1,240,925
1920..........	1,485,561	213,920	1,699,481
1930..........	2,309,886	341,158	2,651,044
1940..........	2,153,279	457,768	2,611,047
1946..........	2,259,392	565,108	2,824,500

number and per cent of children in *private schools* was not, however, so great as the increase in public schools; in fact, it increased no more rapidly than the population itself. The faith of our people is predominantly in public education.

How Much Schooling Have American Grownups Had?

Summing up the situation to the present moment: How far has this swift growth actually affected the people? How much schooling have they had? The situation for the entire country is summed up in the map on page 204. In two thirds of the states the grownup population today has had nearly nine years of schooling; in three of the states — California, Nevada, and Utah — nearly eleven years. For the entire United States the average number of years of schooling completed was

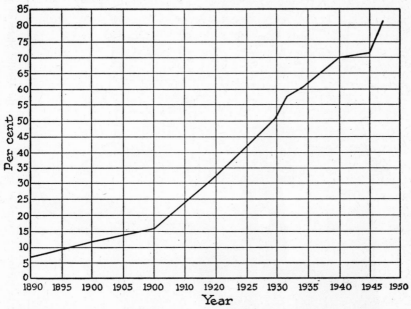

Enrollment of children of high school age in the public and private schools of the United States since 1890. (Adapted from Newton Edwards, *Equal Educational Opportunity for Youth,* Report to the American Youth Commission, American Council on Education.)

eight and eight tenths. The graph of high school enrollment throws more light on the increase in interest in education. In 1890 only 7 per cent of the children of high school age were enrolled in schools; in 1947, 81 per cent — nearly twelve times as many.

The Achievement: Schools for All Children in Every Community

As a consequence of these educational achievements, nearly every American child can today have access to a school. In every district of

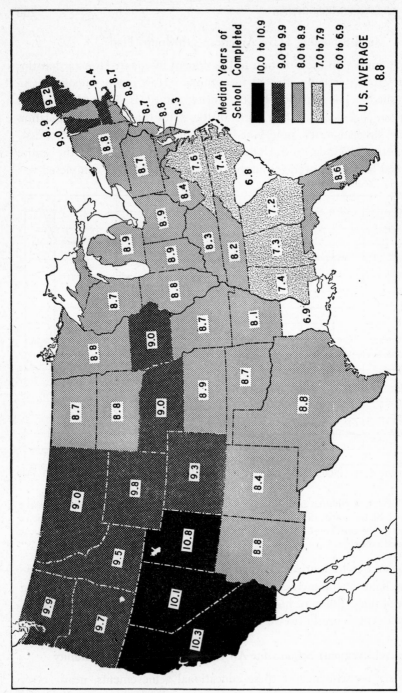

Median years of schooling completed by persons 20 years of age and over in the United States in 1940. (From F. L. Schaigle and W. E. Gibbons, *NEA Leader Letter*, No. 34, March, 1945. Used by permission.)

the 18,000 chartered communities (villages, towns, and cities) of our country a child can find a public, tax-supported school. In many of the larger communities there are nursery and kindergarten schools for children under the age of six. In his own community the child can go to an elementary school. Either near at home or within a few miles of home one of America's 28,973 public secondary schools is ready to receive him.

Number of Schools Available to Children under Six Years of Age (1942) [1]

SCHOOLS	NURSERY	NURSERY-KINDER-GARTEN	KINDERGARTEN
Private	300	478	309
College laboratory ...	69	53	73
Special (Handicapped children)	25	10	10
Public	30		
	424	541	392

[1] U. S. Office of Education, Bulletin No. 5, 1947. No public school nursery-kindergarten and kindergarten data are given, since they are grouped by the Office of Education with elementary schools.

The Office says: "Limited reports for 1946–47 suggest a continuing demand for these neighborhood schools for young children."

Number of Elementary and Secondary Schools in the United States [1]

SCHOOLS	PUBLIC	PRIVATE	TOTAL
Elementary ...	169,905 *	10,285	180,190
Secondary	28,973	3,011	31,984

[1] Biennial Survey of Education Statistics of State School Systems, 1945–46, Chapter II. U. S. Office of Education, 1949.
* This figure includes 24,314 kindergartens and one-teacher schools.

According to the latest survey, the nation offered its youth 1768 institutions of higher education. In more than 700 cities and towns the young student will find a college or university. In over 200 of these communities he will find a public college, giving him a complete 14- to 16-year system of education.

Higher Educational Institutions in the United States, 1946–47 [1]

Universities and colleges	764
Technical and professional schools	287
Teachers colleges and normal schools; of these 217 are public, 36 are private ..	253
Junior colleges	464
Total	1768

[1] Facts from the U. S. Office of Education *Statistical Circular*, April, 1949.

So much for the 30 million children, youth, and grownups who are devoting themselves primarily to the work of education. But in addition to these, 25 million other Americans are taking part in some kind of systematic *adult* education. Expressed in approximate round numbers, the major groups are as follows:

–6,000,000 are studying in one form or another of agricultural extension.

–5,000,000 are brought together regularly in various kinds of educational radio programs.

–1,000,000 are engaged in *each* of these four types: private correspondence schools, library groups, lyceums and Chautauquas, men's and women's clubs

–2,000,000 are in each of indoor recreation groups and adult groups organized under public schools.

Recall the vast machinery that has been created for adult study and discussion — tens of thousands of government-organized groups, thousands of local branches of a score of big national organizations, several thousand centers in public libraries, a huge program over the radio, motion picture, and theater, and groups in hundreds of museums, associations, and conferences.

In short, totaling full-time and part-time participants, *more than a third of the American people are actively organized for education. This is the tremendous enterprise in which you, as a prospective educator, are about to embark.*

America's Financial Capacity to Support Schools

When citizens ask local officials and politicians to expand the facilities of education for their children, one chronic answer is given: "Can't afford it! Costs too much! Haven't got the money!"

Is that true? The picture we have just sketched does not convey a feeling of a poverty-stricken nation unable to finance good schools for its children. But it is very important that every American teacher know the facts of the nation's financial resources if he is to be a missionary for the improvement of our schools; therefore we shall review the matter briefly.

The National Purchasing Power and Its Use for Schools

Perhaps the quickest way to get at our capacity to support schools is to look at the facts of the "real" national income. The graph on this

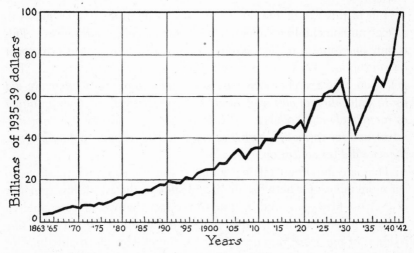

Real income produced in the United States from 1863 to 1942. (From Paul T. David, *Postwar Youth Employment*, American Council on Education.)

page pictures the facts for eighty years, covering both the periods of prosperity and of unemployment and depression. In the middle 1930's, for example, in the worst stage of the Great Depression, with 15 million people out of work and factories, mines, and farms standing still, the

American people altogether received a total "real" income of less than 42 billion dollars. This was only a little more than half their total income — 70 billion dollars — in 1928, just before the beginning of the economic depression.

Social engineers and economists who made careful studies of our producing system in the 1930's agreed that if the factories and farms were fully put to work, three times as much income could be produced for the people. Many cautious and conservative economists ridiculed this view. But when World War II came, the entire production was put to work; all the people did get employment. The great crisis gave impetus to the entire economic system, and the engineers' predictions came true. The graph shows that even in the first year of the war 100 billion dollars of "real" income was produced. Since 1945 the amount has reached 125 billion dollars, three times that of 1932.

Here is a gigantic natural income, yet many experts expect it to be doubled in the near future as the economic system becomes even more efficient.

But of this 125 billion dollars we spend only three billion dollars to give 25 million children and youth a school and college education. This is only *one fortieth of the national income, two to three per cent spent on education!* Do we truly have faith in education? Let us see. The graph on page 209 shows that *we spent more for tobacco than we did for the education of all the children. We spent twice as much for liquor as for schools and colleges. We spent more for jewelry to adorn ourselves, and for cosmetics, barber services, and admissions to amusements, than we did for education.*

Here are important talking points as you campaign with citizens to get more money for better schools. In spite of the astonishing progress of the past fifty years, and in spite of the fact that we educate children and youth better than any other country in the world, *we use but a tiny fraction of our giant resources for education.* The shortsightedness of our people is shown by the fact that *without at least universal secondary education they cannot come to understand their social-economic system — how to keep it running efficiently and how to maintain peace in the world under the democratic method.*

Study this problem carefully in order that you may take part in discussing it with the citizens of your community. Show them that if we

can avoid economic depressions and keep the farms, mines, and factories working full tilt, our people can have an abundant physical life
under the democratic way of living, and also have enough money to
put a vast amount into the development of good schools. The citizens, not knowing the facts, will consistently ask you: "But how much

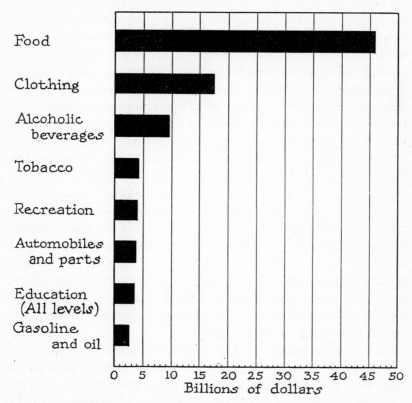

Expenditures for selected goods and service compared with public elementary and
secondary schools, 1942.

will good schools cost? Do we really have a great enough national
wealth to give us the kinds of schools educators say our children need?"
One of the first ways to become informed about the nation's capacity to
support education is to look at the problem historically. How much
have we actually spent for education in previous years, and for what
did we spend it?

How Well Do Americans Support Schools?

A glance at the graph on page 211, covering the growth in educational expenditures for a period of 75 years, will perhaps bring the answer: "Very well indeed! What an astounding development!" Yes, the growth has been swift. In 1870 the American people spent less than 100 million dollars in a year, on all their public schools. In 1940 — even before the beginning of World War II and the full running of the economic system — they spent $2,400,000,000; this was twenty-four times as much. The contrast with the growth of population during these years is impressive. *The number of people multiplied only threefold, but they spent twenty-four times as much money on their schools.* (This is not an accurate comparison, for the dollar in 1870 did not have the same value as in 1940, but the general conclusion to be drawn is approximately the same.) Here, then, is another graphic revelation of the faith of the people in free, publicly supported education.

Such a general over-all curve can be supplemented by more detailed facts; such, for example, as those shown on page 216. There are states, such as New York, in which more than $4000 is spent per year *on a single classroom*, while in half the states of the country approximately $2000 per classroom is spent. Is this a large amount? It is indeed! If an educated citizen of Yugoslavia or any other eastern European country, or any Latin American country, should hear such a statement, he would gasp with astonishment, for it is vastly more than their people can spend on the teaching of their children.

What kind of teacher can New York school boards get if they spend $4000 on a classroom? Remember that half of them — the larger and richer communities — spend more than this amount, half of them less. Can they pay a $4000-a-year salary to the teacher of the class? No, they can pay not more than $2000 to $3000, for only about two thirds of all school expenditures can go to teachers, principals, and other supervisors. The other third must be used for general expenses of heating and care of buildings, supplies, equipment, administration, etc. Similarly, a $2000 expenditure per classroom means probably that not more than $1400 or $1500 is being paid to the teacher. If these salaries seem small, remember that they are several times as large as those paid in most of the countries of the world today.

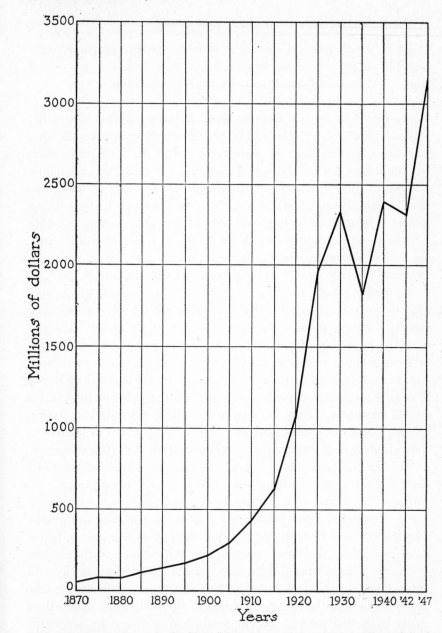

Public school expenditures in the United States from 1870 to 1943. (From *School Expenditures in War and Peace*, NEA Research Bulletin, October 1945. Used by permission.)

Where Does the Money for Schools Come From?

Even though three billion dollars is much less than progressive educators think we should spend for schools, nevertheless, it is a lot of money. Where does this revenue for schools come from?

In 1943–44, 65.6 per cent of all school monies came from a local property tax, 33.0 per cent from the state, and only 1.4 per cent from the national government. Thus, most of our school money comes from local taxes, that is, *taxes on property owned in the local community*. No doubt this is what you would expect in a country that constantly emphasizes the "grass-roots." There are, indeed, states in which the town or the city contributes practically all of the support; about 96 per cent of it is so raised in Iowa and New Hampshire. But at the other extreme there are states in which local support is almost entirely lacking — as in Delaware, where it is approximately only 12 per cent. In Delaware the state contributes 87.7 per cent of all the money spent.

Formerly, almost all school support came from local taxes; from 1920 to 1930, 80 per cent of the cost of public schools was obtained from that source, about 15 per cent coming from the state. However, since the beginning of the economic depression of the thirties, many local communities have been unable to raise sufficient money for schools, and the state governments have had to help. By the outbreak of World War II the state governments were contributing nearly one third of the cost of education. Thus, as usual in our variegated American system, you can find every kind of support. But 90-odd per cent of the money comes from local or state support — almost nothing from federal sources.

Within the local school district, monies for schools are obtained chiefly by a tax on general property; this is divided among schools, departments of police and fire, public health, sanitation, recreation, water, roads, streets, parks, playgrounds, etc. Thus the people's faith in education is revealed through the fact that those who own homes, household goods, and other "real" property pay the expenses of the schools. In rare cases "local" means the county, not the village, town, or city. In a few states, as in Nevada, three fourths of the money expended for education is raised in the county; in eleven of the states more than a third comes from that source. But in nearly half of the states practically nothing is received from the counties; in the country as a whole, not more than a sixteenth comes from the county governments.

What about the United States government as a source of income for education? For the carrying on of the basic work of the elementary and secondary school, *the federal government contributes practically nothing.* We boast of the "grass-roots" nature of our civilization, and we exemplify it by not only letting the citizens of the village, the town, and the city decide the amount and kind of schooling they want, but we let them pay for it as well.

Perhaps you are wondering how, when local cities and towns cannot raise the money necessary for the schools, can the state government do so? Certainly the towns in some states constitute a large share of the population and have much of the wealth, too. That is true, but there are special resources in the state governments. One resource is that the states have "permanent school funds." In the first hundred years of our national life, as the states were formed out of the western lands, whole sections (640 acres) of land were set aside for the use of schools. As time passed, many of these lands became very valuable, and the income from them was put into permanent school funds. These funds have been still further built up through other federal grants, taxes for internal improvements, other "surplus revenue" from the sale of lands, and royalties on forest reserves and other natural resources. By and large, however, the total amount from most of these permanent school funds was not over one per cent of the amount spent for the nation's schools.

Summing it all up — remember that nearly two thirds of our financial support of public schools comes from the citizens in the local community.

Shortcomings of American Education

It is true that we have the makings of a great system of education. Our resources and capacity are established beyond question. Magnificent first steps have been taken. But the finished product is far from achieved. Insistent problems and questions confront us. One question stands out above all others: To what extent does the good education that is potentially possible actually reach *all the people?*

The American goal is expressed in the great ideal of the American people, *Equal Opportunity for All.* The American dream is that every individual shall have the fullest opportunity to rise to the highest stature that is in him and to guarantee that he shall be helped in every possible way to make the most of himself.

In practical terms applied to education this means that the people of any region in America shall have just as good schools as those in any other. All of their children would go: infants to the nursery school, children to the elementary school, and adolescents and youth to the high school. Large numbers would go to college, and communities would find the way to give continuing adult education to relatively all the people. This is the ideal.

The Need for Equalizing Educational Opportunity

But the achievement falls far short of the ideal. Opportunities for education are not equal. There are many little communities where children cannot get a secondary education, and where good teachers are not to be found in the elementary schools, just as there are hundreds of counties in America where there are no hospitals and other indispensable services of a good society. There are, indeed, communities in which there are no elementary schools — where, in rare events, fathers and mothers are taught to read and write with the same books used by their six-year-olds. And there are hundreds of thousands of families that lack the money for shoes and adequate clothing with which to send their children to school even if such schools were available. Educational opportunity is not yet equal in America.

The key to the whole problem lies in the dependence on local or state — not national — initiative. The nub lies in the vast differences in the natural resources and the condition of the people in different parts of the country. In some regions the resources in soil, forests, minerals, and other economic materials with which to build a well-to-do society are not and never have been available. Hence the people who settled on the land in such regions and tried to build a competence with which to bring up and educate their children were unable to do so. In some regions the natural resources once were abundant — virgin soil, grass and timber, huge stores of coal and oil — but they were wasted by the thoughtless people who settled and exploited them. The soil was worn out, squandered by the land-hungry. The timber, coal, and oil were taken out carelessly by those who were concerned only to get rich quick. Thus the first owners often wasted the resources. They did not put back into the land and into the forests what they took out; thus they deprived their children of adequate resources for the good life. If these people knew the Principle of the Sustained-Yield, they certainly did not apply it.

The result of such conditions today is shown in clear numerical terms in the graph on page 209. What a picture is presented of individual differences!

Contrast conditions in such states as New York, California, and New Jersey with others such as Mississippi, Arkansas, Kentucky, and Alabama. *Children who study in classrooms in New Jersey, Washington, California, and New York get an education three or four times as well supported as those in Mississippi, Arkansas, Alabama, and Georgia.* The wealth of the nation is heavily concentrated in certain sections — the northeast, north central, and west coast states. It is these, as you can see from the graph on page 216, that support education most liberally — $200.00 and more per pupil. Twelve states spend less than $150.00 per pupil, four of them less than $100.00. In these twelve states live over thirty million people, one fifth of our nation's population, whose schools are sadly lacking in the financial support given schools in the other thirty-six states. It is clear that, barring federal aid, *the people in some of the states of America will have to tax themselves from five to eight times as heavily as those in other states* in order to provide the same amount and kind of education for their children.

Next, consider the contrast between the financial capacity of the rural and the urban sections of America to support schools. The table on page 217, for example, shows that although the rural regions of America have more of the school-age population, nevertheless, the towns spend about fifty per cent more per pupil and more than twice as much for school property. The towns and cities have more wealth, but the countryside has more children. Hence, with their larger financial means the town children go to school approximately 180 days in the year; the rural school children, about 167 days. In the southern parts of our country, children attend school less than 120 days per year. In 1937–1938 the average salary paid to rural teachers was $864; that for town and city teachers was $1952 — over twice as much. Only two thirds as much was spent for current expenses per pupil in average daily attendance in rural schools as in town and city schools.

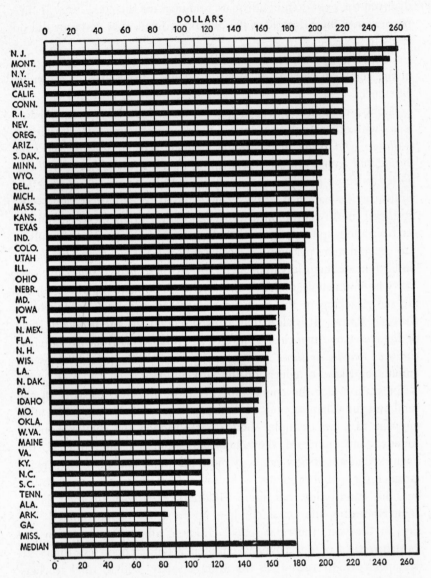

Current expense (including interest) per pupil in average daily attendance during the
school year 1947–48. (Data from *The Forty-eight State School Systems*. Chicago: The Council of State Governments; 1949.)

Yet the bulk of our national school system is located in rural schools, especially in one-teacher schools. In 1945–46 there were 184,541 elementary and secondary schools in the country; 86,563 of these, almost half, were one-teacher schools! Three states, Illinois, Iowa, and Missouri, each have more than 5000 one-teacher school units. This generally means a poorly paid teacher, an inadequate amount of materials

Comparison of Urban and Rural Public Day Schools 1941–42 [1]

	URBAN	RURAL
Population 1940	74,423,702	57,245,573
Population 5–17 years of age, inclusive 1940	14,703,957	15,041,289
Average length of school term	181.3	167.2
Number attending daily for each 100 enrolled	84.2	87.3
Average salary of instructional staff	2013	1018
Current expense per pupil (excluding interest) in average daily attendance .	114.61	80.44
Estimated value of property per pupil enrolled	429	200

[1] Source: U. S. Office of Education, *Statistical Summary of Education* 1943–44, page 12.

given the teacher, and building and equipment far below what young Americans should be using. Yet the table on this page shows that while the number of human beings of school age (5 to 17 years inclusive) is almost exactly the same in rural and urban regions, the estimated value of school property per pupil enrolled was $429 for the urban schools, but only $200 for rural schools — more than twice as much for city as for country schools.

Consider also the discrimination between whites and Negroes in educational opportunity. In the towns and cities the average white person 25 years old and over has completed 9.6 years of schooling; the Negro, 6.8. The rural farm native whites have completed 8 years; the rural farm Negroes, 4.1 years — half as much.

Or consider the educational differences among the varying income groups in America. Howard Bell, in his *Youth Tell Their Story*, shows that twelve out of thirteen of the professional-technical fathers went beyond the eighth grade of school, but only one out of eight of the laborers on the farms of the United States went as far as this. Two out of three of the skilled mechanics and five out of six of the managers of business and industry went into high school, but only one out of three of the unskilled mechanics. Such facts measure the inequality in educational opportunity in America.

These are the facts. For fifty years forward-looking citizens and the nation's educational leaders have faced these facts. Decade after decade they have sought various ways out of the impasse.

Federal Aid for Education

One solution of the problem of educational inequality has been to try to get the federal government to give financial aid to the poorer states. Time after time bills have been proposed in Congress, granting from 100 to 300 million dollars to equalize financial inequalities among the states. Paralleling these attempts to get federal aid, additional provision for taxation has been sought to help the poorer states. On the great democratic principle of equal opportunity for all Americans, these plans would take from those who have and give to those who have not. Behind the plan is the idea that *all the children of all the people should be financed by all of the resources of all the people* — that the chance of being born in a land-poor, resource-poor region should not work against the educational rights of the individual.

Yet, up to the present moment all of the proposals for direct federal aid for education to the states have been defeated. In some instances the House of Representatives has passed the Federal Aid to Education Bill; in other instances, the Senate. In rare cases both houses have passed the bill, only to have it vetoed by the President. Year after year the forces against it have been too strong. What are these forces? Who is against equalizing the vast inequalities in educational opportunity?

One body of opposition has been the private educational interests, the big private colleges and universities. These include both nonsectarian and church schools and colleges. Their leaders insist that if federal aid is to be given, it must be given for private institutions as well as for public ones. Other opponents use the argument that American democracy is built on the fundamental principle of local initiative, responsibility, and control. They point out that if the national government grants money to help regions, states, or local communities, it will "follow the money" into those regions and communities and control its instruction.

It is *federal control* that this latter group fear: the destruction of the historic American idea of local, or "grass-roots," initiative and control. They point to the fact that the Smith-Hughes Act — the Vocational Education Law of 1917 — did that very thing in appropriating and distributing money to the schools of the states to assist in the development of vocational agriculture. The opponents of federal aid say that the administration of the Smith-Hughes funds specified, and thereby controlled, the kind of instruction to be given. They cry out against bureaucracy in government. With that, they also state dramatically and with local pride that their state must not be forced to become the "stepchild" of the national government.

In 1938, President Roosevelt's Advisory Committee on Education discussed and proposed federal aid in their report. They urged only a limited amount of control, such as would guarantee honest and efficient handling of the funds, but insisted on leaving real control of instruction to the states and localities. They recommended that a general fund for elementary and secondary schools be created; also, that in the states which segregated Negro pupils, the funds must be equitably distributed between the two. But the bill that grew out of these recommendations was also defeated.

The American Ideal Applied to Financing All the Schools of All the Children

There are other educators and citizens who maintain that federal aid is not the solution — that it is only patchwork. The true idea, they insist, is that the nation's gigantic resources shall be viewed as a great national pool of wealth upon which the children of any one state have just as much right to draw as those of any other. As there is a federal income tax that now raises $40,000,000,000 a year, so, says this school of thought, there should be included a federal tax for schools that would raise whatever sum of money is needed to give every child in America as good an education as the resources permit; this money would be distributed to individual states in such a manner that the children of any one state would have the same educational opportunity as those in any other.

While this proposal is in accord with the American ideal, to carry it out would involve such drastic changes that no one has any expectation of early enactment. The wealthy states oppose it, of course; and they have the larger proportion of the population and control the Congress. Unless the amount now spent for all education in the nation (over $3,000,000,000) were to be vastly increased — tripled, quadrupled, or even multiplied more than that — the education in New York, California, and other richer states would be seriously curtailed. The idealists say: "Of course it should be enormously increased! We, a rich nation, are niggardly in educating our young people." Let us spend 10 billion dollars . . . no, 15 billion dollars a year, or more, for education. We spend more than that for *war*, even in peacetime. The best way to guarantee permanent peace is to educate all the people, not to build armies and navies.

This is the ideal held before our eyes as we study the actual condition in our schools.

What You Can Do about the Problem of Equalizing Educational Opportunity

Certainly one thing you can do is to understand the educational situation in your own community and state, and in the state and community in which you teach.

1. Make a study of a recent annual school report of your own community. Find out the answers to such questions as:

–How many children and youth are in elementary and secondary schools?

–What percentage of high school graduates go to college? What percentage do not go to college? What are the reasons?

–How much is spent on education — elementary, secondary? How much per pupil? How does this compare with the total income index of the community? Do you think the community is adequately supporting education?

–Are there educational needs which the community has not met?

2. Have committees of your class coöperate in making a historical study of the growth of your local school system. The chief facts can be assembled from reports of the board of education and the superintendent of schools.

3. It would be stimulating to make a study of one of the newest school surveys. Try to get a copy of "A Look at the Springfield Schools" (a survey made by the Illini Survey Associates of the University of Illinois; published in 1948).

From some of these latest survey reports you can find good answers to questions like these (answered in the Springfield report):

–What are the earmarks of a good school?

–What is the determining philosophy of the schools?

–What does the public want in its schools?

–How far is the curriculum geared to life needs?

–What is the ability of the community to finance schools? Does the community actually provide the best schools it could achieve?

4. Get copies of your current state school reports and make similar studies of the state system.   For example, see such surveys of the curriculum, one aspect of state-wide programs, as the following:

–Alabama: *Course of Study and Teacher's Guide for the Elementary Schools, Grades One to Six.*   Curriculum Bulletin No. 8, State Board of Education, Montgomery, Alabama, 1941.

–Washington: *Temporary Guides for the Senior High Curriculum,* Bulletin No. 13, 1943; and *Temporary Guides for the Junior High School Curriculum,* Bulletin No. 14, 1944.   Office of the Superintendent of Public Instruction, State of Washington.

–New Mexico: *Curriculum Development in the Elementary Schools of New Mexico.*   State Department of Education, State of New Mexico, 1947.

–Maryland: *A Curriculum Study Guide.*   State Department of Education; Baltimore, Maryland, 1941.

–Virginia: *Course of Study for Virginia Elementary Schools, Grades I–VII.*   State Board of Education, Richmond, Virginia, 1943.

5. What percentage of the total cost of education in your state is provided (a) by the state, (b) from local sources?   Does your state get any federal aid for education?   How does your state rank with other states in its ability to support education?   Do you think this is satisfactory?   Justify your answer.

6. How have social and economic conditions in your region, in the last 25 years, brought about changes in its educational system?   Can you see any trend toward future development?

What to Read

On the growth and development of the American education system there are many detailed histories. R. Freeman Butts's A Cultural History of Education, Chapters 21 and 22, gives the overview story of its development. Harold Rugg's American Life and the School Curriculum, Chapters VI to XI, inclusive, is an elementary account of the rise of the American graded school and of attempts to reconstruct it. Edwards and Richey's The School in the American Social Order is the best history of the system in relation to population and social changes since 1860 and is an excellent analysis of its reorganization to meet the needs of society.

One of the most recent studies of the system is in American Education in the Post-War Period, Part II, "Structural Reorganization," the Forty-fourth Yearbook of the National Society for the Study of Education. The scope of public education today is discussed in Douglass's The American School System, and in other introductory volumes in education.

For brief current summaries of the statistics of the American educational system see such reports as the following:

NEA Research Bulletins:
    School Expenditures in War and Peace, 1945
    The Nation's Schools after a Year of War, 1943

NEA Discussion Pamphlets:
    No. 3. Planning Post War Education
    No. 4. Paying for Schools

United States Office of Education Bulletins:
    Biennial Survey of Education in the United States, 1943–44:
    "Advance Statistics of State School Systems," 1945–46
    Fall Enrollment in Higher Educational Institutions, 1947
    Statistical Circular, May, 1948

For current evaluations and appraisals of the American school system, including criticisms and proposed reorganization, see the following: Who Shall Be Educated?, by Warner, Havighurst, and Loeb, a careful discussion of the question of equality of educational opportunity; Howard Bell's Youth Tell Their Story, describing how Maryland schools met the needs of youth by reorganizing educational programs; Harold Hand's What People Think about Their Schools, a discussion of the techniques and values of obtaining the opinions of parents, students, and teachers regarding the school system; and an NEA Research Bulletin: *What People Think about Youth and Education.*

With special reference to the colleges, see the excellent report of the President's Commission on Higher Education, entitled *Higher Education for American Democracy*, especially the chapters dealing with the equalization of educational opportunity through a better financial program. President Conant of Harvard, in his *Education in a Divided World*, Chapters 4 to 8, appraises our present high school in terms of general education.

CHAPTER 9

"A teacher affects eternity; he can
never tell where his influence stops."

The Education of Henry Adams

OUR STUDY now comes to questions that you may well ask regarding certain practical aspects of teaching as a career.

–How important is education in American life?

–Is it merely a trade, or is it a high-ranking profession?

–How adequate are its rewards?

Perhaps the central problem of all is security. There are several kinds of security:

–economic security throughout life — the problem of tenure and pensions

–personal and psychological security — a deep sense of belonging and achievement, freedom to teach what you know to be true and believe to be right, freedom to lead your pupils in studying the personal and social problems of our people

One of the keys to security is organization of workers. We shall see how well the teachers have used it in providing security.

The American Profession of Education

IN THE EARLY DAYS of American education the teacher was a person hired to "keep the school," often with little preparation and background for teaching. After one or two terms he would go to another school or to an entirely different type of work. Teaching was a "way-station" job; few people thought seriously of making it a professional career. Then, as you know, the growth of schools and colleges paralleled the economic expansion of our country. Consequently, if you become a teacher today, you will join the largest professional group in our country.

Education: Profession or Trade?

There are now about 1,300,000 workers in education — more than in all the other professions — such as medicine, law, the church, and engineering — put together. Consider a typical city of 10,000 inhabitants, in which about a quarter of the people (2640) will be of "school age," and about a fifth (1980) will actually be attending schools. The teaching staff of 75 will play an important role in guiding the lives of *one fifth of the people*. In addition, these teachers will have close contacts with another third of the city's population, namely, the parents of the children attending the schools. As for the other professional people in the community, there will be: 13 lawyers and judges . . . 13 physicians and surgeons . . . 10 clergymen . . . 6 dentists, and others — a total of 42. Thus, in such a characteristic town there are nearly twice as many workers in education as the total number in the four other established professions.

225

Moreover, the number of educators is increasing; between 1920 and 1930 the number rose by 282,250. If our national school system should be reorganized to provide teaching in small classroom groups and if it should carry on all the special kinds of work that are needed and that our resources now make possible, we could use more than twice the number of individuals now employed in the profession. Some students

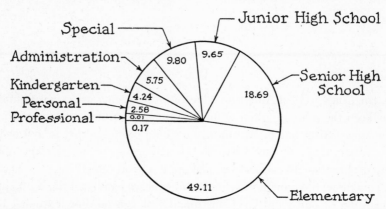

Percentage graph of various types of educational workers in 14 representative cities in the United States. (From Marjorie Rankin, *Trends in Educational Occupations,* Teachers College, Columbia University, Contributions to Education, No. 412, 1930.)

of education insist that in the not too distant future we shall have 3,000,000 trained and experienced educators in America.

Astonishing Variety of Jobs from Which to Choose

Had you thought that the educational profession would offer you narrow choices as to the nature of your work? Did you think of elementary education as only the teaching of reading, writing, and arithmetic — of high school teaching as history, language, the social studies, or mathematics? This might be true of your *first* teaching job, but if you go into education with the thought of staying in it permanently, you will find a vast range of opportunities opening before you.

Study the graphs which give the kinds of jobs available in the entire country. In the elementary schools there are more than 700,000 educational positions; in the high schools more than 200,000.

Marjorie Rankin's study shows that 93 per cent of the jobs fall into the five divisions described on the next page.

–Half the workers are in elementary schools.

–One fifth are in senior high schools.

–One tenth are in junior high schools.

–One tenth in special kinds of work.

–One twentieth are administrators — principals, superintendents, supervisors.

–Other jobs — about 7 per cent.

This study, made in fourteen small and large cities of the United States, showed that the schools provided 603 *different kinds of jobs.*

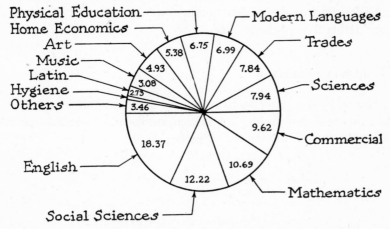

Kinds of high school teachers according to subject matter in 14 representative cities in the United States. (From Marjorie Rankin, *Trends in Educational Occupations.*)

Half of these were in the subject-matter fields, such as aeronautics, agriculture, architecture, biological sciences, commercial subjects, and languages. Each of these broad fields is subdivided into many specific "subjects." They offered 364 different teaching opportunities, certainly enough variety to suit the widest range of interests and abilities.

But in addition to these 364 teaching jobs, Miss Rankin found four other main kinds of work, each minutely subdivided. For example:

–37 different jobs which fall under the heading of "Personnel Maintenance," such as accountants, cafeteria managers, various kinds of business office clerkships, publicity and purchasing agents, etc.

−29 different kinds of work in professional service, such as architects, electrical or heating engineers, psychologists, and statisticians.

−44 different kinds of work in personal service, such as nurses, athletic coaches, librarians, placement officers, visiting teachers, etc.

−finally, at the supervisory level, 129 different kinds of jobs, such as curriculum directors, directors of examinations, supervisors of the various subject departments, specialists in the teaching of the arts and of the physically handicapped.

Most of these nonteaching and nonadministrative jobs are new to the educational system. You will find, indeed, that the expansion of educational opportunities is an amazing and exciting story. To give our profession its true dignity and prestige, we should speak of the "educator" rather than of the teacher.

Education as a Profession

One of the clearest ways to answer the question: "How important is education in American life?", is to compare it with the professions and distinguish it from the trades. A profession, it is said, is marked by no less than ten definite characteristics. A profession

1. is regarded as a lifework.

2. exalts service over personal gain; that is, is devoted to the welfare of the people, gives public service, regards itself as obligated to give more than is required by law.

3. insists upon the highest standards of character and ability.

4. recognizes the status of the worker on the basis of his worth.

5. develops organizations and organs of expression.

6. evolves a code of ethics governing work and behavior.

7. relies upon a highly developed body of scientific and philosophic knowledge.

8. requires extended professional education and internship.

9. exerts real leadership in the communities of America.

10. has its legal status defined by state laws.

If you appraise these characteristics carefully, you may conclude that the first six points are true of trades as well as professions. To a certain extent this is true. For example, the skilled trades, such as stenography, bookkeeping, carpentering, plumbing, (1) all have status as a lifework, (2) are expected to contribute to public service — at least within the limits of the general level of morality set by the community, (3) require of the worker recognized standards of ability and character, (4) base the worker's status in the trade upon achievement of accepted standards of workmanship, (5) have organizations and organs of expression, and (6) in the case of the more prominent national trade unions are, perhaps, as effective as the professional organizations in maintaining codes of ethics for their members. Hence, it does not appear that these first six characteristics draw a clear line between a profession and a trade.

It is in the other four measures that we must look for the real distinction, particularly in the extensiveness and depth of the knowledge and study required to enter a trade or a profession and to develop leadership within it. A trade makes use of a body of manual or intellectual skills. These can all be learned by apprenticeship — that is, by working with a master craftsman. There is little necessity for complex understanding of the theory underlying the skill. The skilled tradesman learns to measure and to start and stop machines by rule of thumb; he learns formulae and applies them. But the professional man, who also masters precise skills and uses formulae, has to make, in addition, an elaborate study of the theory upon which the rules of thumb and the formulae are based. In many instances he could himself reconstruct the formula from his knowledge of the scientific theory.

To gain this thorough understanding of theoretical foundations necessitates extended professional education — our eighth characteristic. But this can be acquired only through years of attendance in technical and professional schools and additional years of internship. The medical profession, perhaps the most demanding of all, can be entered only after completion of an undergraduate college course, three or four years of professional medical education, and a year or more of internship in a hospital, clinic, or research institute. The other professions are all tending to set up similarly rigorous requirements.

Finally, there is the factor of legal status and community leadership. The legal status of a profession is defined by state laws. Members of the professions look upon these laws as a means of imposing upon the

CHARLES HUBBARD JUDD (1873–1946) was one of America's pioneers in building the graduate study of education and in furthering its scientific study. Trained by Wilhelm Wundt at Leipzig (1896), he was the outstanding exponent in America of Wundt's interest in precise laboratory analysis of human behavior and in the psychology of social forces. As Professor of Psychology and Director of the Psychological Laboratory at Yale, between 1902 and 1909, Judd helped build the first courses in educational psychology. He was a leader in the development of the psychology of the school subjects and was the chief defender of the "generalization point of view in the controversy over transfer of training. From 1909 to 1938, as Director of the School of Education of the University of Chicago, he developed one of the country's outstanding centers for the scientific study of education.

Dr. Judd's influence on the administration of the public schools was nation-wide, as shown by his contributions to the junior high school and by his leadership in outstanding educational organizations.

individual certain obligations to society and of making the profession a group distinguished by preparation, experience, and certain personal qualifications. The members of our professions have, throughout American history, distinguished themselves for their leadership in community and national life. They have always been well represented in public office, on welfare commissions, and in community reconstruction.

It is, therefore, in these last four characteristics that we find the clear distinctions between a profession and any other occupation: in the scientific and philosophic understanding required, in the extensiveness and depth of education, and in the creative leadership in the community.

To our question: Is education a trade or a profession? the answer is direct and clear. If you become a teacher today, you will enter a profession. You will be a member of a profession that has defined its standards of entrance, promotion, and continuation very carefully. In the first place, you will not be permitted to teach until you have satisfied a long list of requirements. School boards are prohibited by law from hiring unqualified teachers, and a teacher becomes legally qualified only when he has been certified by the highest authority — generally, the state board of education. The regulations of the state boards specify in great detail the requirements for teaching. In no state can these legal requirements be satisfied in less than two years of education in a teachers college or some other comparable collegiate institution. For a permanent certificate most states require four years of college education, the bachelor's degree, and a specific diploma or certificate for teaching. To teach in high schools almost all states require four years of higher education, and some demand a master's degree.

Specific courses in professional education, such as you no doubt are taking at the present moment, are required in all teacher-training institutions to meet the standards set up by the various states and by the profession itself. Consider, for example, the study of psychology, which in most teacher-education institutions is now required for at least two years. Psychology, now generally respected as the science of human behavior, is over a hundred years old. In that time, through a vast number of scientific investigations in psychological laboratories and schools, a large body of precise knowledge has been discovered and organized. Upon this knowledge teaching depends. It supplies answers to such questions as: How do children learn to read? to write? to solve problems? In short, how do they learn to live? The answers to such questions are no longer left to mere practical experience.

There is a corresponding body of scientifically established facts concerning human personality — physique, temperament, intelligence, and the other raw materials with which people are born. Great strides have been made in defining clearly the nature of these, their rate of growth, and the extent to which they are inherited or are developed by training.

Similarly, during the past three generations the scientific study of society and the culture has been developing a new economics, sociology, geography, political science, history, and anthropology. Today many curriculum directors as well as administrators insist that members of our profession must become thorough students of this new scientific knowledge of civilization. Only in this way, they insist, can we build a program of studies that will successfully introduce young people to our changing industrial society — its races and nationalities, its social and racial stresses and strains, and the nature of our American way of life. The American teacher must have this foundational knowledge, but he can build it only by prolonged study in the college and the graduate school. It is this accumulating program of advanced study that state boards of education are now increasingly requiring of candidates.

You see, then, that in proposing to enter the field of education you are joining not only the largest professional group in the country, but you are indeed entering a *real* profession.

The Rewards of the Teacher

In considering education as a lifework, you have a right to ask: If I join the educational profession, how well shall I be rewarded? To what kind of income may I look forward? How secure will my job be? Will I have fairly permanent tenure? When I become old, what protection can I count upon? Will there be a pension, a retirement allowance? Shall I be recognized by the community both as a person and as a member of a chosen profession?

In education there are several kinds of rewards: First, there is the obvious economic one of salary and assured length of tenure — that is, permanence of job and security in old age through a pension or annuity. Second, there are social rewards which come from the prestige given the position by the community, from the recognition for work conspicuously well done, and for contributions to community life. Third, there are personal satisfactions of great importance — a life of constant stimulation with creative associates, the sense of one's personal development, the inner sense of work well done, and pride in the integrity of one's profession. Because these rewards are of real concern to you, we shall consider each a little more fully.

A Major Issue: the Economic Security of the Teacher

We encounter the problem of economic security on every hand. All around us are people too old to work, infirm people, and others unemployed for one reason or another, without adequate income. Insecure and afraid, their lives are marked by anxiety and possibly ill health.

Is that the outlook of the young man or woman who today takes up teaching as a lifework? A generation ago it was all too true; most educational workers had no further protection than a small, guaranteed, annual salary. Tenure was inefficient, and pensions or annuities hardly existed. But today, as the result of heroic work by the officers of such organizations as the National Education Association and the various state teachers associations, many gains have been made. Recently the NEA Executive Committee spoke out boldly and clearly:

"The days of economic servitude and insecurity for teachers must be brought to a close. Teachers must have public respect, professional earning power, and economic security. They must be able to afford professional study, books, travel, and other means of enriching their minds and renewing physical strength to meet the heavy and exacting daily tasks of the classroom."

Mr. Willard E. Givens, the Executive Secretary, has added:

"Today thruout the nation people believe that teachers should be paid reasonable professional salaries. Legislatures are taking steps to increase the state revenues for local school districts. Many communities have raised their millage rates for school taxes so as to enlarge the sums available from local sources."

Security and Teachers' Salaries Most people forget that the school-teachers have a kind of security that most Americans lack. This is an *annual* salary guaranteed by a written contract. Countless workers are employed on a weekly basis, and most of them can be dismissed or laid off on short notice. But the teachers' salary, small though it may be, is established in advance.

What, you will wonder, can the teacher expect as an annual salary? Consider the salaries paid in the smaller communities, for that is probably where you will begin to teach. The table on page 234 shows that in 1946–1947 the median teaching salary in elementary schools in communities of 2500 to 5000 was approximately $1864 a year. This figure means that about half the teachers received more than $1864 and half received less than that amount. Teachers in high school received about $400 more than those in the elementary school. If you were to serve as a supervising principal, or principal of a junior or senior high school, you could count on about $3000 a year. As you gain in experience and move into larger communities, where more money is spent on education, your salary will tend to increase.

The NEA research studies of salaries made in 1946–47 show a major upward shift, as indicated in the graph on page 235. The first ten years — those of the economic depression of the thirties — were years of sharply declining salaries for educational workers, just as they were years of sharply declining income for nearly all Americans. But from 1935 on there was a sharp increase. The American national income of 90 billion dollars in 1929 had advanced by the 1940's to approximately 200 billion dollars. As production, employment, prices, and the cost of living increased, teachers' salaries, in spite of their lag, tended to increase also. For example, the minimum salaries for 1947–48 were reported "as $375 higher on the average," and maximum salaries averaged $675 higher than those in 1946–47.

The Executive Committee of the NEA kept the issue constantly before the American people.   In February, 1947, it answered the question: How much should a qualified teacher receive? by declaring: "The

Median Salaries in School Systems in Cities 2500 to 5000, 1946–1947

CLASSROOM TEACHERS:
Elementary school $1864
Junior high school 2087
High school 2274

PRINCIPALS:
Supervising elementary school 2900
Junior high school 2625
High school 3197

ADMINISTRATIVE AND SUPERVISORY STAFF:
Superintendents of schools 4225

National Education Association stands for a minimum annual salary of $2400 for a qualified beginning teacher who is a college graduate." In 1948 it asserted that experienced teachers in city systems should be assured of a top annual salary of $6000.

Median Salaries in School Systems in Cities 10,000 to 30,000, 1946–1947

CLASSROOM TEACHERS:
Elementary school $2118
Junior high school 2354
High school 2595

PRINCIPALS:
Supervising elementary school 3031
Junior high school 3425
High school 4071

ADMINISTRATIVE AND SUPERVISORY STAFF:
Superintendents of schools 5856

You will have noticed from the accompanying figures that an elementary teacher may not be paid as much as a high school teacher. Progressive educators have tried for many years to change this practice. A generation ago, the NEA went on record as favoring a single schedule of salaries for elementary and high school teachers of equal qualifications.   There was no evidence, they said, that the teacher in the elementary school needs less ability, less training, or is to be considered less important to society than the teacher in the high school. On the contrary, the NEA leaders proposed that all teachers, men and women, in elementary and high schools be given like treatment in the matter

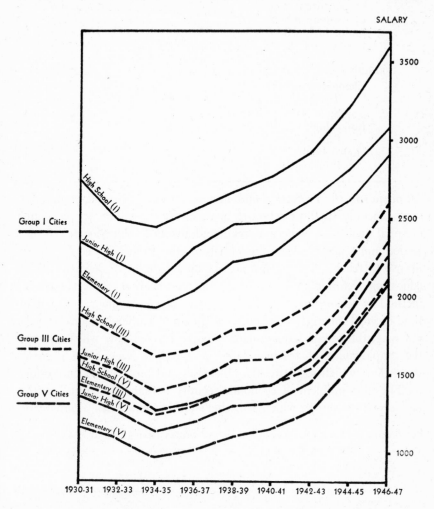

Trends in teachers' salaries from 1930–31 to 1946–47. (From *Salaries of City-School Employees*, 1946–47, NEA Research Bulletin, XXV, No. 1, February, 1947.)

of income. Twenty years later, 31 per cent of the cities had adopted some kind of single salary schedule. By 1946–1947 the number had doubled; 63.9 per cent of the nation's school systems paid all elementary and secondary school teachers on the same basis.

Median Salaries in School Systems in Cities over 100,000, 1946–1947

CLASSROOM TEACHERS:

Kindergarten $2696
Elementary school 2897
Junior high school 3075
High school 3593

PRINCIPALS:

Elementary school:
    Teaching principals ....·.................. 2815
    Supervising principals 4953
Junior high school:
    Principals 4953
High school:
    Principals 5741

Admission to the Profession and Tenure As we have said, professions are open only to those who are qualified by education, training, and personal qualities. A person seeking admission to the educational profession must present legal credentials in the form of a certificate or license to teach. Today laws are set up by the state departments of education defining and regulating the certification of teachers, the method of appointment, and the contract of employment. Except in time of great emergency, school boards cannot employ persons who do not meet these state requirements. There are also laws which prevent the employment of teachers below a specified wage and, in many states, laws which regulate salary increases and professional promotion.

The next problem of economic security is that of "tenure," or the period of time during which a teacher's job is guaranteed. Perhaps no

Percentage of Men Teachers in the United States from 1880 to 1944 [1]

YEAR	TOTAL NUMBER OF TEACHERS	PERCENTAGE THAT ARE MEN
1880..........	286,593	42.8
1890..........	423,062	29.9
1920..........	679,533	14.1
1930..........	854,263	16.5
1934..........	847,120	19.1
1940..........	1,104,283	27.3
1944..........	1,053,646	21.5

[1] U. S. Office of Education: *Statistical Summary of Education, 1943–44.*

economic problem causes more anxiety than does the possible loss of job. In most trades, for example, there is little assurance of permanent tenure, although contracts between labor unions and employers give some protection. But today the laws of most states provide permanent tenure for public school teachers. Although the tenure laws vary in different states, in general they guarantee the teacher against dismissal except in cases of proved inefficiency or misconduct as defined by law. The teacher wins his tenure, however, by passing successfully through a probationary period of three or more years.

It is clear that the struggle of teachers for economic security has resulted in considerable success. The question: "For how long a time should a person's job be guaranteed?" has another side. Society, especially the children, must be protected as well as the teacher. Does the permanent tenure law for teachers insure that? By guaranteeing the job of the competent teacher, it removes from his life one of the chief incentives to good work. It is probably true that all people need stimuli to keep them alive and alert. A graduated schedule of economic and other rewards is one of the important incentives. It is an unhappy fact, therefore, that in many of our larger school systems, laws guaranteeing permanent tenure have removed a most important incentive to continued professional study and development.

Security in Old Age Most young people are not consciously concerned with the needs of old age. To them it is a remote problem to be faced when the time comes. But the leaders of modern society have learned that it must be provided for far in advance, and many private and public plans have been tried. These include private forms of insurance and annuity and, on the public side, various plans for pensions and retirement allowances. Recognizing that most people neither earn enough nor are foresighted enough in their younger years to protect their old age by setting aside and investing adequate savings, wise leaders have created pension and retirement plans for teachers. A pension is defined by the NEA leaders as

> "a benefit to which the beneficiary does not contribute; it is usually paid from the general funds of the state government or by the local school system. A retirement allowance is a benefit to which both teacher and the employer have contributed. Such a plan is usually referred to as a joint-contributory retirement system."

Although the state systems of pensions and retirement allowances vary greatly, several features are common to most of them:

–Retirement is permitted at sixty-five and compulsory at seventy.

–The financial reserve to provide retired pay is accumulated monthly or yearly in payments made by both the teacher and his employer.

–On leaving the profession before retirement age, the teacher may take with him the entire annuity accumulated under the retirement contract.

–Credit for experience elsewhere is often allowed.

–Some retirement systems include disability benefits.

As a result of the deep interest of the leaders of our profession, teachers now retire in practically all of our larger cities and in many of the smaller ones at the age of 65 or thereabouts with an annual income guaranteeing them at least a modest living. Thus education compares very well with the other professions and with government service.

Protection against Illness or Accident   Most states have given their teachers the right of absence due to sickness and accidents. The amount of time varies, but in a school year the average is five days' sick leave with full pay. Some systems allow unused sick leave to accumulate to twenty or twenty-five days, but in this case the pay received by the absent teacher is his salary minus the pay of the substitute. It is clear that, in general, much gain has been made to elevate the profession and to protect the economic conditions of the teacher.

Security and the Problem of Personal Satisfactions

Can a young person about to enter the teaching profession feel confident that he has before him a life of personal happiness — a life that will furnish opportunity for his own development and growth as a person, a life symbolized by worthy and meaningful satisfactions? In an earlier chapter we have discussed this question quite fully, but let us pause a moment and bring together all the facts.

First, teachers can enjoy the peace of mind that is assured by a steady, guaranteed income. The salary is usually higher in the beginning years

James Earl Russell (1864–1945) will long be remembered as the man who built Teachers College, Columbia University, into the largest and most influential professional school of education in America. Preceding this work he had been Professor of Philosophy and Pedagogy at the University of Colorado (1895–1897). As student of higher education in Europe, he produced in his early years *University Teaching in England and America* (1895), *German Higher Schools*, and *The History, Organization, and Methods of Secondary Education in Germany* (1899).

For a generation Dean Russell was the key figure in the development of graduate teacher education, making a unique contribution to the development of the doctorate in education. Individual freedom of teaching and learning was a basic concept in his outlook and policy. In time, adult education became his profound concern. He played a leading part in forming the American Association for Adult Education, and was its first president, in 1926. He was the editor of the widely influential American Teachers Series.

of teaching than in most other occupations. This fact alone, with the certainty of fixed increases of salary, enables a teacher to plan his future to an unusual degree. A sure and steadily increasing salary makes possible the planning for further study, travel, family life, and the following of special interests.

Second, the teacher falls heir to the blessing of time. His job is one which carries long vacations and certain periods of leave, which may be used for travel, study, relaxation, or personal expression.

Third, the teaching profession offers unlimited associations with other human beings. Go to the wisest people you know and ask them what experiences they consider most important. The chances are that they will tell you "contacts with my fellow man" . . . "warm and good relations with other people" . . . "being able to help others" . . . "feeling oneself useful in the world — needed by others." In a school, the teacher is closely associated with children, youths, parents, and colleagues. His relations are as warm and rewarding as he has the capacity to make them. He has the satisfaction of knowing that he is giving very real help to hundreds of young people; he has the pleasure of watching them grow as a result of his efforts.

And lastly, the teacher has vast opportunity to develop fine personal traits — leadership, resourcefulness, self-control, sensitivity, understanding, and imagination. As a strong and wise citizen, he may have deep influence upon the life of the community. There are certain professions that stimulate in their members joy in their work and deep personal satisfaction in their contribution to humanity. Teaching is one of these.

Security and Freedom of Teaching

The teacher must face the fact that in most communities he will find prejudices and conflicts — social-economic, political, racial, and religious. Consciousness of social class and resulting class conflicts may be so intense in the community where you start your teaching that tensions will be reflected in the children, and hence in the school. What position as a teacher will you take on these conflicts and issues? Will you uphold the concept that one task of the school is to maintain channels through which its students may communicate and explore their ideas freely? If so, you must assume your responsibility as educator to face controversial issues. To keep these out of the school is to keep thought out, to denude it of intellectual life. The life of the community must be brought into the school — this means the problems and deficiencies of the community as well as its magnificent achievements.

"But," you may say, "if I discuss such problems as race minorities, the rights of the Negro, youth and sex, or the menacing monopolies in our competitive economic system, I shall be criticized by the parents and community, and I may even lose my job. Am I free to teach what I know the young people must have if they are to become intelligent participating members of the community and leaders in a future society? Even if I have the support of the school staff, must we as a group face alone the struggle of freedom to teach? Does the teaching profession offer any form of security and protection? Are teachers organized as are labor and other occupations for the protection of professional rights?"

Teachers' Organizations and Teachers' Security

Americans are said to be the greatest organizers in the world. One wag commented that if two Americans were shipwrecked and landed safely on a desert isle, their first act would be to organize as "Americans, Inc." One would be president and the other secretary-treasurer! Teachers are no exception to this generalization. Most of the million belong to at least one organization. Nearly all are members of their state teachers' association, and approximately half belong to the National Education Association. Each of these organizations gives them something of value, including some element of security. Since the largest and most powerful of these organizations is the National Education Association, we comment first upon that.

The National Education Association   About ninety years ago (August 26, 1857) the NEA was started as the National Teachers' Association, with this stated aim: "To elevate the character and advance the interests of the profession of teaching and to promote the cause of popular education in the United States." For a half century it grew very little, although it was incorporated as the National Education Association in 1886. When America entered World War I, sixty years after its birth, the Association had only 10,000 members.

In 1920, a group of vigorous, professionally conscious leaders reorganized it and developed a new organization reaching out into the classroom workers of the country. In ten years its membership grew tenfold! By 1929 it had 200,000 members, property valued at nearly $400,000, and a national headquarters in Washington, D.C., with a permanent staff of administrative, research, and clerical workers. A score of departments were organized, and every major division of the profession was brought within its framework. By 1948 it had registered nearly half a million members. As a single example of its influence, the annual meeting of its administrators' department (the American Association of School Administrators) today gathers an attendance of approximately 10,000 members from every state in the Union. With the association, meet leaders representing every kind of work found in the schools. Each of the departments from which they come has its own national organization, leadership, an elaborate program of work, and a magazine reaching thousands of teachers. The *Journal of the NEA* now reaches nearly half of the teachers of the country.

Here is a gigantic achievement — the very cornerstone of an American profession of education. The platform of the NEA stands for:

–a competent, well-trained teacher in every classroom in America.

–improved facilities for their education, and inducements to attract the highest type of young Americans into the profession.

–the profound understanding and interpretation of education.

–an equally well-founded program of research.

–the national recognition of the profession through the establishment of a federal Department of Education with a Secretary in the President's Cabinet.

–equal salaries for equally qualified teachers.

–a democratic, classroom-teacher determination of educational policy and program.

For a generation the NEA has devoted itself with great vigor to the attainment of these ideals. In our judgment the building of the American profession of education can be achieved effectively by using the National Education Association as the nucleus. We urge you to become a member and to throw yourself vigorously into its work, contributing to its *Journal*, its research, the work of its professional committees, and to one or more departments of the Association. Here is an instrument through which you can make yourself felt.

Your State Teachers' Association   In close affiliation with the National Education Association are the state teachers' associations, now organized in nearly every state in the Union. Naturally these associations vary greatly in size, effectiveness of organization, and contribution to the schools, but almost all enroll a large percentage of the public-school workers in the state. From their large incomes, obtained from annual dues, they maintain professional secretaries, departmentalized office headquarters, monthly journals with professional editorial staffs, and public relation and information services. They hold annual state conventions, and through their field organizations reach into the local school systems of the state. Their legislative committees have worked vigorously for the improvement of the profession through higher salaries and legalized tenure.

Join your state organization. If you find its platform and program exciting and interesting, and if it promises a constructive program for teachers and young people in your state, take active part in its work. If you are disappointed in it, that is all the more reason for joining it, becoming an active leader, and helping to build a great profession of education.

The Role of Independent Organizations in Teacher Security

In controversies, who protects the teachers? You will find as you work in the national and state educational organizations, that in education, as in government, business, and the other professions, these big organizations tend to become cautious and conservative in their policies and programs. While they have done a magnificent job, working to better the welfare of teachers, analyzing laws and court decisions, and building more secure salary schedules, tenure legislation, and retirement and pension plans; nevertheless, there are still areas in which the organizations have done little. For example, while these associations have issued liberal statements of platform and position and underwritten documents of liberal general principles, yet they have done very little to implement their policies in cases of community controversy over school affairs.

Every year witnesses the dismissal without just cause of teachers and administrators in various local or state systems. Some of this, no doubt, is inevitable in a period of sharp and accelerating social change, when problems are manifold and controversies are constantly arising. Moreover, in a teaching staff of a million there is bound to be a vast range of individual differences in points of view about social problems. Some educational workers, seeing a real need for reform and improvement, try to make bigger changes in the schools than their boards of education and the majority of the citizens are willing to accept. The result is conflict, and, in some cases, the dismissal of the teacher. Since the close of World War I, every year has revealed instances of this, and rarely have the larger associations been vigorous in their protection of the teacher.

During the past generation, because of this fact progressive citizens and educators have created other security organizations devoted to academic freedom, to the promotion of forward-looking ideas and ideals, and to the defense of teachers and administrators who have been improperly attacked by partisan groups. This is a reflection of the established fact that no single individual is strong enough either to bargain with or to defend himself against a strong group. In every society a few energetic, shrewd, ambitious persons tend to secure an undue proportion of the wealth, the comfort, and the power. The whole history of democracy, therefore, has witnessed the union of the weak to maintain bargaining power equal to that of the strong. We cite four examples of such independent organizations:

–The Progressive Education Association

–The American Association of University Professors

–The American Civil Liberties Union

–The American Federation of Teachers

In each of these cases a group of educators, confronted with actual situations with which they as individuals could not cope, bound themselves together. Each has made an important contribution to the improvement of our society and to the security of educators.

The Progressive Education Association Since we described in Chapter 5 how the vigorous group known as the Progressive Education Association developed, we need say little more at this point. Recall, first, that their chief interest was psychological, and that during their initial fifteen years they worked to improve the teaching of young children. Second, that after the beginning of the Great Depression, the PEA was unusually successful in laying the groundwork for the reconstruction of the American high school through the work of its Commissions (1) on High School and on the College, (2) on Reorganization of Secondary Education, and (3) on Human Relations. In addition, it maintained (4) a vigorous Commission on Academic Freedom.

This organization, now called the American Education Fellowship, has a national membership of some 5000 teachers and parents scattered throughout the cities and towns of the United States. It has a national headquarters in Urbana, Illinois, at the University of Illinois, a paid director, and a professional research staff. It holds annual conventions and regional meetings and prints the journal, *Progressive Education*. It has recently issued a strong social platform and under its new administration will be moving vigorously in further development of education.

Security for College Educators: American Association of University Professors A few months before the outbreak of World War I a group of eminent university professors, feeling the need for the solidarity of their profession as protection against the dictation of college governing boards and unfair discrimination of various kinds, launched a study of academic freedom which led to the organization (January, 1915) of the American Association of University Professors. John Dewey was its first president. Since then it has defended the interests of the profession and the morale and efficiency of higher education by maintaining the freedom of the college teacher to think creatively and independently, and to deal with controversial issues on the basis of evidence.

In the ten years from 1926 to 1935 the Association dealt with 120 individual instances of attacks upon professors, "ascertained the facts by correspondence, by conferences, by informal visits to the institutions concerned, or by formal investigations. In 62, or slightly more than 50 per cent of these cases, satisfactory adjustments were reached." In some instances the Association prevented the dismissal of professors; in others it arranged satisfactory financial and tenure adjustments, and in fifteen of the cases "the complainants were specifically cleared of the charges against them." Many of the cases were handled without any public discussion in the press or adverse comments on either the institution or the professor. There have been instances, however, when institutions suffering the disapproval of the AAUP were so discredited among educators and the public that they were compelled to improve their standards of practice and their relations with the teaching staff. Today there are chapters of the AAUP in approximately 300 colleges and universities. The association has attained a position of national respect and real statesmanship.

The American Civil Liberties Union   As a result of the attack on civil liberties during the First World War, the American Union Against Militarism was formed under the leadership of Roger Baldwin. In 1920 the Civil Liberties Bureau of that union became the American Civil Liberties Union. To quote from its own statement:

> "The American Civil Liberties Union is the only national non-partisan organization defending our Bill of Rights for all without distinction or compromise. For more than a quarter of a century it has championed the right of every American to freedom of speech, press, religion, and assembly. An unrivaled record on a dozen fronts is testimony to its complete impartiality and proof that the Union has no 'isms' or other objects to serve. It is dedicated solely to the cause of civil liberty — to the task of preserving these freedoms for each of us against all inroads."

Since 1920 the ACLU has participated in every major issue where the constitutional rights of Americans have been challenged — "from the Sacco-Vanzetti and Scottsboro cases to countless unpublicized instances where prejudice or arbitrary law has threatened an individual's civil liberties." It has been a champion opposing censorship of the press, radio, movies, or stage; it has led in fighting segregation and discrimination against any minorities and in promoting the civil rights of organized and unorganized workers and employers. In schools and colleges it has supported freedom of thought and expression on international issues. In its pamphlet entitled "The Gag on Teaching," issued in January, 1940, are presented the facts on legislative restrictions on public-school teaching in the form of anti-evolution laws, required Bible reading and patriotic instruction, teachers' oaths of loyalty, control of history textbooks. The Union believes that society can continue to be democratic only if its citizens are free to speak, publish, worship, and assemble without restriction. It believes that all issues must be discussed freely. There should be no restraint upon expression. The Union leaders quote Jefferson:

> "It is time enough for the rightful purposes of civil government for its officers to interfere when principles break out into overt acts against peace and good order."

During the past fifteen years, the problem of free speech has become crucial in the general field of communications because of the increased national and international concentration of power. The ACLU has moved promptly into this field, as shown by the following resolution:

> "The following resolution has been adopted by the Union's Board of Directors, with the approval of the National Committee and affiliated bodies, as a guide to working out solutions for particular problems handled by standing committees:

> "Freedom of speech, press and assembly imply freedom to hear, read and see without interference by public authorities, save for a few incidental exceptions involving the public safety. When public authorities restrict such freedom, they should be resisted. When the same freedom is restricted by private agencies, they too should include not only forbearance from interference with the liberties of its citizens, but also restraints on interference with those liberties by private agencies."

American Federation of Teachers   In those years when American education was establishing itself as a profession, groups in different parts of the United States formed local teachers' welfare leagues.   In Chicago, Gary, Oklahoma City, Scranton, Washington, D.C., and New York, leagues were organized to protect teachers' tenure, salaries, conditions of work, and retirement and pension systems.   These organizations "felt that the essence of professional standing was personal freedom." As Ruth Hardy says in her historical sketch of the Federation:

> "That is exactly what a profession means; it is any group banded together to secure proper support in place of exploitation from the community it serves, aware of a common background and outlook, and free to carry on the work to which its members are dedicated as a matter of the honor of the profession."

For more than fifty years the local teachers' welfare leagues found themselves constantly under attack by the community and the administrative leaders.   Such conditions led the Public School Teachers Association of San Antonio, Texas, to seek affiliation, in September 1902, with the American Federation of Labor; the Chicago Teachers Federation followed soon after.   Organized labor had always been a valiant supporter of public education.   Under increased attacks from powerful minority groups, these locals, in 1916, organized as the American Federation of Teachers.   They affiliated with the American Federation of Labor, and organized a magazine, *The American Teacher*.   This was not a political action, but was governed by the desire to protect the rights and privileges of the teaching profession.

In the next few years local groups were organized in various cities and towns.   By the end of the First World War the membership totaled 10,000, more than a hundred local chapters had been formed, and sufficient funds had been gathered to support a paid, full-time central staff. This rapid growth alarmed citizens and boards of education, who became hostile to the unionization of teachers.   Superintendents of schools, professors of education, and college administrators opposed the new trend.   Dr. Samuel P. Capen, Chancellor of the University of Buffalo, stated very fairly the attitude of most administrators:

> "I am measuring my words when I say if this movement spreads it will be fatal to the academic profession . . . as individual citizens we are at liberty to join any group within the social order that is not

prescribed by the law . . . but the academic profession cannot identify itself with any of these organizations. In our capacity as university professors we cannot join a labor union and thereby commit ourselves to support the interests of organized labor. If the academic profession, or any considerable part of it, decides to cast in its lot with organized labor, then it becomes partisan. Then, should a clash of interests arise, its allegiance to the cause of truth can properly be called in question. Then it no longer has any right to demand immunity which other groups of citizens do not enjoy. Then it must abandon its claim to academic freedom. We cannot have it both ways." [1]

In the early 1920's a nation-wide attack was made on unionization of schoolteachers. Union leaders were dismissed from their jobs. Membership declined. Locals in small towns went out of existence; only in the big cities were the unions able to maintain their membership. Throughout the attack the Federation managed to survive, and by 1940 had a membership of 40,000.

Thus the AFT has been in existence a little over a generation. In that time it has rigorously refused to enter local or national politics, and has devoted itself to the task of securing state legislation and local board action in protecting the professional status of American teachers. Speaking of the AFT in New York, Ruth Hardy says:

"We have gained, since 1916, a pension law which is a model to any community, based on city and teacher contributions, actuarily sound, giving full insurance benefits, and on whose governing board the teachers are equally represented with the city. We have increased salaries, all teacher associations coöperating, but under the leadership of the Union's legislative agent, a teacher whose bold yet well-considered propositions often take away his colleagues' breath, until for various grades they are 75 per cent to 120 per cent higher than in 1916. We have secured liberal allowances for sabbatical leave and have fought off various censorship laws. And we have learned immensely."

The AFT learned how to work with the other agents of the labor movement. It learned that with wisdom and persistence and in spite of their small numbers, it could improve working conditions, the morale

[1] Bulletin of the American Association of University Professors, March, 1937, page 190.

of the teachers, and professional standards. It learned to become competent in the field of school finance. For years in the city of New York the Teachers' Union published studies of school finance that were masterly and professional appraisals of the problem. By and large, the members of the AFT have come to support progressive movements in education. Above all, they have learned that they "stand or fall as professional people, . . . as citizens, in standing for the best possibilities for society, for peace, and international coöperation."

This, then, is the brief story of the development of the educational profession. As we look back on it, we can be proud, indeed, of what has been done. Young people approaching the task of teaching in American schools need no longer fear that they will be part of an unimportant enterprise. The old idea held by our grandfathers — "If you can't do anything else, you can teach!" — is gone forever. With it is gone the mood of apologizing for the backwoods character of our civilization. In not much more than a century our farseeing forefathers transformed an almost illiterate people of homesteaders and artisans into a populous literate nation, with elementary and secondary education for all; in this process education has not only become the biggest profession, but, more important, its standards compare well with those of professions that have been longer established.

Things to Do

The profession needs to have you become an active, vigorous member. Join it, therefore, in the fullest sense, and help to develop it. Your first task is to understand its role in American life and its problems and needs. We suggest a few things to do. You can no doubt discover many others.

1. Ask representative teachers in your community such questions as:

–Do you enjoy your life as a teacher?

–What is especially satisfying? least satisfying?

–What are the chief obstacles to developing your work to its fullest?

–On what problems should teachers study as a coöperating group?

2. Find out about your local and state teachers' organizations. Study their programs and policies. Have a round table on the question: To what extent do the present organizations satisfy the needs of teachers?

3. Hold a forum discussion on the question: Should teachers belong to a teachers' union? Interview members of a teachers' union for their personal opinions and reactions. Get the opinion of members of the local board of education and the superintendent of schools.

4. Have representatives of both the labor unions and of employer associations of the community come before you, if possible in the same meeting, to discuss the role of teachers' organizations in the educational system.

5. Gather evidence on the statement: "Teachers and members of the profession have freedom to teach, to explore ideas freely, to design the curriculum in terms of the needs of the community and nation."

6. Acquaint yourself with the various means of providing security for teachers in your state: tenure laws, appointment of teachers, retirement systems and pensions, school leave, etc.

7. Study the educational salaries of classroom teachers, principals, special teachers, and supervisors in your community. How do these compare with salaries of other occupations in your community and with educational salaries in other communities in the state? in the nation?

What to Read

No prospective teacher should be without Benjamin W. Frazier's *Teaching as a Career* (Bulletin No. 11, 1947, U. S. Office of Education). Two general interpretations of the teaching profession are *Teachers for Our Times*, the general report of the Commission on Teacher Education of the American Council on Education, and Elsbree's *The American Teacher*.

On more specific aspects, see the following NEA Research Bulletins:

–*City Teachers: Their Preparation, Salaries and Experience*, January, 1940

–*The Status of the Teaching Profession*, March, 1940

–*Teacher Personnel Procedures: Selection and Appointment*, March, 1942

–*Teachers' Salaries and the Public Welfare*, December, 1943

–Statistics of State and Local Teacher Retirement Systems, 1943–44, April, 1945

–The Teacher Looks at Personnel Administration, December, 1945

Also see the following NEA Discussion Pamphlets:

No. 1. *Teacher Tenure*
No. 2. *Teacher Retirement*
No. 5. *Ethics for Teachers*
No. 6. *Credit Unions for Teachers*
No. 7. *Teacher Leaves of Absence*
No. 8. *Salary Scheduling*
No. 10. *Teacher Rating*

On teachers' organizations, teachers' unions, and their role in the profession, see the following three yearbooks of the John Dewey Society:

–Teachers in Democracy, Fourth Yearbook, Chapters 1, 10, and 14

–Educational Freedom and Democracy, Second Yearbook, Chapter 9

–Mobilizing Educational Resources, Chapters 5, 6, and 7

On the problem of freedom of teaching, by far the best book is Howard Beale's *Are American Teachers Free?*

On the social-personal aspects of the profession, Chapter IX of Prescott's *Emotion and the Educative Process* discusses the problem of maladjusted teachers, their personality needs and personal relationships. The American Council on Education's *Cultural and Social Elements in the Education of Teachers* is a series of essays on the role of teachers as citizens.

For a discussion of the preservice education of teachers, see Nila B. Smith's *Adventures in Teacher Education.* On the professional education of experienced teachers, Heaton, Camp, and Diederich's *Professional Education for Experienced Teachers* is an evaluation of teachers' summer workshops.

CHAPTER 10

The Widening Conception of Community Life

WE FACE NOW one of the most important ideas of American life and education:

> In a truly democratic society, *the life of the entire community is centered in education.* Government and social life are *the process of education.*

If you are baffled by this assertion, the following chapter will help you understand it more clearly.

The key to such understanding is found in three important meanings of "community":

–The first two — the school as community and the community-centered school — are clear and easy to understand.

–The third — the education-centered community — is the goal which a democratically minded people may well set before their coöperative efforts.

The leadership in building the creative life of the whole community should reside in the board of education and the superintendent of schools; of any local neighborhood, it must rest with the principal of a single school and the teachers. This conception of an education-centered community involves a community-wide organization of creative study and planning groups, continuously using their experience, knowledge, and imagination to produce a better design for living. In the leadership of this thrilling enterprise educators must take an important part.

The School and the Community

IN THE OLD DAYS it never occurred to the teacher that he had work to do outside the school; his place was in the classroom. But today his conception of education reaches into the wider "community," wherever people are living who affect our lives.

To describe this ever-widening radius of the area in which education takes place, teachers have learned to use the term — COMMUNITY. What does it mean to you? Perhaps the place where you live: your village, town, or city? That is no doubt its most obvious meaning, but there is another that is of more subtle use to us now. It springs from the old French word meaning "common," and carries the sense of likeness, common character, or belonging together. Sociologists, anthropologists, and other students of community life today use it in building an understanding of social life. Their study of a culture — whether of a primitive tribe or a twentieth-century American city — is a study of the community life of the people.

A community is any human group, living in village, town, or city. The group may be a clique of friends, or the members of a mutual aid society or of a political party. It may be a group of persons holding common viewpoints about world affairs, such as the advocates of the United Nations Organization, or the readers of any particular publication, such as the *New York Times*, the *Atlantic Monthly*, the twenty million who read *Life*, or the six million who read the *Saturday Evening Post*. In using the term community we shall be giving it its anthropological meaning.

Three Important Concepts of Community

In the building of better schools in America since 1890, educators have moved through three stages in their use of the concept "community."

First: the conception of "The School as a Community"; for example, Colonel Parker's school in the 1880's and John Dewey's in the 1890's.

Second: the idea of "Community-Centered Schools," illustrated by the study of the surrounding community by the progressive schools in the 1910's and 1920's.

Third: the conception of the "Education-Centered Community," school and community seen as one; illustrated by Elsie Clapp's Ballard and Arthurdale Schools and many other experiments.

The First Conception: the School as a Community

Sixty years ago Francis Parker built his Practice School around the idea that a school is itself a community. It was more than child-centered; it was a community in a fourfold sense: parents, children, teachers, and administration. Ida Heffron described it:

"The picturing of school as a community was a revelation to many . . . to see the school as a unit made up of groups, each group thoroughly interested in different lines of work, unified by the one aim — the good of the whole.

"It is a wonderful school . . . some six hundred of us from a child of six to the white-haired student of sixty gathered from all parts of the Union and from foreign lands, all drinking at the same fountain. All joined in the same family, which had no law save the family law, 'each for all.' Each striving to do his best, driven by no goad or lash save enthusiasm and the glimpse of a great idea." [1]

Parker himself described it:

"The social factor in the school is the greatest factor of all; standing higher than subjects of learning, than methods of teaching, than the teacher himself . . . the mingling and fusing and blending of each with all, give personal power, and make the public school a tremendous force for the upbuilding of democracy." [2]

[1] Ida C. Heffron: *Francis Wayland Parker*, pages 40–50. Copyright 1934 by Ivan Deach, Jr., Publisher.

[2] Francis Wayland Parker: *Talks on Pedagogics*, page 421. Reynal & Hitchcock, Inc.; 1937.

Six-year-olds shop for nipples for their lamb and learn the difference between those used by babies and those used by newborn lambs. (Louise M. Gross photo.)

The true community works together — each for all and all for one. That is exactly what Colonel Parker's little school and scores of later progressive schools did. One of the most significant community conceptions in the school was the morning assembly; the daily common meeting of the children, teachers, director, and — always some parents. That was "the family altar of the school" to which each brought his offering — the fruits of his observations and studies, or the music, literature, and art that delighted him. It was a place where each brought his best and choicest experiences to contribute toward the intellectual and spiritual life of the whole. Here children rose naturally from their seats and spoke simply and purposefully to their fellows; or, if they had something to show, went with it to the platform. For example, a boy of nine, finding difficulty in describing something he had discovered, said, "I can't tell it, but I can draw it." Eagerly he mounted the platform and explained as he drew. Thus, the morning assembly illustrates the first meaning of community in education.

The whole school, seen as the larger community, breaks down into many smaller ones. The most truly educative one is that with which

255

the teacher works directly — his own class group. The total "community" of this teaching group, however, is perhaps a hundred people — the thirty-odd children in the class, their sixty or seventy parents, brothers and sisters, and other elders, with the occasional participation of the school principal or other school officers. Here is the central community nucleus for education.

The school community is a fusion of ten to twenty of these intimate teacher-community groups. Impinging upon these classroom communities are the leading personalities and the conspicuous interests and forces that play upon the neighborhood life, direct it, mold it, and set its climate of opinion. In the larger sense these all constitute the community of a single school. In a wider concentric circle, embracing these school neighborhoods, is the total community of the village, town, or city. In the same way that the neighborhoods are molded by the practical interplay of forces and factors, the larger town community is also poured into a matrix of these coöperating and conflicting influences. Thus the first conception of the school as a community reveals it reaching out through its neighborhoods to the uttermost social reaches of town and region, nation, and distant world.

The Second Conception: the School Goes out into the Community

While the first progressive schools to be established, after Parker and Dewey, all employed this conception of the school itself as a community, they developed, in addition, a second important idea. They centered much of their educational program in the life of the local town and rural region. They took the children out of the classroom and out of the school into its surrounding locale. If the school was in a rural district, hardly a week went by without a trip of directed observation to the nearest urban community. The progressive schools in the larger cities not only visited the stores, docks, museums, post office, fire stations, and library, but also the outlying farms. Thus the directed study excursion, or field trip, became one of the most important instruments of modern education. In some instances, high school students went on long trips to distant regions; for example, (1) a New York high school class spent two weeks studying the exciting reconstruction of life in the Tennessee Valley; (2) another spent a week in a West Virginia coal-mining town studying the life and work of the miners and their families.

And there were examples of young people spending entire summer vacations on study trips in foreign countries.

Responsibility to others and to the community often finds subtle ways of expression in the life of the school. Here is an example:

"In one community the neighbors of a school had been making complaints that their lawns were being badly damaged by trespassing of the pupils. They asked for the assistance of the school in stopping this destruction. The problem was turned over to the sixth-grade class for solution. After discussion from various angles, it was voted by the pupils that talks be prepared by the class and given to the children in other rooms, asking their coöperation in stopping the trespassing.

"To give real point to their talks they decided to present facts about the cost of caring for a typical lawn in the neighborhood. Under the guidance of the teacher a list was made of the items required to get a lawn into shape in the spring. The pupils listed black dirt, fertilizer, seeds, utensils, and labor. The cost of fencing was also considered but dropped as not essential. Questions arose as to the cost of the materials needed for the lawn selected as typical, the amounts needed, the quality to buy to the best advantage, the dependability of various sources of supply, and similar items. Some pupils agreed to interview their parents about these questions, others agreed to get prices at the stores in the neighborhood, others to visit a near-by greenhouse to get advice, and others to inquire of firms that sold the various materials needed. Emphasis was placed on the necessity of getting reliable information. The findings were to be presented to the class in the form of arithmetic problems to be solved.

"The class gained a real insight into the cost of caring for a lawn, and as a consequence their talks were sincere and convincing. The teacher wisely extended the scope of the problem to include such items as the cost of victory gardens, the loss due to vandalism in a near-by park, and ways of conserving all kinds of property in wartime. Reports indicate that there has been a marked lessening of trespassing by the children. Similar problems that often arise in the school can be made the means of giving the children practice in democratic coöperation in the solution of difficulties that can be dealt with by the children themselves." [1]

[1] Leo J. Brueckner: "Vitalizing Arithmetic Instruction," *National Education Association 1945 Yearbook*, Department of Elementary School Principals, page 26. Quoted by permission.

Even the little children at nursery school age can have community experiences that add to their understanding of the interdependence of human beings and their respect for the worth of various life activities.

"A kindergarten group visited a cobbler's shop. A pair of shoes belonging to a little girl in the class was taken to be repaired. Arrangements had been made beforehand with the cobbler. Several days of discussion had keyed the children for the experience. Upon arrival, the kindly owner gave them a brief survey of his one-room shop, then proceeded to put half soles on Ruth's shoes. The fact that the shoes belonged to a member of the class was important; just any shoes wouldn't do. As he worked, the cobbler used practically all the tools and machines he had. He named each, explained its purpose, and demonstrated its use. He showed them the different kinds of leather and explained the source and method of preparation. He was a foreign-born, naturalized citizen, who told them how little and inadequate had been his own education and how wonderful was their school experience. The next day in class Ruth's shoes were proudly placed on display, and the trip was discussed and summarized." [1]

Although these first community-centered schools represented a great advance over the old rigid reading and writing schools, they went only part way toward the ultimate goal. They *studied* the outside community very well indeed, but they were still outside of it, standing off, looking on at the "real" community. Except as "going to school" was part of community life, the work of children was not included in it. They did no socially useful work; they had no part in the government or the industry or business of the town, or of its adult social activities. They were unofficial observers only. Then a third conception of education and community began to take hold.

The Third Conception: the Education-Centered Community

Ellsworth Collings and His Oklahoma School Occasionally a truly pioneering teacher brought his school and the community into closer integration. The first case we know about occurred thirty years ago. It is that of Ellsworth Collings, who showed how a one-room rural

[1] G. N. Hufford: "Field Trip Experiences," *National Education Association* 1945 *Yearbook*, Department of Elementary School Principals, pages 39–40. Quoted by permission.

school in Oklahoma could become a part of the real life of the community. Starting from a real problem — instances of typhoid fever in the school — Collings and the children conducted surveys of the actual health and work conditions in the local region and from the results built the local educational program. The results were encouraging. On academic tests the children stood higher than those in neighboring schools, higher also than the national norms. But very important non-academic outcomes were also achieved. More students and parents were drawn to this particular school than ever before. Attendance increased, and the students advanced farther into high school. Families represented in the school stood out in the community for their enlightenment, good citizenship, and farm efficiency. Even today the Collings experiment is pointed out as an example of what can be done in rebuilding the school through its participation in the community, and in rebuilding the community by centering it on education.

Elsie Clapp's Community Schools   Ten years after Collings's innovation — 1929 to 1934 — Elsie Clapp went far beyond her predecessors in the extent to which she centered the whole life of the community in education. She did this by developing a new kind of school — first the Ballard Memorial School in Jefferson County, Kentucky (1929–1934), and later the Arthurdale Community School, Arthurdale, West Virginia (1934–1938). Dr. Clapp, beginning with the people of the community, grownups as well as children, made the school the new center of their lives and made their living the center of the school life.

Ballard became a real community school: farmers, dairy owners, gardeners, mechanics, owners of estates, truckmen and handymen, business and professional men, and farm tenants. The children all went to school together, and with the parents learned to use the school and develop it as a democracy. Teachers and parents became neighbors and partners, irrespective of economic and social differences. The parents shared in the work of the school: they ran the lunchroom, the movies, the lending library; they carried on the women's exchange, the school country fair, and many projects of school decoration and community beautification. Through the Men's Club a fire department was organized.

Most important of all, *the living experience of the community became the subject matter of education.* The school raised its own sheep,

ELSIE RIPLEY CLAPP has lived the great adventure of teaching. After ten years in both public and private schools, and six years assisting John Dewey at Columbia University, she pioneered in two outstanding experiments in developing the community school. The first was her creation of the Roger Clark Ballard Memorial School, Jefferson County, Kentucky, and her work there from 1929 to 1934; the second was her development under the sponsorship of the Federal Resettlement Administration of the Arthurdale Community School, Arthurdale, West Virginia, from 1934 to 1938. In these two projects the school and the community became one, each growing through participation of teachers, children, and parents.

Out of this rich educational experience in educational and community experimentation Miss Clapp wrote *Community Schools in Action*, an original contribution to the new education. "All I know about teaching," she says, "I learned from John Dewey and the children and teachers whom I taught."

chickens, cows; planted and cultivated its vegetable gardens; conducted a labor bureau that helped the local artisans find jobs; established a coöperative market in which were sold the chickens, eggs, milk, cream, pumpkins, mincemeat, sausages, cottage cheese, crullers, pies, fruitcake, jams, and preserves produced in the school. The students renovated the old building, repainted the classrooms and hallways, repaired broken plaster, and reinforced floors.

Thus the community school organized the people, old and young, to meet the urgent needs of the community — its work, its health, its recreation. There was no distinction between school and life outside. *Instead of having the school go out into the community to observe, survey, diagnose, and recommend, the school and community became one.* The whole enterprise became a real School of Living — "a used place where learning and living converged." The schoolhouse was the recreation center, the intellectual center, and the spiritual center.

At both Ballard and Arthurdale a school took form that was both child- and society-centered, and the human *community became centered in education.* As more communities reach this mature stage of human development, *the people,* aware of their culture and thêir personal and social growth, *understand that all the social processes of a democratic society ARE education, and deliberately organize their government and all community enterprises in terms of education.*

A Rural Elementary School as a Community Center   In the war years a
two-teacher rural school in central Florida became an exciting community school in action.   The teachers joined hands with civic, religious, and welfare groups and turned their McIntosh Elementary School
into a real center of community leadership.   The school lunchroom
became a food-canning center and in one year canned 2600 quarts of
vegetables; in addition, twelve families did their own home canning
there, school and families sharing administrative care and expense.

> "The health program made real headway in realizing its aims
> to reduce malaria, to prevent hookworm, to get 100 per cent im-
> munization, to raise the level of sanitation, to reduce and prevent
> anemia, dental caries, to correct physical defects, to improve nutri-
> tion in the community, to provide health instruction in the com-
> munity."

The reading of the school consisted of booklets on food, clothing,
and housing written by the local groups to improve the actual living
in the community.   The exhibits and shows of the school community
fair, held in May, 1944, graphically portrayed the progress that had been
made in better community living.   The baby show, which illustrated the
care and feeding of babies, led to a summer conference with mothers.
The food show exhibited the seven basic foods, "glorified the produc-
tivity of the community, and indicated that with foresight, planning,
and work, all families in the area could have a more wholesome diet."

Radford, Virginia: Community Action through the School   In Radford,
Virginia, a ninth-grade class launched a study unit called "Improving
Urban Culture," using their own town as textbook and source material.
Almost at once they were faced with a problem very close to them —
a high rate of juvenile delinquency, with no playgrounds and supervised
recreational facilities.   They decided to do something about it.   The
members of the class went to work.   They studied playground facilities,
located new sites, got estimates on needed equipment, collected the facts
and causes of delinquency and discussed the problem with the student
body of the entire school.   They sought the advice of the commonwealth's attorney and issued to the leading businessmen a questionnaire
on the need for a playground.   Seeking to make one themselves, they
got volunteer help from the boys in the school.   They prepared a

petition for the city manager. A delegation of twenty-five ninth-graders presented it to the city council, and finally affected the passage of a city-wide ordinance providing for a program of recreation. Within four years the city had a new Recreation Commission, a Superintendent of Recreation, a center costing $160,000, and several playgrounds for both white and Negro children. Here was real leadership of pupils and teachers in community development.

The Community Seeks the Aid of the School   One more example of school-community integration and democratic action! In a small one-industry town, which had grown rapidly during the war years because of the increased demand for its one product, rubberized surgical bandages, the crowded conditions of the schools had become a serious matter. Attempts to solve the problem had failed; something had to be done.

A committee of citizens, teachers, school board members, town planning board members, finance committee members, businessmen, and parents was called together by the superintendent of schools. The question was: Shall we build more school buildings, get more equipment, and increase the teaching staff, with the possibility that much of the new plant will stand empty when the war emergency is over? An even larger issue was: Shall the community develop a long-range program, or merely a war emergency plan? As the discussion advanced, it was soon evident that no one had any facts or figures on which to base a decision. The first step was clear — namely, to study the community: its population trends, industries, money income, and all its resources. Who would do it: the business and industry of the town? The town planning board? A group of parents? The school staff? Who?

Finally the high school principal said: "This is a problem for the youth of this community. They are most vitally concerned. Let them study it. I would like to recommend that the problem be turned over to the high school students for study and recommendation. Their work will be done with the coöperation of community agencies."

The plan was approved, and the next day the principal called a meeting of all high school students and teachers and presented to them the problem that faced the community. Did the students feel it was their problem? Could they take it over for study and planning? Student body and teachers responded with enthusiasm, and the principal capitalized upon it: "This is a very serious matter. It may cost the

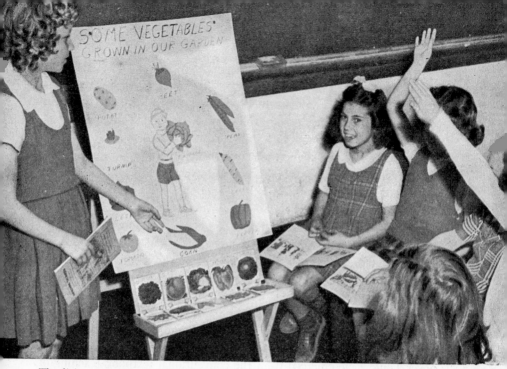

The living experiences of the children both in and out of school are the subject matter of education. (Frank G. Dickey photo.)

town, and therefore your parents, many thousands of dollars. To take over the study and planning of this project is a heavy responsibility. You will have the help of mature and experienced persons in the community — the town planning board, leaders in the town industries, etc.

"Let's begin at once. I suggest that you and your homeroom teachers put aside other plans for the day and make a preliminary canvass of this problem. Report back here tomorrow morning, and we'll see if we as a school can undertake the study and planning of this community project."

The students spent the day exploring the issues involved. They broke up into special groups as areas stood out that needed careful study; those interested in population called on the mathematics and social science teachers for help; those who were to study the relation of changes in industry to the needs of new educational facilities worked with the teacher of economics and business education; and so on. The next day the students and staff decided unanimously to accept the community problem for study in the school.

From that point on, the curriculum of the entire school was reorganized in terms of this study. General planning committees and special study-area groups were set up. Traditional subject matter was vitalized by the need so close to the lives of the students. Classes in economics became practical and full of meaning as the study of the industrial life of the community took shape. Classes in art, industrial design, woodworking, metalwork, and home economics studied building materials, architectural plans, types of construction, and the health, social, and æsthetic needs for an ideal school in their own community. Classes in mathematics went into costs of production, materials, the earning capacities of families, and the projected economic status of the community ten and twenty years hence. The social studies groups explored population trends in the community. The whole student body became actively concerned with the life of the town. Every group worked with community organizations as well as with individual citizens. Again school and community became one.

The project changed the life of the school and of all the people within it. There was a drive and motivation in learning and teaching that never would have emerged from the conventional textbook teaching of high school mathematics, English, and science. The students gained more than skills and facts; they formed social attitudes of respect for people, of social coöperation, and of civic responsibility.

Suddenly, it seemed, they "grew up"; they began to find themselves as adults in an adult world. They were working on an adult problem with the adults of the community, and receiving adult recognition. Finally, the whole episode was an example of democracy at work — students, teachers, and parents attacking problems together. Each for all, and all for each one.

Summing up the Three Concepts of School and Community

The few examples we have given of the building of better schools in America through the integration of education with all the other phases of community life could be multiplied many-fold. Enough have been given, however, to illustrate the three stages through which educators have moved in the past half century. Two of the conceptions of school and community that we have discussed are now coming into acceptance.

–*First:* the school itself as a coöperative community — each for all and all for each.

–*Second:* the good school is community-centered in the fullest sense.

The third concept, that *in a democratic society the life of the community is centered in education*, is just beginning to be put to work. Enough examples of its practice have been found to reveal its tremendous potentialities in the American way of life.

With these concepts of community and school in mind, we can dig more deeply into the task of understanding the baffling problems of our civilization. The key to such understanding is the fullest use of the study of local community life.

Building an Understanding of American Culture through Community Study

Using the Physical Resources of the Community

During the years that educators were struggling to integrate the schools and their communities, the sociologists, anthropologists, and other scientific students of civilization were laying bare the fundamental nature of modern community life. Today as a result of their half century of work they bring to teachers several indispensable ideas. Two particularly are of central importance: the culture and culture patterns, which we discussed in earlier chapters.

In the old school the teacher's conception of the educational resources available to him for use was limited indeed. It consisted of little more than his meager textbooks and his own personal experience. But the modern school is richly endowed with educational resources. In Chapter 14, "The Materials of Teaching," for example, we shall illustrate from new buildings and ten different kinds of materials how a good education grows best in an environment of rich experience. Here we need only recall the great variety in such materials: (1) those needed for direct firsthand experiences, illustrated indeed in most of the chapters of this book; (2) those required for demonstrations and field trips, in which the teacher does something in order to guide systematic observation; (3) the various designed groupings of materials such as audio-visual collections and museum exhibits; and (4) the use of the printed word in books, pamphlets, bulletins, encyclopedias, almanacs, magazines, and newspapers.

We have also illustrated in earlier chapters the vast resources that the teacher commands in the community's natural resources. How can one teach geography effectively except through the direct study of "the land" in the local region, the industries which it supports, the special services and productive enterprises that have grown up there? How better can one develop an understanding of the leisure-time activities of our people than through the direct firsthand study of the recreational and art activities of the local community — its parks, playgrounds, and museums; its concerts and plays, movies and art galleries? Every community provides its concrete exhibits of the conditions and problems involved in transportation and communication: The local power plant dramatizes the story of the production of power; the public reservoir purification plant and pumping station clarifies the problems of public water supply.

To cite a single additional example: A sixth-grade group found themselves studying the natural resources of the state of Illinois because of a half-day trip taken to a local coal mine to study strip mining. The group saw the miners

> "uncovering the seam with giant steam shovels; dynamiting the coal loose; picking it up by machinery and loading it onto special cars; conveying the coal to the tipple where it was washed, cleaned, graded, and loaded on cars for shipment — all by modern, complicated machinery. Then the members of the class went fossil hunting and with the fossils before them heard the dramatic story of coal formations." [1]

Using the Human Resources of the Community

But if the school is conceived as the center of coöperative living, it must learn that its greatest single resource lies in the grownup human beings outside the school. The teachers and administrators within the school have had comparatively little firsthand experience with the industries, businesses, occupations, and the social institutions of family, government, and community. With rare exceptions their knowledge has come from the reading of books, conversation, observation, and thought. How important, therefore, to build in the community the conception that every human adult within it has something in his own experience, understanding, and philosophy that at some time or other

[1] G. N. Hufford: "Field Trip Experiences," *National Education Association* 1945 Yearbook, page 42.

Citizens of Jackson County, Kentucky, study their needs in community workshops that provide useful library material. (Frank G. Dickey photo.)

he should be contributing to the schools of the town. Who is equipped better than the newspaper editor, reporter, or printer to dramatize the publishing of the newspapers and magazines of the country? In all the creative art work of the school, who can teach better than the artist, the painter, the sculptor, the lithographer? Let the fruit grower show the young students how he prunes his fruit trees to improve the quality of his fruit. Let the poet read his poetry and discuss the creative process with working groups of school students. Capitalize on the amazing reservoir of human resources in the local community by using it in the schools.

The cultural heritage of a community is too often overlooked as potential resource material for education. Fletcher Collins, as director of drama and music at the Arthurdale School, told of activities of the community that he found to be of educational significance to the youth:

> "there was square-dancing on Saturday nights, with its concomitants of fiddle-playing, guitar-picking, and mouth-harping. There were also ballad-singing, and nursery songs, and jigs. On Sundays there were sometimes gospel songs and white spirituals. Some of the men were making reproductions of early American furniture in the Mountaineer Craftsmen's Workshop at Arthurdale. The women were beginning to think again of making quilts with the traditional patterns handed down from early times." [1]

Some alert schoolmen have recognized the educative power that lies in using the experience of high school youth as demonstrators and as-

[1] Elsie R. Clapp: *Community Schools in Action*, page 218. The Viking Press, Inc.; 1939.

267

sistants in the lower schools. Many youth are themselves active participants in the social ongoing life of the town. Let the school, therefore, use this rich experience, and, in doing so, enhance the very maturity of understanding of the youth themselves.

Not only is the school program and its building of understanding of community life furthered by this interpenetration of school and outside world; the community life itself is enriched by the sharing of experiences and by the inevitable increase in the improvement of community life. Almost every village, town, or city in America possesses a considerable gamut of human talent that can be used in its schools.

Thus Widens the Community Vista!

Thus education marches on step by step toward the day when truly school-centered communities will cover America. Then we shall be a society in which home, government, industries, trade, farms, organizations, and all the social agencies will perceive their educational functions. Is not that the goal toward which we are moving? As the essence of living is growth, so the very basis of maximum growth is education. The task of transforming our communities into cultivated societies, therefore, is essentially the task of making every social agency in the community conscious of its educational possibilities and determined to live up to its obligations.

At their very best today, government, industry, business, and agriculture devote themselves merely to maintaining society as a going concern, to producing food, shelter, clothing, comforts, and luxuries, and to regulating economic, political, and social affairs. As integral, interdependent elements of the community, however, they have a far more important function than that. They have the educational task of studying the problems of community and nation, of planning and launching experiments that will bring about a progressively better individual and group life. Indeed, the supreme function of local, state, and national government should be the development of an expressive program of life in the community. Not only policing and keeping order among individuals and groups, but advising them and leading them — these are the true functions and obligations of government. How far we are from approximating them today has been more than hinted at in the foregoing chapters.

Safety signs of the community enter into the children's play, serving as both education and recreation. (Frank G. Dickey photo.)

Our conception must be of a coördinated system of adult and child education reaching actively into every phase of community life — homes, government, industry, and trade. The director or superintendent of education and his board of education would constitute a planning, thinking body and only incidentally an administrative, legislative body. Far from being a political or an economic and social gang, as so frequently is the case today, it would be a study and discussion group. It could, indeed, be the chief agency for the organized, coördinated development of cultivated groups throughout the community. Its meetings would constitute open forums attended by all interested members of the community. Its constant aim would be to transform the community from its present norm as a place of bare existence in which human beings are provided with food, shelter, clothing, leisure, and amusements. It would embrace adult education as well as the improvement of child education in its program. It would stimulate the formation of discussion groups, the development of artistic centers of expression, and would coördinate government, industry, and trade with the schools of the community.

One of the functions of the school system would be to experiment with the most effective inducting of youth into participation in government, industry, and trade in the community. Its experiments would bring youth into the community government itself. The best mode of educating understanding and participation in government is to let youth

269

carry on government — in the home, in the school, on the playground, in the church, in social organizations, and in the government of the community itself. Governing officials, therefore, instead of merely policing youth and preventing their attempts to study government, would interrelate their activities intimately and continuously with the established public school system. Indeed, community government would regard itself as responsible for education, not merely for financing and supervising it, as it does today. There would be constant scrutiny and evaluation of its activities. Government would not be "invisible," monopolized by those who obtain a strangle hold upon its privileges and emoluments.

Similarly, there would be a close relationship between the industrial and commercial agencies of the community and the educational system. Whenever technical skills needed by considerable numbers of young people could be more effectively developed through intimate "short courses" within manufacturing plants, on farms, and in stores and offices than in the school, these community agencies would carry them on. In doing this they would not be serving as grudging or even willing collaborators of the school. Instead, they would take over this function as their own, a necessary obligation and opportunity. If they did so, the technical skills would be mastered in a minimum of time and with maximum efficiency and retention. Furthermore, the understanding of the relation of the processes of industry and trade to our civilization and culture would be enhanced. The historical development of the community and the nation also could be taught much more effectively in the matrix of these community activities. There would be gains in understanding and tolerance as well as in the habit of participation. The education of the rank and file of our youth would be vitalized.

This, you will say, is ideal. Yes, it is; but there are many school systems that are striving to reach such an ideal. The fundamental key is *community coördination*. The school is the educational agency in the community that can best plan and work toward this coördination. But it needs the support and coöperation of all other agencies: the home, church, welfare organizations, business and labor groups, and youth and professional groups. When this is achieved, education will be conceived as all one with living.

Next Steps in Studying the Problem

1. Make a study of some community with which you are familiar, determining how the school could make better use of community resources in building its curriculum.

2. Outline a community service project that could be carried on in your local community by (a) an elementary school, (b) a high school, (c) college students.

3. What are the community agencies that should be used by, or allied with, the schools? How do you see them working together, or failing to work together as they should?

4. Study a specific school building in the community as a possible educational center: (a) as it is, without little reconstruction; (b) if funds were available for reconstruction, but on a long-term basis. In this study consider the use of available space for materials, equipment, and types of programs to be established in their relation to community needs and their stated aims and purposes.

5. Evaluate, with your fellow students, any community project on which one of you may be working.

What to Read

Lewis Mumford's *The Culture of Cities*, especially Chapter VII, although geared to the vocabulary of advanced students, is one of our finest interpretations of the school as the center of community life. Lloyd Cook's *Community Backgrounds of Education* illustrates the manner in which community activities and resources condition teaching and learning.

Perhaps the best single illustration of the small education-centered community in action is Elsie Clapp's *Community Schools in Action*; this presents two examples of rural community reorganization. Jean and Jesse Ogden's *Small Communities in Action* tells the story of the rural school's leadership in revitalizing communities in the Southeast. Other projects developed at the University of Virginia under the Ogdens' leadership are reported in their *These Things We Tried*; also see the list of pamphlet reports in that volume.

An excellent description of how the school is rebuilding community life (through examples in Florida, Vermont, and Kentucky under the leadership of Harold F. Clark) is given in the Sloan Foundation's report, *Learn and Live* by C. M. Olson and N. D. Fletcher. Samuel Everett's (Editor) *The Community School* reports nine experiments in community education — urban, metropolitan, rural, and suburban. In *Adventures in Coöperation*, issued by the Bureau of Adult Education of the State Department at Albany, one of New York State's central school districts reports how the community took on new life through educational leadership. Genevieve Bowen's *Living and Learning in a Rural School*, especially Chapters V to VII, is a simply written, anecdotal account of the integration of school and community life. Perhaps one of the best systematic interpretations of schools and communities rebuilding the curriculum together is *Developing a Curriculum for Modern Living*, by Florence Stratemeyer and others.

For advanced students of education the growing library of firsthand studies of communities by the anthropologists and sociologists is indispensable. Of a long list we recommend particularly the following:

–Lynd, Robert S. and Helen M.: *Middletown* and *Middletown in Transition*

–Hayes, Wayland: *The Small Community Looks Ahead*

–West, James: *Plainville, U.S.A.*

–Davis, A., and Gardiner, B. and M.: *Deep South*

–Davis, A., and Dollard, John: *Children of Bondage*

–Warner, W. Lloyd, and Lunt, Paul S.: *The Social Life of a Modern Community*

PART TWO

The Art of Teaching

WE TURN now to the essence of your work as a teacher —
namely, guiding the personal development of your students. Basic to
that task is the search for understanding. There are many pathways to
understanding the boys and girls whom you will teach, but five are important above all others. The first three we shall follow in Chapter 11:

–studying the individual children and youth in the school

–building and using cumulative files of important data about them

–studying and diagnosing individual and social needs through tests

In Chapter 12, "You and the Parents: Guiding Personal Development," we shall follow the other two pathways to understanding:

–visiting the homes and working with the parents

–forming child-study groups of parents and teachers

Both of these take us to the most important source from which to learn
about the children — namely, to their parents and their home environment. There beliefs and traits are largely formed. There you must
go to work out coöperative plans by which home and school education
may become one. This guidance of personal development is not easy,
but it will be intriguing because no two personalities in your groups
will be alike; each will present a novel study in human behavior.

To make sure that young people learn effectively, the teacher must
know what to teach and how to teach it. He must design the activities
in which the students are to engage, and collect and organize the materials for these activities. We call these things that constitute the life
of the school "The Curriculum," and make it the theme of Chapter 13.

It may be true that "teachers are born and not made"; nevertheless, a natural teacher may be hampered by lack of effective materials with which to teach. As an enriched American culture emerged in the last century, rich materials with which to teach were cumulatively gathered by the modern teacher. How this happened and what came out of it is the theme of Chapter 14, "The Materials of Teaching."

The teacher teaches, the pupil learns. To teach well, the teacher must understand the psychology of learning. A rich body of knowledge has accumulated from the studies of psychologists and other scientific students of the human sciences. Much of it has been confirmed by the writings of the great teachers. The practical essence of this knowledge, as the heart of the educative process, is presented in Chapter 15, "The Art of Good Teaching: Guiding Learning."

How do you know when teaching has been well done? Altogether in the old school and too much in the present one, it was left to the unreliable subjective judgment of the teacher. But in the development of newer and better schools in the last fifty years, the process of evaluating the work of the schools was revolutionized by the development of scientific methods of measuring human behavior. Thus in Chapter 16, "Evaluating the Work of the School," we shall return to one of the five approaches to understanding stated in Chapter 11 — the study and diagnosis of individual and social needs through the use of scales and tests.

While you as teacher will be very much the center of every educational scene, there are many important jobs of the school that must be turned over in part to others, called administrators. These jobs include the legal, financial, and building problems, classifying and promoting the children, developing the curriculum for the whole system of schools, and making supplies and materials available. But even in these jobs the newer and more democratic schools utilize the special abilities and experience of the teacher. This we shall see in Chapter 17, "The Teacher and Democratic School Administration."

We return finally in Chapter 18 to the teacher, the individual who, in the total school system, is closest to the student. What ideal do we conceive as the Teacher of Americans, as the builder of well-integrated personalities? None other than the Teacher as a Mature Person.

CHAPTER 11

Understanding the Children: Guiding Personal Development

OF ALL YOUR TASKS as a teacher, that of teaching will transcend all others. Most of your hours will be spent with your pupils — in the classroom, about the building, on trips in the neighborhood and the community. "You and the children" becomes, then, the absorbing theme of our study. In conventional schools, where the pattern of life was drab and standardized, this was not considered important. There the children sat quietly in long rows, studying silently, paying attention and obeying the teacher, learning "lessons," and memorizing and reciting. In this listening school, little was done to guide the living of young people. But today few of these schools are left. Even in the most traditional ones, you and your fellow teachers can doubtless find ways to create a more living atmosphere. We have already given examples of this conception of education — children conducting assemblies and open forums, dealing with modern problems in social studies groups, making exciting laboratory studies, using motion pictures, and taking trips into the community to study the water-supply system, the government, and the many other activities of community living. But there are numerous other ways in which children and youth can be guided in the recognition of their own strengths and abilities, in using these assets to work out their problems and responsibilities in healthy group living.

Guidance depends upon a general knowledge of the stages through which children develop and of the behavior characteristics of the various phases of growth. It depends, too, upon your understanding of each individual child. Your course in psychology will give you a background, but the ability to deal with problems as they arise in the school is something that comes gradually and only through actual experience.

From your first day at school, knowing your children becomes your major concern. As soon as possible, you will want to learn how far each individual child has gone in the continuous process of growing and developing. It is no simple task, for each child is an incredibly complex personality, and no two are alike. Just as children are different in physique, so they differ in intelligence, in emotions, and in temperament. In physical make-up some boys and girls in the class will be several inches taller than others and many pounds heavier, and they will vary widely in physical energy and strength. If you test their mental ability, you will find that some have Intelligence Quotients thirty or forty points higher than others in the same class; some are quick and alert, while others are slow. Some will read ten times as fast as others in the same group. Some will be fluent in verbal expression; others will express themselves better through the materials of paint, wood, or clay. The same variations will be found as the children meet mathematical or scientific problems. They will differ in their patterns of adjustment; some are secure and independent, others need success and intimate relationships with a helpful, encouraging adult. Thus the school and the teacher must know the abilities of the children, their potentialities and their limitations.

Five Ways of Studying Children

There are many ways in which people get inside each other's lives. Some ways are more effective than others. But children, like grown-ups, are so complex that you will want to employ several approaches in trying to understand these young people for whose progress you are responsible. We suggest five such approaches:

–Study the pupils in their active work in the school and the class.

–Build and use a cumulative personal record file for each child.

–Analyze and diagnose individual and social needs through tests.

–Visit the homes and work with the parents.

–Form child study groups of teachers and parents.

The first three of these approaches we shall study in this chapter; the other two in Chapter 12.

The teacher has the opportunity of observing the child in both his work and his play. (Photo from Play Schools Association, New York City.)

First: Studying Children in Their Active Life in Class

The obvious way to study individuals is to observe their behavior in the work of the class groups. In the elementary school much can be done, for the teacher is with the pupils five to six hours a day throughout the year. In the high school, where the students study with four or five different teachers and the teachers deal with a hundred to two hundred individuals, the conditions for developing understanding are not very good. But even there, the pooled judgments of the teachers can throw much light on each boy and girl.

To gain an understanding of individuals, the teacher needs to see them in many kinds of situations. This was not possible in the subject-organized school with thirty or forty children sitting rigidly in their files of seats all day long, reading, writing, and reciting. But under the varied, active living of our better schools, which brings the teacher and the children together in many friendly informal situations, it is possible.

Imagine yourself at the beginning of the year visiting a modern rural school of thirty children who range in age from five or six to the post-adolescent years. The teacher and the children are getting ready for a year of busy, coöperative living. A great variety of things is going on. They paint the soiled walls and buy materials to make new curtains for

277

the windows. The older boys repair the furniture, hang pictures, cut the grass, and clean up the grounds around the building. This is the ideal kind of situation in which to get really acquainted — to observe the special skills and the ways of working of individual boys and girls, to distinguish those who are imaginative and resourceful from the lethargic, docile, or less creative ones. Here one can observe how the children get along with one another, the little cliques that form, the bullying tendencies of some children, the submission of others. The rural school provides such a rare opportunity to work intimately and informally with individual pupils and small groups.

But many examples abound to show that equally good conditions can be created in a city public school. In Chapter 13, for example, we describe the exciting fourth-grade unit of work in the Lincoln School of San Jose, California. Consider the work of the fourth-grade teacher in the Lincoln School. The over-all course of study for the system was planned so flexibly that the teacher was free to choose the unit of work with which she would open the year's study. She and the children decided to carry on a study of the life of their own community of San Jose. She took them on walks to study the life around the school. Returning to the school, they discussed with animation what they had seen.

Later, as they discussed various aspects of community life, many informal activities developed. The children made maps and sketches, planned trips, held round-table discussions, made models of special buildings, and the like. One trip was planned to find out how the city got its food, another took the children to the water department, another to the city hall to study the government of the town, still others to study the public school system and the community's transportation and communication. Their study of the city had stimulated special interests in individuals and groups. The informality of the San Jose fourth-grade study illustrates how a teacher can deliberately set the stage on which to study the children at the very start of the year's work. Such personal and intimate experiences bring the teacher and the pupils close together, draw the children out, help the teacher gain their confidence and thus discover their needs and potentialities.

Another phase of the new school program which contributes to the teacher's understanding of the children is the creative work in poetry, painting, music, dance, and the arts of the theater. Although the ex-

There are many ways in which children can express themselves dramatically. The moving picture is one way. (Play Schools Association photo.)

pressive products of children may be difficult for the young teacher to interpret, yet they will give many clues to the emotional life of the young people. To get their children to express themselves, the teacher must create an environment in which the child feels free, released to say what he really feels and thinks.

As you work to get close to your children, try to create situations in which there will be many casual conversations, much personal "give and take"; easy, friendly relationships emerge only in the natural living experiences. In addition, the teacher will plan personal interviews, which may take place during group work, in the corner of the classroom, on the playground, or after school hours. Here also is a way of discovering the answers to many questions about the pupils. The teacher gets specially pertinent facts — bursts of enthusiasm, expressed likes or dislikes, light on new interests or friends — all of which help to build a deeper understanding of the child. And he, in turn, feels he has a friend in the teacher and begins to see his own personal world more clearly.

Second: Developing and Using Records

The increasing concern over the importance of understanding the personality of the child has led to a second fine resource for the teacher. This is the cumulative personal record begun in the earliest nursery or kindergarten years of the child, built up as he develops, and following him year by year throughout the grades of the school. A brief reference will be made to the four chief kinds of cumulative files — the Behavior Diary Record, the Cumulative Record Card, the Behavior Description Card, and the Cumulative Record Folder.

Behavior Records The behavior diary is an anecdotal commentary on observations, interviews, and other significant facts, written day by day by the teacher. Such diaries, often written in a loose-leaf notebook, provide a running record of the child's intellectual, social, and emotional development. The record should not by any means consist of the teacher's personal reaction to the child's behavior. The teacher should record as objectively as possible the exact happenings, her estimates of their causes, and the judgments of other teachers and administrators.

To illustrate the behavior diary, we quote from four different kinds written by teachers for the Commission on Teacher Education: [1]

First: statements that merely judge behavior as "good" or "bad," "acceptable" or "unacceptable"; for example:

"Julius talked loud and much during poetry; wanted to do and say just what he wanted and didn't consider the right working out of things. Had to ask him to sit by me. Showed a bad attitude. . . ."

This is the traditional way of describing young people — to pronounce them either "good" or "bad." Actually, such descriptions are of little help, either to teachers, to parents, or to the principal.

Second: records that interpret the child's behavior on the basis of a point of view, or a single fact about the child; for example:

[1] Commission on Teacher Education: *Helping Teachers Understand Children,* American Council on Education, Washington, D. C. Quoted by permission.

"for the last week Sammy has been a perfect Wiggle Tail. He is growing so fast he cannot be settled. . . . Of course the inward change that is taking place causes the restlessness."

Such records, while definitely more helpful than the first type, are nevertheless very limited.

Third: statements that characterize the child's behavior in general terms, for example:

"Sammy is awfully restless these days. He is whispering most of the time he is not kept busy. In the circle, during various discussions, even though he is interested, his arms are moving or he is punching the one sitting next to him. He smiles when I speak to him."

While this is better than the first two, nevertheless it, too, is lacking in details that would make it meaningful and helpful.

Fourth: specific descriptive statements that tell precisely what was said and done in a given episode, that describe fully the interplay of the important personalities involved; for example:

"The weather was so bitterly cold that we did not go on the playground today. The children played games in the room during the regular recess period. Andrew and Larry chose sides for a game which is known as stealing the bacon. I was talking to a group of children in the front of the room while the choosing was in process and in a moment I heard a loud altercation. Larry said that all the children wanted to be on Andrew's side rather than on his. Andrew . . . remarked 'can't help it if they all want to be on my side.'"

The Behavior Description Card Paralleling the Behavior Diary Records most commonly used in the elementary school is the Behavior Description Card developed by the Commission on the Relation of School and College, of the Progressive Education Association, for the six years of the junior and senior high school. It consists of:

First: A listing of characteristics, and under them several descriptive classifications.

Second: Spaces opposite the classifications for notes covering the pupil's six years of junior high school and senior high school.

Third: A key system for use in recording the judgments of teachers.

The Behavior Description Card is designed so that a teacher can quickly evaluate a child's characteristics. He is judged on a sliding scale on the following traits:

–Responsibility and dependability
  –varying from type 1, those who are thoroughly responsible and resourceful, to type 5 — those who are definitely irresponsible

–Creativeness and imagination
  –varying from type 1, the child who does everything with active imagination and originality, to type 5 — the child who reveals no originality or creativeness

–Influence on others
  –varying from type 1, those who habitually shape what others do, to type 5 — those carried along by the nearest or strongest influence

–Inquiring nature of the child's mind
  –varying from type 1, those who respond actively and consistently to intellectual stimuli, to type 5 — those who show little or no ability in exploring and investigating

–Open-mindedness
  –varying from type 1, one who welcomes new ideas and studies them with suspended judgment, to type 5 — one who is intolerant of any interference with habitual beliefs, ideas, and procedures

–Power and habit of reaching conclusions on the basis of evidence
  –varying from type 1, he who habitually assembles the facts and thinks them through to well-founded conclusions, to type 5 — he who is unable to analyze even simple situations and accepts statements and results without thought

–Social concern
  –varying from type 1, a pupil who shows an altruistic social concern, to type 5 — one who shows no concern for the common good

–Emotional responsiveness to (1) ideas, (2) difficulty, (3) ideals, (4) beauty, (5) order

–Seriousness of purpose
  –varying from type 1, one with definite purposes carried through, to type 5 — one who drifts without decision and persistence

–Social adjustability
  –varying from type 1, he who feels secure and is accepted by his groups, to type 5 — he who habitually is not accepted
–Work habits
  –varying from type 1, a pupil who has highly effective habits and reaches maximum accomplishment, to type 5 — he who lacks efficient work habits

The Behavior Description Card is most dependable and useful in those classrooms where the teacher is in close contact with the pupils.

Cumulative Record Card   One of the accepted techniques of modern education is the Cumulative Record Form.   One of the best on the market is the Cumulative Record Card of the American Council on Education.   You will want to study it carefully, for this is the kind of personal file that you will find used increasingly in the more progressive schools.
Note especially these following characteristics:

–It is compact and comprehensive, giving on the four sides of an 8½ by 11 folder a detailed picture of the whole pupil: his inheritance, his environment, and his personality.

–It is cumulative; that is, it shows the pupil growing.   It records in a single file the facts of his development for six or more successive years.   A copy of this record should move with the pupil as he advances from grade to grade, from school to school, and from community to community.   By reading across the card the teacher can see the trends in development over a period of years.

–By reading down, he sees each listed item in relation to the others, for example:

–The child's family background; the raw materials of his personality: physique, intelligence, temperament; his school-attendance record; his academic achievements of study; his various skills, understandings, and creative expression; test results; personal traits: interests, abilities and limitations, evidences of leadership; work experience, notable accomplishments, and educational and vocational plans.   Studying the information on this card gives a teacher some understanding of the individual.

Cumulative Record Folder   Even more useful is the Cumulative Record Folder. This combines all the descriptive material just discussed, together with quantitative materials: samples of pupil's work, letters to parents, records of interviews with school psychologists and others, copies of health certificates and medical information, and more personal autobiographical material. These, plus other cumulative records, give a fairly complete summary of trends in the individual's growth and development. These move from the file of one teacher to another as the pupil advances through the grades.

As you prepare for the work of the school year, the study of the personnel records of your individual pupils becomes a prior demand on your time. Either at the close of a school year or before school opens in the fall, you should study the cumulative records on file in the principal's office for each of your prospective pupils. Even for those children who are entering school for the first time, you will find records of interviews with parents, health records, some test results, and anecdotal material based on the child's preschool visit. After such study you can meet your pupils on the first day of school armed with some knowledge of who and what they are.

Third: Analyze and Diagnose Individual and Social Needs through Tests

The third important avenue through which understanding of pupils grows is the modern test. As you know from your personal experiences, tests can be used to measure the outcomes of schoolwork — for example, competence in arithmetical computation, reading, language usage, and other skills. In Chapter 16 you will find a systematic discussion of modern ways of appraising the results of schoolwork through the use of tests. It would be useful at this time to scan that discussion of evaluation, including tests and measurements, for a fuller understading of this way of knowing your children. Here we shall deal primarily with the light that can be thrown on the capacities of the children through the use of standardized tests.

First we remind you that in your daily experiences you are constantly evaluating people and situations. Whenever you make a choice about anything, you make it in the light of an evaluation of certain factors, abilities, or human events. These are chiefly subjective, conditioned by your attitudes and personal experiences, and these, as you can well understand, are apt to be unreliable. It is because of this unreliability that psychologists have felt the need to construct more exact and objective measuring scales and tests. These scales and tests can be used to supplement the teacher's conclusions based on the three types of records we have already discussed — cumulative records, observations, and behavior diaries.

Standardized tests are constructed to measure specific responses. They are called "standardized" because they have been carefully designed and have also been tried repeatedly with large groups of school children. After a significant number of trials, they underwent the necessary revisions. One important outcome of this is that we know the typical or "average" performances of children under normal conditions. With these averages, teachers can compare the work of their own pupils. Specific test scores below or above average give the teacher some indications of the pupil's need for guidance.

The purposes of standard tests are twofold: first, to measure both aptitude and accomplishments; second, to diagnose the specific needs for help and guidance of individual pupils. Teachers and administrators make a grave error when they give tests, tabulate results, store the records away in files, and do nothing more about them. The only true value of tests lies in the *educative use* made of the test results. Every teacher should insist on the careful interpretation of all test results as a means of guidance. If she does not feel competent to do this herself, she should seek the aid of testing services offered by the state departments of education, by county psychologists, or by guidance directors within the school system.

What Outcomes of Schoolwork Are Measured by the Tests? Out of fifty years of experimentation and research in psychology and education we can now measure with considerable reliability:

–skills: reading, computation, spelling, writing, typing, etc.

–mastery of facts and general knowledge

–thinking and problem-solving in actual human situations

–attitudes and behavior patterns, as expressed in different personal-social relationships: interests, aptitudes, critical attitudes, habits of work, traits of leadership and initiative, coöperation, and responsibility

–physical traits and characteristics: weight, height, sight, hearing, etc.

–traits of temperament

It is important to realize that in giving tests you measure only the individual's performance — that is, his achievement: How many or how difficult are the problems he solves correctly, how many and which words he can spell, what facts he knows. The test results become significant only when you know whether or not the individual did as well as he should have done on the tests for his age and stage of development. You will always want to know: Should I have expected higher achievement from him? This question you can answer only in the light of many other findings and tests.

How Estimate a Child's Intellectual Capacity? [1] We come now to a very important problem: How can the teacher estimate a child's capacity to learn, to grow and develop? In addition to the teacher's understanding of a child that comes from all the ways of studying the children we have just discussed, there is the Intelligence Test, or general mental ability test. These are of two types: the individual test, such as the Stanford Revision of the Binet-Simon Test, to be given by a trained psychologist to one pupil at a time; and the Group Mental Ability Test, such as the Terman-McNemar. The latter has now been taken by millions of children and youths, has been revised carefully several times, and can be regarded as highly valid and reliable. The Binet, requiring a personal hour-long interview and giving opportunity for the examiner to make many subjective observations, is even more reliable. At some time in your school career you may have taken the Stanford Revision of the Binet test. It is a compendium, testing various kinds of abilities:

–Giving information, such as identifying and describing familiar things in one's everyday environment

[1] A more detailed discussion of the measuring of mental ability is gvien in Chapter 16.

–Defining and using words and sentences

–Using everyday facts and skills, such as counting money, telling time, tying your shoe

–Following directions, solving puzzles, etc.

–Observing, discriminating and remembering, judging, reasoning, seeing relations

Valuable as this test may prove to be, it is important to realize that *no one single intelligence test* can give a truly accurate estimate of an individual's potential capacity.   No single test is sufficiently inclusive of all the traits that make up intellectual and personal competence.   There are sources of error in testing which may affect the validity of the score.   Profound changes in the child's physical or emotional condition or in his environmental influences affect, sometimes quite drastically, his test performance.   Studies made of intelligence testing of a group of children over a period of years have established that in *exceptional cases* the same child's IQ may vary as much as twenty to twenty-five points; this is true of only one child in a great many.   As Ruth Strang has pointed out in her discussion of testing, the age of the child at the time of testing is an important consideration:

> "Since the individual is growing and changing, test scores obtained several years earlier may not represent his present status.   In interpreting test results, the teacher should take into account the date at which each test was given." [1]

This means that intelligence test results must be interpreted in the light of the opportunities the child has been given to realize his potential capacities.   A teacher should not accept the too familiar verdict: "He is just dumb; there is nothing I can do about it."   For a fair appraisal of the individual child, many factors must be brought together and taken into account, such as

–the emotional adjustment: Is he insecure and unstable or is he resourceful, secure, able to assume responsibilities?

–home and racial background: Has he had broad or limited experiences?   Does he come from a recent immigrant home in which the

[1] Ruth Strang: *Reporting to Parents*.   Bureau of Publications, Teachers College, Columbia University, page 63.   Quoted by permission.

habits and ways of living are different from, or even in conflict
with, his newly adopted culture?

–physical condition: Is he in good physical condition, or are his
energy, drive, and alertness lessened by undernourishment, decayed
teeth, diseased tonsils, poor eyesight, or imperfect hearing?

In other words, has the child had those very experiences and contacts
that tend to bring out the greatest potential that may be in him? That,
perhaps, no one can ever answer, for in spite of the most accurate testing
and the wisest guiding programs, educators and psychologists cannot yet
determine the *exact potential capacity* of any individual. The best we
can do is find the truest *estimate* of potentiality and use it as a partial
basis for our understanding of the child.

How Estimate a Child's Total Ability?   The educator must not be satisfied with IQ's alone. As other reliable objective tests are given and
analyzed, they will add bit by bit to the total understanding of the
child. We have already mentioned the achievement tests that show
growth in such basic skills as reading, arithmetic, social studies, languages, critical thinking, etc. Some of these tests may also evaluate
work-study skills: ability to read maps, charts, and graphs; to use tables
of contents, indices, and encyclopedias; to take adequate meaningful
notes, etc. The results of these tests are often recorded in terms of age
— for example, Reading Age or Arithmetic Age. You may also find
references to Educational Age (EA) in your cumulative records; this
represents the composite score of the child on a series or battery of
achievement tests.

Along with these achievement tests you may find that your school
gives tests that show growth in ability to use facts, to assemble pertinent
data, to draw only those inferences that the data warrant, to see relationships, to apply given facts in the solution of problems.

An important and valuable means of understanding the child is
through the personality questionnaire, which reveals specific attitudes
and emotional reactions. Such tests are skillfully set up, using problem
situations; for example, "If you were riding in a crowded streetcar and
saw a person, upon leaving the car, drop a five-dollar bill, what would
you do?" The questions that are asked offer a choice of various reactions, and these throw new light on the child's interests, ambitions,

Children respond with eagerness and trust to the understanding, sympathetic teacher. (Bremerton, Washington, Public Schools photo.)

motives, frustrations, values, likes, and dislikes. Such questionnaires often support the teacher's own observations and conclusions; at times they explain a child's puzzling behavior.

The foregoing is a brief statement about the measuring program that you may find in operation in your school system. Do not be frightened by its immensity, for you will have the assistance of the principal, the school psychologist, the school nurse or physician, and the guidance director. Nevertheless, you, as the classroom teacher, are the most important person in any measurement program, for it is you who can best use test results for the benefit of your students. This means that you must be *a student* of the various means for evaluating and understanding your pupils. In your teacher-training program you will be required to take courses in tests, measurements, and guidance. Your knowledge of all this material will be of the greatest help to you in teaching.

It must be clear to you that such a program of teaching and understanding as we have been discussing in this chapter could never exist in company with the old system of grades and promotions. A child, if properly understood and guided, will hardly be given an "A" in reading merely because he is the best reader in the third grade. The goal in modern schools is to have his reading reach the maximum level of his own reading *capacity*. This might not mean that he is the best reader in the room. Nor will another child be made to remain in the fourth grade because he failed to meet the grade requirements in arithmetic. Physically and socially he may need to go ahead with his group. We now realize, too, that if he is held back, his arithmetic is unlikely to improve and his whole personality may become affected because he feels he is a "misfit."

These two illustrations merely introduce the problem of marks, promotions, and reports. We shall treat this problem more fully in a later chapter.

These, then, are three of the most effective approaches to the problem of understanding the children and youth who are placed in your charge during their school years:

–Studying them directly in the school and the class

–Studying their individual cumulative record files

–Analyzing and diagnosing their needs through tests

While you will want to study the individual pupil through these three approaches, there is still another source that will yield rich and valuable information: the home and the parents. The child is influenced by his home much more than by the school; as we said in an earlier chapter, nine tenths of his life from infancy to adulthood is spent outside the school, and the ties with father and mother are generally stronger and more enduring than those with any person outside the family. We turn in Chapter 12 to a consideration of the vital role of the home and family in the development of the child.

Observing the Developing Child

1. Taking yourself as an example, write a short psychological autobiography of your own growth and development.

a) If in the elementary school your teachers had really understood you as a person, had known what was happening in your home, in your play, and in other groups in the neighborhood, would they have been able better to direct your development?

b) Did you get respect for yourself as a person, a sympathetic understanding of your needs, tastes, temperamental traits?

c) How far did your teachers understand your motives?

d) Did they give you personal responsibilities and opportunities to think and choose for yourself?

e) How could the environment have provided less strain?

2. It is imperative, if we are to become skillful as well as sympathetic in understanding the potentialities in young people, that we begin to work with them as early as possible. As you advance in the study of education, find opportunities to work as an observer and student teacher in a local school, or in a Sunday school, or in some such community group as Boy Scouts or Girl Scouts. One effective way is to get acquainted with a single child in such a group. Make yourself his friend, see him in his home, study the teacher's diary records about him and other material in his cumulative record file, and study the social conditions surrounding him in neighborhood and town. Try to get at his needs, special interests, and purposes.

3. Write a cumulative diary record of one of the children in the school in which you are an observer or assistant teacher. Look especially for activities that seem to be particularly well designed for the all-round growth of the children. Bring this diary record back to your college class for group discussion.

Further Reading on Understanding and Guiding the Growth of Children

The study of this chapter has focused our attention on the most profound basis of the life and program of the school — namely, the growth process and the development of individual personality. The literature on the subject is vast, and we select for you only a few of the best things. Perhaps the simplest with which to begin is Caroline Zachry's Chapter XII of *Democracy and the Curriculum.*

For a vivid picture of the life style of the individual and the drive of his motives, the factors molding his physical, mental, and emotional growth, and the pressures upon him from the culture, see Chapters II to VIII of Cole and Bruce's *Educational Psychology;* also Bossard's *The Sociology of Child Development.* On the problem of the development of the person and the psychology of personality, see Chapters XX–XXII of Gardner Murphy's *Personality,* and Harold Rugg's *Foundations for American Education;* these last two are particularly for the advanced student.

For insight into the development of young children, one of the best books is Arnold Gesell and Frances Ilg's *The Child from Five to Ten*, a biographic-clinical approach to the development of some fifty young children — their physical and emotional development, personal hygiene, self and sex, and their interpersonal experiences.

See Chapters II and III of Pressey and Robinson's *Psychology and the New Education* for applications of the psychology of physical growth and health to the work of the teacher; see also Chapter VII for the social development of childhood, and Chapter X for the influence of the family. Hughes Mearns's *Creative Youth* and *Creative Power* will give you illustrations of literary expression.

For those who will teach in the nursery school, the young child can be studied further in *Education and Training: a Report of the Committee on Infant and Preschool Child*, of the White House Conference; Chapters III and IV of Elizabeth B. Hubbard's *Your Children at School: How They Adjust and Develop* will give you interesting case studies of children and graphic eyewitness episodes of child life with special attention to social and psychological adjustment.

Those who teach in the junior and senior high school should see Peter Blos's *The Adolescent Personality*; for personality case studies that use teachers' reports and observations, interviews, family histories, and the expressive writing of youth, Part III, "The Theory of Adolescent Development," shows the strains and conflicts revealed in typical adolescent behavior.   Caroline B. Zachry and M. Lighty's *Emotion and Conduct in Adolescence* is a "must" book in this field.   A third source is H. S. Dimock's *Rediscovering the Adolescent*.   The Educational Policies Commission of the NEA issued a companion volume to their *Education for All American Children*, in *Education for All American Youth*; Chapter II gives personality pictures of a dozen American youth, showing their common interests, traits, and problems as well as their educational differences.

If you encounter need for material on the exceptional child, both the socially or physically handicapped, or the exceptionally gifted, see Arch O. Heck's *The Education of Exceptional Children* and N. V. Scheidemann's *The Psychology of Exceptional Children*.

Four books are particularly useful on problems of guidance and mental hygiene.   The role of the school nurse, psychiatrist, and school psychologist and the use of tests in understanding children are graphically described in Part I, "The Child as a Person," of Carleton Washburne's *A Living Philosophy of Education*.   Suggestions for helping the individual to perceive and solve his own problems, the building of a guidance program around the relationships of pupils and teachers, and the continuation of guidance after school days are over, are discussed in Leslie L. Chisholm's *Guiding Youth in the Secondary School.* One of the simplest and most interesting sources is Ruth Strang and Latham Hatcher's *Child Development and Guidance in Rural Schools;* this gives firsthand material on the special conditions of the rural school. Modern views of *Mental Hygiene in Modern Education* have been described by a number of authors in the book of that name, edited by Paul A. Witty and C. E. Skinner.

One of the most useful of all books is *Helping Teachers Understand Children,* brought out by the Commission on Teacher Education; see Chapters I and II for the use of observation in school and home and for the study of cumulative records. One of the most widely used sources is J. Wayne Wrightstone's *Appraisal of Newer Elementary School Practices.*

The Home as a Key to Personality

THE KEY IDEA presented in Chapter 12 is "Seeing the Child as a Member of the Family." Bearing in mind that a child is influenced even more by his home than by his school, that nine tenths of his life is there and the ties are stronger and more enduring, a major job of the modern teacher is to work with the parents.

"Seeing the child as a member of the family" is as indispensable to understanding and guidance as seeing him in the school.

Therefore the theme of this chapter is: the two-way process of getting parents into the school and the teachers into the home.

As you read these eyewitness accounts, ask yourself:

–What should the teacher try to observe in the home?

–What should be the focal points of his visits?

–What can he find out about his children as he establishes rapport with their homes?

You and the Parents: Guiding Personal Development

RUTH STRANG and Latham Hatcher describe the striking transformation which occurred in a child's work when the teacher suddenly discovered a specific deficiency that had been hampering development.[1] It was the case of eleven-year-old Mildred, failing in the third grade of a rural school. She rarely followed instructions, seemed uninterested either on the playground or in the class, and accomplished almost nothing in her schoolwork. Blocked by the whole problem, the teacher went to Mildred's home and met the mother. But this personal visit threw no light on the cause of Mildred's retardation. Weeks passed, with Mildred "the same lost child, indifferent, unconcerned about the world around her." In desperation the teacher went to the home again. In a long conversation about Mildred the mother casually said: "I think Mildred is doing very well considerin' she can't hear good."

At last the teacher understood the real difficulty. From that day she changed the school conditions. She stood near Mildred and spoke loudly and distinctly. She told the other children about Mildred's hearing, and definitely shaped her teaching to help this individual child. "A grand awakening" took place in Mildred, in the teacher, and in the class. In every subject Mildred improved — learning to read, doing other kinds of schoolwork, taking an animated part in the play of the children. By the end of the year she was well adjusted and trying hard to catch up in her work. When she reached the eighth grade, her achievement was up to the level of the class.

[1] Ruth Strang and Latham Hatcher: *Child Development and Guidance in Rural Schools*, pages 14–15. Harper & Brothers; 1943.

There are many ways by which the teacher may acquire an understanding of his students. (Play Schools Association photo.)

Understanding the Child through the Child's Home Life

"Children are not born anew every morning on the doorstep of the school." This apparently obvious remark is said to have come from the experiences of a student [1] of the problems of parents and teachers in guiding the living of young people. Dr. Plant was pointing out that a child's life, as in the case of Mildred, is deeply affected by everything around him in home and community as well as in school. Each child is an individual personality, living in his own special world and developing from a long succession of experiences. The teacher goes as far as he can in understanding each individual through direct study of his behavior in the school. But we know that is not enough; the forces of the home play an even more important part.

The teacher must not forget that the school has the child for no more than a tenth of his life; he is in the home most of the remaining nine tenths. So the home provides valuable material for understanding each individual child. The parents can supply many otherwise unobtainable facts about him. They can give the history of the child's birth, his infancy, and his development during the very early years. From them the teacher can discover much about the child's emotional life at home: his place in the family, his relations with his mother, father,

[1] James Plant, Director of the Essex County (N.J.) Juvenile Clinic.

brothers and sisters; possible pressures under which the family may be living, such as financial worry, overwork, crowded living conditions, concerns about health, or frustrated social ambitions. The teacher can learn from parents how a child is handled at home: whether he feels loved and wanted, whether there is a calm and consistent attitude toward the child and his behavior, whether the standards set for him are geared right for his age or are beyond the possibility of his achievement. Only through close contacts and coöperation with the home can the teacher set the stage for each individual child to grow at his optimum rate.

The school parents, too, are the chief link between the school and the community. The children in the schools constitute nearly a fifth of the population, and their parents make up perhaps a third more; with them the other relatives — brothers and sisters, middle-aged and older people — add up perhaps to a total of three fifths of the entire population. Thus the direct way for the school to reach the community is through the homes of the children and youths who are in school. If anyone in the town can be counted on to work for the improvement of the schools and community living, it is the parents of the school children. They are the ones who have most at stake because it is their own children who are concerned. Here, then, is an important concern of the teacher; for the greatest growth of the individual boys and girls cannot come about unless home and school work together.

And yet, until our own day this coöperation has been almost entirely neglected. As the Commission on Teacher Education said:

> "Failure to understand boys and girls in terms of their family . . . relationships remains one of the most disturbing deficiencies of American school people." [1]

In former times few teachers visited the homes of the children, and few parents came to the school unless forced to do so by problems of discipline. The school has traditionally been an institution aloof from the community, in spite of the fact that three fifths of the inhabitants are directly and intimately concerned with it. There were many reasons for the neglect. One was the educators' ignorance of the necessity for close teamwork with the parents. Another was the habitual attitude of the citizens that school had little or nothing to do with life, the

[1] The Commission on Teacher Education of the American Council on Education: *Helping Teachers Understand Children*, 1945.

conviction that education was merely what went on in the schoolhouse from nine to three.

The traditional attitudes of the teachers themselves had much to do with it. Most of them resented the idea of visiting the home and saw it as an additional burden on an already overworked profession. Their job was in the classroom, behind the desk, hearing lessons and correcting papers with thirty, forty, fifty in a class and much "office" or "book" work to do after class. Their load was heavy enough without having to "call on comparative strangers." And in all likelihood the "strangers" would have felt just as embarrassed by their call. So, for generations the school and the home — each an indispensable factor in education and each ignorant of its dependence on the other — went their separate and isolated ways. The children, the parents, and the teachers — all were losers.

But in the educational awakening of our times the school is concerned with whatever affects the life and environment of the children. Education begins at birth and is a continuous process throughout life. And it uses everything in the child's world — home, school, and all community agencies. So the school has acquired leadership in the community, and the teachers work as teammates of the parents in the development of the best possible education.

The collaboration of parents and teachers is a two-way process. The school not only goes out to the parents in the homes; the parents should find their way into the school and become the closest partners and coworkers of the teachers. Thus coöperation works both ways, and we must study both. First, getting the parents into the school.

Getting the Parents into the School

In One School: 83 Parents on the Staff Helen Halter Long, Principal of the Chatsworth School, Larchmont, New York, says in a Bulletin of the Department of Elementary School Principals of the NEA: [1]

> "If the eighty-three parents who are on the staff of the Chatsworth School, in Larchmont, New York, were to neglect their school duties, the school library would not be open, ten hobby groups would not meet, milk would not be sold during the noon hour, the

[1] *Twenty-fourth Yearbook*, "Community Living and the Elementary School," page 120.

Parents and teachers work as teammates for the best possible development of the child.   (Play Schools Association photo.)

noon hour recreation room would be closed, and the visual education and school publicity services would be seriously disrupted. For these parents do not 'assist'; they are 'in charge' of these activities, being subject only to the supervision of the principal, as are other staff members."

One fifth of the mothers of the Chatsworth children work closely with the teachers in the school; little wonder the parents say: "This is our school."   It began in World War II as emergency war work; nevertheless, it illustrates dramatically many kinds of things that can be done.   The war had taken teachers away from education, and many needed activities of the schools were crippled; for example, there was no school librarian, and the library was open only once a week.   The parents stepped into the breach.   Thirty-five mothers formed themselves into a volunteer, part-time library staff and kept the library open full time.   They improved the library room and facilities, got the board to triple the library appropriation, and secured a trained librarian for the summer months.   As the weeks passed, they came to know the teachers and the children, and the problems of the school became real to them.

Other parents took over the visual education department of the school. They greatly increased the number of motion pictures and lantern slides shown in the school, devised a system of lending visual education materials, developed files for mounted pictures and pamphlets, and increased the visual education budget of the Parent-Teacher Association. Another group sponsored hobby clubs in the school: clay modeling, drawing and painting, music, sewing, dramatics, stamp collecting. Three hundred fifty of the 406 children enrolled in the school joined a hobby group. The PTA paid the expenses of the clubs and trained professional women gave their time as parent sponsors. As interest in the hobby idea spread, adult groups were formed in painting, clay, crafts, and dramatics. Still other mothers supervised the game room and other recreations used by the children at noon; this brought together parents and children for an hour of relaxation.

The publicity department of the PTA was expanded. Mothers wrote newspaper stories about the life and work of the school. At least two school articles appeared in the local newspaper each week. In this way the community learned what was happening in its schools. A new interest developed among the parents of the entire community in the program of the school. Steadily parents and teachers came closer together, and just as surely the school itself improved.

We cite this Larchmont case because it went most effectively to the heart of the problem of parent coöperation; it brought the parents into the school program as vital participants. It made them *a part* of the school; they felt its needs and cared enough to see that these needs were filled. It is the wise principal or teacher who utilizes such rich opportunities for parent-school companionship.

Neighborhood Parent-Teacher Conferences   There are still other ways in which schools have made the parent a part of its educational program. In some communities new types of parent-teacher meetings have been developed. In Palos Verdes, California, for example, parents and teachers met together in the evenings in neighborhood homes. The groups were small — twenty-five or less — and many fathers were present. The primary aim was to build up understanding and friendship between parents and teachers and to help the parents see that education goes on in the homes, in the movies, on the neighborhood playgrounds, and in the churches, as well as in the school. Based on a plan made in advance by the school administration, the parents came with questions, pertinent problems, and suggestions. Vigorous discussions and the study of family, neighborhood, and community issues created an understanding of the joint responsibility of parents and teachers for child development. Another benefit growing out of these activities was the increased confidence in the school's educational program.

A Parents' Room at School   Some schools have set aside a room for the parents — a room that is open to them at any time for conferences, group meetings, informal teas, and many social activities. In one school, situated in a low economic area of foreign born, such a room became a vital and important center for the community. To it mothers came with many of their everyday family problems of nutrition, clothing, language and other social problems. Their needs stimulated the forming of little groups through which they would help each other make over clothes for their family, speak the English language, or discuss with the teacher or principal some common problems of child growth.

The school staff equipped the room informally with a radio and interesting magazines and books. An informal bulletin board was used as a means of suggesting radio programs and magazine articles that discussed phases of child growth or neighborhood activities of interest to the whole family. The room became a stimulating agent for the exchange of ideas and news of interesting happenings in the community. Often the principal or a teacher dropped in to ask the parents if they would like to see a film which had to do with children's interests and growth. This particular "parents' room" became a subtle educational force in the family life of that community. Almost any hour of the day or evening one could find there a little group of parents at work.

Each neighborhood and each school must sense its own special problems and needs and must find its own most appropriate (or effective) way to initiate this vital process of getting the parents into the life of the school. You as a teacher will find a score of things that you can do almost immediately. For example, early in the year — within a week after school starts — invite the parents personally to come to group parent meetings. Get the mothers of your children into the school for an informal afternoon tea. Form a mothers' club to discuss and study their everyday problems arising out of child growth and development. Bring several of the parents into the work of the school kitchen, advising you on school lunches. Have parent and school picnics. Hold a school fair. Form a garden club, a school or community council, a book club. Build up community forums for the discussion of current problems. Open the school in the evenings for adult study groups and for workshops in music, painting, weaving, and other crafts. To achieve success in such activities takes time and patience; a month or two may pass while familiarity and confidence are being built up and friendship and enjoyment established. But in the end the results will be rewarding.

Parents Should Know Their Child in His Classroom There is one other phase of parent-school relationship which, while taken more or less for granted, exercises a deep influence in the life of the individual child. It is the parent's visit to the child's own classroom. This is as important to the high school student as to the elementary school child. Too often the parent comes only on invitation, on a special occasion, to ask a question or to "talk with the teacher," but that is not enough.

The parent should be encouraged to come to the school and classroom freely, spontaneously, and naturally. He should be encouraged to see the school activities as a part of the child's life and to make them a real part of the family experiences. The parent needs to know the child's room, his teacher, his friends, his life in the school. Only then can he have a sound, intelligent basis for understanding and appreciation of the work of the school. The child, then, can take home his school experiences with joy and anticipation. It is especially good for the child to sense a friendly, close relationship between his parents, his teacher, himself, and his school.

So much for one half of the two-way process — bringing parents into the school to study it and work for it with the teachers. In the brief examples and suggestions we have made only a partial approach to the problem.

Getting the Teachers into the Homes

Important though it is to bring the parents constantly into the school, it is even more important for you to go into the homes. Nothing can take the place of your seeing and feeling at first hand the home life of the individual children — of knowing them in their homes. If the

At school picnics, fathers, of course, are the ones who know most about fishing.
(Louise M. Gross photo.)

parents work with you closely in the school and mutual confidence is
built up, they will of course let you know more and more of their home
problems.

A new generation of understanding superintendents and principals
is coming into the schools. They see the importance of arranging time
for the teacher to make such home visits. In some systems, during the
first week of school, classes are held only in the mornings, thereby giving
the teacher the afternoon hours to plan and hold conferences with the
parents. In such systems the teachers *are expected* to become acquainted with the parents. Some plan parent meetings in the school;
others take the five free afternoons to call on parents and children in
their homes.

There are many ways of introducing yourself in the homes and many
effective "rules of conduct" which should govern your visits. First of
all, be guided by the mood of the parents. Let them feel at home with
you. Let their ideas develop the conversation. Don't pry. Their
casual off-guard comments will give you great light about the children.
Talk about the children's interests, their hobbies, what they like to do
outside of school. Seize upon any opportunity to show the parents
that you would like to carry these interests, hobbies, and inclinations
over into the work of the school. Give them the feeling that home life
and school life form one continuous educational and developmental

303

experience. Above all, ask yourself how you would feel and behave if you were the parent in the same situation. If they are reticent, be gracious and leave fairly soon. Do not make any notes while you are with the family. Remember that the best home visit is one that is natural and consequently significant.

Some Typical Reports by Teachers of Their Visits to Children's Homes
In many schools nowadays the teacher writes careful reports of his visits to the home, and these are filed in the pupil's Cumulative Record Form. These reports give the teacher's observations and his recommendations. Let us look at a few.

"When I visited Manuel's home the mother had finished a large washing and was hanging out clothes in the back yard. So I visited with her and talked about many things while she hung the clothes on the line. I told her about some of my interests in my own home, and I learned about her busy days and some of her experiences. She has an electric washing machine and the clothes she was hanging up belonged to a neighbor. I guess she was paid for doing the washing. She didn't tell me.

"The father and mother, six children, and an aunt live in a four-room house. I didn't see inside the house but the back porch was cluttered up and things didn't look neat in the yard.

"The mother said they were having a hard time. She said that they had got behind financially. Recently the milk cow that they depended on so much had died. She said things were easier for them in the summer when they didn't have fuel to buy and could have a garden. The oldest boy had recently joined the Army. For some time before this he had been without work. An older brother of Manuel's needs some medical attention. The mother said that they were anxious to have this attended to but didn't have the money at present.

"The mother said she couldn't help Manuel much with his school work since she had only finished the third grade. She said she could read better than she could work arithmetic. She was anxious for Manuel to do better in school. She told me that the father was not pleased with his report. As I have mentioned before, Manuel's book money and different fees were paid early in the school year. I am sure they must have made sacrifices to pay these fees.

"The baby is about two years old. The smaller children looked soiled and not well kept, but they seemed to be healthy. A neighbor came visiting in the back yard while I was there. The mother introduced her to me in a pleasant way.

"I encouraged the mother to visit the school. She said she would when she could, but she had so much to do. She agreed with me that Manuel responded better to encouragement than to being 'fussed at.' She seemed to appreciate my coming to see her and asked me to come back." [1]

* * *

"Donald (age 10) tells me falsehoods, and even though we knew or saw him do a thing he would deny it. By visiting his home I found his mother did a great deal of switching, and if he told her a story he would escape. I tried to make him feel that I was his friend and tried to build up his confidence in me. We laughed and joked together a great deal and I would often let him stay in the afternoon to help me and to run errands. Then he got to the place where he sometimes told me secrets and begged me not to tell his mother. His mother says he continues to lie to her at times, but I have had a long talk with her, and I hope she changes her way of dealing with Donald." [2]

One teacher had been trying to get the fathers, as well as the mothers, interested in the school. She had tried several means. Here is an example of one way she got the friendly interest of the father. A skilled mechanic, he had never been in his son's school. He was urged to come to help Patrick and his classmates build the scenery for a play:

"*April 22:* Patrick thinks his daddy may help us build some stage wings tomorrow. I wonder — he never comes to school. Is a very good carpenter, I think.

"*April 23:* Patrick came saying, 'I think Daddy is coming to help.' Shortly afterwards he (the father) appeared. He worked for an hour and a half with two other fathers and seemed to enjoy it. He did the directing on the job. After lunch Pat came back and said, 'Daddy said he had a good time at school helping us today.' If I am not mistaken Mr. W. has never been to the school before. He has several children in school. I taught one for two years — a

[1] The Commission on Teacher Education, American Council on Education: *Helping Teachers Understand Children*, pages 51–52. Used by permission.
[2] *Ibid.*, page 55.

problem boy — during that time he never came. I feel that maybe we have a closer friend in him now." [1]

Consider what one teacher learned, through a visit to the home, about a child's emotional problems:

"*First visit:* I went to visit Maria's mother this afternoon. Maria (an only child) was playing in front of the house. I asked her if her mother was at home and told her I would like to see her. She said her mother was at home but she knew she was asleep because she had told her to go out and play and stay away from the house while she took a nap. Maria did not go to see if she was asleep or not.

"*Second visit:* This p.m. I went to see Maria's mother again. I had a nice visit with her. They have one half of a house — an apartment. It is very attractively furnished. Everything is spotlessly clean. Mrs. K. said that Maria was beginning to be a problem, that up until recently she hadn't been. 'She is extremely jealous,' she said, 'but will probably outgrow it.' She said she (Maria) was jealous of her (Mrs. K.'s) attention to the dogs they have. She still likes a lot of attention. Her mother says she does not pet her, but that Maria still loves to sit on her father's lap. The baby is expected soon. I talked with the mother about the necessity for providing extra attention and affection for Maria. . . . The mother seemed to appreciate the help. Maria loves to read. Her mother says she reads nearly all the time when she is at home inside the house. Maria has never cared for babies or small children.

"*Third visit:* I visited in the home this noon and saw the baby. She was very sweet. Maria was proud of her and watched her carefully. Her mother says she is very fond of the baby." [2]

Isaac was "a problem" about whom the teacher learned much by visiting the home:

"I visited the home and talked with the grandmother who was visiting in the home because of the mother's illness. The mother had gone to the doctor. The father was at work. The grandmother (maternal) said that Isaac (age 9) has 'spells' and because of them his parents do not make him mind. The other children have to give up to him. The mother can do nothing with him now.

<hr />

[1] *Ibid.*, pages 48–63.   [2] *Ibid.*, pages 60–61.

He fights her if she crosses him, and she isn't well enough to manage him without the father, so she never crosses him if she can help it. The only way the father can make him mind is to whip him, and he seldom does that. The parents let him go places by himself. Sometimes he has a spell, falls into ditches, runs into things, almost gets run over by cars, breaks or loses whatever he has with him. He stays away for hours and they don't know where he is. If they don't let him go when and where he wants to go, he cries, screams, fights, etc., until they're afraid he'll have a spell so they let him go. He often goes off without permission." [1]

That Hugh and Harper were not "problems" was partly due to the wise guidance of parents, as their teacher discovered in visiting the home:

"When I visited Hugh's (age 12) home the mother and father and little sister came on the porch to greet me. I saw Hugh through the door combing his hair but he didn't come out until I called him. The father and mother said he had always been a very neat and clean child. They seemed fond of the children. I learned from the father that Hugh had a back-yard garden. We went through the house to see the garden. The house was kept neat and clean. The parents are proud of Hugh's garden. They said that things of that kind keep children at home instead of on the street." [2]

"Mrs. G. came to PTA and I showed her some of Harper's (age 7) work. She just sat right down and read every one and simply beamed at the way he had worked. She was selected for a grade mother. On the night of the Halloween party she came to help at our booth, complaining of being so tired. We were selling apples. Mrs. G. helped some but very often she just left the booth to talk, laugh, and play with the children. Harper seemed to be having a grand time; so did his mother. She forgot all about being tired. Harper was so proud of the fact that she was enjoying the party." [3]

If there were space to print them, we could bring you thousands of teacher's reports like these. One of your most important tasks as you visit the children's homes is to build up graphic files of such descrip-

[1] Ibid., pages 55–56.   [2] Ibid., page 49.   [3] Ibid., pages 57–58.

tions. In fact, before you start visiting, read all such reports that the files of your school contain.

What Do These Reports Tell the Teacher? As the result of visits to the homes, what can the teacher observe that will enable her to guide the development of each individual child? We give a few examples. You will find many more as you go into the homes and write records of your visits.

–The father is regularly employed; typical jobs — milkman, painter, policeman, accountant, machine-shop worker.

–The mother works full or part time as sales girl, waitress, laundress, telephone operator.

–The home is broken; child lives with mother; parent has remarried.

–Bill is one of a large family, or, Bill is an "only child."

–A large family lives in a two-room flat — very crowded, little space for the children's play.

–A common bathroom serves several families. Is that why Jane comes to school without clean hands, teeth, etc.?

–The home is meagerly furnished, but it is very neat and clean. There is a good feeling of group enjoyment, and each member of the family makes a contribution.

–Many parents attended school themselves for very few years; hence a seemingly unfriendly attitude toward the school. Frequent visits to the school establish a better feeling.

The Teacher's Task: to Understand a Hundred Unique Personalities
Summing it all up, perhaps you can see now the great task and the problems that confront you on the side of understanding. In Chapter 3 we saw how important and how difficult it is to *know* the thirty-odd children in your class. But now you see that in order really to *know* them — you must learn something at least about sixty or seventy more human beings — namely, their fathers and mothers and the homes with which they have surrounded their children.

A *hundred unique personalities really constitute your class* — that is, if you are really to understand the human beings in your class.

Each parent is himself an individual; each is probably striving to become a person in his own right. As you study these parents, you will discover that each one has very special hopes and longings for his individual child. In these homes you will observe a vast range of differences, not only in the physical and mental conditions but also in the vast contrasts in the ways the children are managed when emotional disturbances arise. You will see a wide range of interests, *variations* in level of understanding and appreciation of life, widely *differing attitudes* toward education itself. The parents will differ in the *reasons* for wanting the children to go to school, in the parts of the program of studies they are interested in, in the careers they look forward to for their children, and in their own peculiar appreciations of aversions to and animosities toward the life and problems of the community.

To name these pronounced or subtle differences that you will find in the homes of the children is merely to remind you of the difficulty of understanding the parents and the families. Nevertheless, as we have said, it is a task of such importance that it must be taken on as a primary obligation of the teacher.

The Written Report to Parents: an Important Bridge between School and Home

Another means of bringing about a close and secure understanding between the home and the school is the Report to Parents about the growth and achievement of their children. Since a detailed treatment of the content of such school reports is given in Chapter 16, "Evaluating the Work of the School," we shall confine ourselves here to their educative value and effective kinds of use.

You know only too well the conventional method by which schools have handled and still do handle this problem. The dreaded "report-card day" is only too vivid in your memory. This was the day, once or twice a semester, when your parents asked: "Why did you get C in arithmetic?" Or, "You are falling down in French!" Or, "Sally Smith gets A's in everything, why can't you? We work so hard to keep you in school!" Throughout most of our educational history reports to parents have consisted simply of sending home a letter or numerical grade: A, B, or 90, 70 — the school's evaluation of the children's work in each school subject.

As school people came to understand the problem better, they saw that such marks told little about the true life and achievement of the child in school. And there was little that the parents could do about it, or did about it. Many were fairly indifferent; these merely signed the report card and sent it back to the school. In cases of lack of achievement or inadequate progress, some blamed the teacher and the school; or, overprotective of the child, they shielded him from his weakness. In one such case a girl

> "was continually falling below the level of achievement desirable and possible for her. When the teacher talked to the mother about it, she just shrugged her shoulders and said, 'Mary told me it was awful rough stuff and she did not like it'; so I said, 'Why bother if it makes you unhappy.'"[1]

In the cities many foreign-born parents were unable to comprehend the report. Still others used the report card as a whip, comparing their child's standing with that of a neighbor's child, or with a higher record than their child could have achieved. Thus the conventional report card failed.

What Is the True Function of the Report? The wise development of a growing child can come about only through the continued study by the teacher and the child and the parent working together. The school report to parents, therefore, is an indispensable tool for carrying on this study. It can be one of the most important instruments with which to bring the parents into close understanding of the work and purposes of the school. Perhaps its most important function is to give the parents a graphic picture of the growth and progress of their child. In doing so, it can also be used to elicit information needed by the teacher and the school. As Strang says in her recent book:

> "From the report, parents also learn something about the teacher. If the teacher has good judgment, his report will coincide with the child's actual achievement. If the teacher is humane and friendly, the report will indicate enough positive trends in the pupil's development to prevent him from feeling undue discouragement or a sense of failure. . . . The effective report will give parents con-

[1] Ruth Strang: *Reporting to Parents*, page 92. Bureau of Publications, Teachers College, Columbia University; 1947.

fidence in the teacher's ability and will assure them that their children are being treated as individuals." [1]

Succinctly stated, what is the new educational point of view about the child's school report?

First: The report itself should be a descriptive, rounded picture of the boy or the girl. It should carry over to the parent a feeling for their child's life with the other children in the group, his daily behavior (ways and habits of working), how he coöperates with the others, his special traits and interests, his achievement on tests, and his creative and original work.

Second: Parents themselves should be encouraged to contribute to the making of the report. They have much valuable information concerning the out-of-school life of the child during the period the report covers. They should be brought into the school to talk over the making of the report, or the teacher should fill in the information on a visit to the home, or letters can be written by parents which can be incorporated as part of the report.

Third: After the report is written, it should either be taken to the home by the teacher and discussed, in part at least, with the child and parents together; or parents should be brought into the school for conferences on remaking it. This is indeed a subtle way of developing the educational understanding of the parents, perhaps the best way to give the parents a feeling for the philosophy of the school.

Fourth: After the report is finished, conferences during which it is discussed can build the coöperative home and school education of the children. Many experiences that the child needs can be provided only in the home and the other out-of-school activities. Some children, for example, need a more carefully planned health program, some need more planned social life, others guided experiences with reading and study, while still others need physical development. All of these can be adequately carried out only with the fullest help in the home.

Fifth: In one sense the interpretation of reports to parents is a continuous matter. Week by week throughout the school year it can be done whenever the teacher visits the home or the parents are in the school, or by the friendly note from the teacher commenting on the excellent progress or growth that Johnny made that particular day or week.

[1] *Ibid.,* page 2.

Report to Parents, as Used by Walt Whitman School,
New York City

FINAL REPORT OF BERNARD — GRADE VIII   MAY, 1947
KNOWLEDGE OF ENVIRONMENT — SOCIAL SCIENCES

Bernard continues to be enthusiastic about his work. He participates actively in discussions; is well informed as to facts; his reasoning reveals good judgment and insight into problems; little interest in written expression; he is enthusiastic in beginning projects but not always in completing them. His ideas are very good; written work not up to the standard of oral contributions.

Test score: 11.0 (Grade)

PHYSICAL AND NATURAL SCIENCES

Bernard is more interested in the practical side of science than in acquiring knowledge. He is not too much concerned in learning per se and does not absorb information too easily. The more exciting aspects of science fascinate him greatly. This is as it should be, but unless he settles down and learns to appreciate information and directions, his performance will suffer.   Test score: 11.0 (Grade)

SKILLS

SOCIAL FORMS

Well taught; impulsiveness sometimes causes him to disregard forms; continues to interrupt; should be more aware of forms at the lunch table.

SPEECH

Needs to control his voice in small groups; very forceful in large groups.

MATHEMATICS

Bernard's attitude in class is generally good. He has a strong interest in mathematics. His achievement is average.

Test score: 9.5 (Grade)

CREATIVE EXPRESSION AND APPRECIATION

Dance and Theater   Bernard's growth has been excellent this year. In both dance and theater he has disciplined his work and as a result has accomplished a tremendous amount in both areas. His interest in mechanical things has made him valuable both in lighting and construction. His work has been most creative.

Art Bernard does excellent work in chalk and water colors. His designs are like creative explosions — free, strong, sudden, even wild — and like explosions they cease to stream and flow when he has temporarily satisfied his craving for creative expression. His whole work proceeds in waves of extreme energy and lack of energy. He has done the most creative work in the group, or better, the purest creative work; that is, purely creative, unhindered and undirected by intellect.

Bernard's problem is to combine creative activity with the activity of conscious reasoning and intellect, in which he also indulges, but separately, at intervals. Such a combination, which is the ideal of mental activity in perfect balance, would probably modify his creative explosions but give them continuity. His reasoning periods would then be creatively enriched. At present he seems to create or reason as two separate activities, as somebody might go swimming or horseback riding. This is the reason for the strange wave-rhythm in his work.

Shop Bernard shows keen interest in all craft work and needs but to develop patience to become a good craftsman. He works steadily to develop his ideas and seems to find much satisfaction from creating with his hands. He is highly coöperative and pleasant to associate with.

Music Bernard has been somewhat inactive in any singing or rhythmic expression but his general support of the group program has been most commendable. He did a good job in his interest and discussion periods regarding "Music in Greek Culture."

Creative Literature and Writing Bernard has done a fairly good job of understanding and contributing to class discussions. He has gained in assurance and does well in his oral presentations. He needs a great deal of practice in written work, and must continue to improve in his spelling and technical grammar. He is much more willing and able to coöperate than before, and has made some strides in his effort to become proficient in self-expression.

Reading Score: 11.0; Spelling Score: 5.8

PARK AND SPORTS' CLUB

Bernard is very interested in games and has a strong competitive spirit. He is physically active and has good coördination. His execution of fundamentals would be much better if he would learn to relax.

PERSONAL TRAITS

Bernard is eager and responsive, which makes it a delight to work with him. He is generally responsible, but still too blunt in expressing his differences with his classmates. He needs help in controlling and redirecting his impulses; should stress neatness in his work as well as in his desk and person. He was a very responsible member of the "Alice in Wonderland" committee; his keen sense of humor was revealed in his characterization of Alice.

ADJUSTMENT TO GROUP AND SCHOOL

Bernard enjoys and does well as a leader in the group and in the school. This spring he has shown development in all areas of the program.

ATTENDANCE RECORD FOR 1946–1947
Present: 146
Absent: 14

Child-Study Groups of Parents and Teachers

For more than a generation the best of our schools have been bringing parents and teachers together in parent-teacher child-study groups. The Commission on Teacher Education investigated this matter very carefully and drew up several important suggestions for developing such groups:

First: The study must be based on the gathering of many significant facts about each child; only these can throw clear light on his motives and behavior. Such collections of facts have already been discussed as teachers' cumulative behavior diaries, and other records on the children.

Second: These diaries are important, but they must be validated against other kinds of evidence — facts secured in home visits, others developed out of the discussions of study groups, as well as those that appear in the objective test records of the child, and those got by consultation with the school psychologist. It is important for teachers to get parents' help in studying and interpreting the behavior diaries, for parents will point out many instances in which patterns of behavior familiar to the home and indispensable to an understanding of the child have been missed by the teacher. Thus the study group helps the teacher in many ways: It checks the facts on an individual child, un-covers blind spots, and cites significant exceptional happenings. It identifies chronic patterns of behavior that need study and suggests hypothetical explanations for certain patterns of behavior. It helps the teacher to see these in the light of the total life of the child and in terms of his life style and to plan practical ways of helping specific children.

Third: The concrete studies of the group should be centered in those boys and girls whose behavior, or lack of development, constitutes a problem.

Fourth: The real clarification of cases will come most fully, however, only as the parents and teacher become a true *study group.* This means a definite program of reading of theoretical and practical books on the biopsychology of growth and development of behavior problems and learning.

Fifth: Of great importance is the selection of a wise and skilled leader of study and discussion. The special needs of each group will finally determine the type of leader to be chosen, but one of the uni-versal needs of all groups is the constant presence of trained and ex-perienced consultants. Left to their own devices, parent-teacher groups all too frequently bog down over difficult problems and become im-patient at lack of progress.

Sixth: Above all, the teacher and the parents should organize them-selves as a group and develop their own plans of work.

Finally, the function of the study group should be kept constantly in mind — namely, to build knowledge of a body of psychological prin-ciples against which their ideas and discussions of behavior can be checked. Such a statement of principles, summed up from what we have learned about the understanding and guidance of children in earlier chapters, would deal with:

–the nature of different stages of physical, mental, emotional growth of the child

–knowledge of his relations with parents and friends in the home, neighborhood, and community

–knowledge of him as a unique individual and a developing per-sonality — of his satisfactions and frustrations, his interests and skills, and his special aptitudes for expression

–in general and recurringly, the factors that will favor his total growth and development as a person

From this brief sketch it should be clear that the development of a parent-teacher child-study group will be one of the most important steps in your teaching. It will give you great pleasure as well as added security in your daily guidance of the pupils, and it will build you as a person into the neighborhood and community life about the school.

Thus we see that the coöperation of the parents is the greatest single resource the teacher can bring to his aid. Work constantly for it, but make sure that it is much more than the raising of money for the PTA or helping out at special school functions. The educative process will go on well only when the parent and teacher work together in building an understanding of the child, learning his strengths and his shortcomings, studying his total development and growth. Parents want the "best" for their children, but this they can get only if they can work with the school in fitting its life and program to the needs and interests of the children and to the problems of the community. Finally, it is parents who can lead best in educating the community to the needs and purposes of the school.

Things to Do: See a Child in His Family

1. Select one of the children in the class in which you are working as a student teacher, and assume responsibility for building up an understanding of his home life. Make a plan for getting the collaboration of the parents. Invent new ways of bringing them into the child's school, supplemental to those discussed in the chapter. Remember that work with the parents is a two-way process — getting them into the school to work with you and getting yourself into the home.

2. It is the first visit that is most important. Find a way to establish friendly and happy relations, beginning with such suggestions as those made in this chapter. Appraise your plan in class discussion, and in the light of it, and in the light of what you know about the specific child, decide for your-

self what to do and how to do it. This prior plan is of great importance. Not only should it help you to prepare your own attitude in advance, you should in addition visualize the kinds of questions you will ask and topics of mutual interest that can be discussed; for example, the specific achievements, capabilities, interests, and hobbies that the child has revealed in the school, knowledge of which would encourage the parents. Be on the alert to find instances of the child's life in relation to his parents, and to his home interests, hobbies, special aptitudes, and so forth that will help cement friendly relations with the parents and that can be carried over and built up in the school.

3. Is there a particular "style of life," a unique "climate of opinion," that seems to mark the family that you visit? Can you see its reflection in the behavior of the child? Do they look at the school in a characteristic way? How do they seem to view their community, its government, its economic life? What is their reaction to the church and religion?

Further Reading on This Question

Among the many new treatments of this problem, two books of Ruth Strang's seem to us to be especially worth recommending. Her *Reporting to Parents* is a fine discussion of the use by parents and children of new types of reports. Strang and Hatcher's *Child Development and Guidance in Rural Schools*, with its eyewitness accounts of home visits by teachers, is equally helpful for teachers in town and city schools.

Among the best books is the Commission on Teacher Education's *Helping Teachers Understand Children*, especially Chapter III, "Seeing the Child as a Member of the Family." Don't forget the Educational Policies Commission's *Education for All American Children*, especially pages 246–259, for its description of newer tendencies in the use of home visits, study groups, and reports to parents.

For the nursery school, see Part II, "Parents at School," of Dorothy W. Baruch's *Parents and Children Go to School*. On the adolescent level see Katharine W. Taylor's *Do Adolescents Need Parents?*, which gives an emphatic "Yes," in a background of graphic description.

For the social setting in community and nation see the White House Conference Report, *Children in a Democracy*; J. K. Folsom's *The Family and Democratic Society*; and the *Twenty-fourth Yearbook* of the NEA Department of Elementary School Principals, "Community Living in the Elementary School," especially pages 90–144.

CHAPTER 13

The Curriculum — a Guide to Personal Development

THE OLD NOTION of the curriculum as a formal "course of study," rigidly governing the details of teaching, is being supplanted by the new conception of it as the entire life and program of the school.

Three major ideas now engage our attention:

–Education as *guided experience*

–The curriculum based on the *needs* of children and youth, and on the *needs* of society

–The curriculum as a program of activities

Guided experience, needs, action — the three basic conceptions of the curriculum.

In building the new curriculum the teacher must work at the age-long problem of subject matter. It is twofold:

–What shall we teach?

–How shall we teach it?

The meaning of subject matter has changed also. Success in developing the new curriculum will hinge on the teacher's success in grasping the new concept.

You and the Curriculum: Guiding Personal Development

WHEN A PERSON who has not been in touch with schools for many years enters a modern school today, he is immediately impressed by the variety of things the children are doing and the great range of materials they are using. "What a change from the school I went to," the visitor almost always exclaims. "We merely sat still at our desks, reading books or writing or reciting." But in modern schools children are moving about, going to other buildings and even to other parts of the town. They seem to read and write as much as their elders did. But, in addition, they measure and make things; they sew, weave, bind books, and learn to repair automobiles and furniture; they take part in forum discussions, make maps, study motion pictures; and they find time to paint, draw, model, and play musical instruments. It looks very interesting, but it certainly raises some problems.

"For example," the visitor adds, "in my day we knew what the curriculum was. It was the printed Course of Study, made by the state department or the superintendent's office. It told us what to teach, and when, and how to teach it. But now? Everything is all mixed up. What *is* the curriculum?"

There is of course a clear answer.

The curriculum today is *all* of these things that have been named. It is everything the young people do and everything they use — all the activities and all the materials of the school. Our democratic values must be translated into action. Hence schools will be places where children in their day-by-day experiences learn to see the worth in each individual and respect his contributions; learn to face situations, make choices and put them into action, and develop curiosity and insight which will enable them to use the potentialities of our society.

319

The Changing Elementary School Curriculum

What Is the Meaning of the Modern "Course of Study"?

The change in the meaning of "curriculum" does not imply that school systems no longer make city-wide or state-wide courses of study. As the activities and materials have increased in the modern school, the necessity for careful planning has become even greater. In the best of school systems, the supervisor or the principal of the school will give the young teacher a printed volume at the beginning of the year, saying: "This is the new course of study. Our teachers have made it themselves with the help of the curriculum bureau. It is *the general outline of work followed by all the schools* in the city. But within its general form, it is flexible; and you and your pupils will be quite free to make changes needed to suit their special interests and needs."

We have a number of these modern courses of study before us; to cite a single example, the curriculum outline of the elementary schools of San Jose, California. It defines for all the elementary teachers of the city "certain areas within which each teacher is expected to remain when choosing units of work." These, for example, are the areas the teachers planned for the first six grades: [1]

GRADE	AREAS IN WHICH THE CURRICULUM IS DEVELOPED
First	Home and School . . . Community
Second	Primitive Life . . . Food, Shelter, Clothing, Occupations
Third	Children around the World . . . San Jose and Santa Clara Mission
Fourth	Santa Clara County . . . California
Fifth	The Americas . . . United States
Sixth	Europe . . . Asia, Africa, Australia

Within this general outline the course of study suggests ten or a dozen illustrative "units of work" from which a teacher can plan the work of the year. For example, the first-grade units are:

The Family	Pets	Indoor Garden
Play (or Doll) House	Thrift	Holidays

[1] Albion H. Horrall, Lydia E. Codone, Mabel S. Willson, and Leah Smith Rhodes: *Let's Go to School: Integrated Experiences in a Public Elementary School,* page 24. Copyright 1938 by McGraw-Hill Book Company, Inc.

Community Helpers   Safety Club   Outdoor Garden
Post Office   Citizenship Club   The Farm

Not all of these must or can be used. A first-grade teacher is free to choose, even to make up others that serve her purpose better.

The theme for sixth grade is Europe. Units for "low" sixth are:

Europe, the Home of Our Ancestors

Greece, the Land of the Glorious Past

Rome, the World Empire

United Kingdom, Great Britain, an Empire on which the Sun never Sets

France, an Agricultural and Manufacturing Country

Germany, a Powerful Industrial Nation

The Lowland Countries of the Western Empire

Switzerland, Playground of Europe and Peace Center of the World

Norway and Sweden, the Land of Seamen

The Iberian Peninsula

Modern Italy

The Danube-Balkan Countries

Modern Greece

In this school the teachers were free to create the curriculum for any part of the program, the only restriction being that they design their new units of work to fit into the over-all plan made for the city. Working with their new freedom the teachers regrouped the children into eight groups and made a new curriculum plan for each one. The titles of the new units of work are as follows: [1]

FIRST (YOUNGEST) GROUP

The Family
Doll House
A Pet Shop
The Circus
A Market

THIRD GROUP

Trees
Primitive Life
Eskimos
Pueblo Indians
Ports of the World

SECOND GROUP

The Theater (creative English)
The Farm
The Garden (indoor and outdoor)
Mexico

FOURTH GROUP

Indian, Spanish, Mission Period in San Jose (This group had studied modern San Jose the preceding term.)

[1] Horrall, Codone, Willson, and Rhodes: *Op. cit.*, pages 28–29.

FIFTH GROUP

Transportation and Communication in Santa Clara County
Industrial Development in the County
Gold
Water
Our Community

SIXTH GROUP

The Search for Gold in the New World
The Making of the United States
Westward Ho!
How Invention Changed American Life
The Union in Danger
Our Neighbors in the South

SEVENTH GROUP

Ancient Greece
Feudal Life
Spain, Past and Present
Architecture Marches On (famous buildings of old Europe)
Peoples and Homes of Modern Europe

EIGHTH (OLDEST) GROUP

The Mediterranean Countries
Australia and the Islands of the Pacific
The Scandinavians
The Hot Dry Lands

What Goes on in These Units of Work?

You know, no doubt, what goes on in the old-fashioned teaching of a subject of study. Each child is given a textbook, and assignments covering certain pages are made from it. At stated periods in the day, for example — 9:15–9:45 . . . 10:20–10:40 . . . or 2:00–2:20, the children read the assigned pages and answer questions on them. In addition, they do certain writing assignments, solve arithmetic problems, or spell the words in certain lists. This goes on all day long in the "subject" curriculum.

But what happens with the modern curriculum of the better public schools? We shall illustrate with a single example from a sixth-grade social-studies unit of San Jose's Lincoln School. The unit is centered on European architecture.

Who Plans the Unit of Work? This unit is an admirable example of the new tendencies in curriculum building. First, it was developed in a public city school in which the size of class (averaging 30–35) and the intelligence and home conditions of children were representative of many

In a modern school, materials of this kind become imperative as a means of developing understanding. (Denver Public Schools photo.)

American schools. It will give you a clear idea of what progressive teachers can do in curriculum development under good public school conditions. Second, the unit was planned and developed by the sixth-grade teacher, with the advice of the principal and other teachers in the school. It grew out of the coöperative plan for the program of the six grades that all the teachers, who had been studying in a teachers' workshop, had devised together. That plan called for study of Europe as the central social studies theme of the low sixth grade. The suggested units included:

–Europe: The Home of Our Ancestors
–Greece: The Land of the Glorious Past
–Rome: The World Empire

and similar ones for ten European countries today. The Lincoln School teachers, after getting suggestions from many published units,[1] decided that they could carry on a fine study of European civilization if they took European architecture as their central theme for the social studies in the sixth grade.

[1] In their study they used a published report of a similar unit in another school: Emily Ann Barnes and Bess M. Young's *Children and Architecture*. You would be very much interested to get this book for your library.

Note carefully one point about the newer methods of curriculum planning: the teachers, not the superintendent or supervisors, choose the general area of study, and the group teacher makes most of the decisions about the central theme and general plan of the work. Do the children help choose and decide? Yes — they *help*. But the teachers say in their report, *Let's Go to School*, "Although the desires of the children are given consideration, the teacher is responsible for choosing the unit." And again — "Whenever valuable suggestions come naturally from the children, she takes advantage of these 'leads' and turns them into channels that will point toward the new unit."

Only the teacher knows enough of the whole problem to choose the theme and make the big plan for the unit of work; "to leave the choice of units entirely up to the children might lead to a series of disconnected unrelated experiences." Each year's work must fit into the total plan devised for the six years of work and study. It is the total plan for growth and development, from six to twelve, that must govern the choice of work to be done in any one year. Little children cannot know these things; hence, they are not competent to make the over-all plan. But they can help plan the immediate work of each day or week; they alone know their real interests and, if encouraged, can make these known to the teachers. Many of their suggestions *are* valuable guides to the moment-by-moment development of the work.

Launching the Work: More Planning The skilled planning of the teacher was in evidence from the very first day. When the children appeared for the new term, their room had been arranged to lead them naturally into this European study. On the reading table were such interesting storybooks of life in Europe as *The Twins Series*, *Wisp*, *A Girl of Dublin*, *Made in France*, *Tono Antonio*, *Children of Other Lands*, *Our Little Spanish Cousin*; these were eagerly read during the first few days. On the walls the teacher had hung attractive posters of European life and picture maps of Europe that other classes had made. In one corner was a model of the Alhambra; on several tables were dolls and other articles from European countries. During the first few days group discussions and much reading aloud brought the children interesting facts about the lives and customs of European people. Thus the teacher skillfully set the stage for developing the children's interests in the study of European architecture. Finally, a personal incident, which concerned the European relatives of one of the children, gave the teacher the needed lead, and soon the group was launched on its study of European architecture.

But the planning of the effective teacher did not stop there. She had prepared in advance a list of the activities that might profitably be carried on by the group and the materials that would be needed. Holding this in abeyance, she stimulated the children themselves to make up such a list. The children's list included:

–read books	–appoint committees, each one
–look at pictures	assigned to a certain architecture
–draw plans	–build something
–find out kinds of architecture	–take some trips
–write stories	–make small architecture
–put on a play	–make up our own songs

The teacher's list of activities and materials included some of the things the children had suggested, as you can see from this selection from it:

–dramatizing stories related to types of architecture
–giving reports
–building vocabulary
–writing reviews of books
–reading biographies of architects of famous buildings
–making trips to outstanding examples of architecture in the city —
to those showing European styles
–making drawings of these buildings
–creating original poems of each period, etc.

Thus the wise teacher takes advantage of the suggestions of the children, but never relies upon those alone. He builds the feeling that the children are helping to decide what they will do, yet his eyes are always on the total growth of the children — both the year's growth and the long-time growth in the program of the whole school. Every unit of work, therefore, is designed in the light of what other teachers in the school have already done or are going to do in the years ahead, and also with reference to the activities in which the children are taking part in other hours of the day. Nothing is more important, therefore, than the most careful design of the program of work and study.

A *Trip to Study the Architecture of the Community* Knowing that
much of American architecture was really European, the teacher decided
to have a trip about San Jose to look for examples. To prepare for it
there was considerable reading in books; the teacher had drawn up a
list of books and articles within the vocabulary range of the children,
and these she and the children assembled. Out of the reading and
discussion the children prepared booklets in which they had drawn and
described the columns, capitals, and characteristics of Greek, Gothic,
Roman, and other types of European buildings.

Forewarned by careful preparation to know what they were looking
for, the group went about the city finding and studying examples of European architecture. Of the best ones they made notes and sketches of
doorways, roofs, columns, and other aspects; special attention was given
to the ways in which the European styles had been used in the buildings
of the community.

The children returned bursting with facts and questions to which they
wanted answers; for example:

–Are there other types of architecture?
–Were the Greeks the first people to use pillars?
–Are all the temples still standing?
–Were there many temples?
–Why were the temples built?
–Were the homes built like the temples?
–What was in the temples?
–Did the Greeks have any public buildings like ours?
–Did other people in Europe build temples like those of the Greeks?

Reading to Solve Problems The teacher used the questions as the immediate incentive for reading from the books she and the children had
already collected. Soon the town, including the school library and the
town library, was being ransacked for other material. From encyclopedias they assembled systematic facts; for example, countries and styles
of architecture were arranged in approximate order of the time in history
when they flourished. The class divided into eight groups, each group
reading on its chosen topic and reporting to the class with a blackboard
outline. These reports formed the basis for animated class discussion.
New questions arose, new words were added to the children's vocabularies, and the study developed in many directions.

What kinds of houses does America need and build?   (Frank G. Dickey photo.)

Constructing Miniature Buildings and Other Activities   One of the most absorbing activities was the construction of models of well-known buildings — for example, the Egyptian Pyramids, the Greek Parthenon, a Roman triumphal arch and the Pantheon, St. Mark's Cathedral in Venice, and the Cologne Cathedral in Germany. This led to other building activities — floor plans and elevation drawings of buildings, designed book ends, block prints for wall hangings, large charts on such themes as "Archways through the Ages" and "Types of Greek Pillars." A competition developed for the best floor plan and front view of each type of building.   For days the classroom was a busy workshop humming with these construction problems.

The Reading and Study of History and Geography   Questions arose which could be answered only by the reading of history and geography; for example — "Why didn't the Greeks have windows in their temples?" . . . "Why were the roofs of the Gothic cathedrals so steep?" Preliminary informal discussion developed into blackboard outlines which emphasized the geography and history of the countries and the customs, amusements, and religious ideas of various peoples. Reading and research groups under pupil leaders devoted several days to gather-

327

ing and organizing the needed facts, which were the basis of class discussion.

More trips were taken, and examples of other kinds of architecture were found within walking distance of the school; for example — the Byzantine, Gothic, and modern American. Each of these trips was a fine educational experience. All involved careful planning and discussion and the building up of a rich architectural vocabulary. Some led to creating prospectuses for European trips and making moving pictures and lantern slides.

The Conclusion: Conference, Exhibit, and Pageant   For several months the daily social studies work of this sixth-grade group continued under the general stimulus of their theme, European Architecture. *Actually, their studies took them into every phase of European civilization; architecture was only the beginning point and the guiding theme.*

Finally the work culminated in a general conference and pageant, entitled "Architecture Marches On," given before the whole school. Cardboard miniatures and descriptive charts of famous buildings were on exhibition. In addition, the culture pageant — scenery, costumes, children's songs, dramatic stories, and lantern slides — all had been prepared by the pupils, including such things as the writing materials of the Greeks, Romans, and Egyptians, their arts and crafts, and examples of Gothic stained windows. Peep shows and notebooks containing drawings and vocabularies illustrated the children's talks. The dances of the Greeks and other early peoples were reproduced, and their myths were dramatized. There was much creative composing of verse, prose, and song.[1]

Here, then, is a single example of modern curriculum making in a public, city, elementary school. You can find many others like it in America today. But most of these will deal, as this does, with the elementary schools. Perhaps you are asking: What about the high school? Is curriculum development advancing there, too? How does the new curriculum meet traditional subject-matter requirements? We shall see.

---

[1] You will find a hundred pages describing this unit and a large amount of similar matter about other units of work in the book written by four educational workers in the San Jose schools — *Let's Go to School: Integrated Experiences in a Public Elementary School,* by Albion H. Horrall, the Assistant Superintendent, and three of the room teachers: Lydia E. Codone, Mabel S. Willson, and Leah Smith Rhodes. McGraw-Hill Book Company; 1938.

The Changing Curriculum in the High School

A Platform for Secondary Education

If you had taught in a high school a generation ago, you would have had little difficulty getting acquainted with the curriculum. It was practically all in a set of textbooks. The mathematics was in an "Algebra" and a "Plane and Solid Geometry." Science instruction was governed by a "Physics," a "Chemistry" or a "Biology"; history by corresponding books in "World History," "European History," "American History." The other subjects were similarly defined. Curriculum planning was little more than (*a*) choosing the textbook . . . (*b*) dividing its content into the number of reading units that would fit into the semester or year . . . (*c*) assigning these day after day as reading and study lessons . . . (*d*) hearing lessons "recited" from these assignments. Curriculum making in the schools of yesterday was not a severe tax on one's imagination or creative ability. *Even today there are many schools in which the practice is not much better.*

But in the past generation great changes have come about in many high schools, and in the best ones curriculum development is becoming as creative as it is in the elementary schools. Since we cannot give many examples, we shall refer to a single study which summarizes nation-wide tendencies and also has the endorsement of the National Association of Secondary School Principals.[1] We present below *"The Common and Essential Needs That All Youth Have in a Democratic Society"*:

1. "All youth need to develop salable skills and those understandings and attitudes that make the worker an intelligent and productive participant in economic life. To this end, most youth need supervised work experience as well as education in the skills and knowledge of their occupations.

2. "All youth need to develop and maintain good health and physical fitness.

3. "All youth need to understand the rights and duties of the citizens of a democratic society, and to be diligent and competent in

[1] See their Bulletin for March, 1947: *The Ten Imperative Needs of Youth of Secondary School Age*, in which you will find hundreds of specific examples of new types of activity actually carried on in public high schools.

the performance of their obligations as members of the community and citizens of the state and nation.

4. "All youth need to understand the significance of the family for the individual and society and the conditions conducive to successful family life.

5. "All youth need to know how to purchase and use goods and services intelligently, understanding both the values received by the consumer and the economic consequences of their acts.

6. "All youth need to understand the methods of science, the influence of science on human life, and the main scientific facts concerning the nature of the world and of man.

7. "All youth need opportunities to develop their capacities to appreciate beauty, in literature, art, music, and nature.

8. "All youth need to be able to use their leisure time well and to budget it wisely, balancing activities that yield satisfaction to the individual with those that are socially useful.

9. "All youth need to develop respect for other persons, to grow in their insight into ethical values and principles, and to be able to live and work coöperatively with others.

10. "All youth need to grow in their ability to think rationally, to express their thoughts clearly, and to read and listen with understanding." [1]

This statement of needs was made only after years of experiment and research by leading principals of American public high schools. Study this list carefully. Note that, as in the elementary schools, the high school leaders are studying *the needs — the imperative needs — of the students*. These needs are becoming the chief focus of curriculum building — not the mere passing on of academic knowledge through encyclopedic textbooks.

Space is lacking to discuss and interpret all ten of these imperative needs. We shall illustrate only one, but it is, perhaps, the *most* imperative need of youth today.[2]

[1] Adapted from *Planning for American Youth*, The Bulletin of the National Association of Secondary-School Principals, Volume 31 (March, 1947), Number 145, page 2.

[2] The whole youth problem — the problem of those who go to high school and college — is discussed in Chapter 6.

Providing Work Experience in the High School Curriculum

At the very head of their list the principals place "Work Experience." (See No. 1.) Work, a part of the regular high school curriculum? Given credit for graduation? Yes, a beginning has been made; for example, in forty-six high schools, according to the March, 1947, Bulletin of the National Association of Secondary-School Principals. The Committee on Curriculum Development opens its report thus:

"Work experience should be considered an important part of general education and as such should be integrated with other phases of the school program. Both the schedule of the school and the curriculum should be arranged to accommodate it. Work experience should be available to all youth regardless of social, economic, or academic status. The 'poor little rich boys,' the 'Quiz Kids,' or the son of the Negro porter are just as much in need of work habits, attitudes, skills, and understanding as is the son of a garage mechanic. A work program should not be used to further the present class structure."

The Committee illustrates this principle with nearly fifty examples of ways in which work experience is incorporated into the regular school program. One school illustrates its part-time program, to enable

"students . . . to acquire skills best learned on the job. . . . In this coöperative, part-time work program, the typical pupil attends classes in the morning and some of his classwork relates to the job (on which) he works from three to four hours in the afternoon. As a part of his school social life, he may belong to various clubs which meet in the evening. He earns credits both in his work and in its related subjects as well as in his regular classwork. He graduates in the usual four years."

The schools are definitely fitting work programs of the youth into community needs. One school

"is fortunate to have the service of a student group which owns a spraying rig. In one year they used 60,000 gallons in four sprayings. They charge by the gallon, and the proceeds are used for the maintenance of equipment and for the student workers. Farmers are happy to get this service at one half the price charged by commercial firms."

Another school

"maintains an air strip and offers a course in aeronautics. During the season, the student pilot (with proper license) maintains a regular schedule in dusting the vegetables and fruits of the community. The school charges a fee to maintain the service."

In another town

"students manage teen-age canteens, assist in hospitals and clinics, entertain the aged and the sick, help with collections of food and clothing, assist in cleanup campaigns and in community chest drives. These activities are done under the supervision of various interested faculty members."

Practical farm experience, including agriculture and experimentation, is given in some schools; one school

"owns a farm [which] . . . gives practical operation sites for students' projects . . . makes possible sound experimentation and serves as a successful proving ground for the farms of the community. It provides the school cafeteria with fresh vegetables and fruits, with eggs and milk and meat and thereby contributes a measure of good health to all the students of the school. A part of the land is taken up by a timber lot. This is tended with care, thinned of young growth, dead wood cut out. . . . Along with learning rotation of crops and care of animals, boys on the farm operate electric brooders . . . [and the] machinery in the farm shop where the boys repair farm machinery, make self-feeders, grain boxes, sheep dips, and other farm needfuls."

In other schools the students keep the buildings and equipment in repair:

"Whenever possible . . . equipment needing repairs comes to the school shop to be redone. . . . Students, too, act as assistants to the engineer in heating. They repair electrical and mechanical equipment under direction. . . . Students plant and replace shrubbery and flowers and seed and care for the lawn. Responsibility for projects of beautifying, preserving, and caring for the grounds, greenhouse, in civic community projects, such as a cleanup campaign, in the mathematics of buying and planting, in soils for agriculture. Everyone is encouraged to make suggestions for and to have a part in maintaining the school property in good condition, for use by the whole group."

In some schools the program is tied in with the home conditions; for example:

"the extent and nature of homework done by the students can be influenced decidedly by the school curriculum. Many students redecorate their rooms as part of their home living course. Boys and girls in industrial arts are encouraged to repair and refinish furniture and to fix electric cords and leaky faucets. Home gardens are a part of the science curriculum. Girls through their home economics classes are stimulated to cook and sew at home. The unit on budget making in mathematics gives every student the responsibility to plan his own expenditures in terms of his allowance and/or income." [1]

These brief reports could be multiplied many fold, but they will serve as examples of what is actually going on in the public high schools of the country. Bear in mind that these illustrate only *one* of the "ten imperative needs" of high school youth. For each of the other nine listed, active programs are now being carried on in our best schools.

The Newer Meaning of "Curriculum"

From these examples of newer elementary and high school practice, you yourself could define what is now meant by the term "curriculum." It certainly means much more than an outline of reading and writing assignments. The very names that pioneers have given their newer types of schools indicate this. Caroline Pratt called hers the "City and Country School"; M. Decroly, the great Belgian schoolmaster, "The Active School." Still others have used the title "Home School." Years ago, influenced by Francis Parker, we coined the name "Child-Centered School" to emphasize that the whole child in action was the center of the teacher's attention. But even that was regarded as too limited, for it seemed to minimize the coördinate need for the school to be *Society-Centered*. That has led us to reflect the broad scope of the new education by the term *"Schools of Living."*

[1] All quotations, pages 331–333, from The Bulletin of the National Association of Secondary-School Principals: *The Imperative Needs of Youth of Secondary-School Age*, pages 11–20.

Whether or not that name is given to them, educators have come to conceive of the schools today as enterprises in living. Hence, although they still use the term curriculum, they mean by it everything that goes on in the school. The "curriculum" becomes — "The Life and Program of the School"; every aspect of a truly vital education partakes of life itself. Not only is the new curriculum all that goes on in the school; the good teacher sees to it that *more* goes on, more rich and varied experiences than ever went on in the old school. Learning is viewed as living through new situations, and the curriculum becomes a continuing stream of activities that constitute the life of the young people and their elders. Thus the school does, indeed, become a School of Living.

The Meaning of "Subject Matter"

The conventional schools have always regarded the reading, writing, arithmetic, mathematics, language, and science of the liberal arts curriculum as the subject matter of education. Indeed, they regard it as the only valid kind of material one could properly call subject matter. The leaders of these schools have always denounced the progressive schools on the ground that they got a lot of activity out of the children but mighty little "subject matter" into their heads. By this they meant that literary and mathematical skills and scientific and historical facts were slighted, the classics were well-nigh ignored, and these, they said, are the true subject matter of education.

We can be very sure, therefore, that the problem of the proper subject matter of education is not only important; it is difficult. Throughout history, philosophers and students of education have wrestled with it. Perhaps, as John Dewey said long ago, it will never be solved. Nearly a hundred years ago Herbert Spencer, the distinguished British philosopher, wrote a book about the classic question: What knowledge is of most worth? We can restate his question as our problem today: *What experience can be used most educatively?* We know now that subject matter and experience are synonymous. *Any human experience that can be used educatively is potential subject matter.* Notice the phrase "that can be used educatively"! There never has been any quarrel with the proposal of the formal schools that mathematical symbols, words, and other linguistic forms are subject matter — *provided they are used educatively.* The real inadequacy in their subject matter is that

The environment poses countless questions for the eager, inquisitive child who has not yet lost his sense of wonder. (Louise M. Gross photo.)

to the present day they have ignored an enormous range of human experience that would have been just as good subject matter as their mathematics and language, perhaps much better. The kinds of activities that we have described throughout this book *all constitute excellent subject matter for education provided they are used educatively.* Let us recall a few:

–Planning a visit to a community industry, coöperatively stating the significant questions and other aspects of the trip, means of transportation, cost if any, contacting the right individuals in the industry, etc.

–Having vicarious experiences by using films, filmstrips, visits by competent individuals from the community

–Caring for school property: respecting it, repairing the old, planning the purchase of the new

–Participating in activities that are necessary for the total program of the school life — cafeteria, school council, newspaper, etc.

–Creating things, by individuals and groups

335

All these and similar experiences of the progressive schools can become fine subject matter, *if used educatively*. The chief difference, with respect to subject matter, between the old book-learning schools and the newer types is that while the former restrict the subject matter of education to narrow verbal fields, abstractly linguistic and mathematical, the latter employ *the entire range of human experience*. But it is important to reiterate: *any human experience, if used educatively, is potential subject matter for education*. The critical test is the educativeness of the material.

What Shall We Teach?

In planning and designing the curriculum of any school, you will confront two problems: What shall we teach? How shall we organize it? Let us consider the first.

In the examples of *curriculum development* that we have studied, what were the teachers "teaching"? What was the subject matter when a group went on a trip around the community to study the buildings? Or when the children were having a vigorous class discussion? Or drawing up lists of problems to study? Planning excursions? Listening to reports made by individuals or groups? Studying lantern slides or motion pictures? In each of these cases, what was the subject matter of education?

Since World War I, educators have blazed many trails on the curriculum frontier, but all have finally emerged on the broad, clear highway of *human* needs. Some saw the program of education in terms of adult needs today, some in terms of child and youth needs, and some, indeed, in terms of society's need of preserving its traditions; but all saw the solution in terms of need.

1. *The Curriculum Built from the Personal-Social Needs of the Students* The ways of life and the doings of 40 million young Americans constitute, educationally, the most important part of the culture. It is around the needs of the children and youth, at any particular time, that the activities of the curriculum are developed. What are these needs? If you are in a high school, ask your students. Notice how closely their responses agree with the "Imperative Needs" of secondary school youth listed by our high school principals.

This personal-social-needs approach was well illustrated recently by the teachers of the Ohio State University High School. In designing their curriculum they made preliminary surveys of pupil backgrounds and needs. They chose those experiences which promised to fit best into both pupil and social needs; [1] to cite a single example, the seventh-grade class in mathematics built its quantitative problems out of the data they collected from their own physical measurements of height, weight, chest expansion, etc.

In Denver, Colorado, high school classes organized a unit of work from their personal interests called "Living in the Home." Such ques tions were asked as: How can I make the most of the home I live in? What is the relation between poor housing and crime? How can a home be made attractive on a limited budget? What are the advantages and disadvantages of home ownership as compared with rental? What proportion of income should be devoted to housing? What should be the contents of the home medicine cabinet?

In five senior high schools over the country the students and teachers built a "core curriculum" out of such activities as:

–studying the personal living of the youths

–understanding themselves and their neighbors

–developing interests and appreciation in reading, gardening, the arts, and the sciences

–exploring problems of living in the family, and in many social-civic relationships

–discovering the characteristics of American democracy and comparing them with the traits of other cultures

–studying the actual workings of our economic system

2. *The Curriculum Built from Society's Need to Preserve and Pass on the Social Heritage* The ancient and honorable principle of curriculum building, followed by all the old schools, was to pass on the heritage in the society. Finding a deep sense of heritage coursing through contemporary history, the schools today, too, have insisted that the curriculum must build an abiding appreciation of our past.

[1] See their report in *Thirty Schools Tell Their Story*, Vol. V of the Eight-Year Study of the Progressive Education Association.

A good example is the Culture-Epoch approach of the Horace Mann School during its participation in the Eight-Year Study of the Progressive Education Association.[1] The program of the high school was built around two major themes:

1. The Story of Man through the Ages
   Grade 7. From the beginning through ancient period . . .
   Grade 8. To the discovery of America
   Grade 9. From the discovery of America to life in the modern world
2. Modern Civilization and Cultures
   Grade 10. American civilization and culture
   Grade 11. Other modern civilizations and cultures
   Grade 12. Modern problems and issues in America

The staff was consciously seeking to use the history of earlier cultures to enrich the present, to show how "progress or retardation in the life of man have affected the life contemporary with the child," and "to emphasize the elements of permanence as well as change in a society." In the junior high school it was carried on under the homeroom teacher's supervision but utilized the services of teachers in fine arts, science, industrial and household arts, mathematics, language, and music. Pupil-teacher planning recognized the personally expressed interests of the students as one basis for selecting the themes of study and organization of materials.

In the senior high school a broad study of American culture was carried on. A large amount of time was devoted to the study of American literature, the making of things by hand, such as a model New England village, painting of a mural which showed the growth of the Bill of Rights, writing and producing a play on the theme of the farm problem today. Regional studies of American life built on understanding of the culture of the region. In upper years, the growth of democracy, nationalism, imperialism, and fascism became the controlling theme, as being significant to the future of American life.

3. *The Curriculum Built from the Needs of Society: the "Social Demands" Approach* A third group of students have built their curriculum around social or adult needs. "Teach the arithmetic facts and

---

[1] See Vol. III, *Exploring the Curriculum*, by Giles, McCutchen, and Zechiel, pages 36–40, and Vol. V, *Thirty Schools Tell Their Story*.

Los Angeles high school students learn Greek dishes at first hand from a visiting student from Greece. (New York Herald Tribune photo.)

skills that our people will use," said Guy Wilson, *et al.*, in 1915. "Teach people to spell the 4000 words they will use in writing," said the group around Ernest Horn. "Teach the grammatical forms human beings use, particularly those that are hard to learn to use correctly," said W. W. Charters. This is the curriculum Doctrine of Social Use: *teach the skills and knowledge that people are going to use.*

"Society's needs? Society needs a generation of informed, skillful, thoughtful young citizens," said the new curriculum makers. "Society's need is not adequately met by preserving and passing on the social heritage alone. There must be emphasis placed upon activities of present-day living." Hence, there has been a concerted emphasis on "Areas of Human Activity and Problems of Life."

In the Los Angeles schools the physical-science instruction in the junior year of the high school was outlined around such problems as:

"our water supply . . . the Metropolitan Water District . . . the building of Boulder Dam . . . water purification, softening . . . conservation of watersheds. Approaching these problems, the students make models, demonstrate artesian wells, make model amphibian planes, traps for bathtubs, sinks, construct birdbaths, demon-

339

strate water coolers, test carbonated water, and the like. In stating their aims the teachers insist that the subject matter should be chosen from those elements of science of the greatest significance to understanding and that the teacher should be free to select and organize his subject matter to fit the needs of the particular learning situation."

Many schools have come to lay great stress on relating schoolwork to the actual life of the community. One recent report states:

"Visits to newspaper plants, factories, farms, libraries, museums, social-service and governmental institutions are common practice in schools generally. To be of greatest value, the thirty schools have found that such firsthand investigations should be part of a well-planned study with definite purposes clearly understood. In one school, located in Boston, the work of the ninth grade centers upon the study of history and present life and problems of that community." [1]

These are the three unique approaches to developing the curriculum.

How Shall We Organize the Curriculum?

Kinds of Activities

That the curriculum shall consist of many varied activities those who have developed our new schools agree. They have emphasized living, making, and doing; and the passive atmosphere of the old school is fast disappearing. Learning is no longer conceived as giving back words and mathematical symbols that have been read, or heard, and memorized. Today we employ no less than seven types of activities.

1. *Activities of Observation and Orientation* These include trips, excursions, and field studies; trips to stores, factories, markets, farms, warehouses and banks, libraries and museums, to the offices of local and other government, to railroad and steamship facilities, to art galleries and artists' studios. For the young people of the city, in addition to the foregoing, there are trips to the surrounding countryside for the study of the geography and life of rural regions; for those in the country, cor-

[1] W. M. Aikin: *The Story of the Eight-Year Study*, page 63. Harper & Brothers; 1942.

responding trips to town and city. Here, then, is one guiding activity of the school — the dramatic orientation and introduction of young people to the life of the local community and the nation.⟩

2. *Activities of Research: Finding Out* The schools of the past half century have taught us to use all possible ways of finding out things:

–Gathering data from the libraries of the school, the town or city, the country or state, and from national libraries and museums

–Gathering information in local industrial technology and agriculture from strategic centers in the neighborhood

–Studying the past through the experiences of old residents and the documentation of old records

–Reading from books of drama, travel, romance, biography

–The building up of collections of technical bulletins, pamphlets, monographs, survey reports, and statistical reference materials through correspondence with county, state, and national bureaus of reference and research

–Lectures from scholars in near-by universities, colleges, and museums

–Motion-picture materials in school motion-picture libraries

3. *Activities of Physical Construction* Acting on the dictum of free the arms and legs, free the body generally, as the first step toward freeing the mind, forward-looking schools have taught us to incorporate a vast range of building activities into the curriculum. These in the elementary school reproduce in miniature the outstanding characteristics of community and national life — stores and homes, courthouses, post offices, and other public buildings; in the junior high school — water supply and power plants, transportation and communication services, the making of a designed object in the form of a model as well as a drawing or drawn plan.   In the high school there is the manual work of the school plant itself, the repair and extension of the building, the making of physical equipment, electric wiring, designing and weaving of rugs, drapes, and other furnishings, the framing of pictures, and the making of wall maps as decoration.

It is important that young Americans learn to know their own towns and cities and to appreciate the beauties of their environment. (Play Schools Association photo.)

4. *Expressive and Appreciative Activities*   The deep-running role of creative and appreciative production in the new education has taught us to increase markedly the amount of time devoted to the aesthetic act. The great purpose of building sensitive persons out of aggressive and competitive individuals leads us to build into the new program a wealth of creative activities.   These will range throughout all the sciences and the arts of expression as well as the mastery of technical skills.   The material facilities of the school expand accordingly — a great range of physical or intellectual materials supplanting the pencil, paper, and pen of the old mass school.

5. *Activities Leading to Mastery of Skill*   The measuring movement in education, now nearly a half century old, has taught us to respect the concept of mastery.   One hundred per cent mastery, not seventy, or sixty, is the goal.   A new psychology of skill, a psychology of the repetition, of building habit through recurring but varied situations, has given us the instruments with which to achieve it.   Thus the new program will

have incorporated into it an economical and efficient body of techniques — the mental skills of arithmetic, spelling, and scientific and mathematical manipulation; the manual skills involved in handwriting, typewriting, and business practice; the craft techniques in using tools and machines; the social skills involved in organizing people.

6. *Forum and Discussion Activities* Years ago pioneers of educational psychology added a new concept to our educational equipment: free the larynx of the child, they said, if you would free his mind; practice him in the formulation and presentation of his ideas and in the give and take of interpenetration of minds. Skill in the technique of study and discussion has been a central aim of the coöperative new education. The study group, with either adults or young people, is now recognized as being an educational resource of profound importance. Thus the new education provides conference tables at which young people and their elders exchange and validate ideas, learn the art of coöperation, and grow under the stimulating impact of personalities upon one another.

7. *Lecture and Assembly Activities* From Colonel Parker's Morning Exercise to the current Town Meetings of the post-war school, the new education has learned to retain the school and group assembly as an important educational technique. The function is manifold: to create a feeling of the community of the school, to bring before the young people constant exhibits of their own creative productions, to provide a forum in which individuals can present their ideas and develop aesthetic and forensic skill, to provide a place of community criticism of the work of the school, to give young people practice and guidance in the art of listening, and to introduce them to the best that the local community and region can supply in the way of public address. The new school finds important educational assets in the art of the lecture, even though the extremists among the progressives frowned upon it as a stiff and outmoded instrument. It is an instrument through which the drama of human civilization can be presented by means of grand examples of the spoken word. Keep the lecture, says the new school, but keep it in its place — and require it to be creatively and aesthetically of a high standard.

Here, then, are seven examples of the dynamic activities that make up the life and program of the new school.

Two Opposed Curriculum Designs

As one acquires experience in teaching, he learns that the educative process will advance smoothly and effectively only if the materials used in learning and teaching are organized in orderly fashion. The complexity of the social world and the necessity for drastic selection from the multitudinous samples of human experience, as well as the intricacy of the learning and teaching processes, make this imperative. The materials of the curriculum must be carefully selected, grouped, and organized if the school program is to produce maximum growth in the children and youth.

But, we hasten to add, the curriculum designers of today agree that there is no royal road to social understanding. There is no one best plan. There are many different ways to start, many different sequences of material, many different uses of excursions, discussion, reading, open forum, practice activities, studies of episodes and historical movements, and treatments of social problems. One organization of these might prove to be as educative as another.

In the past half century educators have devised several different principles of organization of the subject matter of the curriculum. But they all reflect either one or another of two opposed theories of life, education, and curriculum design: School Subjects vs. Experience, or the Subject-Centered vs. the Experience-Centered programs.

Three Plans of Reorganizing the School Subjects

While the progressives were experimenting with the more far-reaching experience-centered plans of curriculum reconstruction, the college and public school reformers were struggling to find acceptable forms of reorganization that would improve matters but leave the curriculum in some form of subject organization. Many plans were tried, but all fell into one or another of three types:

1. Reorganization within a school subject and correlation of subject matter within or between school subjects

2. Building new courses from "Broad Fields" which embrace related subjects; either (a) "General" courses, or (b) "Fusion" . . . "Integrated" courses

3. The "Core Curriculum"

Sensitive observation is important to growth. (Louise M. Gross photo.)

1. *Attempts to Reorganize and Correlate the School Subjects* In our earlier chapters we have shown how the curriculum was made by committees of state and national associations. These contented themselves with a kind of patchwork rearrangement of the standard school subjects. Although slight rearrangements of content were made, most of the content of English, the languages, mathematics, science, history, and other subjects was preserved. No fundamental reorganization of the program to fit the needs of young people or of society was achieved.

A second attempt to remedy was that of the correlation of subject matter in the various school subjects. In every decade since 1890 educational reformers tried to improve the organization of the school curriculum by this method; in the 1890's it was a popular movement; in the 1910's and again after World War I it was frequently discussed in educational conventions. To illustrate it briefly: Courses in history, geography, and literature were taught "in parallel," the same chronological epochs being studied at the same moment in various subjects. Mathematics and science courses were designed with close reference to one another. The written work of courses in English was based upon the content of the social studies and the physical and natural sciences. Under such constant urging, teachers felt so much compulsion to "correlate" that they frequently went to absurd lengths in artificially bringing together the content of the various subjects. Looking back upon it, we can see that the correlation movement was a step in the direction of a more meaningful organization of the curriculum.

Nevertheless, these two plans — changes made within single school subjects and the correlation of subjects — can be considered to be no better than makeshift tinkerings with the curriculum.

2. *Grouping Together Related Subjects within Broad Fields of Knowledge* The second plan, to which we turn next, was *the dominant idea that gripped the reformers throughout the half century.* This was a forty-year attempt to broaden the groupings of subject matter, to merge or fuse or integrate subjects, or at least to blur the boundaries between them. By one plan or another the curriculum makers of our time have tried to organize curriculum materials by putting them into broader units and giving them longer and more flexible allotments of time. You will find them referred to by various labels, such as "Broad Fields," "Fusion," "Integration," "General Courses," but all of them fall within the "subject" conception. This trend engrossed the attention of most curriculum makers from the turn of the twentieth century until well into the 1930's.

By the 1940's the practice of organizing curriculum materials in groupings broader than those customarily represented by the school subjects was definitely recognized. The idea of "broad fields" was being widely accepted, and the parallel "General Education" movement was being extended into the liberal arts colleges and universities.

3. *The Core Curriculum: the Current Trend* Today in the most progressive public schools you will find much discussion of the "core curriculum." (The plan consists of setting aside a large block of time in each school day — quite generally the entire morning — in which to meet the common social and personal needs of the young people in one broad and continuous unit of work. A multitude of new types of organization have appeared under the general name "core curriculum." They all are visualized as bodies of activity and material central to the whole curriculum. The long period provides enough continuous free time to engage in extensive community and regional studies. Since the core curriculum builds common knowledge and skill, it is required of all the young people. It draws a cross section of the entire school community together into one group, made up of youth of all shades of interests, social status, and family backgrounds.

Such a comprehensive study requires expert knowledge on the part of the teachers and most careful design and organization; hence the use of a single Core Teacher who directs and is always present, aided by specialists in the various fields who are "on call." Applied to the high school, this is the kind of program with which the early progressive schools experimented in the years immediately after World War I. In a sense the core program is the systematic expansion in content and in time of the earlier experimental "units of work."

Summing up, then: The core curriculum

–is the broadest of the broad fields — providing for the common experience of all the pupils

–is based on a combination of pupil needs and social demands

–in subject matter replaces several narrow school subjects, drawing upon general areas of "knowledge and culture that seem to promise the help needed"

–utilizes a large amount of time, generally half of the working day

–provides for much active experience in the direct study of family, neighborhood, and community life, group projects, civic investigation, and the building and maintaining of physical and emotional health as a common need of the people

–assumes responsibility for the common skills of communication and computation

–necessitates careful planning and direction under the leadership of a single Core Teacher, but with the coöperation of specialists in the study of physical and natural sciences, health, the arts, the society, and mathematical and linguistic techniques

–makes learning and guidance of critical importance through the coöperation of specialists and the Core Teacher

–is, therefore, the latest attempt to unify the best of the broad fields approach and the experience-centered plan of curriculum reorganization

These, then, are the three principal plans of organizing the curriculum by school subjects. If you go to teach in a formal school of the older type, you will find some form of Plan I, the work organized by subjects — reading, writing, arithmetic, history, geography, etc. Or you may find yourself in a school in which many of the subjects have been fused or integrated into a "broad fields" curriculum of more "general"

subjects — that is, Plan II. Or, you may be working under Plan III —
the "Core Curriculum." But in all of these you will still be dealing with
some modification of the "subject-centered" organization.

Experience-Centered Plans for Curriculum Organization

Of the subject-centered plans, the core curriculum resembles most
closely the plans followed by the pioneering progressive schools.
Throughout the fifty years of work since Parker's and Dewey's experiments, these schools asked one basic curriculum question:

–How shall we organize the life of the school and its program of
work to guarantee *the greatest possible personal and social growth?*

They gave many different answers to this question, but they all reflected
one central theme:[The curriculum shall be built directly out of the
experience, needs, and aptitudes of those for whom it is designed, and
directly from their culture and its historical development. Broken down
into a fourfold detail, their curriculum question becomes:

How can we guarantee maximum growth in

–interest in man, his earth and universe, and his changing society?

–understanding it all intellectually, and appreciating it with feeling?

–capacity to express oneself, to make one's personal statement?

–technical competence enough to live well?

Earlier in this chapter we have illustrated the answer given by the
elementary schools in the examples from the San Jose schools. To
enable us to interpret the answers, however, we reproduce the outline
of a unit of work — the "Study of Boats" — from the third grade of the
Lincoln School of Teachers College, Columbia University. Although
this example dates from the 1920's, we have found no better one in
studying the results of the twenty years of curriculum experimentation.
It is one of the most effectively reported curriculum units we have ever
seen. A careful study of this chart[1] will answer several curriculum
questions: How did the study start? Who planned it? What questions did the children themselves want answered? What subject mat-

---

[1] Harold Rugg and Ann Shumaker: *The Child-Centered School*, pages 100–101.

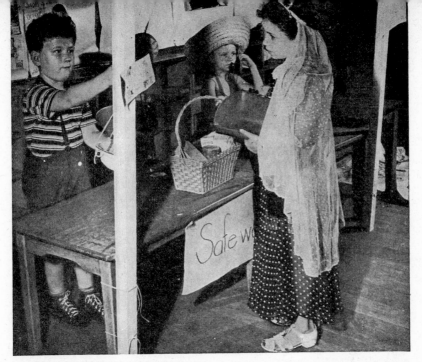

Young budget-minded shoppers often argue vigorously about the cost of living. (Play Schools Association photo.)

ter was used by the children and the teacher in answering these questions? How well was it organized? What outcomes did the teacher visualize? What new interests were developed which would lead the children to build further educative activities? In general, how were the total personalities of the children modified?

Three Major Differences between the Subject and the Experience Activity The study of the Lincoln School unit of work will bring out sharply the distinctions between the subject-centered and experience-centered curriculum. First, an experience unit is infinitely broader than the traditional school subject in its scope of concepts and ideas, problems and interests, and, hence, of understanding human life and activities. The third column of the chart shows that the subject-matter content which the children drew upon came from no less than ten school subjects, including the several social studies, the fine and industrial arts, reading, and science. An experience curriculum ignores all the boundaries between the conventional school subjects.

The second difference concerns the children's motive for learning. "The new school organizes itself around the child's intention to learn."

STUDY OF BOATS

THIRD GRADE

THE LINCOLN SCHOOL

STIMULATION

In the spring of last year many of the boys of this group were interested in trains and other means of travel.

Many summer experiences with boats.

Wood in supply box cut in shapes suggestive of boats.

Bulletin prepared by the teacher.

Trip to see Half-Moon.

Trip to see boat models.

PROBLEMS-QUESTIONS

To construct boats that will look like a certain kind and with which children can play.

How do boats "go"?

Who first thought of making a sailboat?

How did people get the idea for different shapes for boats?

To know more about the people who traveled on the seas in early times.

To find out about the making of boats.

How many different kinds of boats do we have today and how is each kind used?

How did early people use their ships?

To find out about the different parts of a boat.

How do people know how much to put into a boat before it will sink?

This chart was drawn up by Miss Martha Groggel. It outlines what Miss Nell Curtis did in her units on the study of boats, which were developed during several years of her work in the Lincoln School. This chart has been made from notes and records kept by Miss Curtis at the time that the units were in progress.

SUBJECT-MATTER CONTENT WHICH HELPED SOLVE THE PROBLEMS

INDUSTRIAL ARTS
Construction of boats: – making pattern, shaping hull, making sail, making keel, casting weight for keel, making rack for boat, and testing boat.
How boats developed from early times to the present day.
The difficulty involved in building a toy boat so it will balance in water.
Different kinds of sailboats.
The need for a keel on a boat.
Different methods of propelling a boat.
Modern inventions in connection with the propulsion of boats.
What makes boats float?
Different uses of boats today.

HISTORY
The Half Moon directed interest to Hendrick Hudson and his ship.
Historic Ships: – Santa Maria, Mayflower
Reference work, reading and discussions about : –
Vikings : –What color and kinds of clothing did they wear?
What did they eat? What kind of houses did they have? What were their boats like? Did Vikings have stores? How did Viking writing look? Story of Leif Ericson. The gods of the Vikings. Their beliefs.
Phoenicians – Scenery, boats, people, trade, beliefs, clothing, cities, industries, etc.
Egyptians. – Scenery, country, boats, beliefs, tools, writing, etc.
Story of the building of Solomon's Temple.
Early Mediterranean peoples.

GEOGRAPHY
Pictures of boat from newspaper which interested children in world geography.
Geography related to countries studied.
Norway – Country, climate, people and occupations.
Phoenicia: – Country, climate, people, trading routes, daily life of early people compared with that of today.
Egypt: – Country, climate, trading, etc.
Map interest: – Norway, showing ancient home of the Vikings.
The Mediterranean countries, showing cities of Phoenicia and routes on which the King of Tyre sent materials for Solomon's Temple
Plasticene map of Mediterranean Sea and surrounding countries on which children sailed cardboard models of early boats.
Globe in frequent use to locate places mentioned.
Outline world map, locating countries.
Interest in determining distances (reading scales on map).
How far is it from Norway to Phoenicia?
How far is it from Norway to America?
Building Lower Manhattan on floor with blocks to exhibit boats.
Map was drawn on floor buildings in New York City that helped most with sea travel.

ARITHMETIC
Measuring for boat patterns and measurements in boat making.
Figuring the number of board feet used by class in building boat racks.
Arithmetic problems in connection with science experiment of water displacement and floating objects.
What is a gram?
What is a cubit?
Dimensions of Solomon's Temple compared with dimensions of the Lincoln School.
Children saw a cubit measure at the Museum.

FINE ARTS
Sketching and painting pictures of Half-Moon.
Sketching and painting boat models.
Drawing blackboard frieze showing history of boats.
Ten easel pictures showing story of Leif Ericson.
Cut paper pictures of boats.
Painting Egyptian boats seen at Museum.
Painting Viking pictures showing clothing.
Painting modern boats.
Making clay tablet.

COMPOSITION-LITERATURE
Stories written about the trip to see Half-Moon.
Stories of other trips by individual children.
Original poems about boats and the sea.
Labels and invitations for boat exhibit.
Written and oral reports about boats, Vikings, Phoenicia and Egypt.
Stories for bulletin, room paper, council news, or absent class members, telling of class interest and study.

READING
Reference material pertaining to topics under discussion, found in school library or at home.
Children's reading material – Leif and Thorkel, Viking Stories, Early sea people, Boat Book prepared by other Third Grade, material prepared by student teachers.

SCIENCE
How can we tell if our boats will float and balance? Try out in delta table.
Three experiments – Why do some objects float and why do some sink?
How do people know how much to put into boat before it will sink?

DRAMATIZATION
Play-Story of Leif Ericson, spontaneously prepared by class.

MUSIC
Old Gaelic Lullaby.
Volga Boat Song.
Sail, Bonnie Boat.

PROBABLE OUTCOMES

NEW INTERESTS LEADING TOWARD FURTHER ACTIVITIES

DESIRABLE HABITS AND SKILLS

Better skill in sketching
Better skill in handling brush and paints.
A beginning of the development of how to sew.
Developing the habit of making a pattern before constructing an article.
Developing skill in shaping wood by means of plane and spokeshave.
Developing skill in using gouge and mallet.
Developing skill in reading distances on map.
Rapid growth in map drawing.
Developing habit of reading the newspaper.
Better skill in measuring.
Ability to gather information on a certain subject and reporting to class.
Increased ability in writing.

ATTITUDES AND APPRECIATIONS

Economic:—
An appreciation of the use of weights and measures.
What it means to construct a real boat that will float and balance properly.
Appreciation of the change in the lives of the people caused by the discovery of iron and the use of sails.
Appreciation of paper as a writing material.
Appreciation of the modern inventions in connection with the propulsion of ships.

Social:—
What the early people contributed to the world.
The number of people and industry it takes to supply materials for the construction of one building.
Comparison of the ideas of fairness of the early people with the present day.

Recreational:—
Developing a joy in painting, sketching and drawing.
Growing interest in reading books about historical peoples, inventions or boats.
Playing with boats made.
Interest in the construction of a toy boat.
Interest in the construction of a real boat.
The pleasure in making maps.
The pleasure of playing with maps.

Aesthetic:—
Appreciation of the beauty in line and construction of boats.
The adventure of the ship.

INFORMATION

Knowledge of the development of the boat from raft to steamship.
Who Hendrick Hudson was.
General idea of historic ships.
An interesting acquaintance with Vikings, Phoenicians, and Egyptians.
General geographical knowledge of the world.
What a cubit measure is.
Knowledge of how to draw maps.
Some idea of what makes objects float.
Some idea of how to make boats balance in water.
Some idea of how to construct a toy boat.
How the early people made their clay tablets.
How to make a clay tablet.
The need for molds in casting metals.
Some idea of how iron is made into different shapes.

TOTAL PERSONALITY AS MODIFIED BY THE FOREGOING EXPERIENCES

Interest in world geography and travel.
Maps and actual distances between given places.
The time it takes to get to certain places.

Interest in silk through answering the questions:—
What kind of clothing did the Vikings wear?
How is velvet made?

Interest in what clay is: how it is prepared for our use and how it was prepared by early people for making clay tablets.

Interest in the Egyptian and Phoenician alphabet and how our alphabet was developed from it.
The materials the Egyptians used for writing.

Interest in metals.
Interest in weight of different metals through casting of lead for keels.
How metals are shaped.

Interest in the construction of modern buildings through reading about Solomon's Temple and comparing it with the construction of the Lincoln School.

Interest in other phases of transportation.

The first two columns of the chart illustrate the point clearly by showing that the children's own questions played an important part in guiding and propelling their work. This does not mean that the unit was made completely on the spot. On the contrary, as the first column of the chart shows, the whole unit was planned very carefully in advance, its stimulation being designed by the teacher in the light of her rich experience in teaching children of that age. It sprang from work they had done the previous year, from experiences many had had in the summer, from materials the teacher had carefully arranged in the room, from excursions the teacher organized and led the children to take in the community. All that we have said about the necessity of planning in advance was illustrated in this study.

The third difference between the subject-centered and the experience-centered curriculum lies in the emphasis upon "the total personality," upon attitudes and appreciation (see the right-hand section of the chart). The experience curriculum practices the school's responsibility for transforming the Individual into the Person. The concept "the whole child" becomes much more than a new shibboleth in education; the curriculum is consciously designed to get as much as possible of the child into action at any moment. The "centers of interest" or "units of work" are good educatively to the extent that they branch into the total experience of the children; witness the anticipated outcomes in the fourth column of the chart. The teacher not only asks himself the question: Can the children read, write, reckon, and spell better? But in addition: Can they handle tools better? Read maps better? Are they more appreciative? Have they had a good time while they have been learning all these things? Have their feelings been developed constructively? Have they learned to work together coöperatively, in groups?

Summing up, then, we come back to the one great principle of curriculum selection: educativeness.

The Curriculum — a Powerful Guide to Personal Development

But the curriculum is even more than the living that goes on in the school. It is *guided living.* Throughout this book we have emphasized the *central role of guidance. To educate is to guide human experience.* All human living is experience, but educative experience is unique in this one respect: It is *guided.* A wise and mature person — that is, a

WILLIAM HEARD KILPATRICK (1871————), master teacher and Professor of Education at Teachers College, Columbia, from 1909 to 1938, was in that period perhaps the foremost interpreter of the progressive education movement in modern education. With John Dewey and Boyd Bode he has been an outstanding international leader in the reconstruction of the educative process. His influence was shown conspicuously in the development of the art of group discussion, both in America and in other countries. His thinking was followed for a quarter of a century by thousands of graduate students who thronged his classes from all parts of the world.

He was a prominent founder of the John Dewey Society and of *The Social Frontier* (1934–1939). He served as editor of *Frontiers of Democracy* (1939–1943) and was an active participant in the work of committees of the National Education Association and of the Progressive Education Association.

"teacher" — has entered the scene and *planned the experience so that it will educate.* As we said in Chapter 2, the teacher has arranged the experience to satisfy definite conditions of educativeness. These conditions are as follows:

–Freedom to investigate and experiment

–Opportunity to confront problems, compelling the individual to choose between alternatives

–Evaluation of one's successes and failures in terms of goals and growth patterns

–Material adapted to the individual's level of maturity and appropriate to his interests and abilities

–Stimulation of incentives and self-effort

–Incitement of personal creativeness and social coöperation

In short, we said that:

An experience is educative to the extent that the person who undergoes it is prepared, as a consequence of it, to live another experience more fully, more competently, more sensitively.

Using the great concept of growth, we said:

An experience is educative to the extent that the person who has undergone it has *grown* as a result of it.

More specifically recalling the three definite measures of growth:

> Can he manage himself better? Has he learned? . . . Has the experience been planned with the teacher's conscious anticipation of the fullest possible growth?

And finally:

> An experience is educative if it has been meaningfully personal to the learner.

This recall of our criteria of educativeness points to the powerful role of the curriculum in guiding human development. The curriculum is the total body of experience that the teacher plans for the children's living. It serves, therefore, as the constant guide in the development of the young people. To the extent that the teacher and the school plan well, the children grow well; to the extent that the teacher and the school fail, growth is stunted.

Continuing the Study of the Curriculum

1. We suggest that you begin your further study by gathering examples of old and new courses of study, showing the differences between the old subject-matter-set-out-to-be-learned point of view and the newer one which builds on the experiences and the needs of the young people. Appraise these old and new curriculum practices, answering such questions as these:

a) What are the striking differences in the kind of subject matter used?
b) To what extent does each make use of activities?
c) How closely does each type of program relate to what you know of the needs of children or youth?
d) Which kinds of experiences do you find most educative? Illustrate from the programs of study.

2. Study the kinds of planning done in making the newer types of curriculum. Who, for example, makes the over-all grade plan for the schools of the community, for the individual elementary school, and for high school? What part do the teachers play? the supervisor and principals? Pay special attention to the question: How are the children included in the planning?

Is there a special curriculum department in the school system? What does it do in the development of the curriculum?

3. If possible, get permission to join a group of teachers engaged in the development of a school curriculum. Write a paper describing and appraising their methods of working and the outcomes they seem to be achieving.

4. Prepare a paper on one of the current issues of curriculum development; for example — contrast the subject organization of the curriculum with the "broad fields" curriculum and the core curriculum. What is the real difference between the experience-centered and the subject-centered curriculum? As the result of your study make a succinct statement of what you understand to be the newer type of curriculum development.

5. Sum it all up by illustrating how the curriculum can provide favorable conditions of educativeness. Include your view of the conditions of growth.

Further Readings on the Curriculum

A concrete way to begin collateral reading is to gather from the curriculum laboratory of your college, or from local or near-by school systems, copies of "old-type" courses of study and compare them with such new type courses as are exemplified in *Let's Go to School* by Horrall, A. H., and others; *Willingly to School* by Zyve and others; or, for the nursery school, Dorothy W. Baruch's *Parents and Children Go to School*.

An over-all description and analysis of eight different school programs is given in Rugg and Shumaker's *The Child-Centered School*. Chapter II of J. Wayne Wrightstone's *Appraisal of Newer Elementary School Practices* describes examples of better curricula in elementary schools, as do Chapters IV–XIII of *Newer Instructional Practices of Promise* (the 12th yearbook of the N.E.A. Department of Supervisors and Directors of Instruction). See also Chapter III of the Educational Policies Commission's *Education for All American Children*.

One of the most graphic high school examples is given in the book written by senior-year students (1938) of the University High School of Ohio State University — *Were We Guinea Pigs?* The imaginative account given in *Education for All American Youth* gives us a glimpse of the improved curriculum that might be brought about in the schools in the 1950's. An interesting account of the potentialities of the curriculum of the high school, written from the personal observations of a professional lecturer, is Dan Stiles's *High Schools for Tomorrow*.

In many communities the curriculum will be governed by the state course of study. In the last fifteen years some of these have been made over, along newer and more progressive lines. You should study one or more of the reports which publish descriptions of the new programs and how they were developed. The best sources in which to find these are the following:

–Mississippi Program for the Improvement of Instruction, Study Program, Bulletin No. 1, State Department of Education, Jackson, Mississippi (October, 1934)

–North Carolina, Suggested Procedures for Curriculum Construction and Course of Study Building, 1934–35, Publication No. 179, State Superintendent of Public Instruction, Raleigh, North Carolina (1934)

–Texas, Handbook for Curriculum Study, Bulletin of the State Department of Education, Austin, Texas (September, 1934)

–Virginia, Organization for Virginia State Curriculum Program, Bulletin (March, 1932) . . . Procedures for Virginia State Curriculum Program, Bulletin (November, 1932) . . . Study Courses for Virginia State Curriculum Program, Bulletin (January, 1932); State Board of Education, Richmond, Virginia

On Principles of Curriculum Development

In your continuing study of curriculum development you need principles to guide your appraisal of old and new programs. A basic book is Smith, Stanley, and Shores's Fundamentals of Curriculum Development. Somewhat older, but important to the teacher, are Harap's (Editor) The Changing Curriculum, and the Third Yearbook of the John Dewey Society — Democracy and the Curriculum. By far the most extensive study of the progressive high school curriculum is Giles, McCutchen, and Zechiel's Exploring the Curriculum — the fourth volume of the report of the Progressive Education Association's famous "Eight-Year Study."

A recent appraisal is given in Alice Miel's Changing the Curriculum. Florence Stratemeyer's (Editor) Developing a Curriculum for Modern Living presents many examples of forward-looking programs for the public schools. The "subject" and "experience" curriculums are contrasted in Hopkins' Interaction: The Democratic Process, Chapters I, II, and IX.

Twenty years of work in building a small progressive public school system is discussed in Carleton Washburne's A Living Philosophy of Education. The leadership of the rural schoolteacher in building a curriculum from child and community needs is well described in Julia Weber's *My Country School Diary*. In *Were We Guinea Pigs?* the high school students themselves tell how they took part in the four-year experiment at the University High School of Ohio State University. On teacher-pupil planning a good source is Giles's book of that title.

At the close of Chapter 10 we gave readings that will be especially helpful in studying curriculum development based on community needs. See the Clark studies of rural schools in Florida, Kentucky, and Vermont, described in Olson and Fletcher's *Learn and Live*. See also Cook's *Community Backgrounds for Education* and Helen Storen's *Laymen Help Plan the Curriculum*.

The basic problem of *Child Development and the Curriculum* is well treated in Jersild's book of that title; see also Hildreth's *Child Growth through Education*.

The advanced students will need to carry their studies into philosophic foundations. They should not miss Dewey's *Democracy and Education* (1916), or his later *Experience and Education*. Theodore Brameld's *Patterns of Educational Philosophy* is a recent and important volume. Harold Rugg's *Foundations for American Education* is a comprehensive interpretation of the whole problem. On the newer curriculum trends in the liberal arts colleges see the Harvard Report, *General Education in a Free Society*.

CHAPTER 14

Continuing the Study of the Curriculum: New
Materials of Teaching

AN EXPERIENCE-CENTERED *education advances best in a rich environment.*

This principle brings us to the second aspect of curriculum development — the materials of instruction. Here, as in the case
of activities, curriculum building is entering a new day, and new
materials emphasize "real," firsthand experiences.

Not only a rich environment is needed to make possible better
teaching, but an *organized* environment; not only dramatic experiences, stimulating, impressive, and expressive, but *organized*
experiences.

And, as you have found through all your study, materials will
not organize themselves — only human beings can do that!

The Materials of Teaching

A PERSON may be a natural-born teacher and yet be seriously handicapped by lack of materials with which to teach. Fifty years ago that was not true, for generally speaking all that a teacher in small communities was supposed to have was a book, his own knowledge, and ingenuity in imparting it. In rural districts his school building was likely to be a single rough room, furnished with crude benches and an iron wood-burning stove, and his library was made up of a few texts and reference books. As you will recall, President Garfield at Williams College said you could give him "a log hut, with only a simple bench, Mark Hopkins at one end and I at the other, and you may have all the buildings, apparatus, and library without him." But how much more could a Mark Hopkins do today with the aid of the new materials of teaching!

New Buildings and Equipment for a New Education

The New Architecture

Visit one of the new buildings — a rambling one-story elementary school, standing in a setting of green fields, trees, gardens, or orchards. Every room in the building opens through great glass panels onto a well-trimmed green lawn. We can well understand that during several months each year this school moves much of its work out of doors.

359

A fifth grade in the Francis W. Parker School, Chicago, in the 1920's. (Photo courtesy of Flora Cooke.)

Grownups, as they walk into it, exclaim: "Why, it doesn't seem like a school at all!" It is much more like a sunlit home — one side of each room is glass from ceiling to floor. There are bright curtains at the windows, and light, movable tables and comfortable matching chairs just the right height and designed for children's work.

Here are space and fresh air and sunshine, and the freedom to enjoy them. Growing muscles demand physical space and freedom of movement. Growing speech requires mental space and freedom to think. Growing spirits also demand space, an environment in which to expand. If the new education aims at nothing less than the fullest development of all the powers of the children, then everything in the environment must coöperate to help bring that about.

Study one of these new classrooms more carefully. First and foremost, unlike the formal school, it is built for working, questioning, and doing, not for listening. Notice especially how the teacher uses the four corners of the room. Over in one corner is the children's library: open shelves filled with interesting books and flanked on each side with

360

panels on which are posted interesting pictures, clippings, and the children's comments. Here, too, are large round reading tables covered with brightly jacketed books. A half dozen small armchairs invite one to read.

That opposite corner is the "work center": a sink with cabinet space underneath it, for young painters, child botanists, or eager scientists; on either side, work counters with cupboard space above and below; beyond, another counter with two tables pushed under it giving more space in the room for other kinds of work. Over the counters are electric wall plugs ready for appliances and equipment.

The third corner belongs to the teacher. Here she has her own cupboard: a built-in closet with open shelves and drawers and a record file set conveniently into the wall. In the corner is her desk, beside it a comfortable armchair that invites a parent or a child to sit for an intimate conference or quiet talk.

In the fourth corner a low platform has been built. Soft yellow curtains pushed back on either side suggest a stage whenever "the play's the thing." A theater in an ordinary schoolroom? Of course, for many are the moments in the daily life of this school when dramatization is an important avenue to education.

Not only is the room cheerful — bright curtains, plants in the sunny windows, and walls colorful with children's paintings — but it is *educationally efficient*. Notice, for example, the wise planning of storage space. Under each window is a brightly upholstered seat for reading or the exchange of ideas; and under the seat is storage space for those "odds and ends" of material necessary to good teaching but unsightly if left about the room. Between the windows are built-in open cabinets, with spaces for the books and materials that are in daily use and for the display of things made by the children — all set in at just the right height for those sitting at the window to use. On the opposite wall are built-in wardrobes and supply cabinets. Blackboard space is ample but does not usurp the walls. There are many panels which have become an exchange of information and communication — bits of news, maps, pictures, and examples of the children's work.

These are beautiful rooms and efficient ones, everything in them designed for specific educational needs and planned in terms of the children's interests and activities. Beauty and use in the school, a setting planned for the maximum growth of all those who will live in it!

The New Equipment

(1)

_____ The materials of teaching in each classroom are organized partly in terms of the chief interests of children of that age. For example, in a first grade one might find a music corner. Drums, tom-toms, resonator blocks, a xylophone, temple bells, rhythm sticks, and other child instruments lie on open shelves ready to be used. Beside the piano are phonograph and records, placed at the right height for the first-grade child. On the display panel are pictures of people playing musical instruments, singing, and doing folk dances; on the shelves near by are colorful books of songs and games. Nowhere is there a feeling of: "Do Not Touch."

In a sixth-grade room a Science Center may carry along the special interest of the class. Here are materials to intrigue the young scientist — dry-cell batteries, doorbells, a magnet, iron filings, prisms, pulleys, marble chips, bottles, rock collections, tin cans, wire, and string. Perhaps there is an aquarium stocked with snails, fish, a turtle, and water plants. Or there may be a terrarium — the home of toads or salamanders. Any intermediate-grade room can have these; all that is needed is water, gas, and electricity, plenty of cupboard and shelf space — and the teacher's imagination and determination to provide them.

We could give many other examples of materials for teaching gathered around important centers of interest, each focal point depending on the ages of the children and their curiosity and growth through previous experiences. In one room the activity may be painting or sculpture; in another, mathematics; in still others, the study of the earth and the universe, of community life or world civilization.

(2)

If we need more illustrations, a backward glance through the earlier chapters of this book will supply many examples of the way the new materials of teaching are offering new opportunities to the teacher. A list of things to do suggested by sixth-grade children of the San Jose schools supplied the cue for materials needed for good education:

Read books	Put on a play
Look at pictures	Appoint committees and have each one study
Draw plans	a certain architecture
Make up our own songs	Build something ourselves
Write stories	Make small architectural models

Special interest corners and rooms such as this meet a particular need in the modern school (Ohio State University photo.)

What a room full of varied materials will be needed to do these things! Yet this is a mere hint of the richness of materials that experience-centered education provides for teaching.

Recall the picture of young democracy at work in the Town Meeting of the Cambridge School. There buildings, rooms, and teaching materials, as well as the understanding and spirit of the teachers and students, were organized to carry on self-government and growth in cooperative living. In the social-study clubroom was the rich resource material for the study of contemporary life — maps and charts needed for the particular problem being studied, reference books, pamphlets, and magazine articles. In a senior science room Mendel's Law was being clarified to the students by a fifteen-minute motion picture. The members of the ninth-grade science class were out in the town working in the community's water-supply department, collecting maps and bulletins, getting the facts for graphs, sketching the working models of the purification plant they were to build, and assembling a rich scientific library of books and other materials. In a mechanical drafting laboratory the young people were drawing maps and charts. The younger children learned something of reproduction and birth when the mother rabbit had five babies. In a real sense every room was a special educational laboratory. At noon the older pupils were carrying on the work of the dining room. In late afternoon many were working for pay on

363

near-by farms or in the shops of the town. Hence, natural materials, needed for education as well as socially useful work, were provided.

The materials of teaching, too, are the natural ones designed for a good educational program. For example, a good physical growth program requires that the nutritional needs of the entire school community must be cared for, and this means adequately equipped lunchrooms. Efficient health service requires special rooms for clinics and equipment with which nurses, dentists, and doctors can carry on their work. Technical work demands technical materials.

As for their expressive needs, children naturally write, paint, dance, make music, and create theater if they are free and encouraged to do so. In the creative media true freedom requires that proper materials be available when needed. This means studios and easels, tables and benches and kilns, paints and crayons and clay. It means wood, leather, cloth, metals, and many sorts of tools and materials. It means an art studio where young people can paint with teachers who are themselves working artists, and a room in which students model in clay and fire their products in a kiln under the direction of a sculptor-teacher. Architecture takes on real meaning to young people who help design their own buildings and equipment and use the new materials with which to build.

In the Shaker Heights High School in Ohio the teachers experimented with movement and rhythm as basic to creative expression. For example: "The class comes into the art room on their first day and are given paper and charcoal. The teacher suggests that they each make a drawing of something that moves — 'convey the sense of motion.'" The music teacher begins with the raw materials of rhythm — movement felt in walking, running, dancing, and in folk songs and dances. The creative-writing teacher puts no restrictions on the statement of some vivid experience. He encourages the use of words that express movement and color; he supplements with the writings of poets.

Living life to the fullest, each day, is the aim of the good school: responding with all the senses — seeing, hearing, feeling, smelling, tasting, and through the moving muscles of the whole body — to develop sensitivity to all the forces in the environment. The teacher utilizes all the resources that will enrich and build this sensitivity. Constantly he calls attention to the unique sounds in the children's world, and encourages the children to experience such things as the crunch of dry leaves on a crisp autumn day, or the express train rushing in the distance.

Experiences employing the sense of touch are encouraged: the texture of sand, of velvet, of worn stones, of new building materials, the current of a brook against the hand. Sight plays an important part: the reflection of street lights on the river, puddles of water after a rain, the beauty of the changing sky, or the trees and hills seen through the classroom window. All these and others are resources for developing sensitivity. As Edward Vernon reported in the *British Weekly*, these are "the loveliest things" the children know, and these are some of the resources that the teacher uses to create an atmosphere of sensitive awareness.

These examples of the new school architecture and materials of teaching confirm important concepts of the new education. The first is that a good education requires a good environment as well as a good organism. The ancient controversy over which is more important — heredity or environment — is again answered: "Neither one more than the other; both are important." Our study of child growth made very clear that a good education is based on the Principle of the Whole. "I teach the whole child" means not only that the whole body is in action, the whole mind, the whole spirit, but the whole situation and *the whole environment*. And this environment is as vast as the richest experience we can possibly give a child. The environment may become a wonderful series of concentric wholes radiating from each boy and girl and his grownup guides: his parents in the home, his teacher in the schoolroom, and others in the neighborhood and the community.

Summing it all up: The enriched culture of our modern life provides a stimulating environment for the children and gives the teacher exciting materials with which to teach. The best of organisms and the finest inheritance can be stunted by a meager environment, while stock only moderately good can be built to its best stature by rich cultivation.

An Experience-Centered Education Grows Best in a Rich Environment

The second great concept that our examples give us is "experience." In the past five hundred years of western civilization-building, the greatest single shift in human thought has been that from a dictatorial philosophy of authority to a democratic philosophy of experience. This

The school garden is one of the sources of meaningful learning experiences. (Frank G. Dickey photo.)

latter philosophy says to all the children and to all the grownups: "You and I are different; each lives his life through unique experience, yet each of us is a Person. Nothing is more important than the supreme value of each individual personality. Through the coöperative distilling out of human experience of thought and decision we build together our better world." Upon this Philosophy of Experience the School of To-morrow is fashioning an educational way of life that is truly educative. The keynote is experience. The new curriculum is being built directly out of the experience, the needs, and the aptitudes of those for whom it is designed, and is shaped by their culture patterns. Thus subject-centered courses of study are giving way to experience-centered programs of living and growing. Educators are grasping the great principle that to educate is to guide human experience. To do this most effectively the teacher must be able, at any moment, to draw upon any needed materials. This problem of materials is so important that we must study it more thoroughly.

New Materials for the Experience Curriculum

In the past fifty years modern schoolmen have devised no less than a dozen kinds of experience materials — to distinguish merely the principal ones. These range from materials used in personally felt, face-to-face experiences, the making-and-doing of things in everyday life, to the most abstract and symbolic ones needed in intellectual work. The good

school uses all of them; for the good education builds skills of body and
mind and social spirit, practices problem-solving, and fosters creative
expression and appreciation.   To avoid a bewildering and encyclopedic
enumeration we bring such materials together under four headings:

1. Materials needed for direct, firsthand experiences, in which pupils
   are "making and doing."

2. Materials required for demonstrations, excursions, and field trips,
   in which the teacher takes the leadership in guiding systematic
   observation.

3. Audio-visual materials of teaching — radio, records, movies, slides,
   collections, museum exhibits, and other designed groupings of
   illustrative materials.

4. The use of the printed word through books, pamphlets, bulletins,
   encyclopedias, almanacs, magazines, and newspapers — in short,
   the written symbol.

Thus the rich gamut of experience materials for learning and growing
ranges from the clear, direct materials for making and doing to the complexities of verbal abstraction.

1. Materials for Direct Experiences

"Real" to the Children: Making and Doing   Creative activities are the
most concrete of all the experiences of the school.   Here the young
people are doing things vigorously, making things, handling things, re-
constructing things, gathering and organizing needed data, expressing
their original ideas and feelings.   In such experience there is strong
motivation, as, for example, when elementary school children organize
and carry on the supply store of the school, buying and selling the things
actually used in the school, handling accounts, making sales, keeping a
set of books, preparing balance sheets and reports, and making budgets.
Similarly, in a school bank they handle the actual pupil deposits, cash
checks, and make financial statements.   These are all *real* to the children
— especially meaningful if they have earned the money themselves as a
part of their everyday lives.

A splendid case in point comes from the Jones School in Ann Arbor,
Michigan, where a street traffic situation was endangering the lives of

those in the school. The following resolution passed by the pupils of the "9A Law Enforcement Class," speaks for itself:

"Whereas, the executive board of the Parent-Teacher Association of Jones School at its monthly meeting on October 10, 1933, sent a request to the Board of Education through Superintendent O. W. Haisley that some means of protection be provided for school children at the intersection of Catherine and Division streets, said request to be presented by the Board of Education to the proper city authorities: and whereas, the said request was presented to Chief of Police, Lewis Fohey; and whereas, apparently nothing has been done about the matter; and whereas, the 9A class, wishing for some first-hand information about law enforcement in Ann Arbor, detailed themselves to check traffic violations at stated intersection as a class project; and whereas, the findings indicated that out of 533 automobiles passing through this intersection between the hours of 9:15 and 9:25 on the mornings of March 9th, 12th and 13th, 344 cars stopped and 189 did not stop; and whereas, such violations are conducive to accidents, since the person crossing the street at this point expects all cars to stop; THEREFORE BE IT RE-SOLVED that these findings be presented to the executive board of the Parent-Teacher Association; AND BE IT FURTHER RE-SOLVED that we, the pupils of the 9A social studies class, suggest to the executive board that this matter be again called to the attention of the proper authorities so that further steps may be taken to insure the safety of the school children and other pedestrians during the busy hours of the day." [1]

This resolution was presented to the Executive Board of the Parent-Teacher Association and later to the City Council. A committee of the Council investigated the situation and got the state highway routed away from the school street. This experience was certainly real in the lives of the school pupils. What materials of teaching were involved in carrying it through? Can you visualize the directive role of skillful teachers with a vigorous sense of social initiative?

Models, Mock-Ups, and Other Things in Miniature   Modern teachers have learned that many "real" experiences are baffling, hard to understand, but that simplified models can be made that will greatly clarify

[1] The *Eighth Yearbook*, Department of Supervisors and Directors of Instruction, National Education Association: *Materials of Instruction*, page 16; 1935.

Experiences must fit the needs, interests, and maturity of the child. (Play Schools Association photo.)

the problem. For example, to learn how to run and care for an automobile, we must understand how its mechanism works. We learn to bear down on the clutch pedal, move the gear shift from low speed through intermediate to high, and put on the foot or emergency brake. While most of us can drive the car, few really understand how the mechanism works; driving alone will never give this comprehension. But the wise teacher of auto mechanics knows that a "cutaway model," a photograph, or, better yet, a moving picture of the interior of the mechanism in action will throw light upon the operation.

Models and cutaways meet us wherever we turn these days. No doubt you yourself have joined a sidewalk crowd watching a cutaway dishwashing machine publicly displayed in a store window. Go inside, sometime, and ask to see an electric garbage-disposal machine; the salesman will take you to a similar cutaway showing its interior workings.

Community planners make models of whole redesigned regions — towns, power lines, transportation, communication, everything in replica — to educate the people to needed changes. Frank Lloyd Wright, the distinguished architect, built a fifty-foot-square model of his ideal planned community — "Broadacres City." Every residence, store, factory, and public building is reproduced in tiny wood miniature; every roadway, street, park, electric line, playground, and place of recreation —

369

all the appurtenances of the community and region — have been built to scale. How much more effective in getting over new ideas than speeches of exhortation!

Confronted by the insistent need for large-scale education of aviators, engineers, and other technicians, the United States armed forces in World War II learned to use models and other "contrived experiences." Moreover, they invented a new one — what they came to call the "mock-up." In this the essential details of any complex mechanism — for example, the electric-lighting system of an airplane — are assembled in "mock" style on an exhibit table or wall board. This makes visually clear things that are mere words when described in a lecture.

A generation ago the imaginative pioneers of the new schools invented many effective learning devices. In hundreds of classrooms today young people develop a better understanding of world seafaring through building models of the ships of mankind, and of land transportation through models of prairie schooners, early locomotives, trains, and automobiles. A clearer understanding of the development of industry comes through making and using models of Eli Whitney's cotton gin, Samuel Morse's telegraph, Thomas Edison's phonograph, Elias Howe's sewing machine. The history of colonial life is made graphic via the building of miniature Indian villages, frontier blockhouses, and forts. Life in other lands is made more vivid by building a miniature African krall or small-scale reproductions of an agricultural scene in early Rome, of medieval castles and villages, or of Inca mountain strongholds.

Dramatic Play   The third form of personalized experience that you will want to use in your teaching is dramatic participation. For a generation the new schools have been rediscovering the theater. Real life experience is of course most vivid and real, but there are definite limits beyond which it cannot be used. It is restricted, for example, to the actual local environment of the children and to the materials they can make and use personally. But dramatization can go as far as our imagination can take us. Any human experience can be dramatized. Both the past and the present, the civilizations of long ago and contemporary ways of living in other lands, can be lived vicariously through writing and staging plays.

With facts obtained from returned travelers, and from photographs or verbal descriptions of ancient and medieval life and of life today on

New York City children discover that part of their city is an island. (Play Schools Association photo.)

the five continents of the earth and the seven seas, modern teachers use the theater to help their young people relive the experience of other peoples. Folklore, folk dances, and folk songs gathered from the cultures of the world are used in the new elementary school pageants and plays as vital curriculum materials. The record of mankind throughout the ages as well as the story of making today's nations are dramatized through such famous episodes as the first Thanksgiving, the Pilgrims' signing of the Mayflower Compact, the Founding Fathers making the Constitution at Philadelphia, Custer's Last Stand against the Indians, the building of the first transcontinental railroads, the meeting of Roosevelt and Churchill in the North Atlantic and the signing of the Atlantic Charter, and a host of others. The dramatic episode provides a better feeling and understanding for those generalizations with which human beings think about human life. The theater is being made part and parcel of the new education.

Here, then, are three ways in which direct, firsthand experience brings to the teacher and her students a wealth of new materials: (1) socially useful experiences, (2) the building of models, mock-ups, and representations in miniature, (3) dramatic play.

371

2. Excursions and Field Trips, Demonstrations, and Other Kinds of Guided Observation

Excursions and Trips for Observation and Study One of the great achievements of the child-centered schools before the great depression was that they took the children and youths out of the school on carefully guided observation tours of their community and of the regions round about it. A few even arranged long trips to distant regions in our country and organized foreign travel during the summers. The excursion and the field trip became an indispensable part of the learning and teaching processes.

Even the four-year-olds in the nursery school now get their first glimpses of the interdependence of human beings in the cities and towns; for example, by watching the driver of the milk wagon deliver milk in their neighborhood. Under the teacher's leadership the youngsters in the elementary school explore their city or town in study trips. The children in these new schools become unofficial observers of every aspect of community life. Junior high school groups sit in on meetings of the Common Council, the Board of Aldermen, or the Board of Education. Senior high school youths in New York travel to West Virginia to study mining conditions or to the Tennessee Valley for a week's personally conducted study tour of that great experiment in the democratic rebuilding of regional life. Hundreds of schools send their young people each year to their state capitals, or to Washington to study the national Congress in action. Thus the environment itself becomes, through directed observation, a primary source of educative material.

But, you may say, such activities are only for the well to do. Here, then, is an example of what was done in a poor rural area in New Jersey. Miss Julia Weber, a rural teacher, describes a unit she carried on in grades four, five, and six in a two-room school:

> "Practically all of the children in the school are of foreign-born parentage, — Polish, Ukrainian or Dutch. The parents all farm and the children have a large share in this work. They are poor and have few conveniences. Only one has a radio, none have electricity, few have ever been to a movie. . . . Newspapers, magazines, and books are scarce. The experiences of the children are very limited.
>
> "When I began in the fall to study the community for resources,

I saw that very obviously nature was its greatest resource. The class was divided into groups according to the nature hobby each child wished to pursue. . . . Each child chose . . . a small piece of ground to observe. . . . If he happened to be particularly interested in water life, he would choose a plot where he could best study water life. He spent a good bit of his spare time sitting quietly in some spot in his plot observing. He recorded his observations, wrote them up, and illustrated them. . . .

"I made weekly trips to the homes and visited their plots with them. . . . Through these walks I learned much about the child, his interests, and his home.

"In these plots . . . the children found a great many Indian arrowheads, spearheads, and axes. These . . . aroused an interest in Indians, the former dwellers of the community. . . . Consequently a study . . . began. . . . The county library furnished the history of Warren County . . . and maps of rock shelters and trails. (These) were visited. I went to visit Dr. Cummins, at the county seat, who probably knows more about New Jersey Indians than any other man. . . . With this material I wrote stories for the children.

"From the discussion of the picturesque names of the Indian clans, as Minsi, 'the people of the stony country,' . . . the children got into a study of local topography. . . . They learned about the effect of the glacier, the meaning of terminal moraine, why we have muck lands in the mountains. . . . Many of the parents were dependent on the muck lands for their living. . . . They began to see certain generalizations — that trails tend to follow natural highways, that water supply attracted settlements, that man's home and occupation depend to a great extent upon the environment.

"The class made a rock shelter, which became later the center of a play for the parents. . . . They began individual museums of Indian relics. Their community is now an interesting place in which to live.

"Most significant has been the growth in my understanding of the children, through close informal contacts. . . ." [1]

Demonstrations: "Seeing Is Believing" "Show me how to do it!" "I don't understand it!" "How does it work?" are the constant cries of the learner in confronting new problems in arithmetic, new concepts and

[1] Julia Weber: *My Country School Diary*, pages 21–23. Copyright 1946 by Harper & Brothers. Used by permission.

processes in algebra, the new formula in the chemical laboratory, or the complicated machine. So the teacher "demonstrates." In baseball the athletic coach shows the novice how to hold the bat, in football how to pass the ball and tackle the runner, in tennis how to lob or volley. The mathematics teacher breaks down the complexities of the equation in algebra, shows how to factor or clear of terms. The chemistry teacher illustrates the processes of electrolysis, the physics teacher the relation between gravity, velocity, and time.

But, the demonstration over, the wise teacher requires the learner to duplicate the process. "Now you do it" carries demonstration into first-hand experience, and understanding emerges. So the new school builds its laboratories for every aspect of the schoolwork — the social studies laboratory for the study of civilization, and the physics and chemistry laboratories for experiments in the physical sciences, to name only two.

3. Audio-Visual Teaching Materials to Aid Observation

Museum Collections, Libraries, Exhibits   Good teachers have always known that one of their chief functions is to *create the most favorable environment for learning and growth.* An important aspect of this is to help the student find the data he needs in meeting any problem. Recognizing that the teacher's resources are limited, the modern school and community have taken steps to help the teacher. The most obvious and widely used source of help is, of course, the school and community libraries, of which we shall speak later.

The museum has come to stand beside the library as an equally important resource for community education. As a consequence, all the largest cities today have their natural history museum, their art museums (classic, or modern, or American), their aquarium, their museum of science and industry, their historical society, and their zoos — perhaps both a "live-animal park" and a "dead-animal park," as the children sometimes name them. (In southeastern Africa is an enormous live-animal park where the governments of that region drove elephants, rhinoceroses, lions, giraffes, and other kinds of wild-animal life of Africa into a rectangular tract of 100 by 200 miles. As we traveled through it some years ago, we thought frequently: What an opportunity to study wild animal life this is for the fortunate young people of eastern Africa who can come here!)

The intelligent leaders of modern civilization have used large sums of public money to collect significant specimens of the culture for public study and appreciation. The natural history museum gathers in one building the artifacts of animal and plant life of the entire earth — both the dead past and the living present. Another museum interprets the wonders of science and industry for us. A third gathers the greatest paintings, drawings, and sculptures of man's recorded history. Another, the fish of the seven seas. So it is that any class near a metropolitan center can use these organized collections for exciting and authentic study. On a modest scale hundreds of smaller communities are serving their youth in this way.

Such collections have now become one of the most valuable organized resources for education. As a consequence, the children of our good schools spend many hours each year working and studying art, natural history, science, and other things in the museum. Not only do children visit museums; many museums have interesting illustrative materials which they lend to schools. These traveling collections have the added value of becoming for a time a real part of the classroom work. On a smaller scale single schools, and even a few departments and individual teachers, build their own collections of plant life, stuffed birds, fossils, photographs, slides, films and filmstrips, coins, stamps, etc.

This is sense education: building understanding through seeing and touching, measuring, examining with a microscope, comparing species or types, analyzing, generalizing. So the organized collection of any materials needed for learning becomes one of the indispensable resources of the new education.

The exhibit is another form of collection, more temporary than the permanent collection, but organized at the moment for a definite educative purpose. It, too, has many functions. The class spontaneously organizes the materials used in a unit of work. They make an exhibit of charts, photographs, and specimens to illustrate an important idea. When these spontaneous collections are made, the children can take a large share of responsibility in collecting the desired material. The exhibit takes on special meaning when they have assembled it themselves. They are particularly interested that the gay, striped scarf was brought from Guatemala by Mary's aunt, that Virginia brought the silver necklace and bracelets to school, that Phil, beaming, came one morning bearing an earthenware bowl nearly as large as himself. And it helped Phil, too — Phil who was quiet and shy and who up to that moment had found it hard to contribute in any way to the class. When things come from the homes, the families become interested and identify themselves with the school and the work going on in their children's class.

Following through such an exhibit project, one senses that many good things come from the doing of it. Recall the San Jose sixth-grade exhibit and pageant at the close of their unit "Architecture Marches On." Whatever may be the content, the exhibit may be used as an important way to organize ideas, to help in drawing generalizations, and to build meaning of principles.

Motion Pictures and Radio   Each of the types of the materials that has come into the modern school to further good teaching has contributed something special to the new education. The motion picture and the radio are doing this magnificently. Consider what the motion picture can do that other educative instruments cannot accomplish. It can present in designed and selected form episodic and technical details of the paraphernalia of industrial life. It can present to us just those data needed at a given moment to illustrate a scientific concept or principle. It can foreshorten the passage of time, as in scientific agricultural films which illustrate the growth of plants. It can take us through space, in visual imagination, to the uttermost parts of the earth. Through its imaginative reconstruction, we can relive the dramatic incidents of human history. We can actually see James Otis telling off the British business lords in Boston in 1765, Patrick Henry making his famous "liberty or death" speech in St. John's Church at Richmond, Virginia, or Senator Lodge of Massachusetts denying President Wilson his League of Nations before the American Congress.

The motion picture can do most of the things still pictures can do — either photographs, filmstrips, or slides — and in addition it can move us by making the still pictures move. It can integrate, on a single screen, people, facts, and verbal meanings by animated maps, charts, pictographs. It can teach the sequence of events in history by creating the sense of moving events on a pictorial time-line and with them portray the dominant human beings of strategic historic episodes. It can integrate dramatically material from history, geography, economics, anthropology, sociology, and all the social sciences.

But this mechanism has further meaningful educative possibilities.

For example, whenever the processes of study and learning require a long-time exposure of any part of the film, the running of the reel can be slowed down or completely stopped, giving the study advantages of still photographs, filmstrips, or glass slides. Of course, the showing of a film will be repeated as many times as needed for careful study and analysis. A new development in visual aid to teaching is the movie projector set up on a small wagon that can be wheeled from one classroom to another. The film is shown, by reflection, on a glass plate and is clearly visible in a lighted room; this permits note taking by the students. It also means that while the film is being shown, the teacher can watch the faces of the students (or "observe the students") and see if there are portions of the film that are perplexing, and thus need elucidation or a repeated showing, or both. Here is a superb educational instrument of modern education.

And what of the radio and television which let us hear and see things happening around the world? Can you not visualize the well-equipped school of tomorrow — probably in *your* day — in which every classroom in America is wired for sound and pictures? What more effective and up-to-the-minute way of teaching current events can you think of, than by listening in on historic events as they happen? If schools had had the equipment and teachers the requisite imagination and initiative, millions of children could have seen as well as heard King Edward the VIII of Great Britain abdicate his throne, Hitler with his maniacal rantings and screamings exhorting his people to world conquest, President Roosevelt declare war on Japan the day after that country's sudden and disastrous attack on Pearl Harbor.

In some schools today the great speeches on the floors of congresses and parliaments can be carried to our youth, and great musical events brought to their ears. Appreciation of theater can be carried to wonderful heights through great dramatic portrayals on the television screen of the world's classic writings, such as Sir Lawrence Olivier's recent *Henry the Fifth* and *Hamlet*. How better can you bring to young Americans the materials for studying world government than to have them listen to critical debates of a United Nations' Economic and Political Council on such issues as those concerning Israel and the Arab countries? Thus on the screen and over the radio and television the pageantry of mankind moves directly before the eyes and into the ears of young learners.

Already the more progressive communities are building collections of 16mm films for use in the arts and the sciences, and in the study of community and national life.[1] Already musical and dramatic appreciation is growing as schools install efficient phonographic instruments and build record libraries of the world's music and plays.

Still Pictures: Photographs, Filmstrips, and Slides Before the motion picture was the still picture, either drawn or photographed. Its effect, because it is static, is not so moving as the movies. But it is a dynamic supplement to words, and modern schools have long used drawings and photographs to make remote experiences more meaningful. Two generations ago teachers who saw the educative possibilities in still pictures were greatly handicapped by lack of materials; photography was still in its infancy, and the periodical press was just beginning to hit its stride in picturing the world to its readers. But today, what a wealth of pictorial material is available to every rural and village school in America! The pin-ups of all descriptions and dealing with every aspect of life on the thousands of schoolroom bulletin boards are a vivid witness. Newspaper and magazine pictorial clippings can be found, practically free of charge, to illuminate any event, situation, or problem that the ingenuity of the children and the teacher can bring into the school. So, as you begin your teaching, one of your tasks is to help build rich files of still pictures to illustrate every aspect of your educational work.

One of the great contributions of the federal projects of the Works Progress Administration in the depression years was to assemble remarkable collections of photographs, paintings, and drawings of American civilization. These depicted historical events as well as contemporary episodes of community living. To name a single example, there is the remarkable file of photographs of the Farm Security Administration prepared by America's leading creative photographers under the direction of Dr. Roy Stryker. There is also the splendid "Index of American De-

[1] A few examples:
   Free Schools: The Hope of Democracy. Two reels, 16mm. Silent. A broad overview of the many services performed by American public education.
   The Child Grows Up. One reel. 16mm. Silent and sound. Child growth from 1 year old up to kindergarten age.
   The Builders. Two reels. 16mm. Sound. A cross section of the building trades, through the construction of a skyscraper.
   Louisiana Story. Produced by Robert Flaherty. A documentary-art film of the delta country.

sign," consisting of thousands of hand-drawn or painted plates which accurately reproduce the artifacts in our history; again, to cite a single example, there is available the graphic record of the development of glassware and pottery in New York State. The school systems of the future — community and state — will make available to every teaching group a carefully selected body of photographic and hand-drawn materials organized to help the teacher in every department of the school.

Moreover, photography is becoming a "must" [1] as a creative activity in the curriculum of the good school. Hence the building of the file of teaching photographs can now become part of the real experience of the children themselves. Make your own photographs! Yes, and make your own "Index of American Design."

Charts, Graphs, Maps, Pictographs, and Other Visual Materials Our study of the materials of teaching has taken us step by step from those materials used in the concrete, real experiences to those that are more abstract. This becomes especially evident when you turn to the specially drawn maps, charts, graphs, etc., that are coming into schools. Even the basic textbooks are packed with pictorial devices to illumine meanings formerly presented in dull and encyclopedic paragraphs.

Scattered through the pages of this book you will find many examples — pictographs, bar graphs, circle graphs, line graphs, and many others. How much clearer can the facts of the development of machine power in the United States be made, for example, by such pictorial devices as that on page 98. The facts of historical development become meaningful when represented by arranged sequence of bars, as on page 122. Comparative statistical facts of populations can be shown by such figures as on page 100. The facts of growth are presented by various kinds of line graphs, as on page 203. Statistics are made meaningful by the pictographs, as on page 99, or by means of a combined photograph and lettered graph. Thus any facts — those of population, production, exports and imports, climatic facts, facts of pupil ability and growth — anything — can be dramatized through the new pictorial materials.

In the last twenty-five years the dead pages of dull school textbooks have been stirred into life by new pictorial materials. To illustrate this

---

[1] See, as examples, teaching portfolios *Modern Sculpture* and *Texture and Pattern*, published by the Museum of Modern Art, New York City.

Finding places on the map of your own city or town and studying the layout of the city make map reading a vital, personal experience for the student. (Ohio State University photo.)

point for yourself, get a copy of any one of the new social science books from your school library and notice the methods of map making. A generation ago geographies and histories piled on a single map complicated masses of details, packed together thousands of location facts. Today each map is designed to teach just those location facts needed to grasp one concept or a few closely related ideas.

4. The Printed Word: Books, Pamphlets, Magazines, Newspapers — the Verbal Symbol

Having considered the merits of the new pictorial materials so fully, we return finally to the use of abstract symbols — words; indeed, to the teacher's first stock in trade. Modern civilization is above all a world of words — words spoken by people face to face, words uttered from

380

the stage and platform and over the radio, but especially the printed word. One of the greatest achievements of industrial civilization in the nineteenth and twentieth centuries was the bringing about of literacy. In 1800 A.D. not five per cent of humanity could read and write; today, in all the industrialized countries more than ninety per cent can read and write at least simple materials, and in countries changing from agrarian to industrial ways, the people are steadily becoming literate.

Although we teachers will use all nine kinds of experience that have been described in the foregoing pages, one of our most powerful educative resources will continue to be the printed word. The great intellectual aim of education is to develop the ability to generalize from our experience, to think in abstract terms and to use ideas. It is only through this process that we can control our world; through it modern men developed the Indo-European languages, the scientific method of thought, and the instruments by which we observe and understand our world. It was through their success in generalizing concrete experiences into verbally expressed ideas that modern scientists succeeded in creating the powerful engines, machines, and other technical inventions upon which our modern civilization rests. Thus, mastery over the word will continue to be one of our central educational aims and the Book will be man's most powerful single educational resource.

That educators have long recognized this fact is shown by the vast amount of energy devoted to the improvement of reading in the last forty years. As a result, you will be able to find in your college libraries today many scientific reports and books on this subject. In this brief section we can do no more than introduce you to the possibilities.

There are five kinds of reading materials used in our schools:

–Textbooks and accompanying workbooks as outline and resource material guiding units of study

–Supplementary materials: bulletins, current periodicals, and government and other resource reports

–Books for leisure reading

–Self-made reading materials

–Reference books

A brief word about providing these various kinds of reading materials for a school group.

The Use of Textbooks From the time when American public schools were started, much of the pupil's work consisted of reading and discussing a basic textbook in each of the subjects of study — history, geography, the sciences, literature, arithmetic, etc. The textbook was not only an outline; in many instances it comprised the total reading of the students. Occasionally one or two "supplementary readers" were covered in addition to the text.

The progressive schools tended to discard the textbook, building in its place large school libraries and making extensive use of community libraries. Pupils and teachers, in carrying on any unit of work, developed special reading libraries of many kinds of reading material — books, pamphlets, newspaper and magazine articles, bulletins, reports of government bureaus. One consequence was that the amount of reading done by children multiplied many times; it became common practice in intermediate elementary grades, for example, for children to read from thirty to forty books a year.

Another consequence was a radical change in the textbooks themselves. Most of the schools of the country, habituated to textbooks, continued to use them. Hence, forward-moving curriculum leaders and authors, accepting the prospect of intrenched textbooks in the schools for many years to come, said: "Let's change the books so that they will be in line with the new psychological and educational developments." So they did. After World War I, many new series of books were published. These were packed with rich dramatic stories of real life and illustrated by new types of photographic and pictorial material. While they still served as outlines, the texts themselves supplied three to four times as much reading material as did texts of the past. These new books were designed with infinite care, were well graded in vocabulary, and applied the most recent findings of the psychology of learning.

Not the least of the important innovations was the designing of accompanying workbooks. While many of these were superficial devices for recording information, some were designed to build skill in thinking, generalizing, solving problems, organizing material. Some became indispensable materials for teaching.

Supplementary Materials The desire for more reading material than can be found in a single textbook led publishers long ago to develop what came to be known as "supplementary texts." Teachers found, for example, that in developing a unit of work on the subject of "Housing" or "Shelter" they could use such books as: Carpenter, F. G., and Carpenter, Frances: *Houses We Live In*; Cautley, Marjorie: *Building a House in Sweden*; or Maud and Miska Petersham's *Storybook of Houses*. We quote a few titles to illustrate the kinds of books now available as supplementary readers.

Rush, C. E., and Winston, Amy: *Modern Aladdins and Their Magic* (also published in school edition under title, *Science of Things About Us*). Little, Brown, 1927
Lewellen, John: *You and Atomic Energy and Its Wonderful Uses*. Children's Press, 1949
Schneider, Herman and Nina: *How Big Is Big?* William R. Scott, 1946
Sorensen, Clarence W.: *Man in His World: a World View*. Silver Burdett, 1949
Carter, Margaret H.: *The Porters Try Sheep*. University of Vermont, 1949
Bothwell, Jean: *Star of India*. William Morrow, 1948
Brown, Margaret Wise: *Two Little Trains*. William R. Scott, 1949
Canfield, Dorothy: *Something Old, Something New*. William R. Scott, 1949
Mitchell, Lucy Sprague: *Guess What's in the Grass*. William R. Scott, 1945
Untermeyer, Louis: *Stars to Steer By*. Harcourt, Brace, 1939
Wheeler, Opal: *Frederic Chopin, Son of Poland*. Dutton, 1948

Frequently adult magazines run articles not only understandable but interesting to children; often they fit in with the needs of the school program. It not only delights children to read from "grown-up" sources, but it is good to challenge them with such material. Incidentally, we should note that the only way the teacher can be sure to know about interesting articles for her class is by reading comprehensively herself; it is her job to do so.

Another source of supplementary material is pamphlets and bulletins distributed by such organizations as the Bureau of Intercultural Relations, the National Association for the Advancement of Colored People, the Carnegie Endowment for the Advancement of Peace. These organizations put out a large quantity of material that will be sent free if a person writes for it.

Industrial and business corporations also send out materials describing how their products are made; steamship and airplane lines distribute gaily colored posters and voluminous material about the foreign countries they serve.

State bureaus and other government departments are also coöperative in providing information and interesting materials for schools.

Teachers whose classrooms have interesting collections of things; whose bulletin boards are rich with displays of folders, clippings, posters, and notices, and whose classes take stimulating trips through the neighborhood, are men and women who have imagination, resourcefulness, and the courage to ask for the materials they need. They have discovered that by a call or a telephone conversation they can achieve wonders for their classes. Trying it at first, they may be amazed that the head of the large cracker factory is really glad to have their class make a tour of his plant; that the railroad has a man whose regular job it is to take groups of children through the many fascinating parts of the station and aboard a new streamlined train; that the rubber company not only will send written material on the processes of rubber production, but would be happy to lend a two-reel film showing the story of rubber from tree to bright red balloon; that the Bureau of Motor Vehicles will send copies of traffic regulations, and with them a Traffic Safety Officer who will talk to the children and answer their many questions. Yes, a teacher may be amazed at first, but slowly she understands that help can be had from all sorts of unexpected sources *if* she asks. So she and the children ask. These are the teachers whose classes are stimulating, whose children are happy, alert, and interested.

Books for Leisure Reading The revolution in reading materials is splendidly illustrated by the increasing amount of leisure reading done in schools. Some school reading is, and should be, purely recreational. Through browsing and reading for pleasure, children develop a taste for reading, a fondness for good writing. Such tastes can best be formed in a child's early years, and to do this is one of the functions of a good school. Some books are selected because they contribute directly to

Magazines are fascinating for all ages. (Play Schools Association photo.)

units of study. For example, in a unit of communication Joseph W. McSpadden's *How They Carried the Mail* is invaluable. *The Old Curiosity Shop* is a "must" for its period in English history. As the Committee on Materials of Instruction says:

"We find children reading and discussing books of the literary experiences which they are having in the social studies field . . . or in other fields of classified knowledge, and these books give them background and wider understanding. For example, we find children who read *Robin Hood* when they were in the fifth grade using it again in the first year of high school as background for *Ivanhoe*. The familiar *Heidi* is no longer merely a charming storybook; it becomes part of the background for the children's study of life in the mountains. . . . A discussion regarding altitude zones takes place, and the children's understanding of climate is immeasurably enriched. Wilder's *Farmer Boy*, a delightful story of a boy on a typical American farm about sixty-five years ago, gives the background for a lively discussion of the question of natural education gained through living in a rich educational environment. . . .

"Children today travel with the pioneers from New England out to the Genesee country of New York State with Mrs. Orton's *Treasure in the Little Trunk*. They relive the life in the antebellum South with Rose Knox's *Boys and Sally Down on a Plantation*. They discover colonial Virginia through Nancy Byrd

Turner's *In the Days of Young Washington.* Their interest in
certain phases of elementary science is stimulated by Porter's
familiar *Girl of the Limberlost,* and we find them checking its
accuracy in certain respects. As they study Holland, we find them
deep in Daniel's *Broken Dykes* and know that not only has their
historical insight been broadened, but their understanding of the
geography of the country has been immeasurably increased, because this particular book reached the children at the right moment
and through class discussion its hidden implications were brought
out. . . .

"Children do not like biography, we are sometimes told, yet we
find them devouring Lagerlöf's *Memories of My Childhood* in the
secondary school, which with *Marbacka* completes one of the most
original and beautiful autobiographies of our time, and with its
Swedish background contributes much to understanding of that
country. When the French Revolution is being studied the girls
and boys, too, are buried in Eaton's beautifully written *Daughter
of the Seine.* And *Invincible Louisa* proves to be not only a delightful story-biography but also an added source of satisfaction
when it is presented as a true picture of a particular period of
American life and is recognized as the life story of a well-loved
author. . . .

"The slogan is not merely 'the right book for the right child,'
but also the right book at the right time, with opportunity for discussing it with an enthusiastic and well-read teacher who can bring
out its curriculum connections without detracting from the life,
color, and artistry of the work.

"The newer books mentioned in the preceding discussion are
listed here as samples of the type of book which has a close curriculum connection, if it is so used.

Daniel, Hawthorne: *Broken Dykes*
Eaton, Jeanette: *Daughter of the Seine*
Knox, Rose B.: *Boys and Sally Down on a Plantation*
Lagerlöf, Selma: *Memories of My Childhood*
McSpadden, Joseph Walker: *How They Carried the Mail*
Meigs, Cornelia Lynde: *Invincible Louisa*
Orton, Mrs. Helen (Fuller): *Treasure in the Little Trunk*
Turner, Nancy Byrd: *In the Days of Young Washington*
Wilder, Mrs. Laura (Ingalls): *Farmer Boy*" [1]

[1] *Materials of Instruction,* pages 71–72.

You can now understand how, even with the use of a startling variety of nonreading materials, reading is more than ever a vital part of the total program of our schools. That school people see this is shown by the development of reading-room libraries in our best junior and senior high schools. These libraries are the central resources for the reading of the school, and here students are helped to develop better reading habits as well as acquire interest and good taste in reading. We quote Hildur J. Jackson of the reading-room libraries of Seattle, Washington:

> "The reading-room libraries are distinctive in their plan and organization. The library room is equipped with the usual library chairs and tables. These, with built-in bookshelves, magazine racks . . . help to create the setting and atmosphere of a library for work.
>
> "The reading teacher is also the library teacher; and all classes are scheduled to spend one 55-minute period each day in the library. The time spent . . . is divided between instruction in reading and the varied activities that a library suggests. . . .
>
> "The function of a reading-room library is to bring within reach of all children a well-selected collection of supplementary and reference reading material. . . . It is the function of the reading-library teacher to give pupils such instruction in reading as they may need, to guide them in selection and use of materials." . . . [1]

Self-Made Reading Materials A recent development in educational practice has been the local preparation of reading matter. In conducting a study of a community or region it is often difficult to find informative, well-organized printed material. Sometimes local librarians have been inspired to prepare such material. For example,[2] many years ago in Newark, New Jersey, John Cotton Dana, the famous librarian, built up an intense community interest in preparing and publishing historical accounts of the local region. Several short stories were written by Frank J. Urquhart, the editor of a local paper, and published as pamphlets which were lent, or sold at five cents each, to teachers and pupils in the schools. The courses of study in history and geography made increasing use of Newark material, and many more school children

[1] Nellie Apply (chairman): *Pupils Are People*, pages 209–211. Report of the Committee on Individual Differences, National Council of Teachers of English.

[2] Described by Max J. Herzberg, principal of the Weequahic High School, Newark, New Jersey.

used the community library as a resource center. The publication of local material increased. Several books appeared, including *A Short History of Newark*, and forty pamphlets and a large amount of mimeographed material. Elementary school pupils themselves prepared *The Book of Newark* and *A Guide to Newark*. The board of education commissioned the making of many large maps of the city and small maps for pupil use. Out of this developed a systematic course in the civics of Newark.

Other cities have done the same thing. In Lynn, Massachusetts, for example, an intermediate grade project produced a large book entitled *History Stories of Lynn*. The schools of Ann Arbor, Michigan, prepared and published mimeographed source materials on the local region. *Stamford Long Ago* came from the work of the Waterside School in Stamford, Connecticut.

Reference Books Even the smallest school should provide at least one efficient set of reference books especially adapted to the needs of school instruction. It goes without saying that in the larger schools that have well-developed libraries, the reference section should be complete.

For the smaller schools, however, the Committee on Materials of Instruction of the Department of Supervisors and Directors of Instruction, National Education Association, recommends the following:

1. One standard school encyclopedia, such as:
    Compton's Pictured Encyclopedia. F. E. Compton and Co.
    The World Book Encyclopedia. W. F. Quarrie Co.

Until funds are available for the purchase of an encyclopedia, the school may buy a smaller reference work, such as:
    The Lincoln Library of Essential Information. The Frontier Press
    New Champlin Encyclopedia for Young Folks: Persons. Henry Holt and Co.
    New Champlin Encyclopedia for Young Folks: Places and Events. Henry Holt and Co.

2. A standard school dictionary, such as:
    New International Dictionary. Merriam
    New Standard Dictionary. Funk and Wagnalls

Until funds are available for an unabridged dictionary, some schools may purchase a standard dictionary of the smaller type, such as:

The American College Dictionary. Random House
College Standard Dictionary. Funk and Wagnalls
Thorndike-Century Junior Dictionary. Scott, Foresman
Webster's Collegiate Dictionary. Merriam
The Winston Simplified Dictionary. Winston

3. A standard atlas, such as:

Goode, J. P.: *School Atlas.* Rand McNally

4. *World Almanac,* The New York World-Telegram and Sun
Daily News Almanac, The Chicago Daily News

The school will also wish to supply each classroom with several copies of a simplified graded dictionary, suitable for the age group, to be used by children when taking first steps in learning how to use a dictionary.

Teacher's Aids in Selecting Reading Material You have probably concluded that there is plenty of reading material in our libraries and on sale through the publishing houses for any study we may wish to carry on in the schools. That is true, but the teacher's real problem is in knowing what to select from this superabundance. Students of the problem and commercial publishers have collaborated in getting out catalogues and other selected lists. The NEA's Department of Supervisors and Directors of Instruction recommends the following:

BOOKS

Boust, Nora (comp.): *A Graded List of Books for Children.*
American Library Association. Ask for latest edition.
Children's Catalogue. H. W. Wilson Company
The Right Book for the Right Child. A graded buying list of children's books. John Day Company
The Standard Catalogue for High School Libraries. H. W. Wilson Company

PERIODICALS

The Horn Book Magazine. Women's Educational and Industrial Union, Boston, Massachusetts
The Booklist — A Guide to New Books. American Library Association
Schools may subscribe to the Sunday supplements of the *New York Times* and *New York Herald Tribune.* (These include the helpful sections of Book Reviews.)

The "schoolcrafter" is important in the life of Public School 169, New York City. (Play Schools Association photo.)

Materials Will Not Organize Themselves

Have you noticed in considering each of these ten kinds of materials that the materials become truly educative only as teacher and pupils *organize them*? That is, indeed, one of the supreme functions of the good teacher — he organizes the environment. The year's curriculum of activities and materials must be designed — that is, *organized* — to be meaningful. To reach its maximum effectiveness the unit of work must be organized. Every demonstration, trip, and exhibit must be carefully planned. Educative dramatic play is not casual; it is designed, organized. For any educational purpose reading material — books, pamphlets, or periodicals — must be assembled, and to be of maximum educative value must be *organized*. As early as possible, and as far as possible, the pupils must do it themselves; in fact, one of the greatest objectives of the school is to teach them how to do this. But the teacher must lead.

Gather and Organize New Materials of Teaching

No amount of reading *about* the new materials of instruction will give you a true understanding of what you can employ in teaching. The only route to such understanding is the actual gathering of the materials themselves and *using* them in teaching.

1. In connection with an illustrative unit of work which you and the class might develop for the study of the curriculum, include the systematic collection and appraisal of many kinds of audio-visual materials. Examine the newer types of reading materials, pamphlets, bulletins, newspapers, magazines, novels, and poetry. Show how the curriculum using these materials, rather than the old, would build better understanding, more dynamic interest and drive for community participation.

2. Select and plan a radio hour for the class, listening to various kinds of programs and appraising their usefulness in the schools.

3. Show films, including some designed to be educational, and others designed mainly for recreation. Discuss their usefulness for education.

4. Study examples of photographs, filmstrips, and film slides. Discuss their use at various school levels and in typical teaching units.

5. Study examples of the newer types of textbooks and those to which the older curriculum was restricted, comparing them from the standpoint of pictorial materials, charts, graphs, pictographs. Compare also the literary nature of the two — the use of dramatic episodes, of greater richness and concreteness and style in writing.

6. Visit the museums of natural history, science, and industry, and other fields in your neighborhood, gathering suggested materials useful in teaching.

7. One of your most educative activities will be trips and excursions for directed observation and study. Get permission to work with a progressive teacher in your community who takes her children on such trips to study business and industry, government, transportation and communication, etc.

What to Read on the Materials of Education

The New School Architecture and Equipment

Hand in hand with the changing conception of the relation between education and the community, a new school architecture has developed. A fine introduction to this new conception is Englehardt's *Planning the Community School*. In connection with it read the NEA's *Education for All American Children* (pages 227–236 especially) and, for the high schools, similar excerpts of their *Education for All American Youth*.

The whole subject is studied in *The Planning and Construction of School Buildings*, the *Thirty-fourth Yearbook* of the National Society for the Study of Education. If you are concerned with nursery school plant and equipment, see Josephine Foster's *Nursery School Education*. From the United States Superintendent of Documents (Washington, D. C.) you can get a pamphlet on *Functional Planning of Elementary School Buildings*.

Consider how you as a teacher might help in planning a new school building. Assume that the teaching and the curriculum used in the building are to form one of the most forward-looking programs in the country. Draw an outline of principles and criteria that you would use in explaining to the school architect the new educational program so that he, in turn, might design the building to fit the life and program of education.

–Turn through the newer books of the type that we refer to above and such educational magazines as *The Nation's Schools*, *The American School Board Journal*, and *The School Executive*.

–Consider size of classrooms, with space for shopwork, classroom dramatics, and other activity programs.

–Make definite suggestions concerning artificial and natural lighting, the use of glass, ease of exit to outdoor playgrounds.

–Consider the use of wall space in the classroom.

–Make suggestions concerning the design of cabinets, closets, drawers, files, window seats, and other storage spaces.

–Plan for electrical outlets and screens for the use of radio, motion pictures, slide projectors, etc.

–Plan for recreational facilities, science laboratories, and art studios.

–Treat the library facilities as a separate and basic matter; design the central library and the libraries for the separate departments and rooms, reference shelves, bulletin boards, reading tables, etc.

–Provide for the museum needs of the school: wall space for exhibits, showcases for collections, spaces in classrooms for necessary storage.

–Provide conference rooms for committees, councils, small forum discussions, faculty meetings, parent-teacher conferences.

–Plan a combined auditorium, assembly room, and theater for the dramatic work, dance, lectures, demonstrations, etc., of the school.

Audio-Visual Materials

By far the best single book is Edgar Dale's *Audio-Visual Methods in Teaching*. No school should be without it. The next best general source is the *Eighth Yearbook* of the Department of Supervisors and Directors of Instruction entitled, *Materials of Instruction*. After those two volumes comes *New Tools for Instruction* by Doris Bock — a good statement of the whole subject. The best source on the *Radio in Elementary Education* is Willey and Young's book of that name. It is full of suggested projects, activities in the teaching of the various subjects, and excellent bibliographies. On the motion picture, see the story of the work done in Denver high schools in Brooker and Herrington's *Students Make Motion Pictures*. Woelfel and Tyler's *Radio and the School* is an excellent interpretation of a five-year study of the school's use of radio. You can get many ideas from Stolper's *The Bulletin Board as a Teaching Device*.

Materials for the Creative Approach

The development of the more creative approach in teaching has led to the publication of interesting materials. See, for example: Victor D'Amico's *Creative Teaching in Art*, especially Chapter IX; in Chapters XII–XIX inclusive will be found many examples of new materials in painting, sculpture, ceramic art, theater, and other means of expression. See Chapters XI–XVIII of Rugg and Shumaker's *The Child-Centered School*. For the use of sculpture in the schools, see Rich's *The Materials and Methods of Sculpture*. On materials in reading see *The Library in General Education*, Part II of the *Forty-second Yearbook* of the National Society for the Study of Education; also Luvella and Reschke's *The Newspaper in the Classroom*. For music and the arts see Brooks and Brown's *Music in the Elementary School* and Natalie Cole's *The Arts in the Classroom*.

References on the Materials of Teaching

You will need a file of sources from which you can find classified bodies of materials for use in the schools. We give a few selected sources:

–United States Office of Education: *Sources of Visual Aids and Equipment for Instructional Use in Schools*
–Board of Education, Department of Libraries, Newark, New Jersey: *Audio-Visual Aids Catalogue*
–State Board of Education, Kentucky: *Free and Inexpensive Teaching Aids*
–State Teachers College, Montclair, New Jersey: *Free Teaching Aids*. Number 1. Charts, maps, publications, and pictures for all age groups

Many other state departments of education and teachers' colleges have issued similar bulletins on free and inexpensive materials.

–Falconer, Vera M.: *Filmstrips, a Descriptive Index and Users' Guide*.
–Bathhurst, Effie G.: *Phonograph Records as an Aid to Learning in Rural Elementary Schools*. An annotated handbook for educators.
–Wilson, H. W.: *Educational Film Guide*. Cumulative annual catalogue with a two-year supplementary service.

CHAPTER 15

The Artist-Teacher Guides Learning

HERE WE STUDY the total job — the art of teaching. We see the teacher now, not as competent technician but as *artist*, as craftsman. The Good Teacher is the *Artist-Teacher.*

In the art of teaching we put to work the essence of all we have studied thus far under our familiar principle of education as guidance.

–The child's job is to "learn" — hence the teacher's task is to guide learning.

–Thus the new conception of education is the *guidance of learning.*

Our study climaxes:

–first, in the conditions that favor learning.

–second, in the conditions that favor teaching.

The goal of our study is an understanding of the development of the Artist-Teacher.

The Art of Good Teaching: Guiding Learning

"To EDUCATE is to guide human experience."

How many times has that been said in this book? A dozen? Twenty? It does not matter; we cannot say it too often, or too emphatically. You yourself may have concluded that guidance is synonymous with education. Definitions of one certainly sound like definitions of the other. Strang and Hatcher say, for example: "Guidance is the process by which an individual's potentialities are discovered and developed through his own efforts, for his personal happiness and social usefulness." But one can substitute "education" for "guidance" and the definition still holds good. They are, indeed, the same thing.

Teaching and Learning — the Heart of the Educative Process

We come now to what is commonly regarded as the sole job of the teacher — that is, to teach, and, correspondingly, to the pupil's job — to learn. Here are the two aspects of education — teaching and learning. While the old school made the center of the educative process *the teacher's intention to teach*, the new school builds on *the child's intention to learn*. In the one the teacher is the center, in the other the learner. The one stressed teaching, the other learning; but irrespective of the emphasis, the two are inextricably fused. Certainly, if we are to understand the art of teaching, we must first understand the act of learning. This is our next theme for study.

395

"We Live and Learn"

Note the frequent use of "learning" in the advertisements in the papers. "Learn to Dance — in five lessons!" . . . "Learn to express yourself in company!" . . . "Learn to meet your customer!"

Consider how much learning is involved in just growing up. The baby *learns* to feed himself, to sit up, to stand alone, and finally to walk and to speak. The little child *learns* to dress himself. In the neighborhood he *learns* to take care of himself, *learns* to go on errands for his elders, *learns* to go about in the city or countryside alone. In the home he *learns* "the social graces," to meet people and to be their host. He *learns* to take part in the give-and-take of discussion.

In the primary grades he learns to read, to count, to add and subtract. He learns to express himself with integrity, to say what he thinks. He learns to accept the rules of civic life as he takes his place in the community. He learns what not to do as well as what to do, that is, to avoid the manifold taboos that are necessary if complicated community life is to work smoothly. Slowly he learns the irreducible patterns of behavior in the American way of life. Thus, much of living is learning.

Watch your boys and girls grow, study their daily behavior, note the way each reacts to what someone else says or does. They are learning. Most of their behavior is *social* — carried on with others, in an environment, or situation. Study the interplay of this social world — the movements and gestures of people together, the words they speak back and forth, the things they do in the presence of others.

Study the behavior of growing animals, too. See how the puppy learns to get a closed door open by barking or scratching. Notice how the little baby learns that he will be fed if he cries, learns the meaning of the appearance of the bottle and stops crying. So it is that *objects and actions slowly take on meaning, the learning process proceeds.*

We call planned behavior, even such primitive kinds as the crying of the hungry baby, *purposive.* Through such experiences the child builds purposes. The satisfaction of his physical need (like that of the dog barking to get the door open) is a *goal.* By trying various ways of behaving he finds one that is successful. Later, he repeats the behavior. Again he succeeds. Each repetition tends to fix that way of behaving; each is a bit of "learned" behavior. Thus the animal or the human

Planting seed flats and watching the process of growth in green plants are initiated by the child's own purposes. (Louise M. Gross photo.)

being *learns* to use his resources to satisfy his wants, to *control* the world of people and things.

The learning process is not a simple thing. There are no simple formulae which we can follow and so guarantee that boys and girls will learn quickly and effectively. One cannot say: "If I do precisely thus and so, children will learn to read or spell easily; to add, subtract, multiply, or divide accurately; to grasp the significance of broad historical movements." The human learning process is subtle and complex.

In the first place, the *whole* boy or girl is involved in the learning — not just his hands in using a tool or machine or instrument, or just his head in reading or reckoning. All his sensibilities are caught up in the process at the same moment: his whole body — emotions, feelings, and body-responses — as well as his awareness of ideas. Body, mind, and emotions get into every act of human response. Physique, intelligence, and temperament work together. Whether or not a certain boy understands a new step in arithmetic or a new principle in science may be more truly determined by whether or not he is physically well, or by his anxieties over things that have been happening at home, than by the excellence of the teacher's teaching.

No doubt you yourself can illustrate this important fact about learning; it would help you at this point to recall (from your own experience) several concrete instances showing how the child, *as a whole*, learns.

Learning and the Study of Psychology

Perhaps by this time you are thinking, "Learning, for boys and girls in school, seems to be practically the same thing as living." It is, indeed, and your study of the psychology of learning will be one of the major aspects in the study of psychology and human behavior. One of your chief tasks in the teachers college will be *to study psychology*. Before you graduate you will probably have had several such courses: one in "General Psychology," another in "Educational Psychology," still others, perhaps, in "Child Psychology," the "Psychology of Adolescence," and "Social Psychology." Our brief study of how people learn is really a kind of introduction to the study of psychology.

For this study there is an enormous library — more than any one person could read in a lifetime. Thousands of books and hundreds of thousands of scientific reports, monographs, and articles have been published in the last century. The scientific study of psychology began about a hundred years ago in Europe, particularly by German, French, and British students. Not much original work was done by Americans until after our Civil War. In fact, William James's great *Principles of Psychology*, published in 1890 (as absorbing to read as any novel!), was one of the first American contributions to this field. Since that time there have been hundreds of American psychologists — a few of them famous around the world for their discoveries and their publications. You will study their contributions in your courses in educational psychology and in child and adolescent psychology. Here we shall merely sum up a few of their most important agreements and their practical conclusions that guide good teaching today.

Two Opposed Views among the Psychologists

We have already noted that educators divide into two camps on the question: What is an effective way to educate? The view of one of these two camps, a view held by many teachers and administrators, we have called the traditional, or formal, view; the other, held by an increasing number of educational pioneers, we have called the progressive, or informal, view.

The psychologists split in much the same way about the psychology of learning. One camp of psychologists holds to a "mechanical" view

BOYD HENRY BODE (1873————), loved and admired as
a great teacher, has, since 1920, been one of the nation's
chief philosophers of education and perhaps the most influential critic of the theory of American education; witness
his *Modern Educational Theories, Democracy as a Way
of Life,* and *Progressive Education at the Crossroads.* He
was Professor of Philosophy at the University of Illinois
(1909–1921), Professor of Education at Ohio State University (1921–1944), visiting Professor at Fuad University,
Cairo, Egypt (1944–1948), and more recently, Professor
of Education at the University of Florida. As leader in
the Progressive Education Association, he was at the very
center of educational reconstruction.

To Bode, reconstruction means that: (1) thinking advances through the reconstruction of experience; (2) subject matter must be selected so that it illuminates the curriculum; (3) in social matters the spirit of inquiry has the
right of way; and (4) the disposition and habit of cooperative living must be cultivated. Among his many
books are *Conflicting Psychologies of Learning, How We
Learn,* and *An Outline of Logic.*

of human nature and behavior — a view that sees the human being as a
mechanical aggregation of parts. These psychologists emphasize systematic drill and repetitive practice, and center attention on learning very
specific kinds of things.

The other school emphasizes the general or organic nature of human
behavior. It sees the child as a whole organism and stresses the integration and organization of behavior. The teacher who has developed
this psychological point of view will constantly be concerned about the
whole boy or girl — about home influences, interests, hobbies, fears,
likes, and dislikes, as well as the specific learnings of more conventional
subject matter. But, in spite of great differences between them, both
of these opposed groups accept certain basic ideas of learning.

Some Basic and Generally Accepted Ideas

The Principle of Association

One of the oldest and best-established psychological ideas is that we
learn by *associating* our responses with certain stimuli from the world
about us. This is called the principle of association, and our understanding of it goes back at least two hundred years in the history of

thought. No doubt you can illustrate this principle from your own experience. For example:

–Getting ready to go to work in the morning, you look at the sky and say: "It's cloudy . . . may rain . . . better take an umbrella."

–A stamped, addressed letter on the table reminds us that we must mail it at the first postbox.

–A voice on the telephone is associated at once with the name and the face of a friend.

–Familiar slogans illustrate the principle: . . . "The burned child dreads the fire." . . . "Once bitten, twice shy."

–The calendar on our desk reminds us of an engagement that must be met.

These examples illustrate what the psychologists call "association," and nearly all agree that it is fundamental to human learning. All day long, our moment-by-moment behavior is in large measure influenced by, and even determined by, the association of our responses with stimuli from the environment.

A principle of good teaching stems from it — namely, that the teacher always begins "where the individual child is." The new problem must contain recognizable elements from the child's own experience. The new situation must have many familiar things about it, must give cues to the needed response. Each one will be new, but must not be "too new," must not contain so much novelty that response is blocked, learning defeated. This explains the need for careful gradation of all new material or new ideas used by the teacher. The need for such careful gradation applies to the teaching of skills as well as to the solving of abstract problems.

The "Conditioning" of Response The modern form of the associative idea is called "conditioning." The idea itself is as old as human thought, although the name is fairly new. No doubt you could think of scores of examples of conditioning of response in everyday life. Consider the task of conditioning a young dog to his name. At first, by petting, offering food, or other intriguing ways, we get the dog to come to us. As he comes, we call his name. Time after time we do this, each time calling his name as he comes. Eventually he comes to us merely at the sound of his name. A new "conditioned" response has been established; a new "association" fixed. This is basic to learning.

We said that while the idea of conditioning is old, the name is fairly new. Perhaps you would like to know how this modern form of association got its name. It was during some scientific animal-learning experiments carried on in Russia fifty years ago by two Russian physiologists, Bechterev and Ivan Pavlov.

The Pavlov experiment is better known and will illustrate the meaning of conditioning. A hungry dog was fastened comfortably to a laboratory table and fed powdered meat. Each time the meat was blown into his mouth his salivary glands secreted saliva. This was a "natural" response with which the dog's body could respond from birth; it did not have to be "learned." In the experiment a bell was rung each time food was given; the purpose was to build up an association of "food" with "bell ringing"; the objective evidence lay in whether or not saliva was secreted. Through many repetitions of the simultaneous giving of food and ringing of the bell, the salivary reaction was transferred from getting food to hearing the bell. The mere ringing of the bell caused the secretion of saliva. Thus the new response was conditioned from the old. Using the new term, the dog's salivary response was "conditioned" to the ringing of the bell.

In your work in teaching children you will constantly employ this psychological principle. In teaching a young child to read, for example, you will need to use great care in fixing his attention specifically on the printed words the sound of which you are pronouncing. This may be done in various ways. This is a single example of associative learning or conditioning, many more of which you can give from the daily work of the school.

We Learn Only What We Do: the Principle of Active Response

No doubt you have heard teachers or professors in your college use the familiar slogan — "We learn by doing." There is real truth behind it, although a more correct way of saying it is: "We learn only what we have done." Two important psychological principles are illustrated in this common-sense idea. First, it illustrates the principle of association. We learn what we have already done, but our world never quite repeats

Making jack-o'-lanterns can be used to develop many understandings and thus a readiness for reading. (Louise M. Gross photo.)

itself; every human situation is new, at least in some respect. Even the factory mechanic, lying on his back and tightening a single nut on a machine as it moves above him on the assembly line, is doing something "new" each time, though relatively the same general situation is involved. Thus, as life goes on, our behavior takes on new and different patterns. As tiny increments of learning take place, strange stimuli become familiar and serve as "signs" or signals for the new way of behaving.

The second psychological idea in the principle of learning by doing is that of *action*. The more progressive schools are sometimes called "activity" schools because, as we have seen, activity is one of their most important characteristics. We know now that we learn by acting, by responding. We do not acquire meanings in some mysterious, mystic fashion; we respond *with* them. We understand new meanings only by making practical responses which are appropriate to them. Turn to page 417 of this chapter and read the example of the nursery children needing to share the five apples. By dividing an apple they learned the meanings "whole," "half," and "two halves make a whole." Out of the process of dividing the apples came several new meanings. Not only were "whole" and "half" learned, but the first tiny step had been taken toward the learning of the complex meaning "fraction." The important point we are making is that in order to learn the new meanings, they *did something* with their bodies; thus they *responded with meaning*. This is the principle of active response. All learning is based upon it.

The Principle of the Whole: the Organism, and Its Integration or Organization

In our times there has been discovered and scientifically established a third principle which supplies us with much needed guidance. This is the Principle of the Whole, which has directed our thought in the earlier chapters. Briefly, in every human act the tendency is for the whole body, mind, and emotions to be in action; separate parts do not act in isolation. The organism tends to react *as a whole*.

In teaching, remember that the whole situation includes the environment as well as the organism. Thus in any teaching situation the *whole* will include you and your relations with the pupil and his relation to his classmates and to their past and present behavior. It will include the entire gamut of his personal interrelation with home, school, community, his entire world. Teach, therefore, so that you will bring the whole boy or girl and the whole situation into effective action. And never forget that the action of the body is primary in every human act, in reasoning and appreciating as well as in motor skills. Hence, awkward though the term is, we shall call our psychology "*organismic.*"

We have stated three basic principles that psychologists accept and upon which you should base your study of how people learn:

–The Principle of Association (and of Conditioning)

–The Principle of Active Response

–The Principle of the Whole — the Organism and Its Integration

With these three principles at our command we are better equipped to study the chief types of behaving and learning. To these we turn now.

Types of Behaving and Learning

The purpose of learning is clear; it is to live better — to behave more effectively in the moment-by-moment situations of life. This involves being skillful where skill is required, thinking clearly when problems are encountered, feeling deeply and with sensitivity in moments of appreciation, and expressing oneself clearly. And this brings us to one of the tasks to which the good teacher is constantly alert. Moment by moment he studies each teaching situation so that he may adapt what he does to the learner's needs. He knows that no fewer than four distinctive kinds of learning situations must be recognized:

–Skill situations, requiring effective habits

–Problem situations, requiring acts of thought

–Creative situations, demanding expression

–Appreciational situations, calling for acts of deep feeling

He knows also that each of these four learning needs must be met by a separate and special kind of teaching: building skills, developing efficiency in thinking and solving problems, drawing out and enhancing creative abilities, and building appreciative feeling for aesthetic situations.

The good teacher, then, is constantly on the alert to judge which type of learning is involved at any moment. Is practice called for? Is the pupil blocked by lack of facility in recognizing a problem and solving it? Can his aesthetic awareness be extended at this point? Is there some principle of creative work needed that the teacher can give? To be able to distinguish the type of situation confronted is a step in skillful teaching.

Here, then, are four learning situations of the school. We turn to a brief study of each of these.

Habit and Skill

"Everyone knows what habit is!" you exclaim. No doubt, for it dominates much of our waking life. William James, the great psychologist, characterized most human beings as "mere bundles of habits." Much of life is routine, one habit after another, a stream of reactions in familiar patterns. The give-and-take of conversation illustrates it — smiles carry the message of friendliness and arouse corresponding facial gestures and words; frowns, high-pitched angry tones, aggressive gestures produce tensions and characteristic defensive replies. Thus most of human behavior seems to be of the stimulus-and-immediate-response type.

Much of our occupational life is also on the level of habit. Consider the working day of the skilled mechanic running a lathe, power saw, or drill press: hammering, sawing, measuring, fitting, pulling down and building up; the stenographer or typist or accountant in the office, the railroad engineer or fireman, the assembly-line workers in an automobile plant. In some cases the situation met is new every succeeding moment, and habits must be *used* and adjusted to these novel situations. In others, as in much machine manufacturing, the situations are very similar hour after hour and year after year.

In the school you will need to distinguish the different learning processes involved in the four types of skill:

–Motor skills, as in handwriting, typewriting, using tools and machines and instruments

–Mental skills, as in arithmetical computation, algebraic and geometrical manipulation, and linguistic habits

–Expressional skills, the techniques needed in creative acts

–Social skills, the habits needed in dealing with people

Consider an example of the role of habit, which comes from our everyday lives — driving an automobile through traffic. Imagine the driver and his car moving along a highway, alert to the kaleidoscope of changing situations. He drives chiefly "by habit." He puts on brakes, accelerates his speed to avoid pedestrians or other cars, or responds to red lights or other controls of traffic. Here in infinitesimal units of behavior, his whole organism is at work. "Signs" flash up and he responds to them: cars approaching or passing, pedestrians crossing, loose rock or other menacing objects on the road, red lights, the fire engine's siren (or the traffic officer's), the arrow of the one-way street.

Although most of the continuous process presents to the driver tiny episodes of habit reaction, there is still a sense in which each of these consists of solving problems; that is, the driver is facing a constantly changing situation, and to a degree he picks and chooses his way, even though on a simple level. The total ongoing experience is one of continuous reorganization, quite different from the process of the manual and mental repetitive skills — such as running a typewriter or other machine, calculating figures, and the like. Moreover, there is no learning unless new elements come into play; but wherever they do, detection of and response to significant relationships again become central. Nevertheless, the problems are of the face-to-face and short-spanned type, and are to be dealt with on the near-habitual level.

Habits Are Rarely Used Apart from Complex Human Situations   In our modern industrial society certain kinds of jobs have to be carried on in which a skilled workman uses the same trained movements over and over — all day long.   Perhaps the most obvious examples are the assembly-line jobs of mechanized industry, where each workman tightens a nut or screw, fits on a particular part, or does some other simple operation hour after hour.   Here absolute mastery of the specific habit is demanded — and not much else.

But much of our lives is filled with complex changing situations such as driving a car in traffic.   Here also mastery of specific habits is required, but, in addition, quickness and accuracy in calling the right ones into play, because every movement brings a new set of circumstances. Habit control plus speed and accuracy of adjustment to the new is at a premium.

In the school — although our old-school fathers did not know it — most of the habits that are developed are of this type; very few assembly-line skills are ever demanded.   Arithmetical skills are needed in solving problems, but rarely in isolation.   The ability to spell several thousand words is required, but only in order to write letters, briefs, reports, and essay statements of various kinds.   Precise knowledge of word meanings is needed, but only to read the words in varying contexts.   Exact map location facts are memorized, and the connection of occasional dates and events, but only for the purpose of using them in understanding national or world problems.   Specific habits are rarely used apart from some complex situation in which many other human elements are involved. Habits must be so flexible that the individual can adjust quickly to situations that are novel — even strange.   This is of the greatest importance in planning the *kinds of school situations* in which skills are learned and perfected.

The Problem of Practice   What has just been said relates directly to the age-long problem of practice.   The old school believed in the adage that practice makes perfect.   In fact, its curriculum was largely devoted to memorization of facts and mastery of skills.   These it tried to establish by constant repetition, having children repeat a connection

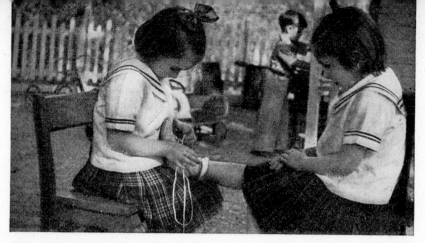

Skills are best learned in real-life situations. (Louise M. Gross photo.)

over and over again in its bare specific form. There is an ancient story of the boy of ungrammatical speech, who habitually said, "I have wrote" and "I have went." He was required to stay after school and write this statement on the blackboard fifty times, "I have written the lesson correctly." He did so, perfectly, fifty times. Then, the job finished, he added his own note to the teacher: "I have wrote your lesson and I have went home."

Now it is known that repetition in some form is useful in perfecting habits and skills. In the case of Pavlov's dog, from ten to fifty repetitions were needed to establish the new conditioned response; in Watson's study of conditioning new fear responses in an eleven-month-old infant eight repetitions were required. Through thousands of experiments in the laboratory and in the classroom in the past seventy-five years many skills have been studied — mental skills as in arithmetic, manual skills as in typing or using tools, linguistic skills, social skills, and many others. These have established the truth which every educator knows, namely, that meaningful repetition is needed in forming habits and skills. Guthrie says: "The effects of practice do not depend on mere repetition, but on the conditions of repetition, and these conditions vary enormously in different learning situations." He adds a conclusion which may surprise you: "In both human and animal behavior, *associations established on a single occasion* are the rule rather than the exception."

You will be well advised in teaching, therefore, while being aware of the necessity of drill, that the conditions under which practice takes place are more important than the number of repetitions. Consider a single example: A child wants to play the violin in order to join the school orchestra. To do this must he practice hours without end —

fingering, bowing, playing exercises — as is done in most formal music lessons? The functional method of teaching the playing of instruments says — NO! Certain rudiments he must know, such as: how to hold the instrument and the bow, that the four strings are G, D, A, and E, and how to draw the bow across the strings. That can be initiated in fifteen minutes of instruction. At that point he is ready to play in a group. "Ridiculous!" you say. "How can he possibly play in a group with so little knowledge and skill?" The answer is: He does have just the bare minimum of skill that is now needed. Most musical compositions have foundational or pedal tones running through the score, as A, D, or G. These the beginning student can quickly learn to play on one open string. With that single skill he can become a part of a musical group; he *is* making music. Neither twenty hours nor one hour of drill was needed to bow the open string. After being shown, with two or three trial experiences, he plays adequately for this particular experience. As he gains in skill, he may next be given a part containing two open strings, as A and D. This is a bit more challenging. He must be careful to draw the bow directly on A or on D. He needs more practice, but now there is impetus for such practice. It culminates in a satisfying experience.

Educational Conditions Which Favor Practice [1] Perhaps you are asking: Are there "laws" to follow in building habits in the school? The tendency today is to say little about "laws" of practice; instead, the psychologists describe *the educational conditions which favor practice.* Stated briefly, factors which effect these conditions are:

1. *Individual differences.* Repeatedly in this book we have stressed "the law of individual differences" used by psychologists to describe the wide differences that exist in any group. Hence, some of your pupils will perfect skills with a small amount of practice, while others, who seem to practice all the time, will be less efficient. One should never lose sight of the wide range of differences in the ability of children.

2. *Meaningful material.* Material that has meaning is learned much more rapidly and retained more effectively than "nonsense" material. This has probably always been a truism of good teaching and, by many studies, has recently been established scientifically.

[1] This section is based upon findings summed up in the *Forty-first Yearbook* of the National Society for the Study of Education: *The Psychology of Learning.*

3. *The use of drill.* By drill we mean the learning by repetition of the same material or process; for example, adding columns of figures, spelling lists of words, locating places on maps, or duplicating handwriting specimens. Certainly there are many habits of behavior that can be learned only by repetition; for example, learning the letters on the typewriter keyboard, or spelling words in the English language. Such skills must be learned by "drill." But that does not mean by *any* kind of repetition; what is needed is just *the right kind* of repetition. Moreover, in planning drill do not expect it to do anything but perfect specific habits; it will not teach leadership or coöperation or build honesty or other character traits. Moreover, your drill will be economical if you are guided by the psychologists' best knowledge. Scientific studies have established, for example, that about three quarters of all the running errors in oral language fall within five classes of errors. The wise teacher concentrates language drill upon those errors that have greater likelihood of occurrence.

4. *Motivated practice.* This is an application of the principle that people learn better when they *intend to learn,* when interests are enlisted. This will be shown in a moment as we state the conditions which favor learning.

5. *Pupil knowledge of his results.* Many studies have been made of the effects of "practice with and without knowledge of results." There is now agreement that the learner forms habits better if he knows how well he is doing; the knowledge guides his practice and provides drive and interest.

6. *Distribution of practice.* Given a certain amount of time for drill, we now know that short work periods are more effective than long ones. Subjects do more work per minute when set to work for a short interval than when set to work for a long interval. Bear in mind that great care must be used in determining how long the practice periods shall be and how often they shall occur. While you should study the problem carefully in your own classes and be guided by your own increasing experience, you will also get great help from the modern types of workbooks and other available practice materials.

7. *Total amount of practice.* The studies show that the building of skill does depend on the amount of practice, but this also is only a general guiding rule. Certainly it does not apply beyond a certain optimum amount of "over-learning."

8. *Maintenance of skills through practice.* There are "laws" of forgetting as well as laws of learning. To be maintained, a skill must be used. This means practice must be kept up. Psychologists are inclined to think now that "moderate initial practice and systematic review" are the best cues to follow.

Thinking and Problem-Solving

Come back again to the example of the man driving his car. This time we meet a face-to-face situation in which impulsive or habitual response will not serve. As he drives along the highway, the driver suddenly notices the odor of heat; a knocking sound comes from under the hood. "Engine's hot." He resorts to one habitual act; he stops the car. Then he stops to think. "Something's wrong; an engine should not be hot." He gets out of the car, raises the hood, and does other habitual things. But he's blocked, a *problem* confronts him, and his habits will not serve to solve it. *Alternatives* confront him, and he must *choose* among them. He must think. Signs flash up from his past experience: Is the oil okay? A glance at the dashboard gauge: "Oil seems okay — but — maybe the engine is out of oil." He measures it with the measuring rod. "No — it's okay." Another flash of suggestion: "Water may be low. Radiator cap comes off. "No, water's okay." The signs to which he responds are suggestions learned in past similar situations. What other factors could cause it? "Oil feed line may be clogged; that's a job for the garage." "The water may not be circulating; also a job for the garage." Suddenly another cue: "The fan belt may be broken." He then sees the belt lying broken below. The "problem" has been solved.

This example of face-to-face problems could be multiplied n-fold from the moment-by-moment living of every one of us. How, then, does the twentieth-century American meet such situations? A generation ago, John Dewey wrote perhaps the best description of this process of ideally successful problem-solving thinking that has ever been achieved. The steps paraphrased in quick review are:

First: We recognize the problem; we confront it directly. Dewey calls it the "felt-difficulty" . . . the "forked-road situation." It

Does a woodchuck drink or lap its milk?   (Louise M. Gross photo.)

has become a problem; impulsive, habitual behavior will no longer serve. We confront *alternatives*; hence, we must choose. The situation is tense; we must confront it directly in *head-on collision*.

Second: We meet it in a rapid process of calling up suggestions . . . ways of behaving . . . from our past experience. In imagination we bring to consciousness things that we might do, find factors that may fit the situation.

Third: We try them, comparing and appraising, rejecting one or another.

Fourth: We accept one and act upon it.

In this analysis the process has been broken down into a series of enumerated steps. Actually they are almost concurrent, flashing up in swift succession, shot through with the mood, feeling, and emotion of the moment, tangled with meanings, desires, or fears.

This is Dewey's famous analysis of the complete act of thought.[1] In the thirty years that have followed the publication of *How We Think*, this analysis has been made the basis of much of the theorizing about

[1] The reader should not miss Dewey's chapter, "The Analysis of the Complete Act of Thought," in the first edition of his *How We Think*.

thinking that has been going on in the schools of education and teachers' colleges of the country.

The Familiar vs. the Significant Relationship   Before leaving the consideration of the concept of thinking, one final word on its relation to
habit.   Involved in both habit and problem situations is the tendency
of the organism to respond impulsively.   The make-up of the nervous
system and its close integration with the glandular and muscular systems
predispose the individual to become a slave of habit; this is as true in
complex social situations as in simple routine ones.   Every social situation presents a complex of elements shot together in a fused on-going
and ever changing process.   Each person responds to the total pattern,
but it always takes on for him a unique organization.   He *impulsively
selects one particular meaning* to which to respond, although without
being aware of his selective process, and, using it as the cue, acts.
Some single phrase, idea, or other element, in conjunction with the
integration of the speaker's gesture and voice, touches off the response.
Hence the tendency is to respond with the act, word, or gesture called
out by that particular fusion of familiar elements.   The habitual reaction is to the *familiar* cue, not necessarily to the *significant* one.   Where
habitual response is called for, this guarantees efficiency, but if thought
is demanded, it may result in the individual reacting with the wrong
meaning.   Intelligent understanding demands that we react to the
significant meaning in a situation, not necessarily to the *familiar* one.
The familiar one may not be the significant one, and our task is to delay
response long enough to analyze the situation and to find the most
significant meaning.

Solving Problems: Practical Teaching Suggestions   No psychological
problem of learning has been studied more carefully than that of thinking, especially the kind of thinking we call problem-solving.   From
the vast amount of work on this subject we can present several
valuable suggestions for teaching: [1]

   –The nub of the process is recognizing the problem: Help the
   children to formulate it clearly and see that they keep it in mind
   constantly.   Recall similar cases, "guess courageously" (but in-

   ------

   [1] See the Forty-first *Yearbook* of the National Society for the Study of Education: *The Psychology of Learning.*

telligently), maintain suspended judgment, build the habit of criticizing suggestions and anticipating objections and consequences. Build outlines and use diagrams and graphs. Let the children use any familiar method. Don't impose a systematic formula. Try to develop a problem-solving attitude.

–Remember that a problem is really solved only *when the learner understands what he has done and why his actions were the appropriate ones.* Mistakes in problem-solving are cleared up only when the young people understand the inadequacies of their own methods, when the needed meanings have been developed. The test is whether the pupil's method of solution can be used again.

–Introduce variety by having the children solve different problems with the same method, also the same problems by different methods. Keep the relationships in the situation well within the understanding of the child and his ability to identify them. Develop the needed meanings and understandings in each situation.

–Give practice in distinguishing between the reasonable and the absurd, the logical and the illogical.

–Remember that organized experience in solving real problems is most important. The scientific attitude can be built only by slow accumulation of experience in problem-solving over a long stretch of years.

This concludes our brief study of learning in connection with habit and thinking. There are two other factors which are very important. They are much less understood and all too little recognized and used in the school. The first of these is the significance of the creative process in learning, which we shall now discuss.

Learning and the Creative Process

In some respects the creative act resembles other types of learning, for it is the active response of the learner. Put in the homeliest of phrases, every human being wishes to *express himself* — to say what *he* thinks or feels and to say it *his* way. Come into a school in which an artist-teacher is working with children in the social studies. Here is a model of a miniature city, there a map of Odysseus's travels, over there an illuminated map of the Mediterranean region. The artistic impulse working itself out in clay produces a model of a medieval castle. Here are paintings illustrative of the birth of Christ; there, tracing the history of our own country, are models of Columbus's ships and a back drop for a play about Hendrik Hudson. The pageant of industrial history also moves before us — a model of the first railroad train, a miniature Conestoga wagon, primitive paintings of early Chicago.

The art aspect of every subject is being developed in the new school. The children paint pictures of things seen on excursions, originate cartoons to illustrate current topics, or design block prints for covers of the school or class magazines. One class makes a frieze depicting the history of printing from its Asiatic beginnings, another pictures harvest, spring, and Christmas festivals; masques, plays, pageants, and puppet plays furnish opportunities for relating dramatics to expressive graphic art. What a range of expressive art: etching, block printing, wood carving; working in clay, marble, copper, bronze, wood, cloth, raffia; map making; toy making; the making of plaster casts and plaques; the making of masks and puppets; the drawing of machine parts and blueprints; cabinetmaking; the building of ship, train, and plane models. The pupils of more than one school have been permitted to design and paint murals and frescoes on their schoolroom or corridor walls and to make, dye, and print designs on curtains. Batik is popular with older girls, while even young children have been able to make very interesting Japanese wall scrolls.

The old school was centered on personal adjustment, on adaptation to the existing order. But in the new school it is the creative spirit within each person that is encouraged, not conformity to a pattern imposed from without. The child as artist, poet, and composer is coming into his own. Today the school assumes that every child is endowed with the capacity to express himself. Some will create with words, some with line or color, others with music. Some will express themselves through the body in dance; others will model, carve, give shape to their ideas in plastic materials. Still others will find expression through oral language, or through an integrated physical, emotional, and dramatic gesture. But whatever the medium, each one has some capacity for expression. And so the pupil is surrounded by an atmosphere conducive to expression.

To understand the creative process consider how the artist-teacher works. Starting with his own imagined conception, the artist selects

Clay modeling — "just make it your own way." (Louise M. Gross photo.)

material and molds it into an organization. The nature of the material may be physical, mental, spiritual, human, or nonhuman. In the graphic and plastic arts it may consist of paper or a canvas or a wall and oil paint, water color, or crayon; music tones produced on metal strings or tubes or bars, or blown through tubes. In the theater, the materials are the living actor and his words, the choral speech of groups, electric lighting, the architecture of the stage, and the concepts and moods evoked by the words of the script. But irrespective of the artist's materials — and they are a miscellany — man works as artist by selecting those that are useful to his purpose, molding them into an organization of unified form that expresses his feeling for order.

And you in the school will be working as an artist. Your task as an artist-teacher will be to work with the raw materials of personality in the young egocentric individualists as they come to you in the school and guide each child in becoming a unified whole, a truly formed personality.

Learning and the Development of Appreciation

The second of the little-understood but very important kinds of human acts is appreciation. We use the term to embrace a wide range of the more intangible responses that enter into every hour of our lives.

415

Every human response is colored by some form of appreciation. Listen to snatches of conversation anywhere, any hour of the day, and you will feel it: Men and women, boys and girls, talking together, enjoying one another; not solving problems or running mechanical contrivances — just "appreciating" things, getting the feel and the joy of life. These are experiences that move us and stretch us and through which we grow. There is the enjoyment of music, the response of the individual to painting and sculpture, the reaction of the whole self to unity in architecture. There is the expression of individuality in rhythmic movement in the dance, the integrated adjustments of the body in physical games. There is the aesthetic enjoyment of ideas, the self-absorbed thrill of meditative reverie, interest in the play of human relationships. But enough of illustration; those we have given have made clear what we mean by "appreciation." Certainly the development of sensitive feeling is one of the great goals of education.

What is it in the atmosphere of the new classrooms that produces creative expression and thereby builds a capacity for appreciation? Consider a single example: the way an artist-teacher develops the appreciation of fine writing. The heart of it, in one case at least, was the development of a "creative reading" environment. Hughes Mearns, author of *Creative Youth*, a great teacher of young people, was a master reader. He read dramatically, and in his classes at Lincoln School of Teachers College he made mature writings intelligible to children through his thrilling use of spoken language. As he himself expressed it, he began with what he had — undeveloped, immature adolescents of junior high school age, relatively uninterested in fine writing, endowed with all the desires for dynamic action typical of young Americans today. He read to them constantly, talking about the implications of his reading as he went along. Through stimulating comments he gradually got them interested in reading. Mearns comments on the reading parties:

"Invitations were issued. . . . We read — and munched! — steadily for fifty minutes. Old favorites, among them *Marigold Pendulum, Stopping by Woods on a Snowy Evening, Good-bye* and *Keep Cold, Eve,* were given with that strange rich effect which comes only with the rehearsing of fine music . . . ; even the teacher, suppressing a native shyness in such matters, read out of his own private store a group that might have been called 'Poems Written in Very Early Youth.'"

Little by little the abler ones among the classes were called into the oral reading enterprises. They read to each other, and as the conviction slowly dawned upon them that they, too, could be critical, that their function in the school was to form their own judgments of writing irrespective of the writer, they matured in appreciation.

This brings to a close our brief introduction to the study of the learning of those four primary human acts that influence behavior and learning:

–The forming of habits and the building of skill

–The solving of problems and mastery of other kinds of thinking

–The expressive or creative process

–The act of appreciation

One other task confronts us with respect to learning — namely, to bring together the knowledge of psychologists regarding the conditions that favor learning.

Conditions That Favor Learning

First: People Learn Better if They Desire to Learn: the Role of Interest and Purpose

Out of long experience educators agree that people learn best when interest is at white heat, when their purposes are engaged. It is *the child's desire to learn* that is important. The teacher's intention to teach is important, too, but he must find the way to build lively interests in the boys and girls. Each situation must embody a need felt by the learner himself. Consider an example:

A four-year-old boy comes to school with five beautiful red apples. The nine children in the group exclaim over them, saying how much they like apples. The boy wants to share his apples with the group. He passes them around, but to his dismay finds he hasn't enough. What is he to do? Some have apples, some have none. Some are happy, some very sad. To his "I haven't enough apples," the teacher replies:

"Is there any way you could have enough to go around?" They face the problem. Several make suggestions: one says, "Go home for more." But it is too far. "Go to the store on the corner." But they have no money. "Save them until tomorrow and we'll bring more." But the apples look so tempting, the children want them now. "My mother cuts them in pieces," one child suggests.

"If we cut each apple once, will that be enough?"

"Let's try and see."

The boy cuts one apple in half. "That makes two pieces," says one interested child. "We call the two pieces of the apple two halves," puts in the teacher. One child fits two halves together; the teacher smiles and says: "Yes, put together the two halves and what do you have? A whole apple!"

The boy cuts the other apples. They count all the halves, and count all the children. Good! With the teacher we have just enough!

This example illustrates several important things about learning, for, as always happens, several things were learned at the same time, not just some new arithmetic facts.

First: Most important of all, the children learned how to confront a group problem and solve it together. They had a fine constructive lesson in coöperation. They experienced the satisfaction of successful achievement and saw how working together brought it about. They had the enjoyment of sharing experiences and learned to respect each other's contributions.

Second: Interest was at a high pitch; the purposes of the children were enlisted. They were intensely attentive because they were concentrating on the thing they most wanted.

Third: The children were *active*, not passively listening; they were doing something about the problem.

Fourth: They were experiencing several arithmetical concepts. They were learning to count; they were learning very important new meanings — namely, the meaning of *half*, and the relation of *halves* to *wholes*. Here was the first small step in the long process that would extend over several years of school life in the learning of fractions.

The Problem of Motivation: Reward and Punishment   In the foregoing example is illustrated the problem of motivation which has been
studied by educators for two generations.   People learn best, they now
conclude, when the children's *motives* are enlisted.   Motivate! . . .
Motivate! . . . Motivate! . . . is the admonition to teachers.   So important is the problem that it has been studied scientifically by the psychologists.   There is a large library of books and reports on the subject;
see for example, Professor Edward L. Thorndike's *Psychology of Wants,
Interests, and Attitudes*.

There are many phases to this problem of the interest of boys and
girls, and many ways have been tried to guarantee that schoolwork will
be based upon interest.   Two ways have been studied particularly: One
is the effect of *punishment* on learning; the other is the effect of *rewards*.

Teacher says: "Johnny, if you can't play in the game without push-
ing and punching the other children, you may leave and play by yourself, where you will have no one to push and punch."   Johnny immediately becomes hostile and resentful, fights authority, and tries to avoid
the necessity of choice — to stay and play fair or to leave.   His undesirable conduct is turned into other undesirable behavior, and he
schemes how he can still be unfair to the group but undetected by the
teacher.

But what would have happened if the teacher, instead of dealing
with Johnny in this negative, disciplinary way, had tried a constructive,
positive lead, something like this: She walks up to the group and says:
"I'm sorry to interrupt your game, but I need someone to do a very important errand for me.   Johnny, will you help me?"   Before Johnny
has time to resist, he is chosen and accepts the errand, namely to take
an envelope to the Superintendent's office in the center of town.   The
envelope contains valuable materials that must be guarded carefully.
The errand will take time out of Johnny's lessons, but the envelope must
go, and Johnny can make up his lost time by a little extra effort, since
he is a smart boy.   Johnny accepts the responsibility and later returns
to the school with a glow of pride in his accomplishment and with added
prestige in the group.   He senses this a bit; the group does also.   He is
still the bully, but to a slight degree less.   Johnny thinks: "It is fun, after
all, to be a leader and take responsibility."   He watches for other opportunities.   The teacher notices this and slowly works him into leadership in small groups, each time increasing his responsibility and status

in the group. Steadily he feels more secure, both in himself and in the group.

You can fill in the rest of that educational picture. Johnny has learned through freedom, not through prison-like atmosphere and restrictions, to find himself just a bit, to appraise his interests and activities a little more effectively, to set himself goals which give him more pleasure and security than he has had before. New values take the place of old ones, along with new experience and knowledge of how to get along with others. Going into the football game no longer means going in to fight; it means going into something where he will be recognized, and accepted for his contribution to the group.

So much for the first important condition that favors learning; people learn better when they are interested, when they see the value of the learning to them.

Second: People Learn Better when Relaxed and Happy

Visitors to our best modern schools, even those who are adversely critical of much that they see, always agree on one thing: "These children are happy — happier than in the schools of a generation ago. Everyone seems busily at work, attending to his tasks. While there is a good deal of moving about, most of it seems to be motivated by something that needs to be done. Under the rigid discipline of yesterday's school the children were both tense and inattentive, restless, not centering their attention on their work."

This brings us to the second condition that will favor learning — namely, a good emotional situation. People learn better if they are relaxed and happy. Efficient learning requires close attention. Anything that will improve concentration will improve learning; anything that will distract attention will hamper learning. While some types of emotion heighten attention, others are real distractions. Sensitive teachers and parents agree that an emotionally disturbed child does not learn well, does not get along well with his fellows. A favorable emotional condition is a prerequisite for good learning and balanced behavior.

To understand learning, therefore, we must understand the psychology of emotions. It is a tragic fact that in spite of the importance of the emotions, the psychologists know all too little about them. Much

Construction materials come from varied sources. These children are taking a box apart. (Louise M. Gross photo.)

of their time and energy for the past fifty years has been devoted to studying other things — the nervous system, how people perceive things, how habits are formed and facts are memorized, and how we think. But in recent years many studies have been made of the physiology of the emotional responses, and some agreed-upon facts have been acquired; the important ones we can pass on to you.

Introducing the Study of the Emotions *First:* What is emotion? Definitions of emotion are legion in number and vary greatly, but certain ideas are common to them. One is that a person "is emotionally aroused whenever he is in an excited condition." Excitement, heightened energy, tapping "hidden reservoirs of energy" as William James used to put it, are words that describe emotional states. All students seem to agree also that it is our emotions that *move* us, drive us on or impede our behavior.

Second: There are many different emotional states, and we have given names to them. Through these names we express ourselves about them: anger, fear, grief, astonishment, rage, hate, love, sympathy, contempt, malice, boredom, casual concern. The total list is long and covers every mood, trait, disposition, or sentiment.

Third: These emotional states vary enormously as to type and to strength. At one extreme are the negative and destructive emotions, at the other the positive and constructive ones. In fact, it is difficult if not impossible to classify the types clearly. Psychologists are not uniformly agreed upon any classification; but, grouped under two captions to indicate the extreme opposites, the so-called "strong" emotions are:

POSITIVE STRONG EMOTIONS CONSTRUCTIVE OF WELL-BEING	NEGATIVE STRONG EMOTIONS DESTRUCTIVE OF WELL-BEING
Love	Hate
Happiness	Despondency
Joy	Grief
Hope	Despair
Courage	Fear
Generosity	Greed
Enthusiasm	Disinterestedness
Admiration	Abhorrence (scorn, loathing)
Respect	Contempt
Tenderness	Callousness
Quiet calm	Rage

These strong, positive emotions — love, joy, hope, courage, for example — give us power and force, lift us over obstacles, give us strength to do our tasks and endure our difficulties. But hate, grief, despair, fear, greed, and the other negative, destructive emotions disturb and frustrate the even tenor of our ways. They break us down nervously, upset our equilibrium, and disrupt our behavior.

To give you a sense of the powerful role of emotions, we quote perhaps the world's greatest expert on their physiology — Dr. Walter B. Cannon. In this excerpt he describes what happens to the body

"as the accompaniment of the powerful emotions of rage and fear. Respiration deepens, the heart beats more rapidly, the arterial pressure rises, the blood is shifted away from the stomach and intestines to the heart and central nervous system and the muscles, the processes in the alimentary canal cease, sugar is freed from the reserves in the liver, the spleen contracts and discharges its content of concentrated corpuscles, and adrenin is secreted from the adrenal medulla. The key to these marvelous transformations in the body is found in relating them to the natural accompaniments of fear and rage — running away in order to escape from danger, and attacking in order to be dominant. Whichever the action, a life-or-death struggle may ensue." [1]

[1] Walter B. Cannon: The Wisdom of the Body, pages 213–214. W. W. Norton & Company, Inc.; 1932. Used by permission.

There are other general traits known by different names, which also appear to be "emotionalized." It is very difficult to draw a fine line between them and others that clearly deserve the name "emotion." Sometimes we refer to them as attitudes, sometimes as moods, at other times as sentiments. To some extent they are characterized by excitement or heightened energy; hence they are in a sense emotions. But they shade off into one another, and it is difficult to set them off from one another sharply. The list of mild emotions includes:

POSITIVE MILD EMOTIONS CONSTRUCTIVE OF WELL-BEING	NEGATIVE MILD EMOTIONS DESTRUCTIVE OF WELL-BEING
Responsiveness	Indifference
Sympathy	Antipathy
Friendliness	Unfriendliness
Altruism	Self-seekingness
Disinterestedness	Prejudice
Relaxation	Anxiety
Sensitivity	Callousness
Impartiality	Bias

As you scan the list you would agree, no doubt, that some of these are mild emotions and can be clearly set apart from the strong ones just examined. But what shall we say of others? For example, we speak of an "attitude of expectancy" . . . "I got myself into a receptive attitude." We speak of altruistic, disinterested, impartial, or sympathetic "attitudes"; also of "moods" or sentiments of altruism or sympathy. We say: "He is a 'sensitive' artist." Are these moods, attitudes, or sentiments? Or are they emotions? Who is to say with assurance? Certainly we do not do violence if we say that they are the "mild" emotions, and if, for practical purposes, we also call them moods or sentiments.

Fourth: But what causes the emotions? What makes people love or hate, admire or loathe, be brave or afraid? A vast amount of theorizing has been done about this in the past centuries and, in the last half century, a considerable amount of scientific explanation. Of the latter, the best work is by the physiologists, particularly those laboratory students who have worked on the brain and on the endocrine glands.[1] But that study is more properly a part of educational psychology; so we shall say no more about it here.

[1] No teacher should miss Dr. Walter B. Cannon's two classic books, *Bodily Changes in Pain, Hunger, Fear and Rage* and *The Wisdom of the Body*.

Third: People Learn Better if the Situation Is within Their Level of Understanding

Here, our guide to better learning is the stage of development of the learner and the careful gradation of learning material to fit it. We must ask constantly: "At what point on the growth curve is this boy or this girl? All that has been said about the individualized rate of development comes to our aid here. Each child develops at his own personal and unique rate. The psychologists give the name *maturation to this natural maturing process that goes on even without training.* They warn us that we must never lose sight of this *unique rate of maturing* of each separate child. Give a child too high a goal, or let the ambitious and over-confident child set himself one that is too difficult, and he will fail. If the skill is too hard to learn, the idea too complicated to grasp, the aesthetic experience too complex to feel, he will be frustrated, become discouraged, stop trying, give up.

Again we meet the problem of guidance. Here is one of the teacher's most critical tasks of guidance — to choose examples, teaching material, readings, and problems for discussion *that are not too difficult, yet are difficult enough to stretch the abilities of the pupil;* not so complex as to defeat him and cause him to give up, yet novel and intriguing enough to prod him to work at high pitch.

Fourth: People Learn Better if They Grasp Understandable Wholes instead of Isolated Parts

It was one of the chief defects of the formal school that it taught things in "bits and pieces." It was ignorant of the Principle of the Whole. The school day was broken up into a score of minute school subjects: 10 minutes of writing, 15 minutes of spelling, 20 minutes each of reading, history, arithmetic, geography, etc. Literature consisted of analyzing into bits great classic poems, novels, or plays that had been written to be read and enjoyed. But the new school, profiting by the psychological findings about learning, has learned to center attention on wholes.

You will need to use the Principle of the Whole. Constantly there is the danger of confronting the children with problems too big for them to grasp at their stage of maturity, and you will have to choose and

organize the subject matter. Questions of selection must be answered:
How much shall I bring to them at this moment? How broad shall
the problem be? Can I break it up into smaller units, into "parts," that
will be within the grasp of the learners? This is the "Part-Whole" problem in teaching, and many experiments have been conducted to discover
the most effective ways of handling it in children's and adults' learning.
In memorizing long poems, for example, shall the whole poem be studied
at one sitting, or shall it be broken up into parts and the separate parts
memorized? Many studies, since William James's famous first one
(1890), have confirmed the Principle of the Whole: Fewer repetitions
will be required if the poem is learned as a whole than if successive bits
are memorized separately. But the studies also show that a judicious
mixture of "whole" and "part" learning may, in some instances, be still
more effective. The optimum length of the unit of learning will depend on the maturity and readiness of the children for this kind of
learning, on the organization of the material, and on other special circumstances. If the new learning is divided into easily felt units, each
may itself become a smaller "whole," to be learned by itself.

The principle will apply in learning in arithmetic, algebra, or geometry, and in the physical and natural sciences whenever you have to
introduce new ideas or meanings. In the study of civilization, also, it is
doubtful if one can find a single social, political, or economic problem
today which can be grasped by either adults or children unless economic
facts, political facts, geographic facts, psychological facts, and other
facts of the whole culture are learned together as "wholes."

This is not only the Principle of the Whole. It is also the Principle
of Related Meanings in learning; that is, if meanings are needed together
for understanding, they must be learned together in "wholes." Thus we
bring together our third and fourth conditions for effective learning.
The subject matter of the school must be graded very carefully in terms
of the actual maturing of the young people. For example, consider the
problem of organizing arithmetic so as to build understanding of the
meaning of a fraction. The newer teaching distributes the study of
fractions over several years — from the kindergarten or first grade, where
the simplest manipulations of halves and quarters of actual objects are
learned, to the abstract generalizing of the fifth and sixth grades. Thus
the modern teaching of arithmetic discriminates no less than seventeen
separate steps in the study of fractions from the kindergarten to the fifth

grade. Each of these steps is not only a "part" of the six- or seven-year process; each one is also a smaller organized "whole" in itself. Thus we see the intimate connection between the Principle of the Whole and the Principle of Related Meanings.

We can perhaps sum up our brief study of the Part-Whole problem by reminding ourselves that we should always use the largest whole that the readiness of the learners will permit. If the parts are too big and too complex, the learner will be blocked; if they are too small, there will be waste in trying to integrate them and grasp them as a whole. Remember, moreover, the application of the Law of Individual Differences to our problem; namely, the most appropriate whole will surely be too big for some children in your class, while too small for others. Thus the Principle of the Whole must be used judiciously.

Fifth: People Learn Better in a Democratic Environment

Finally, we come to the most all-inclusive of the favorable conditions for learning. It is the conviction of our people that the democratic way of life makes for the highest well-being of the largest number of people. It is the corresponding conviction of the educator that *people will learn best in a democratic environment*. This means an atmosphere in which the supreme worth of each individual personality is recognized. People differ widely in physical, mental, and emotional traits, but in one thing they are equal: in the dignity and value of their own Persons. Thus the democratic way of living is one in which each wholeheartedly believes that a "man's a man for a' that," no matter what his property, skin color, race, or religion. It provides an environment in which every member of the group is free to grow to the finest possibilities that are in him.

This is the democratic idea, and we have seen how it has already worked its wonders in many classrooms. New articles of faith have emerged, and the first of these is freedom: "Free the legs, the arms, the expression of a child, and you have taken the first step towards freeing his mind and spirit." Hence the revolution in all the paraphernalia of administration — the disappearance of the ironbound seats and the lock-step rigidity of the old curriculum, the abandonment of the elaborate machinery of mass education. Hence the air of happy, cheerful living, the informal atmosphere, the smaller classes, the free interchange of thought in the newer schools.

Phoenix, Arizona, high school students analyze and judge their own behavior. (North Phoenix High School photo.)

Moreover, such schools believe that the ability to govern oneself grows only through the practice of self-government. They believe that learning takes place more effectively when boys and girls share in their own government, in the planning of the program, in conducting the life of the school. In such an environment pupil-teacher planning marks the beginning of the school day. Learning is at a high ebb; pupils are alive, active, hard at work, inventing and organizing their own ideas, assembling materials, carrying out enterprises. Both as individuals and as social groups, the young people grow in their capacity to govern themselves, as well as in their individual capacity for creative expression. Democracy is put into practice in the school, and education as conformity gives way to education as creative experience. Thus Jacques-Dalcroze's slogan comes alive: "I would have a child say, not 'I know,' but, 'I have experienced.'"

Summing Up

The five conditions that favor learning are:

–*First:* People learn better if they desire to learn.

–*Second:* People learn better if they are relaxed and happy — not insecure and frustrated.

–*Third*: People learn better if the situation is within their level of understanding.

–*Fourth*: People learn better if they grasp understandable wholes, instead of isolated parts.

–*Fifth*: People learn better in a democratic environment in which they can put their ideas into operation and learn through experience.

Having reviewed the principles of how people learn, and outlined the conditions that favor learning, we come to the final phase of this subject — *good teaching as guidance of learning.* Throughout our entire study, guidance has been an underlying theme. But now, because it is so clearly the supreme educational task, we shall consider the subject of guidance more systematically. In doing so, we shall at the same time be discussing its synonym — the teaching process — and the one who knows most about that — *The Good Teacher.*

Conditions That Favor Good Teaching and Guidance

Certainly the basis of good teaching is understanding the children. The secret of good teaching in large classes has its roots in the fact of differences in the children. Thirty to forty individuals and individualists! All different — different in physique, different in intelligence, different in personality traits. All coming to you from different homes, different family backgrounds, different family problems. No two alike — each one to be studied as a unique individual. Hence, teaching, as well as child study and guidance, must be individualized.

Five ways of building an understanding of the individual children have already been discussed (Chapter 11):

–Study them as they are actively at work in the class.

–Study them by using instruments of evaluation and measurement.

–Build and use cumulative record files, elaborate personal histories of each individual.

–Visit their homes, getting to know the parents and getting the parents to work in the school.

–Work with the parents and other teachers in child-study groups.

The advantages and limitations of each of these five ways have been explored. All must be employed, none neglected.

Importance of the Curriculum in Good Teaching

The second factor which determines how well teachers will guide children's growth is the curriculum itself. Does the program permit the teacher to study the individual children? The old standardized curriculum, and question-and-answer teaching, treated all the children alike and treated them all as passive and receptive. Under it the guidance of children was utterly inadequate. The new informal activity program treats them all differently and as individuals. It assumes that they will learn and grow to the degree that they are expected to work, meet problems, think out their own solutions, say what they themselves feel and think, criticize and create — all under their own drives.

The new curriculum enables the teacher to become the friend and fellow-worker of the pupils, and encourages him to study the boys and girls in many different situations. Under these conditions individual differences emerge for the teacher to observe. When, for example, thirty children and the teacher, aided by parents and neighbors, put a rural school building in order, cleaning, painting, and repairing it, and when they clear and plant the land in crops and meet together for the coöperative study of school problems, a perfect situation has been established for child study and guidance. When members of a school community carry out group projects together, barriers are broken down, personal problems and traits emerge, and understanding grows. As one teacher, who carried on an informal curriculum of this type, said: "We by no means had a perfect school, but I do think I left it in a better condition, and our pupils better equipped than we found them. I feel that if it had not been for my guidance training I would have made a failure of my year of teaching."

First and foremost, therefore, the building of an appropriate curriculum is a necessary initial step in providing favorable conditions for guidance.

Necessity for Careful Planning

Good teachers do not just walk into their classrooms on the first day of school and spontaneously develop fine educational experiences for thirty children. No, fine teaching is the product of many hours of careful planning. Many examples have been pointed to in the foregoing chapters that were made possible by the fact that administrators and teachers had together created both the spirit and practice of good planning. Recall the role of planning in the examples cited from the San Jose curriculum (Chapter 13). In such instances there is, first, the long-term planning that the teachers do near the close of each year, outlining and reorganizing the total curriculum from the nursery to the senior high school. Working together, the teachers of adjacent grades appraise the results of their year's work and make over-all decisions concerning grade placement of major themes and units, order of development, allotment of time, and the like. In the light of these group decisions, and of her study of available records on the children, each teacher plans roughly in advance the themes and units to be developed with her new class during the coming year. Thus while each room teacher's curriculum is part of the over-all design of the whole school program, the latter is made so flexible that as the work develops, each teacher can change the plan from one unit to another.

But the teacher's planning does not end even there. How does it happen that when children arrive on the first day of school, they find other children's paintings hanging on the walls, exciting models scattered about the room, pieces of wood in the wood-supply box, needed tools on workbenches and in racks, cloth and sewing materials in the cabinets, books on various subjects on their reading table? These things are in the room because an artist-teacher, knowing in advance what kind of situation he wishes to create, will prepare for it carefully. In the spring of the preceding year she had studied the needs of the thirty children who will be coming to her in September. Even during the summer her weeks in a university teacher's workshop, or some other kind of activity, stimulates her study of the coming year's program, bringing her new experiences and new ideas for curriculum development. Thus a program of planning in the schools is an essential condition of good teaching.

Adequate Time to Become Acquainted with the Group

The third condition favoring or hampering child study is time: Does the teacher have a group long enough to know the boys and girls intimately? No one can question the difficulty of getting inside complex human beings, of discovering individual interests and capacities, disabilities and handicaps. Many examples have taught us that even under favorable conditions months pass, sometimes a year, before a teacher really understands the boys or girls in his group. But the formal practice of promoting children from grade to grade once a year, or even twice, interrupts the teacher-pupil relationship, and the children are passed on to another stranger who begins all over again the struggle to understand them.

This condition has led many thoughtful administrators, during the past fifty years, to keep a teacher with her group for two, three, or even four years. The practice is followed in some schools today, and you can find many articles which report the results of such experiments. There are disadvantages in advancing the teacher with the class; for example, it is found sometimes that certain children do not get along well with particular teachers. In such cases, no doubt, the child would be placed with another teacher. But such instances are the exception rather than the rule. Certainly one great gain comes from letting a teacher take over the responsibility of work with a school group for two or three consecutive years. In this way the time spent in getting to know them thoroughly during the first year brings its reward in the better teaching and guidance of the second and third years.

Closest Possible Coöperation between School and Home

The fourth important condition for wise guidance is the close coöperation between teachers and parents. This was the theme of Chapter 12, and at this point we need do little more than summarize that discussion. Notice especially that the collaboration between parents and teachers is a two-way process: The teacher must go out to the parents and children in their homes, and the parents must be brought into closer partnership with the teacher in the school.

Many examples have been given of the success of teachers and administrators in getting the parents into the school — getting them to do volunteer work in the library and the lunchroom, work as assistants to room teachers, build up the use of motion pictures and lantern slides, develop hobby clubs, write publicity stories for the local newspapers, and hold neighborhood parent-teacher conferences. Thus they become aware of the program of education.

The other half of the process is equally important — namely, getting the teachers into the homes and accepted by the parents and the children. Wise administrators make definite provision for this at the very beginning of the school year by leaving teachers' afternoons free for the visiting. And from diary reports of their visits, you have learned how the teachers' understanding of individual children grew. The teachers came to understand the living conditions in individual families and built up closer relations with boys and girls. Fathers as well as mothers came to know about and show real interest in the progress of their children. Light was thrown on the children's emotional problems through the teacher coming to understand the child's relations with the father and mother and other members of the family.

Guidance Enhanced by Group Size, Grade Placement, and Promotion

Another important factor in guidance is the size of your group, and in our public schools this will be large. In the schools and colleges of America today there are nearly 40 million students, and about 1,300,000 teachers to teach them. This means an average of more than 30 pupils to a teacher, although, of course, many classes are smaller. In our larger cities classes of 40, 50, and even 60 are common.

Because of such large numbers the method by which boys and girls are grouped in classes becomes of vital importance. In the conventional mass school, grouping is done by sheer routine — by chronological age and alphabetical arrangement — six-year-olds in the first grade, seven-year-olds in the second, and so on. But progressive educators, realizing that effective grouping, grade placement, and promotion are important conditions for good teaching, have long studied this problem. The psychologists among them have focused their study on such problems as that of maturity or social age, the administrators on homogeneous grouping and frequency of promotion, and the research students on marks and evaluation. As a consequence of fifty years of study, all the students agree that guidance is enhanced by effective grade placement,

Under the wise guidance of school counselors, learners concentrate on personal and group goals. (Washington State Department of Public Instruction photo.)

wise promotion, and sound evaluation of the work of the boys and girls. These will be discussed in Chapter 16.

Guidance Experts on the School Staff

We have emphasized constantly that in the long run the group teacher knows more about the individual boys and girls than anyone else in the school and hence is the best guidance expert. But the point should also be made that it is impossible for the group teacher to be an expert on all the problems encountered in education. To secure favorable conditions for educational guidance, the staff must include several specialists competent to deal with various aspects of growth. Today on the staff you will find one or more of the following:

–A school physician — a licensed doctor — the professional medical officer of the school. No responsible school today is without the services of such a specialist.

–A school pediatrician — a licensed physician especially trained and experienced in the study and treatment of the health of children and youth

–A school psychologist — especially trained in the use and interpretation of mental and educational tests, rating scales, behavior description records, cumulative record files; a specialist in the diagnosis of specific learning difficulties and other educational handicaps

–A visiting teacher and social welfare worker

–A director of curriculum — especially competent in the planning and development of the activities and materials of instruction

The Teacher's Preëminent Understanding of the Development of the Whole Child

Granted the need for the expert knowledge and direction of school psychologists, educational counselors, or other guidance specialists in the school, still, you, as a group teacher, can become the children's wisest guide. This is especially true if you work in an elementary school. You then will have the children with you all day long, in a great variety of situations. If you work in a school system where the teacher is promoted with the class, you will have the children with you two or three years and will be in an even more favorable position for knowing them. If by chance you work in a rural school, you will find an ideal situation in which to study a community of young people of all ages from childhood to adolescence. The rural school, in spite of its much decried difficulties, provides in reality a fine opportunity for the effective study and guidance of boys and girls.

So, in spite of the great need for the expert knowledge of specialists, the group teacher is in the most strategic position to know *the whole child*. She knows that a boy's general physical condition, his mood and natural way of responding, his worries and joys, hobbies and special enthusiasms, all play their parts with his intelligence and study habits in determining how he gets along in school. Your greatest task in education will be to help transform the egocentric, individual selves that appear in the nursery school and kindergarten into mature persons of adult years. To do that you must make yourself a student of the whole child. Turn to the medical men and physiologists for better knowledge of the child's physical growth. Study the newer schools of psychology and psychiatry to understand his mental and emotional development. Turn to the researches of the sociologists to see the children with their parents and community. Study and use the new mental and educational tests; try out aptitude tests and rating scales with your pupils. Put all this knowledge together, and you will become a wise guide. You will know more about the whole child than any single expert — physician, pediatrician, psychologist, or psychiatrist — can possibly know.

Continuous Guidance from Infancy to Maturity

Guidance is a never-ending process. Just as human growth is continuous, so is the need for guidance. It begins with infancy and continues until real independence has been achieved. In fact, the process is longer than the twenty years which this statement implies. It actually begins before the birth of the child and continues for many people well into adult life. There are, indeed, few grown persons who will make important and difficult decisions without discussing their problem with a close personal adviser. In this sense, guidance continues for all of us throughout life.

But especially are cultivated people agreed that the need for guidance arises very early. The years that customarily precede entrance to school are now recognized as the most important period in human development. New professions of specialists — pediatricians, psychologists, psychiatrists, social workers — are arising to satisfy the growing demand of your parents for advice on the care of mothers, babies, and very young children. Some of the books on this subject are best sellers.[1] The care is extended to include even the critical months before childbirth. With the recent development of nursery schools for children of eighteen months to three years, many mothers are coming to rely on them for guidance in the growth of their young children. Nursery schools are being made a part of the regular school program. In the case of a few progressive schools, such as the Dalton School of New York City, the high school curriculum requires every girl to work in the baby nursery and the nursery school. The school now sees as its function the understanding and helping of children through working with the parents, the child's physician or pediatrician, and in special cases with a psychiatrist, a social worker, and other community agencies. The new point of view is to emphasize the importance of guidance.

[1] See Dr. Benjamin Spock's *Physical Health and Care of the Young Child.*

The Characteristics of the Good Teacher

Who, then, is the good teacher? He is the many-sided person pictured throughout this book. The Good Teacher

–loves to teach — "would rather teach than do anything else."

–loves children, in fact, likes people, is a deep believer in humanity, has great faith in the potentialities of human beings.

–is a friend, comrade, and guide — not a policeman and taskmaster — respects his students and is respected by them.

–is sensitive to others, keeps the channels of communication open.

–is a dynamic creative person — an artist-teacher with great capacity for feeling.

–is a person of integrity, with a deep sense of responsibility.

–is a student of our civilization, of the psychology of learning and the development of personality, and of human expression and appreciation.

–plans his teaching carefully, is a master of the art of developing thinking ability.

These are the qualities of the great teachers, the geniuses of the educational profession. These set the goal for all of us. All who aspire to be good teachers should measure themselves on this yardstick.

As you study the yardstick, perhaps you are asking yourself if, to be a good teacher, you just have to be "a natural" — or whether any amount of training will make a good teacher out of one who lacks these traits. It seems to be true that there are the "naturals" in athletics, and in acting, music, and the other arts. Take Babe Ruth and his batting average of .350 . . . Fritz Kreisler and his virtuosity on the violin . . . John Barrymore playing Hamlet . . . Isadora Duncan on the dance stage. These are "naturals," endowed physically, mentally, and spiritually above most human beings for the particular skill or kind of expression to which they have devoted themselves.

But far more than natural endowment was needed: years of internship and study, years of guidance by experienced and talented artists, years of dogged persistence and practice. Good performance in any field of work is dependent upon knowledge and ideas, and these are obtained by study, by hard intellectual work. You will see in our list of traits: The good teacher is a student of civilization, and a master of the psychology of learning and of the art of communication; that is, he is a student of ideas as well as a natural-born teacher. His native endowment alone cannot give him an understanding of our complex civilization and of equally complex human beings. His natural gifts cannot make him competent to pass such understanding on to others.

The great modern dancer, Martha Graham, exclaims: "It takes ten years to make a dancer." We reiterate her affirmation for an educator: "It takes ten years to make a good teacher." Ten years of study, of getting the facts, working at the problems, digesting the guidance of older experienced teachers.

We see, therefore, that good teachers are both born and made. They must have the needed raw materials of personality. If, for example, they don't like people, are dull and inert, are selfish and dictatorial by nature, have little patience with the disabilities of others, they should choose some other lifework. With such handicaps upon them at the start, no amount of education will turn them into good teachers. So it is true, in the sense of needing a basic endowment in such traits, good teachers *are* born.

But they are also made. Teaching is an art, and the good teacher is an artist. Like all artists he must *know and be able to do, as well as just be.*

Studying How the Artist-Teacher Works

1. As you began your study in this course, you were asked to recall and describe the best teacher in your own school and college career. Suppose now that we are nearing the end of our study, you do it again. Turn back to Chapter 1 and follow the suggestions given there. If you have saved your earlier paper on the subject, compare your later one with it.

2. One of the best ways to study the art of teaching as *guided learning* is to teach another person some new process, skill, or understanding. Try

it now. Teach a girl to knit or swim or play tennis, or a youth to drive a car, run a machine, or use a tool. Keep careful records of the learning process as you saw it revealed, of the factors which aided learning, and make a short report to the class of your findings.

3. In your observation of teaching in the practice school or a local town school, try to study the learning processes of some one child. Apply the ideas and principles developed in this book: Study the whole child in action, be curious about everything he does, question any unusual instance of behavior. Debate with yourself possible causes of behavior in his physical condition and social relations in the home, neighborhood, etc. If the child you observe is not learning successfully, see if you can find the reason. In class discussion compare your findings with those of your classmates.

4. Conduct an experiment in conditioning the learning of a family pet — a dog, cat, or some other animal. Compare your findings with the discussion of learning as conditioning in this and other modern books.

5. Make a unit of workbook material for some selected unit of work for a chosen school grade. Take a topic that children in the school can do something about — for example, the study of how the city or town gets its food. Plan a variety of activities — trips of directed observation, etc. — as suggested in earlier chapters.

6. In your college curriculum department, study examples of workbooks at the junior high and elementary school levels.

7. Have a round-table or panel discussion of the merits and limitations in the use of workbooks in the school.

8. Come to class prepared to tell of some instance in your own experience or in the observed behavior of a child in which failure to learn was due to physical ailment or disability.

9. Be prepared to report to the class one or more examples of the behavior of "anxious" children, whose schoolwork, obviously far below their capacity, is known to be due to emotionally disturbing conditions at home.

10. Select some one person in the community who is devoting himself enthusiastically to a particular hobby — for example, a boy excited about airplanes or automobiles, or an adult devoted to gardening or stamp-collecting, and make a study of the role of intense interest on learning. Show the effect of such an intense drive on the acquisition of knowledge.

11. Have a class round table on the place of drill in various aspects of schoolwork.

12. Bring to the class a creative painter, poet, or other artist from the college staff, student body, or the town, for a forum on the creative process in learning. Find out how the artist works and how this differs from the way scientists and technicians work.

13. Get acquainted with such artists, and talk with them about the creative process. Go to their studios and study their works.

14. Have a class discussion of freedom and control in teaching situations your class has observed. Bring into the discussion situations outside of school.

Further Reading on Learning and Teaching

To teach well, you will want an understanding of the psychology of learning, and you will want to develop your own point of view. In your library you will find many books that deal with the subject. Although there is no completely agreed upon point of view, several basic ideas are generally accepted. Your task is both to know the consensus and to get what you can from the separate points of view.

Of the recent publications perhaps the best is Cole and Bruce's *Educational Psychology*, especially Chapters 9 to 12, which deal with learning. For the advanced student the best scientific presentation is the *Forty-first Yearbook* of the National Society for the Study of Education, *The Psychology of Learning*. Two books by Boyd H. Bode: *Conflicting Psychologies of Learning*, and, in its rewritten form, *How We Learn*, are among the most readable, yet critical, studies of various views of learning. For the clearest defense of the "field," or Gestalt point of view, see Part II of George Hartmann's *Educational Psychology*. For a reinterpretation of the role of body-movement and feeling in education, see Harold Rugg's *Foundation for American Education*, especially Chapter VII, and pages 92 to 97, 438 to 447.

For the newer view of the relation of growth of total personality to the problems of learning, see Gertrude Hildreth's *Child Growth through Education*.

The problem of motives, incentives, and interests is well treated in Pressey and Robinson's *Psychology and the New Education*, especially Chapters 9, and 11 to 13. The classic study of interests and their reconciliation with the problem of effort and control is John Dewey's *Interest and Effort in Education*. See Chapters IX to XI of his *Democracy and Education* for special consideration of experience, thinking, and perception of meanings. The emotional background of interests and their role in the learning process are well treated in Daniel Prescott's *Emotions and the Educative Process*.

For further study of the democratic environment as favorable to learning and teaching, see Chapters V and VI of Dewey's *Experience and Education*; also, Chapter III of L. T. Hopkins's *Interaction: the Democratic Process*, and Chapters IX and X of *Helping Teachers Understand Children*.

On learning and the creative process, see Rugg's *Foundations for American Education*, Chapters XIII and XIV, and his *Culture and Education in America*. For special application to the creative expression in music, see B. Marian Brooks and Harry A. Brown's *Music Education in the Elementary School*; for graphic arts, Herbert Read's *Education through Art*; for writing, the Foreword of Hughes Mearns's *Creative Youth* and his *Creative Power*, Chapter XIII. For an over-all statement applied to all the arts of expression, see Rugg and Shumaker's *The Child-Centered School*, Chapters XI–XIX, and Natalie Cole's *The Arts in the Classroom*. The creative teaching of six-year-olds is vividly illustrated in Hubbard's *Your Children at School*.

For the modern point of view on learning and living see Kilpatrick's Chapter XIII of *Democracy and the Curriculum*, the Third Yearbook of the John Dewey Society. Part III of Carleton Washburne's *A Living Philosophy of Education* might be read in this connection, because of its emphasis on functional learning, integration, readiness, and drill applied to the school subjects. Caroline Pratt tells what she discovered in her school about "growing and learning," in her book *I Learn from Children*. A. Gordon Melvin presents many suggestive techniques, materials, and activities in *New Methods for New Schools* (pages 121–154). The NEA Educational Policies Commission's *Education for All American Children* gives examples of good teaching in classrooms today. On the "core teacher" and other special teachers, see Chapter X of *The American High School*, Eighth Yearbook of the John Dewey Society. See also Umstattd's *Secondary School Teaching* for suggestive usages of radio, visual aids, and other techniques. Yoakum and Simpson's *Modern Methods and Techniques of Teaching* discusses lesson planning, questioning, and problem solving.

On group planning and the democratic process in the classroom see: H. H. Giles's *Teacher-Pupil Planning* (perhaps the best discussion); Grace Coyle's *Group Work with American Youth*; and the NEA Educational Policies Commission's *Learning the Ways of Democracy*.

On questions of discipline and freedom in the classroom, see Chapters XIV, XV, and XVI of Washburne's *A Living Philosophy of Education*;

Chapters V and VI of Dewey's *Experience and Education;* and Sheviakov and Redl's (Editors) *Discipline for Today's Children and Youth.*

But to see the teacher as a Person go to Chapters IV, V, and VI of *The Teacher and Society,* the *First Yearbook* of the John Dewey Society, and Witty and Skinner's *Mental Hygiene in Modern Education.*

And for inspiration and good reading, don't miss Peterson's *Great Teachers* and Barzun's *Teacher in America.*

CHAPTER 16

How Can We Appraise Growth and Development?

WE COME now to another basic job of the teacher and the parent:

–to appraise the outcome of learning and teaching.

Fifty years of scientific study distinguishes the specific abilities and phases of personality; for example, physique, intelligence, and temperament, from the growth and development of *The Whole Personality*.

It distinguishes also the methods of appraisal:

–Specific abilities *measured* by objective Scales and Tests

–Total personalities *appraised* by subjective judgment

But both are aided by "instruments" of evaluation; hence, we study the concept — *Measurement in Education.*

Two purposes of appraisal are also distinguished:

–Administrative purposes: marks, reports to parents, etc.

–Diagnosis of a child's difficulties in learning, for the purpose of expediting growth and development

But *growth of total personality is all important.*

Evaluating the Work of the School

ONE FINAL ASPECT of the art of teaching remains to be considered — namely, appraising its results. How do you know when the pupil has learned? when he is progressing satisfactorily in his school subjects? whether or not he has grown as much as he should have in knowledge and understanding and in the ability to express himself? How does one evaluate the products of education? These are the questions that have confronted educators as long as there have been schools.

Early Studies of Evaluation

The Teacher's Judgment — the Traditional Yardstick

"Leave it to the teacher. He knows what has been happening in his class. He knows how well each boy or girl has progressed in arithmetic, science, or language; how well each one can read, write, and reckon. Leave it to the teacher's judgment."

This is the conventional method. Once, twice, four times a year the teacher sends his marks to the school office, and the dreaded report card comes home; P for passing . . . F for failure. Or, when more detailed evaluation is required: A for excellent, B for good, C for fair, D for poor. Or, if the scale is a numerical one — 94, 80, or 76. These marks are precise, indeed omniscient, for in them our fate is settled by another human being's judgment. On such "marks" rest our very lives, the decision as to whether we are promoted or are branded "Failed!";

compelled to spend another year on the same distasteful grind. Admission to college is also decided by teachers' marks on entrance examinations. Memberships in honor societies, honors — *magna cum laude,* the valedictory oration, many others — all are determined by the personal appraisal of the teacher.

Jobs and prestige in the adult world also are settled by this same subjective judgment; so, too, are money scholarships to colleges, prizes, recognition in community, state, and nation. Civil service systems of modern nations still rest on examiners' judgments. Artists' competitions are settled by the judgments of other artists. Architects are given commissions to design public buildings on similar competitions and prizes awarded them — again in competition. And so it runs.

Human judgment must, then, be a very reliable measuring instrument! But is it?

The Scientific Appraisal of Teachers' Judgments

Forty years ago professors of education began making objective studies of the question: How reliable are teachers' judgments? Since that time hundreds of careful investigations have been made. In some studies a single examination paper was read by many well-respected teachers. In others the marks of teachers of different subjects were compared and analyzed to lay bare discernible tendencies in marking. Other studies appraised the *content* of the examinations. Still others studied marks given in relation to the time when marking was done and the sequence of papers marked. And there were others. But all were concerned with the weaknesses of subjective judgments and sought to find a way to substitute for them more objective appraisals.

One of the most startling of these studies was conducted a generation ago by D. Starch and E. C. Elliott. They had a geometry examination written in a large Wisconsin high school marked by the principal mathematics teacher in 116 standard certified high schools of the North Central Association. The results were astounding — some said incredible! Two examiners marked the paper 92. One gave it 28! Sixty-nine, more than half of the examiners, marked the paper "Failure"; forty-seven passed it — gave it 75 or more. Twelve teachers thought so highly of it that they marked it between 83 and 90; thirty-seven others marked the same paper below 65.

The study caused excited discussion in academic centers. "How could two teachers give marks to *the same paper* that differed by 60 points!" "Impossible," said many. "Must be something fishy," said others. There were many explanations. Meanwhile other students reported similar studies of school and college marks. All confirmed Starch and Elliott's conclusion that such subjective judgments were thoroughly unreliable. In one of the most striking studies Ben Wood reported that a "model" examination paper, written by an expert examiner as his "standard" scoring paper in college history, was accidentally included in a batch of college examinations marked by other expert readers. This "model" paper was marked "Failure" by another examiner. In company with other "failed" papers, it was then marked by the other expert readers. The marks on the expert's model ranged from 90 to 40!

J. D. Falls reported a study in which 100 high school English teachers marked the best composition found in a survey of Gary, Indiana, written by a high school senior who was a journalist correspondent for a Chicago newspaper. Five examiners appraised it as college work; another five as satisfactory for the elementary grades!

Are teachers consistent in their marking? Several investigators sought the answer to that question. Hulton had 28 experienced Wisconsin high school English teachers mark an English composition twice, two months apart. Of those who passed it the first time, 18 failed it the second time. The importance of such a finding stands out especially because most teachers' examinations are of the "essay" or composition type. E. J. Ashbaugh had 49 Ohio State University students, with teaching experience, mark a seventh-grade arithmetic examination three times at intervals of approximately one month. The marks were utterly inconsistent. Only one of the 49 gave the same score on all three markings; seven on any two successive markings. C. C. Ross reported differences of 27 points on successive remarkings of the same paper. Discussing the conditions abroad, Ross reports that in England the situation is just as bad: "Examiners were found to reverse their judgments almost completely when they were asked to mark again the same papers they had scored a year before." Starch had long before that reported the same finding: that college instructors almost invariably give different marks to the same papers when marking them a second time. Thus it is seen how subjective and unscientific teachers' judgments can be.

Causes of Unreliability in Evaluation

The studies of a generation ago laid bare one of the chief factors in the variation in marking — namely, the tendency of teachers to be "high" or "low," "hard" or "easy" markers. A score of investigations established the conclusion that "Pass" or "Failure," 90, 70, 50, etc., does not mean the same thing to any two people. To cite a few studies:

Max Meyer in perhaps the earliest investigation of this kind (1908) studied the marks of 40 instructors in the University of Missouri over a period of five years: Professors in Philosophy gave 55 per cent of A's; professors of Chemistry III gave 1 per cent. In Latin I, nobody was failed in five years; in English II, 28 per cent were failed. Meyer's interpretation: One subject is not harder than another; one group of professors is harder than another.

Thirty years ago in the University High School of the University of Chicago, F. W. Johnson established the tendency of some of the teachers to give high marks and of others to give low marks. The teachers of English failed 15 per cent of the students; the history teachers 8 per cent. In the French department only 9 per cent of the pupils got A, while in the German department 17 per cent received this mark.

Walter F. Dearborn discovered that in one college department ten times as many A's were given to the same grade of student as in another department; only one tenth as many failures occurred in one as in another. Another study reported that the same students, in the same course, taught by one instructor in the first semester and by another in the second semester, "had three times the probability" of receiving a mark higher than 85 in one case than in the other.

Many were the explanations for the variations in marks on the same examinations. One was that already advanced — the lack of a common standard, hence, the tendency for one instructor's marks to fall in a higher part of the scale and those of another in a lower part. There are high markers and low markers. Some never give marks above 80 or 85; others almost never give any below 70 and few below 80! Some said the marks were determined by whim: They depended on the instructor's mood, how he felt the day he read the papers. A British wag put it:

" 'Twixt Right and Wrong the Difference is dim:
'Tis settled by the Moderator's Whim:
Perchance the Delta on your Paper marked
Means that his Lunch has disagreed with him."

One study of the factors involved in marking concluded that the "passing or failing of about 40 per cent depends, *not* on *what* they know or do not know, but on *who* reads the papers"; also, that "the passing or failing of about 10 per cent depends . . . on *when* the papers are read." Such studies have established the fact that the mark on a given paper is greatly influenced by marks given other papers read at the same time. One investigator reports that "a C paper may be graded B *if it is read after an illiterate theme, but if it follows an A plus paper,* it seems to be of D caliber."

Another factor entering into this unreliability is the subjective, unscientific nature of the examinations themselves — the tendency to use obscure, ambiguous questions, to ask trivial details, to use "catch questions," to appraise only certain aspects of the subject. The studies established the unscientific selection of items for the examination, lack of care in choosing precise words and in designing questions to fit the actual content of the course. In some schools an important factor was the tendency to have the principal or other administrative officer prepare the examination without consultation with the teacher.

Edward L. Thorndike, the most eminent of the pioneers in the scientific study of education, appraised the situation:

"these marks and grades . . . were opinions rather than measurements, and were subject to two notable defects. Nobody could be sure what was measured, or how closely the measure tallied with the reality!"

If several people measured the length or weight of a thing, Thorndike said, they could be fairly sure that all competent persons were measuring the same thing, namely, length or weight. But what do marks in freshman algebra measure? Marks in that very precise subject

"might be measures of inborn talent for mathematics, or of acquired power at mathematics, or of mathematical erudition, or of temporary memory, or of docility and fidelity in doing what the instructors ordered, or of sagacious divination of what the instructor desired."

As early as 1922 Thorndike summed up the situation in teachers' marking in school and college: "The general result was scandalous."

All agreed that judging human traits and accomplishments was a thoroughly subjective process, and while society would probably have to

EDWARD LEE THORNDIKE (1874–1949), former President of the American Psychological Association, was perhaps our most distinguished leader in building the first graduate study of educational psychology and in formulating the course that is still widely taught in American teachers colleges. He was the outstanding pioneer in initiating the systematic study of animal psychology, the quantitative investigation of the transfer of training and of the psychology of learning, the design of standardized scales and tests in education, and the design of the subject matter of the school curriculum on the results of scientific investigation. His scientific studies of adult learning gave an important impetus to the adult-education movement.

In World War I, Dr. Thorndike was cochairman, with Robert Yerkes, of the Committee on Classification of Personnel in the United States Army. Among his books are the three-volume *Educational Psychology, Mental and Social Measurements, The Measurement of Intelligence, Human Nature and the Social Order,* and *Man and His Work.*

continue to employ human judgments, everything possible should be done to make them more objective and consistent.

A quarter of a century passed. Society and its schools continued to use subjective judgment in evaluating people. But it did much in addition. It practically revolutionized the techniques of appraising the work of the school. These early studies of grading students' work turned out to be merely a phase of a nation-wide movement to measure human behavior in schools and colleges.

Fifty Years of Scientific Method in Education

Broadly conceived, this phase of the measurement movement was part of a basic effort to make all education more scientific. Two psychologists, trained in laboratory science and exact measurement, led the way — Edward L. Thorndike, to whom we have referred, and Charles H. Judd, for nearly thirty years Director of the School of Education at the University of Chicago. Under their leadership every phase of education was subjected to scientific study and to a vast amount of reconstruction. To wit:

–The processes of learning were studied scientifically in the laboratory, and the classroom and teaching methods improved.

–The curriculum was given careful scrutiny; scientific studies were made of what to teach, in what grades to teach it, and how to organize and present curriculum materials.

–College entrance examinations were reappraised and great improvements made in them; new scholastic aptitude tests and comprehensive examinations were devised.

–Forty years of scientific work was done on "intelligence" — including the design and use of new instruments with which to measure it.

–Rating scales for judging students' work and teachers' efficiency were devised and tested.

–New types of objective examinations and "standard" tests in every subject of study were invented, tried out, and finally given to millions of pupils.

–Administrative studies were made of the age-grade census of children in the school system, promotion and retardation, elimination of pupils from school, the efficiency of school buildings, the financing of schools, and school laws.

–Scores of investigations were made of teachers' marks and marking systems.

This is only a hint of the swift, fact-finding movement that spread across the entire country. Between 1905 and 1925 every aspect of school practice was surveyed, questioned, and measured. From the impetus given by the Thorndike and Judd centers of inquiry, the quantitative mood in education took its drive and its characteristics for a quarter of a century. By 1930 Phi Delta Kappa, the graduate "scientific" fraternity in education, had initiated over 2000 members; the American Educational Research Association was a department of the NEA and its *Journal* well established. Hundreds of professors of education throughout the country were using questionnaires, counting and tabulating everything observable in the schools. Everywhere the slogans proclaimed: "Better schools; better grading, classification, promotion, marking, and certification of pupils by a more exact collecting, classifying, and treating of the facts."

The very nub of the quarter century of work was the evaluation of the work of the school — the problem involved in the studies of the unreliability of teachers' marks. As we have said, those studies were a preliminary part of the quantitative movement. Their findings spurred on the professors of education to devise instruments and methods that would be more objective, more accurate, more scientific.

What Do We Mean by Science and the Scientific Method?

Since the terms science and scientific method will necessarily be employed in this discussion of objective appraisal of the work of the schools, we should be clear about their meaning. So frequently have you encountered these concepts in your previous school and college work that here we shall simply define them. We shall do that, first, by summing up the characteristics of any body of knowledge and inquiry that assumes the name of science.

First: A *science is a body of knowledge founded upon primary concepts unique to it and of clear and universally accepted meaning.* While it makes use of the concepts of another science, its concepts are primary and peculiar to it as a body of knowledge. For example:

- –The science of physics is founded upon such primary concepts as energy, motion, the field, the first and second laws of thermodynamics.

- –The science of biology is built on such primary concepts as growth, evolution, integration, genes, individual differences.

- –The science of psychology rests upon such primary concepts as experience, the self, personality.

Second: A *science has evolved a body of measuring scales made up of equal units, universally understood and accepted, with which it can establish, gather, classify, and interpret "facts."* The concept of precise measurement, with constant reduction of error, is crucial.

Third: A *science has evolved a body of primary theory upon which its inquiries are conducted.* This is necessary because theory must precede design, and design, in turn, must precede construction.

It should be added that *several of the sciences, perhaps all of them, are founded upon a few superprimary concepts which provide the great foundation for all.*[1]

These are the criteria for a science. In all attempts to answer the question: Have we now, or can we build, a science of education? we must apply these criteria rigorously. In what follows we shall mean by the term "scientific" a method of inquiry and work that

–confronts a problem directly as the focus of its inquiry.

–works in the tentative (hypothetical, suspended judgment) frame of mind.

–attacks its problem with an awareness, and statement, of its specific hypotheses and assumptions.

–draws its hypotheses from a sufficient sample of the scientific world's known data — with special care that the data of other sciences have also been scrutinized.

–observes and collects its data with the aid of physical instruments of observation and measurement.

–"measures" with full and frank reservations concerning implied assumptions and possible sources of invalidity and unreliability.

–organizes its data, wherever they are quantitative, in statistical rank-order frequency.

–treats quantitative data with mathematical and statistical methods, presenting its findings via measures of average, dispersion, correlation, validity, and reliability.

–finally, in the light of the foregoing, draws new generalizations from these organized-in-relationship data, these generalizations standing as new hypotheses.

–on rare occasions, when such generalizations have been confirmed by recurring experiments and investigations, announces them as "scientific law"; such statements of law are, however, emphatically regarded as nothing more than hypotheses — the best possible generalizations from the best known data.

[1] For a fuller discussion of this and related problems see Harold Rugg's *Foundations for American Education.*

The Central Problem: How to Measure More Accurately in Education

Let us come back now to measurement, for it plays the central role in the scientific or objective way of working. The scientist insists that he knows only when he can measure the amount of a thing. Thorndike's great slogan was: "Whatever exists, exists in some amount." It was the amount of the thing upon which he centered attention. When Thorndike and Judd began their work, the meaning of the idea of measurement had already been thoroughly agreed upon by physical scientists. The new laboratory psychologists concurred with the physicist Max Planck that "whatever can be measured is real," and with Sir Francis Galton, the eminent British scientist, that "until the phenomenon of any branch of knowledge has been subjected to measurement and number, it cannot assume the status and dignity of a science." It was to be expected, therefore, that our educational pioneers should insist upon knowing the quantity as well as the quality of the things involved in the work of education. And that had been lacking in the teachers' examinations and marking systems. As Thorndike said, the school or the parent who receives a report of 70 as the rating of his child in elementary composition, "does not know what it was 70 of . . . or whether it was really 60, 65, 70, 75, or 80 of it. *Clearly defined units of measure and instruments by which to count them were lacking.*"

But "clearly defined units" implies measuring scales, and the use of these is the very essence of the scientific way of working. A modern measuring instrument has two characteristics: First, it is constructed of materials appropriate to the functions to be measured. Second, its dimensions consist of a series of equal units arranged in numerical rank-order from a zero point. The intervals must be equal units irrespective of their position on the measuring unit; one unit of linear or circular measure, of weight, of electrical resistance, etc., must be equal to another unit; for example, on a handwriting scale sample 80 must be as much better than sample 70 as sample 20 is better than sample 10.

Measurement: Merely a More Acute Form of Evaluation

In the moment-by-moment life of every human being the objects of the environment are constantly being evaluated. Most of this process of evaluation is subjective — the product of personal experience — and, as we saw with teachers' marks, much of it is grossly unreliable. For

Lewis M. Terman (1877————), a leading American psychologist and Professor of Psychology at Stanford University (1910–1942), is best known for his work in the measurement of intelligence. His influence has been world-wide since his revision of the Binet-Simon Intelligence Scale in 1916. In World War I he was head of the Psychological Division of the United States Army. He has been active in research studies of genius, the gifted child, and child psychology and hygiene, and in the design of such group tests as the Stanford Achievement Test and the Terman-McNemar Group Test of Mental Ability. He has made original studies in the fields of psychological factors in marital happiness, sex, and personality.

Among Dr. Terman's numerous books are: *The Teacher's Health, The Hygiene of the School Child, Health Work in the Schools, The Measurement of Intelligence, The Intelligence of School Children, Genetic Studies of Genius, Sex and Personality, Measuring Intelligence, Marital Happiness,* and *The Gifted Child as Adult.* He has been an editor of national and international psychological journals.

example, books like Hugo Münsterberg's *On the Witness Stand* have established beyond question the unreliability of much of the legal testimony given in our courts by persons who claim to have been eye-witness observers. It was to be expected, therefore, that as our educational pioneers began to apply more exact methods of observation to the work of education, they would first want to supplant subjective evaluation with more objective kinds of measurement. They would have agreed with the frequent pronouncement of Robert Fletcher of Dartmouth, who used to say to his students:

> "Young gentlemen, your constant purpose in life will be to reduce error. In the practically observed world there is no such word as 'truth.' There is only approximation to truth which we call 'fact.' Hence you will measure and remeasure the same object many times, using all the instruments at your command; and you will correct your measurements with the best statistical aids. If you persist, you will achieve approximations to the fact near enough for practical purposes."

One basic and obvious conclusion that the young educational scientists drew from the study of engineering and physical sciences, therefore, was that they must first design exact measuring scales and tests if they were to measure and evaluate the work of the school.

The Beginnings of Educational Scales and Tests

Nearly a hundred years ago the Reverend George Fisher, an English schoolmaster, published a series of *Scale Books* composed of "various standard specimens . . . arranged in order of merit." These were used in the Greenwich Hospital School as early as 1864. They covered the subjects of handwriting, spelling, mathematics, grammar and composition, French, general history, navigation, drawing, and practical science. They were far more "objective" than the ordinary essay examinations. The pupil's handwriting was marked, for example, by comparing it with "standard specimens" — as today in the case of the modern handwriting scales. Some historians of the educational measuring movement date the attempt to use objective tests from Fisher's work. Others begin twenty years later with Sir Francis Galton's invention of the questionnaire and other devices for reporting and appraising education more exactly. Still others date the movement from the testing work of the American Dr. J. M. Rice, sometimes called "the real inventor of the comparative test," who in 1894 as editor of *The Forum* reported the results of spelling tests which he had conducted with thousands of pupils in the public schools. His articles, which denounced the "futility of the spelling grind" and other subject-matter grinds, caused great controversial discussion.

Nevertheless, because there was no direct connection between Rice's work and the work of Thorndike, and because Thorndike's work led without interruption into a tremendous nation-wide movement to create standard scales and tests, we prefer to date the educational measuring movement from his work. Not long after Thorndike produced his first scales, Leonard P. Ayres, Director of the Division of Education of the Russell Sage Foundation, published his scales in handwriting and spelling. These are important in the history of measurement because of Ayres's pioneer use of scientific assumptions and techniques.

By the time we entered World War I the measuring of educational products was well launched. The war experience expedited enormously the making of group tests for intelligence, aptitude, and trade proficiency. At its close the measurers hurried home from the war and rushed scores of new scales and tests through the press. Many of these were published without a basis of theory and careful design and without measures of validity and reliability. There ensued a hectic period of mass commercialization of scales and tests — "well-nigh a public scandal," some of the older critics said. Certainly we can agree with Ross's description of the period as one of "overconfidence, uncritical acceptance of test results, naïve assumption that IQ's measured innate capacity and that achievement tests measured the outcomes of teaching." Everybody was "thinking up" tests, giving them to small groups, standardizing test items merely by percentages of correct pupil responses, and determining validity by such superficial methods as correlating test results with teachers' marks.

By the late 1920's this stage had run its course. The professors were moving into the theoretical fields of design and validation. Those more soundly equipped were financed by grants from foundations, notably Carnegie and Rockefeller, through the agencies of the American Council on Education and the leaders of the Progressive Education Association. So a period of more critical design set in, criteria of validity and reliability and assumptions were clarified, and principles were worked out for determining equality of units on scales. Thus the half century that has passed since Rice's original testing of public school pupils constitutes, we feel, a single and preliminary stage in the movement for measuring educational products.

Stock Taking after Fifty Years

It would be impossible, in a few pages, to give an adequate idea of the vast amount of work that has been done since Thorndike and his colleagues began their measuring work, nearly fifty years ago. Hundreds of scales and tests have been devised and redesigned, tried out repeatedly in laboratories or schools, and perfected as valid measuring instruments. Many of these tests have now been discarded, but some have stood the critical test of use in the schools. Some, such as the Stanford Achievement Test, have been given to millions of school pupils and can today be used confidently to check up on the general achievement in the school subjects of a pupil, a class, a school, or a school system. Others, such as the Terman revisions of the Binet-Simon Scale for verbal intelligence, given individually in hour-long oral interviews, can now be used to give teachers a pretty good judgment of the intellectual abilities of their pupils.

To provide you with a general resource outline of the product of this fifty years of measurement, we have reproduced the following chart[1] drawn from another study by the senior author of this book.

EVALUATION AND MEASUREMENT

We distinguish evaluation from measurement:

1. We can *measure* the raw materials of personality, aptitudes, attitudes, and some of the products of education.
2. We resort to general *evaluating* methods (judgment) in dealing with the personality of the whole person, the efficiency of the teacher, and of the school-as-a-whole.

A. EVALUATION

I. THE WHOLE PERSON . . . PERSONALITY

1. Psychoanalysis and psychiatry: the leadership of Freud, Jung, Adler, Rank, et al.
2. The use of questionnaires, interest inventories, personal-history records, standardized interviews, etc.
3. The Rorschach Technique.
4. The Rating Scale: man-to-man, self-rating.

II. EVALUATING THE TEACHER AND TEACHING EFFICIENCY

Rating scales: man-to-man . . . self-rating.

III. EVALUATING THE SCHOOL, OR SYSTEM: GENERAL LEVEL, PLANT, FINANCING, CURRICULUM

Score cards and rating scales.

B. MEASUREMENT

IV. MEASURING THE RAW MATERIALS OF PERSONALITY

1. Measuring physique: varieties and relation to aptitude.
    Cannon, Kretschmer, Cattell, Whipple, Sheldon, Hoskins, Hull, et al.
2. Measuring temperament: varieties and relation to aptitude.
    Cannon, Kretschmer, Sheldon, Hoskins, Hull, et al.
3. Measuring intelligence: relation to aptitude, vocations, etc.
    Forty years of investigation . . . huge library of measurement, experimental and statistical data; such names as Binet, Terman, Thorndike, Otis, Kuhlmann, Stoddard.

V. MEASURING APTITUDES

1. Pioneering by Galton, Cattell.
2. Psychological laboratory tests for specific forms of sensory, motor, and mental efficiency.

[1] Harold Rugg: *Foundations for American Education*, pages 747–749.

3. Aptitude testing stimulated by Psychological Division of U. S. Army in World War I . . . vast and successful program of Army Air Force in World War II.

4. Tests for "general" vs. "specific" factors: a generation of controversial study — Spearman, Kelley, Thurstone, Thorndike, Thomson, Hull, et al.

5. Trade tests stimulated greatly by the two World Wars.
   –For novices, apprentices, journeymen, experts.
   –Pencil-and-paper tests: verbal . . . picture . . . performance.
   –General mechanical aptitude.
   –Miniature vs. abstract tests.
   –Apparatus tests.

6. General mental ability tests: for example, Binet, Terman-McNemar, Otis, National, American Council.

7. Tests in expressive arts; for example, Seashore tests for musical talent.

VI. MEASURING ATTITUDES — RACIAL, SOCIAL DISTANCE, ECONOMIC, POLITICAL, RELIGIOUS, AND ETHICAL

Rating scales of social-economic-political opinions . . . case histories . . . verbal tests of attitude . . . questionnaires on attitudes . . . attitude interviews . . . the Bogardus Social Distance Scale . . . the Keeny Experience-Description tests . . . occupation rating scales . . . scales of ethical judgments . . . tests for clusters of attitudes (general traits) . . . emotional and characteristics tests . . . tests for stereotypes . . . information and opinions on current issues.

VII. MEASURING CHARACTER

1. The Lewin measurements of psychic tensions.

2. Tests of character: honesty, will-temperament, will-power, moral-standard, motor inhibitions, etc.

VIII. MEASURING THE PRODUCTS OF EDUCATION

1. General achievement batteries: Stanford, Metropolitan, Progressive.

2. Diagnostic and speed tests in reading (Durrell and others), comprehension, arithmetic, etc.
   –Pencil-and-paper tests: directions tests, group tests, arithmetic tests, best-answers, synonym-antonym, disarranged sentences, analogies, general information, matching proverbs, sentence completion, cause and effect, related words.

3. P.E.A. experiments in designing tests for organizing things and people, creative production, and appreciation.

TYPES OF TEST INSTRUMENTS

I. The Questionnaire — systematic descriptions of characteristics, traits, opinions, interests.

II. Word Descriptions of Personality, Traits, Physique, Temperament, Intelligence, Knowledge, Sensitivity.

III. The Rating Scale . . . The Score Card.
1. The numerical score card: for the school-as-a-whole, curriculum, buildings, finance, etc.
2. The man-to-man rating scale.
3. The self-rating scale.

IV. The Essay Examination.

V. The Standardized Scale for Measuring Educational Products. Handwriting scales, drawing scales, composition scales, lettering scales, etc.

VI. Standardized Tests of Performance.
1. General achievement: survey of class or school attainment.
2. Specific skill tests.
   Speed ("hurdle race") tests: amount of work done per unit of time, or time required for stated work.
3. Difficulty ("high jump") tests.
   Tests of meaning, interpretation, reasoning, drawing conclusions, etc.
4. Information or knowledge tests, or combined information and thought tests.
   a) Multiple-choice tests.
   b) Matching tests.
      —Completion and true-false tests, much less used than formerly.

Some Important Things Still Evaluated Subjectively

What, after fifty years of effort, can we measure in schoolwork?

Not everything. The chart reminds us that we still distinguish between phases of schoolwork which can now be measured by reliable scales and tests and those in which we must resort to general subjective judgment. While we can measure physique, intelligence, and certain aspects of temperament, some aptitudes and attitudes, and a good many achievements of the pupils, we still are in the subjective evaluating stage when it comes to understanding the Whole Person — the total personality. There we still rely on the specialist — the trained psychoanalyst or psychiatrist using such techniques as those of Sigmund Freud and

FRANK N. FREEMAN (1880————), professor of Educational Psychology at the University of Chicago
(1909–1939) and Dean of the School of Education,
University of California (1939–1948), has made an
important contribution to the psychology of the school
subjects, especially through his scientific laboratory
studies of the psychology of handwriting. He also
made original contributions in the field of mental and
educational testing and in visual education. He was
chairman of the Editorial Board of the *Review of Educational Research*, member for many years of the Board
of Directors of the National Society for the Study of
Education, and member of the American Psychological
Association Council from 1937 to 1941.

Dr. Freeman has been a frequent contributor to the
discussion of the nature-nurture controversy; witness
such publications as *The Effect of Environment on the
Intelligence of Foster Children*, and *Twins: A Study of
Heredity and Environment*. Among his other outstand-
ing books are *How Children Learn, Mental Tests, The
Psychology of the Common Branches, Experimental
Education, The Teaching of Handwriting*, and *Visual
Education*.

followers — and on the judgments of teachers, parents, and others who
know the student.

But in this evaluating process, besides the psychoanalytic methods,
we now have available many instruments to help make our judgments
clearer and more balanced — questionnaires, interest inventories, personal history records, Rorschach test results, and rating scales in which
the traits of one person can be compared with those of another. Likewise, in judging teachers and their teaching we can use rating scales to
define more precisely traits and phases of work. There is the man-to-
man type, in which a teacher is rated by comparing his traits and abilities on a scale with other actual teachers on various traits and aspects of
teaching. There are also self-rating scales, so designed that the teacher
can measure himself by answering specific questions about himself and
his work.

In spite of the gains achieved through the development of those instruments, the best measure of the teacher's work is still the actual behavior of his pupils. How well do they read, write, reckon, solve problems, spell, and use language? Such questions can be answered objectively by the use of quantitative scales and tests, as we shall see in a

moment. How truly creative are they? Are they sensitive Persons, marked by dignity and integrity? For these qualities there are almost no valid and reliable measuring instruments; personal judgment still dominates the process of evaluation. The more profound question to ask about the influence of the teacher's life and teaching on his students is: What was its long-time effect in their adult lives? Did his teaching carry over into their later years? Definite instruments and techniques to aid in answering such questions we do not have.

Neither can we measure the whole school or school system objectively, although forty years of steady improvement in methods of administering schools have produced instruments which greatly clarify and define the judging process. Hundreds of school systems have been "surveyed" by the new professors of education who have sat in classrooms, appraised teachers' methods and results, and scrutinized printed courses of study, financial and pupil accounting, records and reports, and business management. Most of the surveying of what a good school should be and do was done, however, on their own subjective judgment.

But as the years passed, the administrators followed the leads of the measurers and developed "score cards" and rating scales. They saw that the process of judging school administration could be greatly improved if the complex total could be broken down into clearly specified aspects and characteristics. This they did in such score cards as the Mort-Cornell Guide for Self-Appraisal of School Systems, the Strayer-Englehardt Score Card for Junior High School Buildings, and the Bruner Criteria for Evaluating Teacher and Learning Materials and Practices. These have improved the evaluation of the work of a school or school system in various definite ways. They catalogue detailed and hitherto neglected aspects of schoolwork; they bring new and progressive ideas and practices to the attention of a large number of teachers; they standardize the many items of schoolwork and administration, stress the important role of the philosophy of the school, and give emphasis to major phases of the curriculum. In other words, they have put first things first.

Thus, as we catch a glimpse of the astonishing successes in making education more scientific, we shall bear in mind that many of the most important aspects of our work are still in need of further objectification.

Marked Success in Measuring General Abilities, Aptitudes, and Scholastic Attainments

Having expressed this cautious attitude, we hasten to assure the prospective teacher that he is fortunate indeed in the extensive body of measuring instruments that he can call to his aid today. The appraising of many human abilities and achievements need no longer be a vague, subjective process. The situation is far from "scandalous," as Thorndike called it a generation ago. For many of those critical abilities and accomplishments we now have "defined units of measure and instruments by which to count them." We are much surer than we were forty years ago about *what* is measured and *how closely* the measure tallies with reality.

To illustrate concretely, take a quick glance at the rich body of descriptive facts about each pupil that can be given to the teacher as she begins her year's work with a new class. These appear in the cumulative record folder of the pupil if such a file is available in the school.

With respect to the pupil's physique, the teacher should find such routine physical facts as his exact age, his height, and his weight. She should know from experience, or from consulting with the school physician or the physical education department, whether the relationship of the child's height and weight falls within the normal range. She should have the answers to such questions as: Is his vision normal? Is his hearing normal? (Imperfect hearing expressed in loss in decibels.) Is his general health good? Does he suffer from malnutrition, rickets, anemia? Has he diabetes, asthma, enlarged tonsils or adenoids? What is the condition of his teeth, skin, etc.?

If the child's emotional condition deviates markedly from that of the normal happy child, the teacher should try to understand the whole school and home background. As indicated in Chapter 4, each pupil's folder should contain descriptive accounts of teachers' visits to the home, anecdotes illustrative of home and neighborhood conditions, and any other facts needed to give a full picture of the environmental influences surrounding the child. While facial tics (involuntary twitching of the muscles) and cases of acute stammering are easy to detect, there may be facts about the child's home life which should be contained in the records. In the case of the young child, for example, is there enuresis (bed-wetting)? Does the child suck his thumb on going to sleep past the time when thumb sucking is usual? Does he have severe tantrums? repeated nightmares? Is he afraid of the dark or of animals? Has he other fears?

In addition to such important descriptive material, the teacher to-day can draw upon the results of using fairly reliable scales and tests in at least three critical phases of his work:

First: He can know the general mental ability of his pupils, as stated by Mental Age (MA) and Intelligence Quotient (IQ) and obtained from fairly reliable tests of verbal intelligence.

Second: He can discover by means of objective tests special aptitudes needed in most kinds of scholastic work and in some vocational fields.

Third: He can measure the skills and knowledge (and with some reliability the social attitudes) of his students in all the commonly used school subjects of study.

Fairly reliable tests are also available for many newer school subjects and curriculum fields; for example, in health, hygiene, and physical education, home economics, industrial arts, public speaking, reading, the vocations. The changing curriculum has created a demand for tests of qualities and achievements that are not the direct product of the school study, and these are rapidly being made available. One can now find tests for knowledge of contemporary affairs, for social adjustment and development, comprehensive individual history record forms, diagnostic child-study records, study habits and skills, guidance tests and inventory, adult profile, occupational interest blanks, interest inventories, vocational interest blanks, vocational interest schedules.

In addition, the teacher should find in the cumulative record folder descriptions of personality traits, examples of creative achievements, and instances of leadership and followership in the pupil's daily school life.

While many of the most critical facts about the pupils are verbal descriptions — life history records, home and neighborhood episodes, etc. — many are based on definite quantitative measures. It is to those that we shall devote brief attention.

Measuring General Mental Ability

So far has the spirit of science come to imbue our attitudes about schoolwork today, that knowledge of the general mental ability of each pupil in a class is regarded as indispensable. "What is his IQ?" is now the first question asked about any pupil whose schoolwork in reading, mathematics, or some other subject is not satisfactory. "Only 80," comes the answer, perhaps, and with it, a good deal of light on the situation. An IQ of 80 means that teaching will have to be much more elementary, material more carefully selected and limited, and ideas more concretely illustrated than if the answer had been 110, or 120, or higher. "He has an IQ of 140, yet he is doing poorly in his work" tells the teacher that the boy certainly has sufficient general mental ability to master any intellectual problems of the school curriculum. The cause of poor work must lie in other factors than intelligence — perhaps in physical condition or in emotional disturbance.

The teacher today is required to know what such terms as IQ (and MA, EQ, and others) mean and how to interpret any given IQ — whether it is 70, 80, 100, or 120. She should know, for example, whether the test from which the IQ was computed was on

–an individual scale, such as the revised Stanford-Binet (a revision of the original Binet-Simon Scale published in France in 1905 and 1908, and adapted to American use by Lewis M. Terman in 1916) or the Kuhlmann-Anderson Series, the Minnesota Pre-School Scale, or the Detroit Tests of Learning Aptitude;

or whether it was

–a group test, such as the widely used Terman Group Test of Mental Ability, the American Council on Education Psychological Examination, or the Kuhlmann-Anderson test.

If it is an IQ from an individual test, such as the Stanford-Binet, the teacher will put a good deal of trust in its reliability, especially if it is an average from three separate tests given a year apart. He will be cautious in interpreting it, however, knowing that all "intelligence" tests today do not measure native, or inherited, intelligence alone. The IQ is a measure of the interaction of many forces of home, school, and community on the pupil's inherited, or "native," capacity. The teacher knows, moreover, that the IQ is merely a numerical index obtained by dividing mental age by chronological age. Thus a boy 12 years old who performs successfully the tasks that 75 per cent of all 12-year-olds can do has a mental age (MA) of 12. Hence, $\frac{MA}{CA}$ or $\frac{12}{12} = 100$, generally called 100. And in order to interpret the meaning of the numerical IQ, the teacher should know that from millions of pupils tested the mean or average was set at 100; thus half of the American children have IQ's of more than 100, and half less than 100. About 1 per cent fall above 130 and 1 per cent below 70. One third of all IQ's lie between 95 and 106.

The teacher will know also that such measures of general mental ability can be of genuine assistance in advising young people about choices of school courses and in determining their fitness for the academic work of a liberal arts college or the more scientific abstractions of the technical and professional school; it is valuable also as a basis for some general vocational counseling. The teacher will seek such intelligence measures if he is trying to diagnose pupil difficulties and build up specific skills or understandings.

Because of the expense involved in giving and interpreting individual tests, most public school systems do not use the individual mental ability tests with all students. But they are beginning to use group tests. Indeed, to facilitate the administrative work of the school, nothing can take the place of the group test. It is economical and moderately reliable when interpreted cautiously. When the teacher feels that the result of a group test does not seem valid for some one individual, he should ask for an individual test. Hundreds of individuals can be tested at once, and efficient and economical techniques have been developed for scoring the papers — perforated scoring cards, recording blanks, and such large-scale devices as the International Test Scoring Machine.

The history of the group test reaches back to the initial work of Arthur S. Otis and the Psychological Division of the United States Army in World War I. For a full generation the better group tests have passed through a ruthless screen of criticism, widespread administrative use, critical study, and redesign by scientific workers. The chief types of items now used in the subtests are Information, Synonyms, Logical Selection, Classification, Analogies, Opposites, and Best Answer. On the next two pages we reprint a few excerpts.

INFORMATION

Underline the word that makes the sentence TRUE.

1. Our first President was

    1 Adams   2 Washington   3 Lincoln   4 Jefferson
    5 Monroe

2. The piccolo is used in

    1 printing   2 weaving   3 mining   4 music   5 farming

SYNONYMS

Which word has the SAME or most nearly the same meaning as the beginning word of each line?   Write the number in the space at the right.

A. correct — 1 neat   2 fair   3 right   4 poor   5 good (   )

B. content — 1 cheerful   2 satisfied   3 well   4 willing (   )

LOGICAL SELECTION

Underline the word which tells what the thing ALWAYS has or ALWAYS involves.

1. A cat always has

    1 kittens   2 spots   3 milk   4 mouse   5 hair

2. A bird always has

    1 nest   2 eggs   3 bones   4 cage   5 mate

OPPOSITES

Which word has the same number as the word which is OPPOSITE, or most nearly opposite, in meaning to the beginning word of each line?   Write the number in the space at the right.

1. hinder —

    1 attack   2 attain   3 help   4 avoid   5 try (   )

2. brisk —

    1 slow   2 warm   3 heavy   4 soft   5 slight (   )

CLASSIFICATION

In each line below, four of the words belong together. Underline
the ONE WORD which does not belong with the others.

1. 1 dog   2 cat   3 horse   4 chicken   5 cow

2. 1 hop   2 run   3 stand   4 skip   5 walk

ANALOGIES

Blacken the answer space numbered the same as your choice for
the correct answer, as in the sample.

SAMPLE.   Hat is to head as shoe is to   1   2   3   4   5

1 arm   2 leg   3 foot   4 fit   5 glove

A. Army is to general as navy is to   1   2   5   4   5

1 ensign 2 admiral 3 boatswain 4 pilot 5 major

B. Success is to joy as failure is to   6   7   8   9   10

6 work   7 happiness   8 poor   9 luck   10 sadness

BEST ANSWER

Read each statement and mark in the answer space at the right
the number of the answer which you think is BEST.

1. We should not put a burning match in the wastebasket because

    1 Matches cost money.   2 We might need a match later.

    3 It might go out.   4 It might start a fire.   (   )

2. The moats surrounding medieval castles were most valuable as

    5 Water reservoirs.   6 Fortifications against enemies.

    7 Swimming pools.   8 Protection against wild animals.(   )

(Adapted from Terman-McNemar Test of Mental Ability.
Copyright 1941 by World Book Company.)

Two important purposes will be served by the use of such measurements of human nature and general mental ability. The first is the exploration of the abilities of an individual child or youth, the diagnosis
of the factors back of his performance, and the prognosis of development.

STUART A. COURTIS (1874———) has long been a pioneer in the measurement of educational achievement. He was Director of Educational Research in the Detroit Schools, Dean of the Detroit Teachers College from 1920 to 1924, and Professor of Education, University of Michigan, from 1921 to 1944. He himself stresses those phases of his life's work which are concerned with the measurement of growth (witness his book, *Measurement of Growth*) and techniques of coöperation.

As philosopher and teacher, Dr. Courtis has contributed to the development of the coöperative approach in education and to the building of techniques of coöperation, the costs and dividends of social achievement, and the improvement of the democratic process. He served as consultant in surveys of the school systems of New York City and Gary, Indiana, and of schools in Michigan and Oklahoma. Among his other books are *Then and Now in Education* and *Why Children Succeed*.

The second function of the tests is administrative — to help in classifying pupils for educational work and in promoting them through the school system.

We see, then, that really effective instruments are at hand today with which you can know objectively much about the general mental abilities of the pupils in your classes.

The Measurement of Special Aptitudes

You will frequently need to know the special abilities and disabilities of your pupils. Some children in the elementary school are "ready" for reading long before others in the same class; some have distinctive aptitudes for arithmetic, others for creative expression in music and the other arts; some excel in physical activities on the athletic field, and still others in the intellectual abstractions of mathematics or science. Knowledge of these special abilities will help you use the resources of the school in developing the talents of the young people to the very maximum. Knowledge of disabilities will help you concentrate on special difficulties, will prevent you from trying the impossible, and will point the way to needed remedial methods.

The fact of widespread differences in aptitude, and hence in interest, has always been known to thoughtful people. But in our generation scientific psychologists have built on that knowledge a very helpful body of aptitude tests. The history of these tests reaches back more than a generation to the pioneer work in 1890, when J. McKeen Cattell published ten tests for various specific mental performances. Just before World War I (1913) Harvard's Hugo Münsterberg showed that psychological tests could be devised to select girls who would make good telephone operators and men who would become efficient streetcar motormen. He did this by measuring such traits as speed of reaction, attention span, and specific abilities in observation, memory, and accuracy. A few years later, in World War I, the Trade Test Division of the United States Army designed and standardized effective proficiency tests for hundreds of occupations and aptitude tests for trade skills. Three typical tests were used: (1) verbal trade tests, (2) picture trade tests, (3) performance trade tests. This work speeded up the civilian measuring movement enormously, and between the two World Wars scores of trade and proficiency tests were designed and standardized. These proved a great stimulus to the development of aptitude tests in the psychological laboratories. In some instances (as in the test for streetcar motormen or bus drivers), where the test cannot be made under practical job conditions, "miniature tests" have been designed which duplicate key skills of the occupation; for example, the Wisconsin test for engine-lathe aptitude, or the Münsterberg test for motormen.

"Abstract" tests are also used in which specific sensory, motor, or mental efficiencies are measured by psychological laboratory tests. An example is the measurement of reaction time used in the selection of machine operators. The miniature tests are more expensive and require special apparatus but have much higher prognostic value.

In the high school such aptitude tests have been devised as the Iowa Placement Examinations, Aptitude Series, and many other tests used to detect special aptitudes in algebra, geometry, English, foreign languages, mathematics, and the sciences. In the elementary school "readiness" tests in reading and arithmetic have been developed.

GORDON W. ALLPORT (1897———), Professor of Psychology in Harvard's Department of Social Relations and former President of the American Psychological Association, is well known for his contribution to the psychology of personality. This is represented best in his book *Personality — A Psychological Interpretation*. His course, "The Social and Psychological Foundations of Behavior," has long been the largest elective course in Harvard College.

Dr. Allport's interest in the integration of psychological and social relations has led him to the study of the psychology of the social tensions, prejudices, and racial conflicts of minority groups. As a leader in such study he has worked with police-training courses in Boston and with the Bureau of Intercultural Education in New York, and as consultant at the Paris conferences of UNESCO on social tensions. He has collaborated with others on *The Psychology of Radio*, *The Psychology of Rumor*, and *Studies in Expressive Movement*.

Objective Measurement of the Products of the School Subjects

But the signal success of the measurers has been in the school subjects, especially in the fields of skill, knowledge, and reasoning ability. No longer do report cards have to consist of vague teacher opinions, or letter or numerical marks. The efficient school can give the parents clear, definite, and illuminating answers to such questions as, for example: "Can John (Grade III) write, spell, and reckon as well as he should, considering his age and schooling?" Definite answers can be given: "John's handwriting scores 70, average for his grade, on the Metropolitan Primary Cursive Handwriting Scale. His spelling score is above the national spelling norm for Grade III. In arithmetic fundamentals, as shown by his performance on the Metropolitan Achievement Tests, he is clearly doing better than the national norm for the third grade. In arithmetical reasoning and problem-solving his is fourth-grade standard."

Looking back on the forty years of building tests to measure the school subjects, it is clear that we have come a long way from the "scandalous" teacher-marking that Starch and Elliott, Thorndike, and their colleagues condemned a generation ago. The efficient school system today can report to the parents the tested proficiency of any child in the several skills and abilities involved in reading, writing, spelling, language, arithmetic, high school mathematics, science, the languages, history, geography, and the social sciences. It can appraise with a good deal of objectivity his ability to think through novel problems. It can portray his personal characteristics with illuminating paragraphs describing his conduct in school, his leadership and organizing ability, his coöperation, his creativeness and his appreciation in the arts. And it can compare his abilities definitely with those of comparable pupils in American schools. It can, in short, present a fairly complete and objective profile of the whole boy in action.

It can do this by reporting his performances on any one of several moderately reliable and well-validated general achievement tests; for example:

–Stanford Achievement Test. (World Book Company)

–Coöperative General Achievement Test: for the social studies, the sciences, and mathematics. (The Coöperative Test Division of the Educational Testing Service)

–Iowa Every-Pupil Tests of Basic Skills: for reading, language, and arithmetic skills.

–Metropolitan Achievement Tests: for arithmetic, reading, English, and handwriting. (World Book Company)

–Progressive Achievement Tests: for reading, arithmetic, mathematics, and language. (California Test Bureau)

As their name implies, these tests are measures of general achievement, good for over-all appraisal of the work of classes or individuals and for such administrative needs as classification and promotion of pupils, reports to parents, and so forth.

New Measuring Instruments to Diagnose Learning Difficulties and Improve Teaching

But the measurers have given the teacher more effective devices to help him in teaching than mere scores on tests and comparisons with group and national norms, important though those may be. They have perfected a vast body of *diagnostic* tests and remedial instruments in the various school subjects. Consider reading as a single example.

In our modern world of words reading is without doubt the most important single tool of learning in the school, as well as the most crucial skill for general everyday competence. Within the school itself no progress in history, the social studies, the sciences, literature, and the languages is possible without at least a moderate proficiency in reading. Outside the school it is the chief means by which the citizen becomes informed of current events, the affairs and problems of the community, state, nation, and modern world. It is the basis of success in many of the occupations and is, of course, one of our chief leisure activities.

For these reasons a tremendous amount of creative, scientific energy has gone into the study of reading abilities and the techniques of improving reading instruction in the schools. Elaborate analyses have been made of the major kinds of reading, distinguishing, for example, oral and silent reading of leisure types and of work types, essential skills in work-study types of reading and methods of developing them, such obstacles to good reading as low intelligence, visual and auditory defects, defects of muscular coördination, speech and glandular disturbances, emotional factors, disturbing home environments, and so forth. As a consequence of these voluminous studies in reading, many diagnostic and remedial tests have been developed, such as those listed below.

–The Gates Reading Readiness Test.

–Diagnostic tests in oral reading, such as the Gray Standardized Oral Reading Paragraphs or the Gray Oral Reading Check Tests.

–The Gates Silent Reading Tests.

–The Iowa Silent Reading Tests, New Edition, Elementary.

–Corrective exercises in reading, such as the remedial devices by Gates, Gray, Horn, and others.

Appraising Personality

Although we have touched only a few aspects of the problem of evaluating the work of the schools, you can see what impressive additions have been made to the teacher's resources. We still must leave much to the teacher's judgment, but today that judgment can be made more valid and reliable by the use of measuring instruments. To a degree unknown a generation ago we can measure mental abilities, common skills, and knowledge, and with considerable objectivity. In a formal school, where attention will be focused on the learning of subject matter, these will be regarded as sufficient.

But if you are concerned with the growth and development of the total personalities of the children, such measurement of intelligence and school achievement will be far from sufficient. And if you are the teacher of a school grade or a school subject, you will know that past achievement and the capacity for further understanding do not tell the whole story of a child's future work. They only tell the quantitative aspects of growth and achievement. They do not reveal the deep underlying reasons for the behavior of the bright boy who is up with his class, perhaps ahead of the others, but who soon becomes bored, who plays during school hours, tries to disturb the others. He has done well and has plenty of intelligence, but his school accomplishment has already shown a definite slump. Or the quick, sensitive child, so shy that she cannot recite in class; her schoolwork may be poor because she has not gained sufficient self-confidence to work as an effective part of a group. There is still another child who has marked ability but whose only way of work is that of flitting from one thing to another. His eager mind is easily stimulated, easily distracted; his work *could* be good if he held himself to his job, but he has no steady habits of work. He has never learned to concentrate. Then there is the fearful, worried child who dares not trust her good intelligence; she becomes panicky over a test; her work is poor because she is disturbed emotionally.

There are countless reasons why capable children may progress slowly in school. In many cases the roots of the trouble lie in personality patterns, elusive and delicate structures which demand careful observation and study. There is a group among the students of psychology who are interested in the exploration of the total personality: What can we find out about those inner drives, impulses, wishes, and fears that make up an individual's pattern of living? For the past generation they have worked on techniques for the study of personality traits. The most widely used one is the Rorschach Technique, commonly known as the ink-blot test. Another is the Thematic Apperception Test, a picture-story devised by Henry A. Murray. To use either of these requires the knowledge and skill of the trained psychiatrist. Both of the techniques are attempts to get at the conscious and unconscious expressions of the individual's experiences; to find cues to the maladjustment, balance, and control of his personality structure. Although the study of the total personality is in its infancy, it cannot be doubted that such techniques are suggestive ways of adding to our understanding of a student's success or failure in school and life situations.

Classroom teachers are becoming more conscious of the value of play activities, of dramatizing real life situations. Much understanding is gained by the observation of the young child's response to his make-believe activities of family life or neighborhood experiences. As the little first-grade child relives in the play situation his life at home, the teacher can explore his responses to father, to mother, to the new baby brother. He may reveal to the teacher possible insecurities, emotional conditions which may clarify his recent behavior in school. Toys, dolls, miniature pieces of equipment for play and group experiences provide further means of understanding the child. As high school youth put in dramatic form problems of the community and of their personal lives, they too may disclose to the teacher unexpressed interests and prejudices, fears and desires, feelings of dominance or submission, of security and insecurity. All these steps, however, constitute no more than a tentative beginning of the complex task of exploring the total personality structure.

One final type of appraisal needs to be mentioned. This is the over-all evaluation that is continuously being made by the total school staff, the parents, and the pupils. Periodically in conferences, child study groups, and community meetings they examine the educational program of the school. They ask such questions as:

–Is the school really meeting the needs of its students? Is it sending out youth who are equipped to cope with the practical conditions of everyday life?

–Does the curriculum fit the personal and social needs of the community?

–Are there untapped personal or social resources that should be utilized in building the educational program?

–Do the teachers devote themselves to building a better psychological understanding of human nature and behavior, learning and development?

–Do the school buildings and equipment permit the kind of program that is desired?

–Are the life and program of the school designed to stimulate the development of an intelligent, competent citizenry?

This is a mere hint of the never-ending task of over-all appraisal of the work of the schools, yet it illustrates the manner in which educators are trying to evaluate the deeper aspects of personality which are so closely related to the child's success and development in school. The next decade should see great strides in this direction.

Things to Do

1. Arrange to observe a teacher giving a group test to a class; also, if possible, a Stanford-Binet to an individual child. To familiarize yourself with it before you observe, study the test and the directions for giving it. Study how the examiner establishes rapport with the pupils, and the meticulous care with which directions are followed. Arrange with the teacher to go over the child's test blank, studying his specific responses, the ratings given, and the analysis and recommendations for the teacher.

2. Study the cumulative record file of a particular child, extending over several years. Notice his development as shown by test results. What relation do these scores show to his physical record? to his record of special interests and attainments during his school career?

3. Have a panel discussion on the present system of College Entrance Board Examinations, based on your study of recent examinations. Include an appraisal of old and new achievement and aptitude tests.

4. Devise objective tests to measure the student's grasp of selected problems in this book.

5. Write a short list of questions to be incorporated in an objective test for a specific unit of school study; use forms such as true-false, completion, multiple choice, paired associates, and matching. How does a teacher-made test differ from one of the published standard tests? You can get help from Part II, "The Construction of Informal Teacher-Made Tests," of Ross's *Measurement in Today's Schools*. Other sources are E. W. Tiegs's

Tests and Measurements in the Improvement of Learning and Harry A. Greene and others, *Measurement and Evaluation in the Secondary School.*

6. Invite the dean of admissions of your college to discuss the question of present-day selection of candidates. Ask him to compare the process of selection today with that of two decades or more ago. Ask him to appraise the whole machinery of promotion in school and admission to college. How much importance is ascribed by the admissions office to College Entrance Examination Board tests? How much to school records, personal judgments, and other factors?

7. Have a round-table discussion on school marks and reports to parents. Consider their various functions — to reward or punish the learner, to inform the parents, to help the pupil and teacher diagnose strengths, weaknesses, achievements, and progress.

8. In the light of your present knowledge, appraise the use of teachers' marks and other methods of evaluation used to judge your own work as a child or youth in school. How well did they measure what you yourself think you did? Did marks or grades help or hurt you? What was their effect on your development? Do the same thing for report cards and other methods by which the school reported to your parents. In the light of our discussion compare the effectiveness of today's type of report to parents with that used in your own school experience.

9. In case your college library does not have tests for general mental ability, achievement in the school subjects, aptitudes, and the like, write to such sources as the World Book Company, Yonkers, N. Y.; the Educational Testing Service, Princeton, N. J.; the California Test Bureau or the Bureau of Research, or to one of the state universities such as Iowa (Iowa City), Ohio (Columbus), or Illinois (Urbana). Gather sets of the tests. Study the authors' descriptions of how they were made and how their validity and reliability were determined.

10. Throughout history schools and colleges have tried to cultivate the "liberally educated man" through a curriculum of "liberal arts." This is still the aim of many private and public colleges.

Hold a class discussion of the characteristics of the liberally educated man, as the term is used today. See such books as the Harvard Report: *General Education in a Free Society,* the comparable report from Columbia: *A College Program in Action,* and those from Yale, Princeton, or other private colleges. See also James B. Conant's *Education in a Divided World.* The most publicized statement of the extreme "liberal arts" point of view is in the writings of the group of educational theorists led by President Robert M.

Hutchins and Dr. Mortimer J. Adler, both of the University of Chicago. See Hutchins's *The Higher Learning in America*. You will find an over-all appraisal in Berkson's *Education Faces the Future*.

Further Reading on Evaluation

On Measurement and Testing

The best single book on the total problem of evaluation of the processes of education is Ross's *Measurement in Today's Schools*. There you can find both practical and theoretical help on every phase of the problem. Close to it in usefulness are the two books of Greene and Jorgensen: *Measurement and Evaluation in the Elementary School* and *Measurement and Evaluation in the Secondary School*. Another useful book is Tiegs's *Tests and Measurements in the Improvement of Learning*. For an elementary treatment of the problem of school marks and of graphics and statistics, see Harold Rugg's *A Primer of Graphics and Statistics*.

On the theme of measuring intelligence or general mental ability, see either Freeman's *Mental Tests: Their History, Principles, and Applications* or Terman and Merrill's *Measuring Intelligence*.

On tests to detect aptitudes there is one over-all book, namely, Hull's *Aptitude Testing*.

On Evaluating Personality

There are fewer books that will help you on the appraisal of total personality. The best, Murphy's *Personality*, is admittedly difficult, probably only for the advanced students; see especially Part V. Young's *Personality and the Problems of Adjustment* (Chapters 14 to 19) deals with behavior problems from early childhood to youth. For help with the very young children, see Alschuler's *Painting and Personality* (Vol. I), Carlson's *Guiding Children in the Nursery Class*, and Driscoll's *How to Study the Behavior of Children*.

On the evaluation of social relationships in children's groups see Lippitt and White's *Social Climate of Children's Groups*, Hyme's *A Pound of Prevention*, and Axline's *Play Therapy*. Several magazine articles are especially recommended:

–Elliott, Merl H.: "Patterns of Friendship in the Classroom," *Progressive Education*, November, 1941

–Olson, W. C.: "Improvement of Human Relations in the Classroom," *Childhood Education*, March, 1946

–Atkin, Ellen M., and Reggs, L. O.: "Sociometric Experiments in a 7A Junior High Group," *Baltimore Bulletin of Education*, September, 1945

Perhaps the best study of appraising the newer practices in education is Smith and others: *Appraising and Recording Student Progress*, one of the volumes of the Eight-Year Study; see also Wrightstone's *Appraisal of Newer Elementary School Practices* and *Appraisal of Experimental High School Practices*. Part II of Pressey and Robinson's *Psychology and the New Education* is devoted to the total problem of guidance and learning — the mental hygiene of student and teacher. There is an excellent chapter (XXV) on the newer conceptions of pupil growth and evaluation in *Newer Instructional Practices of Promise*, by the NEA Department of Supervisors and Directors of Instruction. Traxler's *The Nature and Use of Anecdotal Records* is very helpful to the teacher.

We recommend Ruth Strang's *Reporting to Parents* for those who need discussions of new methods of reporting.

CHAPTER 17

The Fullest Use of the Teacher

IN MEETING most effectively the manifold jobs of the schools, we must utilize all the human resources. For each job we ask — "Who is competent?"

–Some of these jobs require technical specialists: lawyers, doctors, engineers, administrators.

–Some require specialists in the art of curriculum making.

–Some require artists in teaching.

–Some require a cross section of the citizens of the community.

In school administration, as in every phase of the culture, we shall have to choose between two opposed regimes:

–The authoritarian, command-obedience type: "Do as I say" . . . "Believe what I tell you."

–The democratic: "You do this, and I'll do that" . . . "We'll work together."

We hail the democratic principle as the American way; and we must discover the best ways of putting it to work, using the teacher in administering the schools at every point where she has competence. We shall find a better answer to the question "What is her competence?" if we distinguish three major jobs:

–Making the policy

–Planning the program of education

–Carrying out this program

The Teacher and Democratic School Administration

Dr. Carleton Washburne, for twenty-six years Superintendent of Schools of Winnetka, Illinois, tells a story that takes us to the very heart of the relationship between the teacher and the administrator.

"I remember a dear old lady who was teaching in Winnetka, when I first came — and had been for over forty years. She was, of course, formal and traditional in her methods; but she was imbued with the ideal of loyalty and obedience to her superiors. She attempted to carry out the ideas of her new, very young superintendent. One afternoon I saw her sitting at a table at five o'clock, making some cards for individual instruction in arithmetic. I said: 'Miss Dwyer, you don't have to do that. You were teaching before I was born. You've taught these children's mothers and fathers to read and write. You know your craft — carry it on in your own way.'

"She looked up at me with a great sigh of relief: 'Mr. Washburne, do you mean that? Do you really mean that? Oh what a relief that is! — But,' and she looked down at the cards she was making, 'these are good. I can use them.' And she went right on with her work.

"She was freed. But she was also stimulated. And, old as she was, she grew. She was a coöperative helpful member of the staff to the day of her retirement." [1]

The whole problem of school administration and the teacher's relation to it is wrapped up in that little episode: the old and the new, the

---

[1] Carleton Washburne: *A Living Philosophy of Education*, page 547. John Day Company, Inc.; 1940. All excerpts from this book quoted by permission.

craftsmanship of the teacher and the leadership of the superintendent, the obedience attitude of the formal, authoritarian school, and the freer, creative mood of the democratic one.

School Administration: Authoritarian or Democratic

The Authoritarian Tradition

Frequently in your life as a teacher you will encounter two attitudes in school administration. They correspond to the two opposed views of life that we have commented on — the authoritarian and the democratic. In some communities we have seen children and youth listening and obeying in their regimented schools. In others we have watched young democracy at work, discussing and settling the problems of youth in juvenile town meetings, growing in understanding government by governing themselves. We have observed children and teachers planning their work together. Now we meet the problem again — teachers studying and working with superintendents and principals.

Once more the ancient issue confronts us: Is school administration to be authoritarian or democratic? The answer will depend on the philosophies of life and education of the superintendent of schools and the dominating persons of the board of education. It will depend also on the extent to which strong, democratically-minded leaders have appeared among the teachers. In most towns today the temper of the schools will reflect the ruling climate of opinion of the most active groups of citizens in the community itself.

Throughout all history the societies men have created have been governed by varying degrees of tyranny or freedom. In earlier times, and recently under the Nazis of Germany, the Fascists of Italy, the Politburo of contemporary Russia, and in parts of Latin America, freedom was all too frequently at a minimum; control was imposed by the Dictator from above. Each of these was an authoritarian and totalitarian society. In the schools of such societies there was little or no freedom. The textbooks and all content of teaching were chosen by the Dictator's officials; everything learned reflected the philosophy of life, government, and education of the governing dictatorship. We call

CARLETON W. WASHBURNE (1889————), since 1949 Head of the Department of Education of Brooklyn College, was for twenty-six years (1919–1945) Superintendent of Schools in Winnetka, Illinois. His book, A Living Philosophy of Education, is the product of an outstanding attempt to individualize instruction in public schools and to develop both community-centered and child-centered education in a small American community. Through new textbooks, study guides, and teaching materials, and by his articles, bulletins, and contributions to Yearbooks of national societies, he influenced the subject-centered schools of the entire nation.

As President and Director of the Progressive Education Association of the United States and its world organization, The New Education Fellowship, Dr. Washburne has been an indefatigable worker for better education. In recent years he has represented the United States Department of State in South America and has worked in northern Italy as Director of the United States Information Service.

this the Philosophy of Authority; in it, democratic ideas were utterly lacking.

As we have seen, the Americans, from the first lap of their westward movement, sought to make their schools democratic. They left the people of each state free to provide for their children the amount and kind of education they desired. The state governments, in turn, left those local communities that had become "independent" chartered towns or cities, free to plan their schools. Thus to a considerable extent the legal basis of education was local, and to that extent democratic. But for a long time, that was as far as the democracy went; in most respects the first schools our people set up were authoritarian. That was perhaps inevitable under the circumstances. The schools were set up quickly with little time for either careful planning or for the thorough education either of citizens or of teachers. An enormous number had to be created, and the people lacked the knowledge of how to fit each one to the particular needs of its community. The result was a vast system of identical schools; to see one was to see all of them. The structure of the system resembled the assembly line of industrial mass production — ridiculously large classes taught by a single teacher, children listening and obeying commands, marching and saluting, much like a juvenile army. Flora Cooke, one of the great schoolmistresses of our time, tells how in the early 1880's she actually taught one hundred children in a first-grade class in Youngstown, Pennsylvania. In number-less places in America such "mass enterprise" in education was being duplicated — but without Flora Cookes! Almost overnight our fathers built their schools under the familiar drive of hustle-and-get-it-done. There was neither time for planning nor a mood of meditation; and there were no precedents — never before had man built schools for all the people. Hence, although education was theoretically free to all, there was actually little freedom in the life and program of the schools. So it turned out that the society, where the conditions for the democratic way were most favorable, succeeded in its first half century of free public education, in setting up almost completely authoritarian schools.

In school systems which still follow this authoritarian philosophy you will find the entire direction, planning, and management of the schools in the hands of the administrative officers. All policies and programs are determined by the board of education and the superin-tendent of schools and his associates — not only problems of finance, classification, promotion, etc., but also of curriculum — what is to be taught and how it is to be taught. Everything is decided in the central office, and the teaching of children is governed by rules and regulations made and distributed by the administrative staff. The parents, let alone the teachers and the children, will rarely be included in decision-making with respect to any aspect of education. This is the army "line-staff" method of getting things done. The directive intelligence and energy are conceived of as being centered at the top.

The system is a hierarchy of command and obedience. At the top is the board of education, next below it the superintendent of schools and his associates . . . below them in rank and direction the principals . . . then the teachers . . . finally the children. Thinking, planning, policy-making, creativeness — all are conceived of as arranged in the same hierarchy; each layer below the top one receives its directions from the one above and passes them on to the ones below; each is permitted to interpret the directions, but always in the light of the philosophy of the upper layer. This is the fascist plan of Fuehrer (leader) ruling the followers, and the Leader is the Boss, the one who knows best.

A college president recently said in an address before an alumni association:

"Society is sure to ask two things of the young people whom we graduate from our schools and colleges — that they be able to work

FLORA J. COOKE (1864————), one of our earliest
artist-teachers, will long be remembered as the leading teacher at Colonel Parker's Practice School at
the Chicago Normal School (1889–1901) and as a
founder and the Principal of the Francis W. Parker
School (at Chicago, 1901–1934). She became one
of the nation's leaders in the development of child-
centered education in America. She participated
actively in the work of the Progressive Education
Association and of the North Central Association,
and in forward-looking civic movements. The graduates of her school influenced education throughout
the entire country, especially through the founding
of such progressive schools at the Ojai Valley School
in California, the Edgemont School, Greenwich,
Connecticut, the Shady Hill School, Cambridge,
Massachusetts, the North Shore Country School,
Illinois, the Winnetka, Illinois, Public Schools, and
the F. W. Parker Schools of San Diego, Pasadena,
and Claremont, California.

hard at a job whether they like it or not, and that they find happiness in obedience — the obedience of the apprentice to the master
workman, of the master workman to the superintendent and the
manager, of the manager to the president, of the president to the
board of directors, of the board of directors to the stockholders,
and of the stockholders to society as a whole." [1]

"Theirs not to reason why, Theirs but to do and die." This is the
perfect illustration of the hierarchy of structure and power to be found
either in the army or in the great industrial and business corporation.

Dr. Washburne agrees that this dictatorial procedure is all too
common:

"In some school systems the freeing of the people beneath him
is the reverse of what the administrator does. Instead, he dictates
procedures and expects loyal obedience. This assumes a degree of
omniscience on his part that no one possesses. . . ." [1]

The Rise of Democratic Administration

After 1900, however, the people in many communities built freer,
more democratic kinds of education. Not only was a new spirit brought

[1] Quoted by Carleton Washburne: *A Living Philosophy of Education*, page 485.

into the classroom and into the making of the curriculum; but the philosophy of life and education of the superintendents and principals was changed, and with it the role of the teachers in the administration of the schools. In many of the largest cities the mass-production, army, command-obedience spirit persisted, but in a host of smaller towns more democratic methods began to prevail. Today, therefore, in the thousands of communities of America one can find examples of widely varying degrees of teacher participation in the administration of the schools and colleges. This newer tendency was recently discussed in a symposium of articles in the *Michigan Education Journal*, the organ of the State Teachers Association. Reacting against what was said, one rebel teacher wrote a letter which was, in part, as follows:

"The statement was made in your symposium (November) that the teachers should assume some part in planning the program of the entire school. *Have you ever found one still in the profession who tried it?* [Our italics.]

"As long as our administrators, supervisors, and principals are largely composed of women and little men who have spent years talking down to immature individuals and *were then promoted to executive positions without any preparation in true democratic leadership* and solely because that was the only way to increase their salary; just so long as these people insist that, to satisfy, you must teach the way they taught, scowl the way they scowl, and wear their length of skirt — just so long you will have 'pernicious professional anemia.' . . .

. . . "Let us devise some way of giving the down-trodden a voice that can be heard, a chance, if you please, to promote professional standards in a profession composed of free men and women. Can you have professional standards among clerks and office boys except as they are conceived by the bosses?" [1]

Thus America is growing up, and the old order is passing. Its place is being taken by the democratic order marked by the spirit of the Philosophy of Experience. That way of life will say to you through the community climate of opinion: "The multitude of individuals who make up our people are all different, yet we must live together. Each one is a Person. Each, to use Whitman's term, is a Supreme. Each lives a life of unique experience. Each has some power of original

[1] *Michigan Education Journal*: "A Letter to the Editor," January, 1937, page 225.

William Chandler Bagley (1874–1946) is remembered as one of America's great teachers. He was convinced that the successful teacher must have a rich background of culture and scholarship. His first book, *The Educative Process* (1905), which brought him national recognition at the age of thirty, emphasized teaching as an art. He was a clear, forceful writer and a distinguished master of the English paragraph.

As Professor of Education at Teachers College, Columbia University, from 1917 to 1940, and later as Editor of *School and Society*, Bagley devoted his life to the improvement of the classroom teacher. His deep belief in the democratic ideal led him to question critically the wholesale use of intelligence tests and the position of the hereditarians in the nature-nurture controversy. He was a vigorous defender of the preservation of the common essentials in the curriculum, and from this point of view was a critic of progressive education. He practiced democracy as he preached it.

thought. If we coöperate, we can distill judgment and decision out of human experience. So we shall rule together." As we discuss the manifold jobs of a school system, we shall illustrate the application of this point of view, but to introduce it, consider the way Principal J. E. Jacob of the Lawrence (Kansas) Junior High School brought his teachers into policy making and planning:

"Start with a small problem. — The first feature of the organization to be questioned was an elaborate honor-point system based upon school marks, attendance, deportment and home-room activities. The teachers were encouraged to think carefully about the value of this system to the pupil. A faculty committee was appointed which met from time to time to discuss the problem. Reports of the deliberation of this committee were made at regular faculty meetings. The teachers finally decided that this system was made by the teachers for the teachers and that it had been imposed upon the children from above with little or no thought as to their real interests and needs. At mid-year the honor-point system was officially abolished by unanimous vote of the faculty. The teachers were pleased but surprised when no one questioned this action. It gave them confidence to know their deliberations could be translated into effective action, and that their power was limited only by the extent of their mutual agreement as to what was sound policy." [1]

The Need of Authority in Planning and Direction

In our study of the educative process we have tended to make you, the teacher, the center, and in a real sense that is sound. But there are other jobs to be done, very important ones, that you as a teacher cannot do. Yet some competent person must do them. They are the manifold tasks of policy-making, organization, and management that are called "administration."

If one man is doing a piece of work alone, he plans what is to be done, does it, and appraises it. He is the entire personnel — workman, boss, and supervisor. But if two or more men are doing a job, one man must be in charge. Even though they both take part in planning, doing, and appraising, there will inevitably be differences in opinion; therefore there must be one to assume the responsibility of leadership in making the final decision. Another way to say it is, that in every social enterprise there must be organization and direction. The larger the group, the greater will be the need for separate personnel to organize and give direction. In a very small organization, the "boss" is also a workman, giving only a part of his time to directing. Thus in small, four- or five-teacher schools the principal is also a teacher, sometimes called a "teaching principal," or "supervising teacher."

But whenever the enterprise becomes large enough to need the services of many people — as in a town of several elementary schools and a high school — then the jobs become so numerous and the problem of organizing, directing, and managing the system becomes of such importance that separate administrators have to be set aside to do them. There must be a principal over each school to guide the work of the teachers, watch over the health and well-being of the children and grownups, meet the parents, handle the problems of attendance, grouping, marking, and promotion, and supervise supplies and the care and protection of the building. Similarly there must be a superintendent to guide the principals, the teachers, and other employees to represent the entire school system in all dealings with the community, meet parents and citizens, supervise the administrative acts of other ad-

[1] George R. Koopman, Alice Miel, and Paul J. Misner: *Democracy in School Administration*, page 175. Appleton-Century-Crofts, Inc.; 1943. Used by permission.

ministrators, lead citizens in making policies, interpret the laws affecting education, make reports to the citizens about how well the system is being operated, and act as their officer through the board of education. Hence, in education as in any other social enterprise there must be organized planning and direction.

The Over-All Organization of a Modern School System

To understand the need of planning and direction more clearly, let us glance quickly at the whole system of schools in a modern community, noting the types of jobs to be done, how they are organized, and the qualifications required for doing them. Then we shall be prepared to understand the relation between the work of the teacher and the manifold other jobs of the school system.

The Manifold Tasks of a School System

While teaching the children is the irreducible basic task of education, teaching cannot go on unless many other tasks upon which it depends are efficiently taken care of. In any large and varied enterprise there must be careful allocation of responsibility, discrimination of jobs, and selection of persons most competent to do them. This generalization has been learned in the development of the complex, interdependent life of our industrial society, and schools are no exception to it. A hundred and fifty years ago, when there were no "systems" of schools — either town, county, state, or nation — one man directed the work of such education as was given. But today in most of our schools a good education cannot be given by that method. Scan this list of manifold tasks that must be carried on and the intricate organization required:

–Legal problems to be solved . . . compulsory-education laws necessitating officials to see that the children are in school and, once there, to guarantee that they are given the requisite amount and kind of education; an endless amount of legal detail about this and other problems

–Money to be raised . . . the teachers and others must be paid, supplies and materials bought . . . buildings and their upkeep financed — all requiring continuous study of the financial resources and problems of the community

–Buildings to be built, heated and cleaned, kept in good repair; equipment of varied kinds to be supplied to the teachers and others

–Teachers to be employed, their qualifications guaranteed, their duties planned and regulated, their responsibilities allocated, provision made for their protection in illness and accident and old age

–The curriculum — what is to be taught and how it is to be organized — to be planned and developed from the best the nation has discovered and created . . . and comparable questions of teaching dealt with also

–A vast array of materials to be chosen, purchased, stored, and efficiently distributed to the teachers and the children

–Manifold problems of the relation of the parents and homes to the work of the children in the schools

–A plan of adult education developed and operated, embracing the agencies and grownups of the community

–And other lesser tasks, too numerous to mention here

While it is not the function of this chapter to discuss these tasks in detail, nevertheless, in order to see your role as teacher in the administration of this vast enterprise, you should at least have a glimpse of the over-all organization of education and the nature of the principal jobs.

First, a brief sketch of the over-all structure of the state system of which your local schools are a unit.

How a State School System Is Organized

The town in which you will teach is only one of many hundreds of school districts that make up the state school system. In spite of the centralization of power, control, and leadership that has emerged in a hundred and fifty years of national life in the federal government, education has remained primarily a function of each of the separate forty-eight states and their local communities. The laws that govern education in your town are basically state laws; the only exception is the case of the larger incorporated communities which have been given great independence in matters of education. Without going into detail about the matter, on page 490 we quote a chart that shows the organization and control of education in a typical state — Virginia.

As you scan it, note two things: First, authority is placed in a state board of education of seven members appointed by the governor. While these men are the representatives of the people and make the regulations for the schools of the state, the executive leadership is in the State Superintendent of Public Instruction and the associates whom he directs in the capital at Richmond — the State Department of Education. In most states all schools, except those of independent cities and towns, are under the direction of the state board, but the county and district superintendent's office plans, directs, and supervises the teaching. This includes the rural and village schools not included in the incorporated, independent districts of the towns and cities. Second: The educational work of the state is carried on through seven major Divisions — Instruction, Vocational Education, Special and Adult Education, School Buildings, School Libraries and Textbooks, Higher Education, Research and Finance.

One additional comment about the recurring problem of democracy and the control of education: In a century of history, often only after prolonged controversy, the question of dividing responsibility for the support and leadership of education has been worked out through the coöperation of the state and local communities. Even though the communities have strenuously opposed control by the state, they have had generally to acquiesce in state aid and control because of their inability to finance their local educational needs themselves. The state educational leaders have insisted on prescribing how the money shall be spent by the villages and towns. Thus state support of education has actually helped to bring better schools to poor communities. In some cases it has tended to hamper local initiative and make the towns dependent on such political bureaucracy as has developed in the state capital. In any event, the amount and kind of education given in the rural and village schools — the so-called "common" schools — must meet the requirements of the state laws and the regulations of the state board of education. Although there has been great disagreement about the

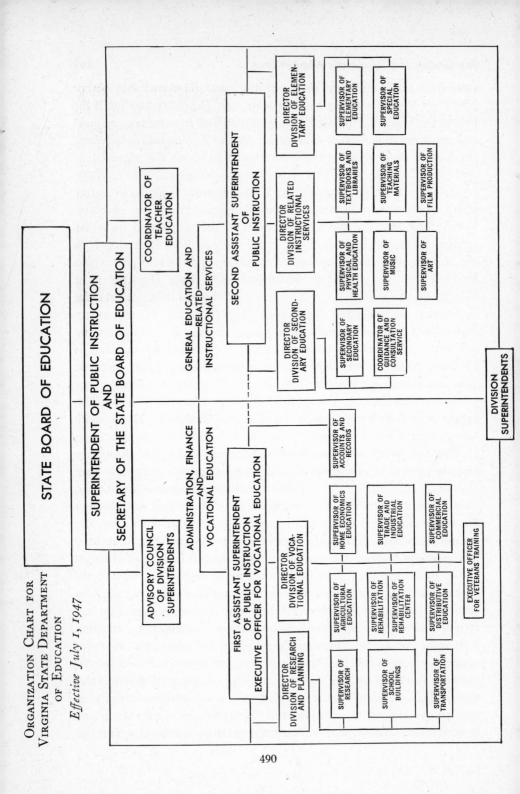

ORGANIZATION CHART FOR
VIRGINIA STATE DEPARTMENT
OF EDUCATION

Effective July 1, 1947

STATE BOARD OF EDUCATION

SUPERINTENDENT OF PUBLIC INSTRUCTION
AND
SECRETARY OF THE STATE BOARD OF EDUCATION

ADVISORY COUNCIL OF DIVISION SUPERINTENDENTS

COORDINATOR OF TEACHER EDUCATION

GENERAL EDUCATION AND RELATED INSTRUCTIONAL SERVICES

ADMINISTRATION, FINANCE AND VOCATIONAL EDUCATION

SECOND ASSISTANT SUPERINTENDENT OF PUBLIC INSTRUCTION

FIRST ASSISTANT SUPERINTENDENT OF PUBLIC INSTRUCTION
EXECUTIVE OFFICER FOR VOCATIONAL EDUCATION

DIRECTOR DIVISION OF ELEMENTARY EDUCATION

SUPERVISOR OF ELEMENTARY EDUCATION

SUPERVISOR OF SPECIAL EDUCATION

DIRECTOR DIVISION OF RELATED INSTRUCTIONAL SERVICES

SUPERVISOR OF TEXTBOOKS AND LIBRARIES

SUPERVISOR OF TEACHING MATERIALS

SUPERVISOR OF FILM PRODUCTION

SUPERVISOR OF PHYSICAL AND HEALTH EDUCATION

SUPERVISOR OF MUSIC

SUPERVISOR OF ART

DIRECTOR DIVISION OF SECONDARY EDUCATION

SUPERVISOR OF SECONDARY EDUCATION

COORDINATOR OF GUIDANCE AND CONSULTATION SERVICE

DIRECTOR DIVISION OF VOCATIONAL EDUCATION

SUPERVISOR OF ACCOUNTS AND RECORDS

SUPERVISOR OF HOME ECONOMICS EDUCATION

SUPERVISOR OF TRADE AND INDUSTRIAL EDUCATION

SUPERVISOR OF COMMERCIAL EDUCATION

SUPERVISOR OF AGRICULTURAL EDUCATION

SUPERVISOR OF REHABILITATION

SUPERVISOR OF REHABILITATION CENTER

SUPERVISOR OF DISTRIBUTIVE EDUCATION

EXECUTIVE OFFICER FOR VETERANS TRAINING

DIRECTOR DIVISION OF RESEARCH AND PLANNING

SUPERVISOR OF RESEARCH

SUPERVISOR OF SCHOOL BUILDINGS

SUPERVISOR OF TRANSPORTATION

DIVISION SUPERINTENDENTS

490

GEORGE DRAYTON STRAYER (1876———) has made a distinguished contribution to the improvement of educational administration in the United States. One of the first to be given the doctorate in education, he was for nearly forty years Professor of Education at Teachers College, Columbia University. From that post he built a new conception of educational administration, leading thousands of administrators in the study of public school finance and other problems.

As a President of the National Education Association and a leader in its Commissions, Dr. Strayer contributed markedly to the leadership of that organization. He is especially well known for his many surveys of school systems. Among his books are *Problems in Educational Administration* and *School Building Problems*.

matter, the more informed students of education have been of the opinion that, in the long run, better "common" schools are maintained by centralizing much of the policy-making as well as financing in the state executive.

As for typical practice, there is only one state in the Union which organizes and administers all of the schools directly under the state board — Delaware. Twelve of the states administer their schools through the county government; there are more than 3000 counties in the United States and they vary in area from 22 square miles (New York County, a part of New York City) to over 20,000 square miles (San Bernardino County, California); while one county in South Dakota contains only 50 people, Cook County in Illinois has over 4,000,000. In the six New England states and in New Jersey, Indiana, and Pennsylvania the schools are administered under the government of the town or the township; in the remaining 26 states, most of them west of the Mississippi River, under the school district. Of the 160,000 independent governing districts in America, 119,000 are *school* districts. You see, therefore, a huge sprawling body of governments ranging from the little local ones of tens of thousands of one-teacher-one-room school districts, up to the nation-wide federal government. In three centuries of history the practice has developed of putting these school districts, tiny though the majority of them are, under the direction of *elected* school-board members. As a result, there are today nearly 400,000 laymen on local school boards — approximately half as many citizen-supervisors as teachers; in some states there are actually more board members than there are schoolteachers!

In recognition of the inefficiencies inherent in these practices in local control, the administration of schools for the rural districts has been rapidly centralized in larger units. Twenty years ago one third of the teachers were in one-teacher schools, but today only 15 per cent of them are. In spite of this advance, there are still some 100,000 one-room elementary schoolhouses in the United States.

The Local System and Its Three Major Jobs

In most things that the people of a democratic society do together, three separate functions have to be provided for:

–A policy has to be decided upon.

–A plan, a design, has to be made.

–The enterprise has to be set up and operated.

This is true of the schools of the community as well as of the public water supply, the sanitary system, the roads and streets, the parks and playgrounds, and the police and fire departments. There are three distinctive tasks: (1) the kind and amount of education to be given the children, (2) a plan for developing it, and (3) the carrying on of the curriculum and teaching. In each of these jobs the teachers, the parents and other lay citizens, the children, and the administrators all should play a part.

1. Who Makes the Educational Policy?

The communities in America agree that the people determine the educational policy. Since all the children of all the people are to be educated, in the long run all the people must decide how much and what kind of education. In some instances — as in the adoption of a bond issue for a new school building — the proposition is actually put up to the people to be decided by vote at an election. But in most instances the American method of representative government is employed. The people choose representatives — members of the local board of education — who act for them. It is they who, in the framework of the state constitution and other special educational laws, decide all questions of general policy — the conditions of compulsory attendance, the number of years of schooling offered, its general scope and nature, and its relations to the constitution and law of state and nation. In short, the board of education is the legal depository of the power of decision over local community problems of education.

But ultimately in our democratic society it is the people alone who are competent to make the policy. If they do not approve what their representatives on the board of education do, they can recall them and elect others in their places. In the last analysis it is they who must decide what they want for their children. Hence, in a democratic society schools of a town, state, or nation can never rise higher than the will of the people will permit or compel. In some instances this results in mediocre schools because the rank and file of the people are mediocre in understanding, sensitivity, and cultivation. It is undoubtedly true that in many instances one could get better schools by leaving decisions to the judgment and control of a wise and benevolent dictator. But to guarantee that the dictator would be wise and benevolent is more of a gamble with the course of events than the American people have been willing to take. They have chosen the democratic method, even though in a transitional period, while the community is growing to maturity, it may give them mediocre schools.

It is the local board of education that makes the educational policy for the people of the community. If the members of the board are wise and truly interested in *all* the children of *all* the people, the community will get good schools. If, on the other hand, the board members represent merely one point of view about life and education and one social class, as has too often been true, the schools will give most of the children a very inadequate education. And if the board of education is a part of the political machine of the state and community — and this also has been true — and uses the schools for the advantage of a mercenary party of politicians, all the children of all the people will get a bad education, exactly as the community gets bad services from its other departments. Hence, "eternal vigilance is the price of a good education as well as other forms of 'liberty.'"

That the question of getting board members who truly represent *all*

the people — not just a single social class — is important is shown by
the facts of the social composition of boards. Of the many studies
that have been made we cite a few.

George F. Struble found that among 1000 board members only 54
belonged to skilled and unskilled trades; all the others were from the
professional or business class — 208 merchants, 70 bankers, 67 lawyers,
57 physicians, 53 business executives. The superintendents who gave
him the facts said it was their experience that by far the more progressive
board members were the professional persons and the younger members
— not the older businessmen and industrialists. Scott Nearing also
studied the background of 1000 board members in larger cities; three
fourths were business and professional men. "The control of our
schools," he said, "lies in the privileged classes of society" because "nine
tenths of the school-board members of the large American cities are
selected from one sixth of the gainfully occupied population, which is
above the rank of wage earner or clerk." George S. Counts studied
1654 boards of education, covering all classes of boards, and found that
of the board members only eight per cent were "engaged in manual
labor." Moreover, *only on the rural boards is the membership drawn
directly from those occupations in which the great majority of the
people are engaged.*" He described the typical city board in these
words:

> "The typical city board of education in the United States is
> composed of six members. These members are elected at large for
> a term of three years. One of the six members is a woman, who
> follows the occupation of housewife. Of the five men, one is a
> merchant; one, a lawyer; one, a physician; one, a banker, manu-
> facturer, or business executive; and one, a salesman, clerk, or laborer.
> Three of the members have children attending the public schools
> of the city. From the standpoint of formal education, *they con-
> stitute . . . a highly selected group.* But one of the members is a
> product of the elementary school only; two have attended the
> secondary school; and three have enjoyed college or university
> privileges. In age, they exhibit a range . . . from thirty-seven to
> sixty-three years." [1] [Our italics.]

Moreover as Counts shows, these facts of social membership of school
boards are of supreme importance, for:

[1] George S. Counts: *The Social Composition of Boards of Education*, page 79.
University of Chicago Press; 1927. Used by permission.

"the fundamental character of public education in the United States is, in the last analysis, determined by the board that controls the school . . . the possibilities which the school possesses as a creative and leavening social agency are set by the good will, the courage, and the intelligence of that membership." [1]

A glance at the broad powers given local boards confirms Counts:

–Appointment of administratives, teachers, and other employees

–Adoption of courses of study

–Acquiring sites for school buildings and erecting buildings

–Financing the schools with necessary estimates and tax levies

–Prescribing rules and regulations for school management

–Enforcing compulsory school attendance

–All other duties necessary to carry on public education

These are important powers to give representatives of the people. But, by and large, there are almost no Negroes, almost no skilled or unskilled workmen, few labor union members, on the school boards of the United States; these three groups alone include more than half of the population of the United States. Certainly the *social or economic composition* of boards of education is not *representative* of *all* the people. Whether or not a one-class social membership can work disinterestedly for the good of all the people and express *all* points of view, especially on controversial matters, is open to question. That it is expected to do so is expressed well by Vivian T. Thayer in *The Educational Frontier*:

". . . the board of education is primarily a legislative and not an administrative body . . . its members are expected to represent the people as a whole. Ideally it is nonpartisan and nonsectarian in character. Representing no special interest, it guards jealously the schools from interference on the part of individuals or groups who wish to promote their own selfish concerns." [2]

The records show that in many cases boards of education have done this. Certainly, taken as a whole, they themselves represent a high order of

[1] *Ibid.*, page 1.
[2] Vivian T. Thayer: *The Educational Frontier*, pages 214–215.

education among the American people, and that is a true asset. But the records also show that in many cases the education given the children has been formal and unprogressive, and that it has totally ignored the controversial issues of our times or has given a very one-sided approach to them in the curriculum. This, then, is a problem of great importance.

So much for policy-making, the first task of educational development in a community. It is clear that the leadership in this task is in the hands of the board of education. But the board is made up of lay citizens and, even in policy-making, needs the guidance of its trained professional executive officer — the superintendent of schools. His role in the entire system will emerge more clearly as we turn to the two remaining tasks of the educational system. We shall consider these two major jobs together.

2. Who Plans and Implements the Educational Program?

To plan and develop the program of education to be carried on in a school, or a system of schools, would require a full grasp of all the kinds of ability and knowledge outlined in this entire book. It is essentially a technical and professional task. No lay citizen lacking such training and experience could contribute to it competently. This is not to say that it would not be highly desirable to have parents and other citizens understand it thoroughly and enter into the discussion and appraisal of it. But to make and carry out the plan requires prolonged thought and professional experience.

Moreover, no one person can possibly know enough, or be wise enough about the society and the culture, the psychology of growth and development, and the problems of teaching to plan and develop the program alone. To carry on the manifold and specialized jobs of education requires *a group of competent persons*. No superintendent of schools, principal, or supervisor can do it alone; certainly no board member has the technical competence required, although on certain specialized tasks — such as public finance, school building, engineering and architecture, medical and health development — his advice might be invaluable in planning.

Ellwood P. Cubberley (1868–1941) was a pioneer educator who, in company with Messrs. Strayer, Judd, and Elliott, created the first graduate study of educational administration after 1900. As Professor of Education, Head of the Department, and Dean of the School of Education (1917–1933) at Stanford University, he is remembered admiringly by his many students. They regarded him as a master teacher, a clear and vivid lecturer, a close friend and constructive critic. He convinced thousands of young Americans that teaching was a worthy life career.

Dr. Cubberley served as consultant on school surveys in cities and states throughout the country. Perhaps his most distinguished contribution to education was in the developing and editing of the *Riverside Textbooks in Education* and in writing such books as *Public School Administration, State School Administration, School Organization and Administration, Public Education in the United States, A History of Education,* and *The Principal and His School.*

A Note on Leadership and Followership The question of the part to be played by teachers — and the parallel roles of the superintendent, principals, supervisors, and the children and their parents — calls for a brief appraisal of the problem of leadership. In a fascist, authoritarian society the perfect model is found in such totalitarian one-party governments as those of Nazi Germany or the Russian Politburo. Each is one-way leadership, the leader on each level of the hierarchy of Fuehrers giving orders to the followers on the level below and taking orders from the one above. This is action by the method of "Heil Hitler." So much has been said about this "leadership" of the dictator and the blind followership of the little people that we need say nothing more about it.

But in American schools today we are concerned to instate *democratic leadership and followership;* that is something very different and is of supreme importance in building the good life and the good education in America, for it presupposes coöperative and total group activity. Individuals on the school staff — teachers as well as administrators — will at the proper moments emerge as leaders, and will at other times be fully coöperating followers.

Granting the fact of individual differences in intelligence, sensitivity, and administrative initiative, it is obvious that some persons will naturally be predisposed to move out in advance, to take the initiative.

Granting, also, that the jobs in a school are manifold and varied and require specialization of competence, certain vigorous personalities, because of their recognized achievements and their creative and organizing abilities, will be accepted by the group as persons to follow. Nevertheless, we know that the product of group intelligence will be better designed and will have greater potentiality and fewer limitations than any plan that springs from a single mind. Thus, in planning and designing, the highest form of leadership in a school or system is that which is achieved coöperatively.

Ideally a democratic social order is constituted for the functioning of such group leadership. It provides freedom for each person to make his ideas and abilities known, and to appraise and criticize the ideas, proposals, and plans of others. When the climate of opinion in a school releases the teachers from their fears and inhibitions so that they express themselves, make suggestions, and appraise proposals, then the highest order of leadership and followership is realized. Not only are the stronger initiating personalities discovered and accepted by other members of the group, but a better conception of authority is put into practice — authority as the expression of all the members of the group.

Summing up, then, there are two kinds of competence to bear in mind in considering who shall do what in a school. There is the competence of the individual especially equipped by experience and training. And there is an optimum coöperative group contribution to the jobs of the school. This dual principle of competence establishes the indispensable role of teachers in many phases of school administration.

The Local Superintendent of Schools   But we must consider that question against the background of the leadership of the superintendent of schools. The discussion will be very brief, for our main concern is the teachers.

Even in a democratic society, leadership organizes itself in a kind of hierarchy. There must be a director, a council of direction, with full and free access back and forth to the creative suggestions of the followership. If the system is really democratic, efficiently organized and conducted, the best competence will rise to the top; that is, of course, if politics doesn't get in the way, and too often politics does get in the way. Moreover, efficiency in any complex organization requires centralization of action and of authority in a single person. Divided control at the top never works. Hence in every good school system there will be a superintendent who is both the leader of the professional staff and the responsible agent of the community as a whole. Briefly, the superintendent of schools

—serves as the executive of the board of education, working with it and its committees continuously but exercising no vote in policy-making decisions.

—nominates for election all administrators, teachers, custodians, and other employees . . . takes the initiative in hiring and firing.

—leads the administrators and teachers in developing courses of study (within the framework set by the state and community laws and ordinances), building up libraries for schools and rooms, selecting textbooks and other materials of teaching.

—makes final decisions concerning all administrative matters authorized by the board under the law; supervises the operation of buildings and equipment and supplies.

—leads the business administration in developing the school budget, conducting continuous surveys of the resources and needs of the community and of its adult and child population.

—is the leader in the fullest sense in educating the citizens of the community in the forward-moving and continuous rebuilding of the life of the community, especially through the cultivation of adult education; is in the truest sense the director of education for the entire life of the community.

There are many other specific functions — legal, financial, operational, maintenance — which burden the hours and energy of any superintendent of schools; but here we are concerned with the superintendent as the leader in community life. As the inspiring leader of the board and the teachers, his thought should be constantly on the life of the village, town, or city, and its relations to the wider world.

And, without considering his functions in detail, note also that in each single school there must be a directing head — a Principal. While, as we have seen, there is a need for some uniformity of program in all the

JESSE H. NEWLON (1882–1941) was one of the
country's outstanding superintendents of city schools.
As Superintendent in Lincoln, Nebraska, and in Denver,
Colorado, he secured widespread teacher and citizen
participation in educational policy making, and achieved
distinguished success in rebuilding the curriculum
through the teacher-committee system. He was Director of the Lincoln School of Teachers College
(1927–1930) and Professor of Education (1930–
1941). As President of the National Education Association (1924–1925) and a member of its Commissions, he was influential in developing a public social
policy in education. This interest was revealed in his
activity in the American Civil Liberties Union, in *The
Social Frontier*, the John Dewey Society and its *Yearbooks*, and in his outstanding books, *Educational Administration as Social Policy* and *Education for Democracy in Our Time*.

Dr. Newlon's colleagues felt in his life three guiding
loyalties — faith in the brotherhood of man, faith in
the common people, and freedom of mind.

schools, the principal should have great autonomy within the single
school in leading both its teachers and the parents and citizens of its
neighborhood. He is a crucial link in the chain of leadership that extends from the community as a whole to the neighborhoods and the
specific families of the town. Visualized from the standpoint of the
community, the superintendent leads the whole town, the principal leads
the neighborhood around the single school, and the teacher leads the
hundred persons in the families of her class.

From this background of the total problem we turn finally to the
part played by the teacher.

The Role of the Teacher The teachers of any one school form the
central social unit. We now raise the question: What is the individual
teacher's responsibility for the promotion of a democracy of human
relationships? First, recall the major tasks of the teacher discussed in
the preceding chapters, and consider them in light of a democratic
school program.

*First: Understanding the individual children; organizing and making
available a cumulative personal file of data about every boy and girl.*
This is the task of the coöperative group-teachers, parents, school

psychologist and pediatrician, principal, and others. But *the teacher is the leader*. The teacher knows most about each child, is the initiating expert.

Second: Planning and carrying on the work of each school day. Here pupil-and-teacher planning is the key, carried out through group discussions. Plans, however, must be coördinated with the over-all plans of the whole school and of other groups.

Third: Designing the framework of the curriculum (a) for the schools of the community — the system, (b) for the single school, and (c) for the individual class. This is the central coöperative group task of the teachers and the system. No single administrative officer can do it. For the entire system and for separate schools, the initiating expert is the director of curriculum. *The over-all planning should be done by committees of teachers* drawn from every level and school of the entire system, coöperating with principals, supervisors, and curriculum special ists.

Similarly, under the direction of the principal, the teachers of eac school constitute a coöperative team to plan the curriculum for t school within the over-all community framework. *And the teachers the chief resource.*

Finally, the specific plan for the single class group is made by teacher of that group, with the definite and constant coöperatio teachers of adjacent classes. *And the teacher of the class is again initiating expert and chief resource.*

Fourth: Planning the coöperative parent-teacher activities: parents into the school and teachers into the homes, buildi continuing adult education of the neighborhoods and the com *as a whole.* For each class, the teacher is the initiating leader, ing with the parents, coöperating closely with the principal other specialists in the school.

For the community as a whole the same principle appli of dynamic teachers work under the direction of the superin schools, the director of adult education, and other leaders tem. But the teachers are the indispensable resources in th of the community.

GEORGE D. STODDARD (1897————) is known as a teacher of psychology at the State University of Iowa, from 1925 to 1942, Director of its Institute for Child Welfare Research, from 1928 to 1942, and Dean of its Graduate College, from 1936 to 1942. During these years he made outstanding contributions to the study of child development and behavior and to the clarification of intelligence, defending the environmentalist point of view in the nature-nurture controversy.

Dr. Stoddard has been a constant collaborator with progressive movements in education in the United States and around the world; witness his membership of the President's Commission on Higher Education, his work in the Progressive Education Association, his chairmanship of the United States Education Mission to Japan, and his service as American delegate to the UNESCO conferences in London and Paris. Since 1942 his psychological interests have been replaced by his work as State Commissioner of Education in New York, and most recently as President of the University of Illinois.

Fifth: Planning and designing the school building and other physical facilities of education for the community. Here also group competence is the key. No single person or section of the staff knows enough to do the job alone. School architects and engineers contribute experience and knowledge of technical construction; administrative specialists carry on studies of growth, mobility of population, and related facts. . . . *But the teachers, the principal, and other specialists who plan and develop the curriculum and teaching* know most about what kind of life is to be lived in each room. Planning a school building is a task requiring the competence of a large coöperative group. The room teacher plays a vital part in this.

Sixth: Planning the development of the professional staff of the school systems — the appointment, cultivation, and advancement of teachers and other educational workers. From time out of mind, this has been done in authoritarian schools solely by the superintendent, with the advice of principals and other individuals. This was, and is in some places, one-way hiring and firing.

But democratic school administration requires that we utilize group competence. The wise superintendent will enlist the help of teachers in the discovery and promotion of teaching and other special talents. While the legal power to recommend and to appoint lies in the hands of the superintendent and the board of education, the wisdom needed to

discover and put to work the finest human talent available will undoubtedly be found in a wider coöperating group of teachers. *A chief resource here will be teachers' councils.*

Seventh: Stimulating the professional growth of the school staff. The leadership lies in the superintendent, but through the coöperation of the teachers, principals, and others will emerge the maximum group competence. As far as possible, the initiation of professional growth activities must lie in the individual teachers, especially in their unions and other organizations.

What effects do these attitudes of the teachers have upon the kind of learning that takes place, and on the personalities of students? First, we know that the atmosphere of any classroom reflects the attitude of the teacher. He, in turn, may merely be reflecting the point of view created by the administrators of the system. In a classroom where there is freedom in the search for knowledge, freedom in interchange of ideas and opinions, and mutual respect and understanding, the authoritarian teacher does not thrive. On the contrary, in such a classroom one finds the teacher who lives by the principle of competence, and accepts the necessity of both leadership and followership in a democratically run school system.

Those teachers, children, parents, and administrators who are working toward the finest in educational leadership, recognize:

–the democratic superiority of group control over individual control.

–that participation is the key to effective learning.

–the need to implement goals and purposes through the utilization of group organization.

–an administration that is broad enough to allow adequate flexibility.

These, then, are the guiding ideas governing the role of the teacher in the administration of the schools. A new day is breaking in this respect as in others. The autocratic command-obedience regime is on the way out; the democratic way is coming in. As that happens, the question is being asked insistently: Who is competent to do this work? And increasingly the answer is: A coöperative group, not any single individual. In that coöperative group the teacher plays a more and more important part.   In the system he, like the principal and superintendent, is finding a place both as leader and as follower.

Continuing Your Study of the Teacher's Part in School Administration

1. Make a report on some meeting that you have recently attended where a group discussed a problem or issue, or proposed to take some action. Summarize the important events or ideas discussed, the attitudes of those participating, the action taken, etc.   Analyze your statement of the meeting in terms of leadership exhibited: Was it democratic or authoritarian?   Who did the planning?   Was the meeting directed by a preselected small group? Were those with special information and experience utilized?   How much group participation existed?

2. Define in the light of your readings and discussion: *democratic leadership; intelligent followership; the expert; authority.*

3. Describe in a short paper the best example of group participation that you have known.

4. Have your class group set up a method of rating student participation. Visit classrooms in elementary, high school, and college, and use your rating sheet to determine its effectiveness.

5. Make a chart to show the organization and administration of a specific school.   Compare it with those described in this chapter.   What are its strengths and its weaknesses?

6. Suggest definite and constructive ways in which teachers may participate in the administrative practices of an elementary school.

7. Invite a local school-board member to come and discuss with your class the problems his board encounters.

8. Attend a public meeting of the school board and then discuss it at the next meeting of your class.   Find out in advance and study the problems and issues to be aired.   Appraise the meeting in the light of the principles developed in this book.

Things to Read

From a large library of writings on school organization and administration we have picked a few that deal best with our problem of the teacher's participation — that is, with the democratization of administration. We think you will get much help from Carleton Washburne's *A Living Philosophy of Education* — clear, episodic, practical, based on his twenty-six years of experience as superintendent of schools in a small Illinois town. Because of its many actual examples of teachers' participation, we recommend Koopman, Miel, and Misner's *Democracy in School Administration*. Moehlman's *School Administration, Its Development, Principles, and Future in the United States* is a good general statement of educational leadership. On the social side, see Jesse Newlon's *School Administration as a Social Policy*. See also:

–NEA's Association of Supervision and Curriculum Development, *Organizing the Elementary School for Living and Learning* (1947 Yearbook).

–The *Eighth Yearbook* of the Department of Elementary School Principals (Michigan Educational Association): *Democratic Participation in Administration*. Part I gives the philosophy of teacher participation; Part II, many examples of current practices.

–The *Eleventh Yearbook* of the NEA Department of Supervisors and Directors of Instruction, *Cooperation: Principles and Practices*, reports examples of democratic supervision and administration.

–The NEA's Educational Policy Commission's *Education for All American Children* and *Learning the Ways of Democracy*.

Julia Weber's *My Country School Diary* has many examples of teacher-pupil-parent planning of the life of the schools.

On group leadership de Huszar's *Practical Applications of Democracy* is a simple statement of democratic action. Ronald Lippitt's *An Experimental Study of Authoritarian and Democratic Group Atmospheres* is an advanced scientific study made with children. See also Baxter and Cassidy's *Group Experience; Group Planning and Education*, by the NEA's Department of Supervision and Directors of Instruction; and Courtis's *Some Social Aspects of Coöperation*.

CHAPTER 18

The Supreme Goal of Human Development

To be effective, the self-education of the teacher must have a powerful goal. Throughout our study we have implied that maturity of personality is that goal. Now we can state it definitely as the Mature Person.

We know that from birth to death the unformed human Individual struggles to become a mature, balanced Person. Education is the guidance of that process.

In this concluding chapter, therefore, we are concerned with the qualities of maturity of personality. We shall ask:

–What has experience to do with it?

–What is the role of physical well-being? of effective intelligence?

–What are the signs of emotional maturity? of the integrity of the Self?

We have made it abundantly clear that teaching is an art and the good teacher is the Artist-Teacher. In concluding our study, the Artist-Teacher becomes the master-student of the development of personality.

The Teacher as Mature Person

WE RETURN finally to the central theme of our study — the teacher in school and society. We return, however, oriented with an understanding of the potential role of the teacher in modern life. It is not beyond the bounds of possibility that the teaching profession could, in the next generation, make itself into an enlightened leader of our culture. Around the teachers the creative forces of the community and the nation might gather, energizing the building of a society of physical, intellectual, and spiritual abundance. But that could happen only if those who are drawn to that profession are themselves magnificently qualified to lead.

It behooves us, therefore, to hold clearly before our eyes the high goal at which our efforts shall be directed. And that goal, it seems to us, is the same for the teachers as for the children and youth of the nation — the Mature Person. For we hold it to be established that only a mature person can sense the characteristics of personality surely enough to fashion a proper program for their development in others. Certainly the principle that any goal of education must be known by the teacher, internally, through experience, was established in the early days of our modern schools. Creative writers, painters, musicians, and other artists have been brought into the schools to teach; as a consequence children and youth have produced a body of expression of a quality hitherto unknown. It is a commonplace of professional college administration that the faculties of engineering schools shall include practicing engineers, the faculties of medical schools shall include practicing doctors, and of law schools — practicing lawyers and judges. So also in athletics, if one would turn out a golfer, he should give the novice a teacher who has *played* golf with some success; a teacher of baseball players must have *played* baseball. Hence the inference seems to follow that to lead young people successfully toward the goal of maturity of personality, the teacher must himself have experienced maturity of personality.

The Person of Rich Experience

In painting a brief word-picture of the teacher as mature person we start, therefore, with the all-pervasive idea of modern education — *experience*. Every phase of this book has pointed to the role of experience. The writings of modern educators center attention upon it; to cite only two: John Dewey's *Education and Experience* and *Art as Experience*, and Jacques-Dalcroze's classic phrase, "I would have a child say, not 'I know,' but 'I have experienced.'"

Frequently we ask: "What made him such a good teacher?", and are told: He has *lived* so richly. He has been everywhere, has felt so many sides of life. Although he is a master of the best that has been written, he is not just a bookish person; he has seen things firsthand. He has explored the life of his community: its docks, lumberyards, fish canneries, delicatessens, artists' studios. Since he has touched these things, his spiritual interests have emerged, the world has widened, he has grown with it and has become a part of it. Indeed, all life, all occupations, coursed through his body, mind, and spirit — bricklayer and Wall Street broker, elevator operator and coal miner, housewife, lumberjack, and soapbox orator. And he is able to sing with Walt Whitman:

> "O the joy of that vast elemental sympathy which only the soul is capable of generating and emitting in steady and limitless floods."

Because:

> "There is something in staying close to men and women and looking
> on them, and in contact and odour of them, that pleases
> the soul well.
> All things please the soul, but these please the soul well."

So, warmth for people, kindled by love in the heart of the mature teacher, makes way the path of understanding those whose lives he guides. As a consequence, he not only knows people but he likes people. This is fortunate, for he will never be a good teacher unless he likes those whom he teaches. If he likes them, he will live well with them. He will work at understanding them, exploring their personalities, and finding their strengths and weaknesses. In a word, he will discover them.

Moreover, the person of rich experience is the person of many and varied interests — outside as well as inside his teaching specialty. As an artist he knows that he can grow only in a creative environment of expression. The teacher of painting or theater works with a master of the dance. The poet-teacher of writing craves contact with the great arts of movement — music, dance, and painting. The sculptor knows he must draw, but to draw people he must know the body, even if this forces him into the study of anatomy. The man of books will find varied outlets for his creative energy, even as Candide, who, tired of philosophizing, said, "Yes, but one must cultivate his own garden." He spends his holidays in other environments — in the country if he is a city teacher, in the city's museums, theaters, and concerts if a ruralite, or in foreign travel.

Experience seems the product of this kind of living, a storehouse of rich resources. But these must become a part of oneself: an experience that has been retained and felt, not merely one that has entered with as easy facility as it has disappeared. Only by holding these things close can they become part of a person, and permit him to grow. A teacher draws upon such resources spontaneously. Thus he not only knows the world in which he lives, *he loves it*, is stimulated and challenged by life itself, by man's follies and foibles as well as by his successes.

The Person of Physical Well-Being

Think of several teachers you know well. What stands out about them, first and foremost? Recall that tired teacher of your fifth grade, petulant, impatient of the needs of children simply because she has not the physical stamina to sustain herself. One such teacher comes to mind who has pampered herself to the point of becoming so fat she cannot walk without help. She rules her little first-graders from her chair, querulous and dictatorial, shouting commands and threats.

She is perhaps about the worst of many bad teachers of the old regime.

But across the corridor from her we see the figure of Miss Alice, as young today at sixty as she was when she took over a first grade at twenty. After forty years she moves calmly about her room, quietly guiding her thirty little individualists as they work at their all-important jobs. Her very bearing breeds security in the children. Here is a person they can count on as a friendly yet incisive critic, a guiding resource of wisdom and good judgment. But it is her physical well-being that, more than other traits, builds this feeling in the children. The children sense this through her sure and active step. As you observe her, you get the feeling that she knows not only what every individual child is doing, but also his unique needs, the current stage of his development, what is happening to him at home and in his play groups. Through her body alertness we sense that she is perhaps the most secure human being we have ever known, a fine ideal of *the teacher as mature person*.

We may well set ourselves the high ideals of the teacher of fine physical well-being. No longer do we have the question-and-answer regime in the school, in which the teacher can sit at a desk up front, issuing orders and checking up on their execution. The new school has come alive with a great range of activities, and to supply it with life continuously, teachers must be persons of abundant physical energy. The children will reflect the teacher; his voice, his mood, his smiles or angry frowns, his personal tensions, will create the atmosphere in which work and play go on. So it is that when a teacher enters the classroom, the children first sense the person, if he is there at all, in the physical being.

In most people's lives energy and physical well-being do not just happen. It is true, a few among us are superlatively endowed. But for most people great wisdom and constant care are necessary to maintain a steady reservoir of physical energy. A wisely planned regimen as well as a strong inheritance of bodily strength is the combination that constitutes the mature person.

The Emotionally Mature Person

The greatest reservoir of strength for fine teaching lies in the teacher's emotional resources. It is from these that he draws the energy he so much needs. The children must feel in him a warm and sympathetic personal friend inspiring them to lift themselves over their emotional obstacles. They need to sense in him a quiet mastery, a feeling that they can count on him no matter what may be ahead. The parents too must feel this confidence. And the teacher must be conscious of that delicate balance between comfort, sympathy and protection, and the nurturing of independence and respect for self. He must not be overprotecting, which might prohibit the full growth of his students. He will respect order, efficiency, and careful workmanship but within it permit freedom to explore, to think, to act in one's own unique pattern of behavior. Can he exert authority without demanding submission? Can he give out spontaneous expression and have the capacity to relax and be the good companion, both with his pupils and his peers? These are the marks of the mature person. At the core is a fine sense of humor, especially the capacity to laugh at oneself. Indeed, the mature person is one who strives day by day to achieve the goal set by the ancient adage — "Know thyself." He has no illusions about his "Self." He is tolerantly amused by his own foibles, knowing full well that he is not exempt from the chronic tendency to rationalize them and compensate for them. To the old adage, "Know thyself," he even adds, "Be thyself."

Above all, the mature person has gone far toward solving the problems of security. In the life of a teacher outside the school there are many crises which can best him. He must be so secure within himself that he can handle each in terms of itself and not according to any fixed patterns. If the crises are met successfully, the teacher will enter the classroom a happy, stable individual. If they are dodged, he will increasingly become emotionally unfit. One question he must answer constantly: Am I a steady mooring mast for these children? Am I in control of myself sufficiently to give them the warmth and understanding they need, and intelligent direction to their growth? To answer "Yes" is to apply oneself to the building of a rich and satisfying life and to solving personal problems as they come up. But let's be honest. Many a fine teacher still knows his immaturity, understands the heartbreak of insecurity, and is therefore able to offset his precarious balance in life by giving out a strength born of his own human frailty.

A teacher who becomes such a mature person will be patient and calmly accept children and youth for what they are. He will not label them "good" or "bad," but will see each one as a whole developing person, often baffled by what life is doing to him and needing friendly and wise guidance. He will know that the basis of the balanced emotional life is a deep sense of *security*. But he knows also that one does not leave the possibility of emotional balance to the chance of either inherited physical constitution or the current of daily life. You *do* something about it, and the first step is to permit no personal problems to go unfaced. The mature person confronts problems head-on, finding constructive solutions rather than resorting to any of the dozen forms of escape and rationalization. Thus the mature person is one who compensates as little as possible, and rationalizes never. It is chiefly because such a teacher is secure in himself that he can give security to children.

Perhaps there is nothing more important to the mature person than success in solving the personal problems of love, sex, and home life. One important sign of this phase of emotional maturity is a balanced understanding of the role of sex in his own life. Rather than treat sex as something to be shunned, he respects it and builds it constructively into the pattern of his life. He is positive and happy in his family living. Life, to him, is good. The capacity for love and the inspiring of trust and affection are the foundations of the mature person's expression in any form of social participation.

Effective Intelligence and Leadership in the Culture

The point has been made abundantly clear that our times and our world cry out for leadership of the younger generation in understanding our changing society and culture. It is a truism now to say that such social education is a twofold process. It consists, on the one hand, of making sure that the essential ideas, beliefs, and values of the people get passed on to our young people; but, on the other hand, there must be those who guide in the interpretation and appraisal of the culture, picking out its salient features, pointing out its strengths and weaknesses.

To do these things requires of the teacher intellectual maturity of the highest order. To build it, he must devote himself to becoming, within the limits of his ability, a student of American life and its role in world culture. If he is to help build a curriculum of activities in the social, natural, or physical sciences, he must have reasonably accurate knowledge of men and their affairs, an understanding of the social conditions and problems which our citizens confront in the communities of the nation. Controversial issues must be honestly faced; the mature person knows that to bar issues from the school is to bar life from it. Hence young people must be led in this careful, balanced study of the problems of the community and our society.

The mature person is alert to the moving trends of our culture, and to new ideas and theories and ways of doing things, because he has constantly put himself in the way of new and stimulating human beings. His life is continuously a life of learning. His friends speak of his good judgment, that his handling of social problems in the school seems always to be based on a careful study of the facts. Such qualities stand out by contrast against the tendency of the climate of opinion of all the community agencies to impose on young people a one-sided and emotionalized body of beliefs and loyalties. Of this tendency the teacher must be aware, while quietly leading young people in a more comprehensive and balanced study of the facts of changing social life.

Thus, difficult though the task is, the mature teacher will strive to make himself a student of the history and current problems of modern industrial society. To lead in the task of developing a generation of mature men and women, he must be generously informed of the social foundations of education.

Effective Intelligence in the Psychology of Development

But, since his chief task is to guide the development of young people, the teacher has another responsibility — namely, that of being a student of the biology and psychology of human growth and development. He must find his way to the rich sources of knowledge about human nature and behavior — that is, to both the scientists and the artists who can inspire, discipline, and inform him. These sources are bewildering in their scope and their depth, ranging from physiology and brain psychology, through all the "schools" of psychology, to the social sciences, which teach how the culture molds our young people. For the teacher's task is one of understanding the whole-acting person — a unique life style, driven by biosocial needs, learning to adjust, to anticipate what to expect from life's situations, and maintaining his balance amidst the storm and stress of human conflicts.

ROSABELL MACDONALD MANN is a painter and a teacher of children, youth, and adults in the graphic and plastic arts. Not only is she one of America's outstanding public school teachers, but she is also a distinguished student of the creative process in education. Born and educated in the schools and colleges of New York City, she was for thirty years a teacher in the high schools of the city. She served successively, over a period of years, as head of the department of art in the Theodore Roosevelt High School, as founder and Director of the Art Division of the experimental Art and Music High School and the Jamaica High School. She has also been a teacher of art in adult-education institutes. Her pioneer study of the creative process in the graphic and plastic arts was published in her book, Art *in Education*. She has long been active in the work of the Progressive Education Association. (Photo by courtesy of Harry Teichlau.)

The mature person talks and thinks with the concepts of growth as well as of skills and knowledge. He accepts children and youth on their level of fun, vitality, and creativeness. He handles the raw materials of their expressions, ideas, and emotions with respect for their individual differences. And he guides their learning activities toward the realization of the best in themselves, whatever that best may be. For the teacher knows the give and take required of life.

A Person of Integrity

The teacher as a mature person must have a personal philosophy of life. Right or wrong, he must know where he stands, what position he takes concerning life problems. If he is a critical student of human relations and world affairs, he will have developed values compatible with the changes and discoveries of each generation's way of life. But the question is: Has his philosophy emerged from his own experiences, his own critical attitudes and appraisals, his own feelings and ideals? Or does he jump on every band wagon that goes by his corner? As the artist would say, "Does his life have Form?" Is there a wholeness, a completeness within himself and his contacts with the world? Can he stand with Whitman and, in the humility of pride, acclaim the democratic impulse:

"We affirm there can be unnumbered supremes and one does not countervail another . . . and that men can be good or grand only in the consciousness of their supremacy within them."

To bring this out — the dignity of self — is the teacher's job, for he is

"Pressing the pulse of life that has seldom exhibited itself (the great pride of man in himself)."

The Artist-Teacher: Master of the Development of Personality

The picture of the wise teacher we have just given you becomes very real when we give him his true title — THE ARTIST-TEACHER. Teaching is an art, and the teacher is primarily an artist. Not merely a skilled technician, nor a scientist, but an artist! An artist is one who takes the scattered and miscellaneous materials of his art and organizes them into a unity. Think of the painter creating his picture, the sculptor carving his statue, the musician composing his symphony. Each, working with his own special materials — color, line, stone, mood, tone — transforms the scattered bits into an organized whole.

This is exactly what the teacher does; so we call him — Artist. The materials of his art are twofold:

–*First:* They are the raw materials of personality with which the children are born: their physiques, their intelligences, and their temperamental traits, their capacities for skill, for understanding and for expression and appreciation; in short, the heredity of the children.

–*Second:* They are the conditions and problems of the world around the children . . . the ways of living in the community into which they must be inducted, the ways of living in their own country and in other countries and regions of the earth . . . the facts of the universe, of our earth, of other earths, and of all living things and creatures upon them . . . and the history of how all these developed; in short, the environments of the children.

The teacher's task is to gather the elements of these two great bodies of material — heredity and environment — and mold them into a great organization or perfect unity. That unity is the whole child, the formed personality. This is the great goal of education. From birth to death the unformed human individual struggles to become a mature, balanced person. In that struggle his great teachers — mother, father, the teacher in the school, or some other elder one — stand at his side as friends and guides, directing him along the difficult path of growing up.

Thus the mature teacher works as artist — not as mere technician or master of the facts of a profession. Because in one human being he integrates the two needed traits, we call him Artist-Teacher:

–On the one hand, as Artist — as master of the materials of his art: the psychology of man's nature and his behavior, the data of his society, his plant and animal world, his ways of thinking, feeling, and expression.

–On the other hand, as Teacher: as master of the art of arranging human situations so that day by day each unformed individual surmounts obstacles, subdues fears, grows in understanding and feeling, climbs the stairs of his problems and stands foursquare as clear, expressive, and whole Person.

This is the Artist-Teacher, true guide in the development of personality.

Bibliography

ALSCHULER, ROSE, and HATTWICK, L. W. *Painting and Personality*. Chicago: University of Chicago Press; 1947.

American Association for Adult Education. *Community Education in Action*. New York: Institute of Adult Education, Teachers College, Columbia University; 1948.

American Youth Commission. *Youth and the Future*. Washington: American Council on Education; 1942.

Association for Supervision and Curriculum Development. *Laymen Help Plan the Curriculum*. Washington: National Education Association; 1946.

––––––. *Organizing the Elementary School for Living and Learning*. Washington: National Education Association; 1947.

––––––. *Toward Better Teaching: A Report of Current Practices*. Washington: National Education Association; 1949.

AXLINE, VIRGINIA M. *Play Therapy*. Boston: Houghton Mifflin Company; 1947.

BARKER, ROGER G., and others. *Child Behavior and Development*. New York: McGraw-Hill Book Company, Inc.; 1943.

BARUCH, DOROTHY W. *Parents and Children Go to School*. Chicago: Scott, Foresman & Company; 1939.

BARZUN, JACQUES. *The Teacher in America*. Boston: Little, Brown & Company; 1945.

BAXTER, B., and CASSIDY, R. *Group Experience*. New York: Harper & Brothers; 1943.

BEALE, HOWARD. *Are American Teachers Free?* New York: Charles Scribner's Sons; 1936.

BEARD, CHARLES A. and MARY R. *The Rise of American Civilization*. New York: The Macmillan Company; 1927.

––––––. *A Basic History of the United States*. New York: The New Home Library; 1944.

BELL, HOWARD. *Youth Tell Their Story*. Washington: American Council on Education; 1938.

BENEDICT, RUTH. *Patterns of Culture*. New York: Penguin Books; 1946.

BIGELOW, K. W. *Teachers for Our Times*. Washington: American Council on Education; 1944.

517

BLOS, PETER. *The Adolescent Personality.* New York: D. Appleton-Century Company, Inc.; 1941.

BOCK, DORIS. *New Tools for Instruction.* New York: Hinds, Hayden & Eldredge; 1948.

BODE, BOYD H. *How We Learn.* Boston: D. C. Heath & Company; 1940.

BOSSARD, JAMES H. S. *The Sociology of Child Development.* New York: Harper & Brothers; 1948.

BOWEN, GENEVIEVE. *Living and Learning in a Rural School.* New York: The Macmillan Company; 1944.

BRAMELD, THEODORE. *Patterns of Educational Philosophy.* Yonkers, New York: World Book Company; 1950.

BROOKER, F. E., and HARRINGTON, E. *Students Make Motion Pictures.* Washington: American Council on Education; 1941.

BROOKS, B. M., and BROWN, H. A. *Music Education in the Elementary School.* New York: American Book Company; 1946.

BRYSON, LYMAN. *Adult Education.* New York: American Book Company; 1936.

BUTTS, R. FREEMAN. *A Cultural History of Education.* New York: McGraw-Hill Book Company, Inc.; 1947.

————. *The College Charts Its Course.* New York: McGraw-Hill Book Company, Inc.; 1939.

CARLSON, JESSIE. *Guiding Children in the Nursery Class.* Philadelphia: Judson Press; 1948.

CHAMBERLAIN, CHARLES D., and others. *Did They Succeed in College?* New York: Harper & Brothers; 1942.

CHASE, MARY ELLEN. *A Goodly Fellowship.* New York: The Macmillan Company; 1939.

CHISHOLM, LESLIE L. *Guiding Youth in the Secondary School.* New York: American Book Company; 1945.

CLAPP, ELSIE R. *Community Schools in Action.* New York: The Viking Press, Inc.; 1939.

COLE, LAWRENCE E., and BRUCE, WILLIAM F. *Educational Psychology.* Yonkers, New York: World Book Company; 1950.

COLE, NATALIE. *The Arts in the Classroom.* New York: John Day Company, Inc.; 1940.

Commission on Teacher Education. *Helping Teachers Understand Children.* Washington: American Council on Education; 1945.

Committee on Infant and Preschool Child, White House Conference. *Education and Training.* New York: D. Appleton-Century Company, Inc.; 1931.

CONANT, JAMES B. *Education in a Divided World.* Cambridge, Massachusetts: Harvard University Press; 1948.

COOK, LLOYD A. *Community Backgrounds of Education.* New York: McGraw-Hill Book Company, Inc.; 1938.

COREY, S. M., and others. *General Education in the American High School.* Chicago: Scott, Foresman & Company; 1942.

COUNTS, GEORGE S. *Education and the Promise of America.* New York: The Macmillan Company; 1945.

COYLE, GRACE. *Group Work with American Youth.* New York: Harper & Brothers; 1948.

DALE, EDGAR. *Audio-Visual Methods in Teaching.* New York: The Dryden Press; 1946.

D'AMICO, VICTOR E. *Creative Teaching in Art.* Scranton, Pennsylvania: International Textbook Company; 1942.

DAVIS, ALLISON, and DOLLARD, JOHN. *Children of Bondage.* Washington: American Council on Education; 1940.

——, and GARDNER, BURLEIGH. *Deep South.* Chicago: University of Chicago Press; 1941.

DE LIMA, AGNES. *The Little Red School House.* New York: The Macmillan Company; 1942.

Department of Elementary School Principals. *Community Living and the Elementary School.* Washington: National Education Association; 1945.

Department of Supervision and Curriculum Development. *Discipline for Today's Children and Youth.* Washington: National Education Association; 1944.

——. *Group Planning in Education.* Washington: National Education Association; 1945.

Department of Supervisors and Directors of Instruction. *The Changing Curriculum.* New York: D. Appleton-Century Company, Inc.; 1937.

——. *Coöperation: Principles and Practices.* Washington: National Education Association; 1939.

——. *Materials of Instruction.* Washington: National Education Association; 1935.

——. *Newer Instructional Practices of Promise.* Washington: National Education Association; 1939.

DEWEY, JOHN. *The Child and the Curriculum.* Chicago: University of Chicago Press; 1902.

——. *Democracy and Education.* New York: The Macmillan Company; 1916.

——. *Experience and Education.* New York: The Macmillan Company; 1938.

——. *Interest and Effort in Education.* Boston: Houghton Mifflin Company; 1913.

——. *School and Society.* Chicago: University of Chicago Press; 1915.

DIMOCK, H. S. *Rediscovering the Adolescent.* New York: Association Press; 1937.

DOUGLASS, AUBREY A. *The American School System.* New York: Farrar & Rinehart, Inc.; 1940.

DRISCOLL, GERTRUDE. *How to Study the Behavior of Children.* New York: Bureau of Publications, Teachers College, Columbia University; 1941.

Educational Policies Commission. *Education for All American Children.* Washington: National Education Association; 1948.

——. *Education for All American Youth.* Washington: National Education Association; 1944.

——. *Educational Services for Younger Children.* Washington: National Education Association; 1945.

——. *Learning the Ways of Democracy.* Washington: National Education Association; 1940.

EDWARDS, N., and RICHEY, H. *The School in the American Social Order.* Boston: Houghton Mifflin Company; 1947.

EELLS, W. C. *Why Junior College Terminal Education.* Washington: American Association of Junior Colleges; 1941.

ELLIOTT, HARRISON S. *The Process of Group Thinking.* New York: Association Press; 1928.

ELY, M. L. *Why Forums?* New York: American Association for Adult Education; 1937.

ENGELHARDT, N. L. and N. L. *Planning the Community School.* New York: American Book Company; 1940.

EVERETT, SAMUEL (Ed.). *The Community School.* New York: D. Appleton-Century Company, Inc.; 1938.

FOLLETT, M. P. *Creative Experience.* New York: Longmans, Green & Company, Inc.; 1924.

FOLSOM, J. K. *The Family and Democratic Society.* New York: John Wiley & Sons, Inc.; 1943.

FOSTER, JOSEPHINE, and MATTSON, M. *Nursery School Education.* New York: D. Appleton-Century Company, Inc.; 1939.

FREEMAN, FRANK N. *Mental Tests; Their History, Principles, and Applications.* Boston: Houghton Mifflin Company; 1939.

GATES, A. I., and others. *Educational Psychology.* New York: The Macmillan Company; 1948.

GESELL, ARNOLD, and ILG, FRANCES. *The Child from Five to Ten.* New York: Harper & Brothers; 1946.

GILES, H. H. *Teacher-Pupil Planning.* New York: Harper & Brothers; 1941.

———, and others. *Exploring the Curriculum.* New York: Harper & Brothers; 1942.

GREENE, HARRY A., and others. *Measurement and Evaluation in the Elementary School.* New York: Longmans, Green & Company, Inc.; 1942.

———, and others. *Measurement and Evaluation in the Secondary School.* New York: Longmans, Green & Company, Inc.; 1943.

GUNTHER, JOHN. *Inside U.S.A.* New York: Harper & Brothers; 1947.

HAND, HAROLD. *What People Think about Their Schools.* Yonkers: World Book Company; 1948.

HANNA, PAUL R., and others. *Youth Serves the Community.* New York: D. Appleton-Century Company, Inc.; 1936.

HARTMAN, GERTRUDE, and SHUMAKER, ANN (Eds.). *Creative Expression.* New York: John Day Company, Inc.; 1932.

HARTMANN, GEORGE. *Educational Psychology.* New York: American Book Company; 1941.

HAWKINS, GAYNELL. *Education for Social Understanding.* New York: American Association for Adult Education; 1940.

HAYEK, F. A. VON. *The Road to Serfdom.* Chicago: University of Chicago Press; 1944.

HAYES, WAYLAND. *The Small Community Looks Ahead.* New York: Harcourt, Brace & Company, Inc.; 1947.

HEATON, K. L., and others. *Professional Education for Experienced Teachers.* Chicago: University of Chicago Press; 1940.

HECK, ARCH O. *The Education of Exceptional Children.* New York: McGraw-Hill Book Company, Inc.; 1940.

HEFFRON, IDA C. *Francis Wayland Parker.* Burbank, California: Ivan Deach, Jr.; 1934.

HILDRETH, GERTRUDE. *Child Growth through Education.* New York: The Ronald Press; 1948.

HOPKINS, L. THOMAS. *Interaction: The Democratic Process.* Boston: D. C. Heath & Company; 1941.

HORRALL, A. H., and others. *Let's Go to School.* New York: McGraw-Hill Book Company, Inc.; 1938.

HUBBARD, ELIZABETH V. *Your Children at School: How They Adjust and Develop.* New York: John Day Company, Inc.; 1942.

HUBERMAN, LEO. *We, the People.* New York: Harper & Brothers; 1932.

HULL, CLARK L. *Aptitude Testing.* Yonkers: World Book Company; 1928.

HUSZAR, G. B. DE *Practical Applications of Democracy.* New York: Harper & Brothers; 1945.

HYMES, JAMES. *A Pound of Prevention.* New York: New York State Committee on Mental Hygiene; 1947.

INGLIS, RUTH. *Freedom of the Movies.* Chicago: University of Chicago Press; 1947.

JENKINS, GLADYS G., and others. *These Are Your Children.* Chicago: Scott, Foresman & Company, Inc.; 1949.

JERSILD, ARTHUR T. *Child Psychology.* New York: Prentice-Hall, Inc.; 1947.

———, and others. *Child Development and the Curriculum.* New York: Bureau of Publications, Teachers College, Columbia University; 1946.

John Dewey Society. *The American High School.* New York: Harper & Brothers; 1946.

———. *Democracy and the Curriculum.* New York: D. Appleton-Century Company, Inc.; 1939.

———. *Educational Freedom and Democracy.* New York: D. Appleton-Century Company, Inc.; 1938.

———. *Mobilizing Educational Resources.* New York: Harper & Brothers; 1943.

———. *Teachers for Democracy.* New York: D. Appleton-Century Company, Inc.; 1940.

JOHNSON, ALVIN S. *The Public Library — A People's University.* New York: American Association for Adult Education; 1938.

KARDINER, ABRAM. *The Individual and His Society.* New York: Columbia University Press; 1939.

KNIGHT, EDGAR A. *Twenty Centuries of Education.* Boston: Ginn & Company; 1940.

KOOPMAN, G. R., and others. *Democracy in School Administration.* New York: D. Appleton-Century Company, Inc.; 1943.

KOOS, L. V. *Integrating High School and College.* New York: Harper & Brothers; 1946.

LILIENTHAL, DAVID. *TVA: Democracy on the March.* New York: Harper & Brothers; 1944.

LIPPITT, RONALD, and WHITE, R. K. "The Social Climate of Children's Groups," *Child Behavior and Development* (R. A. Barker, Ed.). New York: McGraw-Hill Book Company, Inc.; 1943.

LORWIN, L. L. *Youth-Work Programs.* Washington: American Council on Education; 1941.

LYND, ROBERT S. and HELEN M. *Middletown*. New York: Harcourt, Brace & Company, Inc.; 1929.
————. *Middletown in Transition*. New York: Harcourt, Brace & Company, Inc.; 1937.

MARTIN, JOHN. *America Dancing*. New York: Dodge Publishing Company; 1936.
MAYHEW, K. C., and EDWARDS, A. C. *The Dewey School*. New York: D. Appleton-Century Company, Inc.; 1936.
MEAD, MARGARET. *From the South Seas*. New York: W. W. Morrow & Company, Inc.; 1939.
MEARNS, HUGHES. *Creative Youth*. Garden City, New York: Doubleday, Page & Company, Inc.; 1925.
————. *Creative Power*. New York: Doubleday, Doran & Company, Inc.; 1929.
MEIKLEJOHN, A. *The Experimental College*. New York: Harper & Brothers; 1932.
MELVIN, A. GORDON. *New Methods for New Schools*. New York: John Day Company, Inc.; 1941.
MIEL, ALICE. *Changing the Curriculum*. New York: D. Appleton-Century Company, Inc.; 1946.
MOEHLMAN, A. B. *School Administration; Its Development, Principles, and Future in the United States*. Boston: Houghton Mifflin Company; 1940.
MURPHY, GARDNER. *Personality*. New York: Harper & Brothers; 1947.
MURPHY, LOIS B. *Social Behavior and Child Personality*. New York: Columbia University Press; 1937.

National Society for the Study of Education. *American Education in the Post-War Period*. Part II, 44th Yearbook. Chicago: University of Chicago Press; 1945.
————. *General Education in the American College*. 38th Yearbook. Bloomington, Illinois: Public School Publishing Company; 1939.
————. *The Library in General Education*. Part II, 42nd Yearbook. Chicago: University of Chicago Press; 1943.
————. *The Psychology of Learning*. 41st Yearbook. Bloomington, Illinois: Public School Publishing Company; 1942.

OGDEN, JEAN and JESSE. *Small Communities in Action*. New York: Harper & Brothers; 1946.
————. *These Things We Tried*. Charlottesville, Virginia: University of Virginia Press; 1947.
OLSON, C. M. *Learn and Live*. New York: Alfred E. Sloan Foundation; 1946.
OVERSTREET, HARRY and BONARO. *Leaders for Adult Education*. New York: American Association for Adult Education; 1941.

PARKER, FRANCIS W. *Talks on Pedagogics*. New York: E. L. Kellogg; 1894.
PARKHURST, HELEN. *Education on the Dalton Plan*. New York: E. P. Dutton & Company, Inc.; 1922.
PETERSON, HOUSTON. *Great Teachers*. New Brunswick, New Jersey: Rutgers University Press; 1946.
PLANT, JAMES S. *Personality and the Cultural Pattern*. New York: The Commonwealth Fund; 1937.
PRATT, CAROLINE. *I Learn from Children*. New York: Simon & Schuster, Inc.; 1948.

PRESCOTT, DANIEL. *Emotions and the Educative Process.* Washington: American Council on Education; 1938.

President's Commission on Higher Education. *Higher Education for American Democracy.* New York: Harper & Brothers; 1947.

PRESSEY, S. L., and ROBINSON, F. P. *Psychology and the New Education.* New York: Harper & Brothers; 1944.

Progressive Education Association: Commission on the Relation of School and College. *Thirty Schools Tell Their Story.* New York: Harper & Brothers; 1943.

RAINEY, H. P. *How Fare American Youth?* New York: D. Appleton-Century Company, Inc.; 1937.

READ, HERBERT. *Education through Art.* London: Faber & Faber; 1943.

Report of the Commission on Freedom of the Press. *A Free and Responsible Press.* Chicago: University of Chicago Press; 1947.

Report of the Harvard Committee. *General Education in a Free Society.* Cambridge, Massachusetts: Harvard University Press; 1946.

RICH, J. C. *The Materials and Methods of Sculpture.* New York: Oxford University Press; 1947.

Ross, C. C. *Measurement in Today's Schools.* New York: Prentice-Hall, Inc.; 1944.

RUGG, HAROLD. *American Life and the School Curriculum.* Boston: Ginn & Company; 1936.

———. *Foundations for American Education.* Yonkers: World Book Company; 1947.

———, and SHUMAKER, ANN. *The Child-Centered School.* Yonkers: World Book Company; 1928.

SCHEIDEMANN, N. V. *The Psychology of Exceptional Children.* Boston: Houghton Mifflin Company; 1931.

SEAY, MAURICE (Ed.). *Adult Education.* Lexington, Kentucky: University of Kentucky; 1938.

SEXSON, JOHN A., and HARBESON, JOHN W. *The New American College.* New York: Harper & Brothers; 1946.

SMITH, B. OTHANEL, and others. *Fundamentals of Curriculum Development.* Yonkers: World Book Company; 1950.

SMITH, NILA B. *Adventures in Teacher Education.* San Jose, California: Stewart Publishing Company; 1937.

STILES, DAN. *High Schools for Tomorrow.* New York: Harper & Brothers; 1946.

STOLPER, B. J. R. *The Bulletin Board as a Teaching Device.* New York: Bureau of Publications, Teachers College, Columbia University; 1946.

STRANG, RUTH. *Reporting to Parents.* New York: Bureau of Publications, Teachers College, Columbia University; 1948.

———, and HATCHER, O. LATHAM. *Child Development and Guidance in Rural Schools.* New York: Harper & Brothers; 1943.

STRATEMEYER, FLORENCE, and others. *Developing a Curriculum for Modern Living.* New York: Bureau of Publications, Teachers College, Columbia University; 1947.

SULLIVAN, LOUIS H. *The Autobiography of an Idea.* New York: American Institute of Architecture; 1924.

TAYLOR, KATHARINE W. *Do Adolescents Need Parents?* Iowa City, Iowa: University of Iowa Press; 1941.

TERMAN, LEWIS M., and MERRILL, MAUD A. *Measuring Intelligence.* Boston: Houghton Mifflin Company; 1937.

THAYER, V. T.; ZACHRY, C. B.; and KOTINSKY, R. *Reorganizing Secondary Education.* New York: D. Appleton-Century Company, Inc.; 1939.

TIEGS, E. W. *Tests and Measurements in the Improvement of Learning.* Boston: Houghton Mifflin Company; 1939.

TRAXLER, A. E. *The Nature and Use of Anecdotal Records.* New York: Educational Records Bureau; 1945.

UMSTATTD, J. G. *Secondary School Teaching.* Boston: Ginn & Company; 1937.

University High School, Ohio State University, Class of 1938. *Were We Guinea Pigs?* New York: Henry Holt & Company, Inc.; 1938.

VAN DOREN, MARK. *Liberal Education.* New York: Henry Holt & Company, Inc.; 1943.

WALSER, FRANK. *The Art of Conference.* New York: Harper & Brothers; 1948.

WARNER, W. L., and LUNT, P. S. *The Social Life of a Modern Community.* New Haven, Connecticut: Yale University Press; 1941.

————, and others. *Who Shall Be Educated?* New York: Harper & Brothers; 1944.

WASHBURNE, CARLETON. *A Living Philosophy of Education.* New York: John Day Company, Inc.; 1940.

WATSON, GOODWIN. *Youth after Conflict.* New York: Association Press; 1947.

WEBER, JULIA. *My Country School Diary.* New York: Harper & Brothers; 1946.

WELLS, H. G. *Story of a Great Schoolmaster.* New York: The Macmillan Company; 1924.

WEST, JAMES (Withers, Carl). *Plainville, U.S.A.* New York: Columbia University Press; 1945.

White House Conference. *Children in a Democracy.* Washington: Superintendent of Documents; 1940.

WILLEY, ROY D., and YOUNG, H. A. *Radio in Elementary Education.* Boston: D. C. Heath & Company; 1948.

WITTY, PAUL A., and SKINNER, C. E. (Eds.). *Mental Hygiene in Modern Education.* New York: Farrar & Rinehart, Inc.; 1939.

WOELFEL, N., and TYLER, I. K. (Eds.). *Radio and the School.* Yonkers: World Book Company; 1945.

WRIGHTSTONE, J. W. *Appraisal of Newer Elementary School Practices.* New York: Bureau of Publications, Teachers College, Columbia University; 1938.

YOUNG, KIMBALL. *Sociology; A Study of Society and Culture.* New York: American Book Company; 1942.

ZACHRY, CAROLINE B., and LIGHTY, M. *Emotion and Conduct in Adolescence.* New York: D. Appleton-Century Company, Inc.; 1940.

ZYVE, CLAIRE T., and others. *Willingly to School.* New York: Round Table Press; 1934.

Index